# CHILDREN'S SPATIAL DEVELOPMENT

*Edited and Compiled by*

## JOHN ELIOT

*Associate Professor*
*Institute for Child Study*
*University of Maryland*

*and*

## NEIL J. SALKIND

*Assistant Professor*
*Department of Educational Psychology*
*University of Kansas*

*With Contributions by*

**GEORGE E. FORMAN**
**LAUREN JAY HARRIS**
**DAVID R. OLSON**
**STEVEN G. VANDENBERG**

**CHARLES C THOMAS • PUBLISHER**
*Springfield • Illinois • U.S.A.*

*Published and Distributed Throughout the World by*
CHARLES C THOMAS · PUBLISHER
BANNERSTONE HOUSE
301-327 East Lawrence Avenue, Springfield, Illinois, U.S.A.

*With* THOMAS BOOKS *careful attention is given to all details of manufacturing and design. It is the Publisher's desire to present books that are satisfactory as to their physical qualities and artistic possibilities and appropriate for their particular use.* THOMAS BOOKS *will be true to those laws of quality that assure a good name and good will.*

*Printed in the United States of America*
*Y-2*

## Library of Congress Cataloging in Publication Data

Eliot, John, 1933-
  Children's spatial development.

  Bibliography: p. 197
  1. Space-perception. 2. Child Study. 3. Cognition (Child psychology)
I. Salkind, Neil J., joint author. II. Title. [DNLM: 1. Child Development. 2. Space perception—In infancy and childhood. BF469 E42c]
  BF723.S63E42        155.4'13        74-8843
  ISBN 0-398-03210-6

# CHILDREN'S
# SPATIAL
# DEVELOPMENT

*This book is dedicated*
*to*
**Sylvia and Leni**

# CONTRIBUTORS

JOHN ELIOT
*Associate Professor*
*Institute for Child Study*
*University of Maryland*
*College Park, Maryland*

GEORGE E. FORMAN
*Assistant Professor*
*Department of Human Development*
*University of Massachusetts*
*Amherst, Massachusetts*

LAUREN JAY HARRIS
*Associate Professor*
*Department of Psychology*
*Michigan State University*
*East Lansing, Michigan*

DAVID R. OLSON
*Professor of Applied Psychology*
*Ontario Institute for Studies in Education*
*252 Bloor Street West*
*Toronto, Canada*

NEIL J. SALKIND
*Assistant Professor*
*Department of Educational Psychology*
*University of Kansas*
*Lawrence, Kansas*

STEVEN G. VANDENBERG
*Professor of Psychology*
*University of Colorado*
*Boulder, Colorado*

# INTRODUCTION

HOW DO PEOPLE perceive and think about the different visual environments of their daily lives? To what extent does the ordering of objects or events in these visual environments give shape or direction to our thought? Is it possible to arrange the content of specific environments in order to enhance a particular kind of thought? How do children perceive and think about their visual environments differently from adults?

If we knew the answers to this sampling of questions, then surely we would possess solutions to some of the more enduring mysteries about the nature of human thought. By the same token, if we substitute the word "space" for the word "environment" in these questions, then clearly "space" is an important dimension in human thought. Perhaps if we knew more about the ways by which children represent objects or events spatially, we might discover more about the nature of children's thought and the factors which influence that thought.

The emphasis of this book is upon the development of children's representation of space. For the purposes of this book, the term "development" refers to changes in behavior which can be associated with increasing age or experience. Similarly, the terms "representation of space" refer to the imagining, contemplating or taking as an object of thought either one's own or another's multi-dimensional visual environment. Defined in this manner, "the development of children's representation of space" is inclusive of different meanings and different research approaches—a necessary attitude considering how little is known about the topic.

The purpose of the book is to stimulate further research interest in problems of spatial development. To achieve this end, three kinds of resources are included in this book. In Part I, four essays indicate the status of different kinds of research with regard to the study of space. Each of these essays is written by a person who is currently active in spatial research. In Part II, forty experiments involving different kinds of spatial problems are presented as a sampling of the kinds of research which have been conducted with children. Finally, in Part III, an extensive bibliography has been compiled to concentrate the available literature for interested researchers. Except for the fourth essay in Part I, the content of this book is a direct outgrowth of a symposium on children's spatial development held in Philadelphia in March, 1973 at the Society for Research in Child Development's biennial meeting.

The first essay in Part I is Lauren Jay Harris' "Neurological Factors Affecting the Development of Spatial Skills." The thesis of Harris' essay is that the right hemisphere may be the "dominant" hemisphere for infancy and early childhood. In developing his thesis, Harris reviews not only the evidence concerning functional differences, but also the evidence concerning possible structural differences underlying hemispheric specialization.

Steven Vandenberg's "Hereditary and Other Sources of Variation in Spatial Tests" is the second essay in Part I. Vandenberg begins his essay with a brief commentary on the development of spatial tests. He then turns to a short discussion of several possible sources of variance with respect to performance in these tests and concludes his essay with a description of a training program using a new test adopted from Shepard and Metzler's work.

The third essay in Part I is David Olson's "On the Relations Between Spatial and Linguistic Processes." Olson's focus in this essay is upon the recent, non-Piagetian research concerned with the language of space. Olson considers ways in which children acquire and use this language of space and concludes his essay with some comments about the relationship between this language of space and children's spatial perception.

The fourth essay in Part I is George Forman's "On the Components of Spatial Representation." When this book was first conceived, the editors wanted to include an essay on Piagetian research to off-set Olson's emphasis on non-Piagetian research. Forman's essay, however, goes beyond the excellent existing summaries of Piagetian research (Flavell, 1970; Beilin, 1971) in that he considers the evolution of several conceptions of space through history, including Piaget's. Specifically, Forman underscores a number of critical distinctions which a child must make about his visual world and then compares the child's spatial development to man's gradual redefinition of space through history.

Part II of this book consists of forty abstracts of experiments involving children's spatial behavior. Each abstract includes a brief statement describing the purpose of the study, the sample, the methodology employed and the results of the study. A short list of further references is added to provide readers with citations to tangential as well as similar work. The purpose of these abstracts is to identify some representative studies in hopes of inducing further research activity.

Part III of the book is an extended bibliography on spatial abilities and children's spatial development. The references collected in this bibliography refer to a broad range of behaviors inasmuch as the term "spatial" covers many categories whose boundaries overlap. The bibliography is intended to serve as a resource which will stimulate further research interest in the measurement and interpretation of spatial behaviors and the many factors which are believed to affect their development. For the most part, this bibliography is a compilation of research which is concerned with the responses to spatial tasks requiring some combination of perception, imagination and thought.

In short, the editors hope that the different resources of this book will be drawn upon and used by active minds from many different fields. The book is deliberately cast as a transitional statement of problems and possibilities and is not intended as a comprehensive survey of the topic. It was prompted by a conviction that spatial awareness is both a critical dimension in the perception of our visual environments and a major component in our representation or thought about those environments. It was also prompted by the conviction that the study of children's spatial development will become a major research frontier before the end of this century.

JOHN ELIOT

# CONTENTS

Page

*Dedication* . . . . . . . . . . . . . . . v

*Contributors* . . . . . . . . . . . . . . vii

*Introduction* . . . . . . . . . . . . . . ix

## Part I
## ESSAYS

*Chapter*

1. NEUROPHYSIOLOGICAL FACTORS IN THE DEVELOPMENT OF SPATIAL SKILLS—Lauren J. Harris . . . . . . . . 5

2. SOURCES OF VARIANCE IN PERFORMANCE OF SPATIAL TESTS—S. G. Vandenberg . . . . . . . . . . . . . 57

3. ON THE RELATIONS BETWEEN SPATIAL AND LINGUISTIC PROCESSES—David R. Olson . . . . . . . . . . . 67

4. ON THE COMPONENTS OF SPATIAL REPRESENTATION— George E. Forman . . . . . . . . . . . . 111

## Part II
## ABSTRACTS

5. ABSTRACTS OF SELECTED JOURNAL ARTICLES—Neil J. Salkind and John Eliot . . . . . . . . . . 159

## Part III
## EXTENDED BIBLIOGRAPHY

*Bibliography* . . . . . . . . . . . . . . 197

*Index* . . . . . . . . . . . . . . . . 295

# CHILDREN'S
# SPATIAL
# DEVELOPMENT

# PART 1

# ESSAYS

# Chapter 1

# NEUROPHYSIOLOGICAL FACTORS IN THE DEVELOPMENT OF SPATIAL SKILLS

LAUREN JAY HARRIS

## INTRODUCTION: MAN'S TWO BRAINS

OUR SEARCH is for those structures or characteristics of the human brain and nervous system that subserve spatial skills. If there are such structures, how and when do they develop? We begin our search with some basic neuro-anatomy.

The human brain, at maturity, weighs about three pounds and occupies the entire cavity enclosed by the skull. The brain is divided according to its embryological development: early in its growth, three simple divisions can be seen: the forebrain, midbrain, and hindbrain. The forebrain later divides into two parts: the telencephalon and the diencephalon. The midbrain (mesencephalon) does not divide, but the hindbrain divides into the metencephalon and myelencephalon. The adult brain thus is composed of five major divisions, named above in the order from front (telencephalon) to back (myelencephalon). Our interest here is with the telencephalon, the principal part of which is the cerebral cortex (cortex means "rind" or covering), which is gray matter, or cell bodies. In birds and "lower" animals, the cerebral cortex is not very well developed; but in mammals, particularly in the primates, it is extremely well developed. In human beings, the cortex constitutes about a half of the weight of the entire nervous system and is so cramped into the skull that it presents numerous invaginations (the telescoping of an organ in the manner of a pouch) and ridges, thus greatly enlarging the amount of cortex.

5

The cerebrum is divided into two essentially mirror-image halves, or hemispheres, by the deep longitudinal fissure, or slit, that runs along its midline. On the dorsal, or back, surface of the cortex, and slightly posterior to the center is the central sulcus, a deep furrow running laterally and slightly anteriorly from the median longitudinal fissure. On the lateral surface of the cortex, the lateral fissure runs posteriorly and dorsally. These three main fissures divide the cortex into four pairs of lobes, one set in each of the hemispheres: the frontal lobes include all the cortex anterior to the central sulcus; the parietal lobes include the dorsal surface, extending posteriorly from the central sulcus and laterally to the lateral fissure; the temporal lobes are lateral and ventral to the lateral fissure. Finally, the occipital lobes are at the very base of the cortex, immediately behind the temporal lobe and beneath and behind the parietal lobe.

The cerebral hemispheres are joined by a massive bundle of interconnecting nerve fibers called the "corpus callosum." The left side of the body is mainly controlled by the right hemisphere, or right side of the cortex, and the right side of the body is mainly controlled by the left hemisphere. The connections, then, are "contralateral" rather than "ipsilateral."[1] The corpus callosum serves to facilitate communication between the hemispheres, through the transfer of ideational and sensory-motor information from one hemisphere to the other.

From our standpoint, we are most interested in the fact that the two hemispheres have very different functions. The left hemisphere —that which controls the right side of the body—is intimately involved in the analysis of language and symbolic material, while the right hemisphere subserves nonlinguistic, visuospatial functions. Our interest is primarily with the right hemisphere.

The idea that the right hemisphere has any special role at all is quite old but it has only relatively recently begun to get its share of attention from neurologists and psychologists. For a long time the right hemisphere was considered merely a "weaker" version of the "dominant" left hemisphere and its distinctive functional properties were not appreciated. Recently (1972), *Benton* has described the history of this belief. The following summary is partly based on his review.

In 1861, Paul *Broca*, a French pathologist, anthropologist, and pioneer in neurosurgery, reported his discovery of a specific association between aphasia and disease of the left frontal lobe.[2] Broca's discovery was followed by numerous other reports of other aphasic disorders—e.g. impairment in language understanding, disturbances in naming, loss of reading ability—all associated with damage in the left temporal and parietal areas. As Benton expressed it, "Inferring the positive from the negative, students of human cerebral function readily concluded that at least in righthanded persons, language behavior was mediated primarily (if not necessarily) by neural mechanisms located in the left hemisphere" (Benton, 1972, p. 5).[3] The area of the brain in which Broca localized the center for articulate speech—the third convolution of the left frontal lobe—is now known as "Broca's area."

With such a variety of intellectually critical skills apparently served by the left hemisphere, it is natural that the left hemisphere should have been called "major." But by this characterization, Benton notes, the right hemisphere was assumed to be "minor," with no distinctive features or functions of its own. While it shared certain properties with the left hemisphere, whatever it could do, the left could do better.

Some scholars opposed this idea and suggested instead that the right hemisphere had special functions of its own. In 1874, the British neurologist, Hughlings *Jackson*, argued that the posterior area of the right hemisphere was critical for visual recognition and visual memory. Two years later (1876) he described a patient with a tumor in the temporo-occipital region of the right hemisphere. He diagnosed this tumor and its location on the basis of a "kind of mental defect" consisting of visual disorientation, failure to recognize persons ("facial agnosia") and dyspraxia for dressing.[4] Jackson called this array of disabilities "imperception" and argued that it was as specifically characteristic of disease of the posterior right hemisphere as impairment in expressive speech was of disease of the anterior left hemisphere.[5]

During the years following, there were scattered other reports that pointed to the possibility that the right hemisphere played a critical role in subserving certain aspects of visual perception. In the 1880's and 1890's, accounts were published of disturbances in spatial orientation as reflected in loss of geographic memory, difficulty in locating objects in space, inability to find one's way around from place to place, and so on. These "spatial disorders" were shown by patients suffering from focal cerebral disease and with intact central vision acuity, suggesting that the disorders were "higher-level," not merely expressions of sensory defects or significant intellectual impairment. Still further reports appeared, in scattered form, through the next several decades.

Important support for this alternate view of the "minor" hemisphere came in 1935 with the publication of Weisenburg and McBride's study of aphasia. This study compared right-hemisphere-lesion patients with left-hemisphere-lesion patients and control patients. The observed performance patterns of the right-hemisphere patients showed significant impairment in some nonverbal tasks, although verbal abilities appeared almost normal.

Then, in 1936, Hebb described a patient with a large excision in his right temporal lobe. The patient showed superior verbal intelligence but markedly defective performance in visuoperceptive and visuocontructive tests, as well as tests of tactile form recognition.

Major support for the alternative view of the "minor" hemisphere appeared in a 1941 paper by Brain. Specifically, Brain described case studies of spatial disorientation in patients with massive lesions of the right parietal lobe. Judging from the dramatic case reports Brain described, his argument ought to have been extremely convincing, particularly since his case studies clearly indicated profound deficits in visuospatial ability while linguistic ability remained apparently intact. Some patients, for example, got lost going from one room to another in their own homes, although none showed either a loss of topographic memory or an ability to describe familiar routes. One patient, when going downstairs from his bedroom on the first floor to the sitting room, tended to turn to the right instead of the left and would end up in the dining room. He would then recognize his error and become very upset. He showed no difficulty in visualizing the correct route: the problem was to follow it. He also found it was difficult to find the electric switch above his head in the dark, although he could describe where it ought to be. Another patient, a woman, had difficulty recognizing her room and, moreover, could not find her way about her apartment. "When she set out for the bathroom she arrived at the lavatory, which was a door on the right, and when she tried to go to the lavatory she made a similar mistake, took a turn to the right and got lost again" (Brain, 1941, p. 259). Yet this woman obviously "knew" verbally the layout of her house.

When asked how she would find her way to the bathroom, she answered: "I should first go to the cupboard in which my husband keeps his clothes . . . Then I should open the bedroom door and outside would be where the coats are hung up. I should then look for the electric light switch which is outside the bathroom, because the Borough Council won't allow it inside, and I should then find the bathroom and the bath would be in it" (Brain, 1941, p. 259).

## DYSPRAXIA FOR DRESSING

Brain (1941) also noted that some of his patients with right hemisphere disease seemed to be incapable of dressing themselves (dressing dyspraxia)—a symptom described by Jackson much earlier (1876). This disability was later associated specifically with damage in the parietal or parieto-occipital area of the right hemisphere (Hécaen and Ajuriaguerra, 1945, 1955; Arseni, Voinesco, and Goldenberg, 1958; all cited in Hécaen and Ajuriaguerra, 1964). Some of the specific spatial components involved in dressing oneself, however, are implicit in Brain's descriptions: one patient, for example, tended to put her clothes on back to front or upside down, which she attributed to the fact that she did not know the right side from the left. Another patient could put on his pajama coat only if he laid it out first on the bed. He had learned that the handerchief pocket was on the left side, the buttons on the right, and by using these landmarks he could put on the coat. If he tried any other way, he got "in a complete muddle" (Brain, 1941, p. 258).

Benton observes that these reports ought to have had far more impact than they did have—but, in fact, they had no significant effect on prevailing conceptions of hemispherical cerebral dominance. Why not? Perhaps the reports were too scattered. But it also was true that the literature on the left hemisphere was much larger and all of it pointed to the paramount importance of the left hemisphere for thinking and perception, as well as for language. These "minority" reports, too, were not widely disseminated. Jackson's papers, for instance, were published in journals that were not widely read outside England.

Finally, some authors did not draw what would seem to be the obvious conclusions from their own observations—a reluctance, Benton notes, which was unlikely to encourage others to reflect on the implications of these reports. One must wonder, too, whether the diffidence of the researchers, as well as the general lack of interest in visuospatial deficits, did not stem from the much greater value likely to have been imposed by society, perhaps most especially by educated society, on linguistic rather than on nonlinguistic abilities. Linguistic disabilities would be more salient, more likely to be a mark of something gone awry, more likely to invite the interested attention of neurologists and psychologists. Language, after all, is the most distinctly human ability and when it is disrupted our most human characteristic is thereby affected. One wonders whether, for these reasons, more persons with left-hemisphere injuries were selected into hospitals thence to come to the attention of medical and psychological experts. Perhaps it is worth noting that developmental and other psychologists historically have devoted far more research attention to language development than to visuospatial development. One hopes that the present book of essays, if it accomplishes nothing else, will spark further interest in the development of "nonlinguistic intelligence."

Whatever the reasons for the lack of impact of these earlier studies, they nonetheless succeeded in influencing the next generation of workers, such as Zangwill (1960) and Hécaen (Hécaen and Ajuriaguerra, 1945, 1964), whose studies between 1944 and 1951 initiated the modern period of investigation in this field. Much of this new interest undoubtedly was also stimulated by World War II which, because of the large number of wounded men who suffered penetration wounds of the brain but survived, simultaneously spurred the practical necessity for research on human brain functions and provided large numbers of young and otherwise healthy subjects for this research.

## LIMITATIONS OF CLINICAL STUDIES

Clinical studies pose a problem for anyone interested in understanding the neurological bases for the growth of spatial skill in *normal* children. In most clinical studies, the subjects are adults, often elderly, who have suffered one or another kind of damage to their brains. This damage may be either of diffuse character from external injury or it may be of focal character through the spontaneous growth of lesions. The logic of the studies is to write a functional map of the brain by correlating observed behavioral deficits with observed brain damage. These studies are hampered insofar as the damage might have occurred many months or years prior to examination and, moreover, may have affected not only the specific functional systems but their interaction as well. Despite these drawbacks, it is currently these studies that afford us the most detailed analysis of the neuropsychology of spatial knowledge.

Fortunately, we also possess nonneurological techniques for analyzing hemispherical asymmetry and the role of neurological factors in spatial skill in normal subjects. While the bulk of these studies have concentrated on language analysis (that is, left-hemisphere functions) in young adults, studies of spatial functions are beginning to appear, though as yet only a few studies are concerned with children.

## VISUAL FIELD DIFFERENCES

One of the most promising techniques for research on hemisphere specialization for visuospatial perception involves the use of the tachistoscope. The technique is simple enough: a target is projected tachistoscopically either to the subject's left or right visual field. Since for each eye alone, vision in the left visual field is subserved by the occipital lobe of the right hemisphere and vision in the right visual field is subserved by the occipital lobe of the left hemisphere, observed differences in the accuracy of detection of targets in each field can be assumed to reflect differences in hemispheric specialization for type of target.

Though the technique is simple, the effects are often very subtle and many potential confounding variables exist (White, 1969). Generally, however, words and letters are reported more accurately from the right visual field (left hemisphere), and "spatial" targets are reported more accurately from the left visual field (right hemisphere).

Let us review some representative studies. In a recent experiment by Durnford and Kimura (1971), very short lines, varying in length from fifteen to sixty-five degrees, were projected one at a time in either the left or right visual field. After each projection the subjects —college students—were instructed to identify the projected target from a variety of slanted lines on a sheet of paper. Slope identification (or what we could call the identification of the *direction* of the lines) was consistently superior, by a small amount, in the left visual field. This result was also reported in a study with college students by Fontenot and Benton (1972), which, in addition to finding significantly more accurate identification of the direction of lines in the left visual field, demonstrated, in the same subjects, significantly better recognition of nonsense words in the right visual field.

Visual field differences have been reported also for the task of detecting the location of a target. The general procedure in a series of experiments with college students by Kimura (1969) was as follows. A single circle served as the pre-exposure stimulus projected either to the left or the right visual field. Within this field a single dot was presented in one of twenty-five positions. After stimulus exposure, the subject was instructed to report the position of the dot by number from a matrix card containing all twenty-five positions. This card was mounted on the tachistoscope just over the subject's head. The score was the number of correct localizations for each field, left and right, the maximum score being twenty-five for each.

With this procedure, Kimura demonstrated significant field differences, the left-field (i.e. right-hemisphere) scores superior to the right-field scores. To check the possibility that the dot was simply more easily seen in the left field and that increased accuracy of location was the result of ease of detectability, subjects in a separate experiment were not asked to give the location of the dot but simply to indicate whether they had seen it or not, and to say whether it had appeared on the left or right side. The measure was the mean exposure time at which the dots were detected. This time, field differences were absent, indicating that the field differences in the localization task could not reasonably be assumed to stem from differences between the fields in terms of the ease with which the dot could be detected—at least within the range of exposure times used.

In the same study cited earlier, Durnford and Kimura (1971) also reported findings suggesting that the right hemisphere is more critical for distance perception. To the back of a tachistoscope they attached a box containing a fixed vertical central rod in line with the fixation point. On each side of the central rod was a track on which another vertical rod could be moved. The movable rod was seen with both eyes for only a split second and the subject was to judge whether it was nearer to or farther from the central rod. When the variable rod was presented in the left visual field (so that the information was projected to the right hemisphere), the subjects were more accurate.

These field differences appeared only when the subject viewed the movable rod binocularly. There were no field differences with monocular viewing. This additional result suggests that binocular information is processed primarily by the right hemisphere, while monocular information is processed by both hemispheres.

The role of the right hemisphere in binocular depth perception has been studied also through comparisons of brain-damaged patients according to locus of disease. One such demonstration has been reported by Carmon and Bechtoldt (1969). Instead of a distance judgment task, however, these investigators assessed stereoscopic processing ability. They generated random-letter stereograms from an IBM 7044 computer program (Bunge, 1967), slightly modifying the random-dot stereograms developed by Julesz (1964). Essentially, the subject's task is to locate a form in depth. Methodologically, the use of stereograms permits almost ideal conditions for the investigation of binocular depth perception, since the stereograms eliminate monocular figure-ground contours and other monocular cues that could be used in stereoscopic vision. It also permits the systematic varying of such factors as matrix density and degree of retinal disparity, which can influence performance on this task. The results indicated substantial impairment in stereoscopic vision (more errors and longer response times) in patients with right-hemisphere disease, while patients with left hemisphere disease were not significantly different from control patients without cerebral disease. Since publication of this study, these results have been confirmed by Benton and Hécaen (1970) with brain-damaged patients, and with normal subjects (college students) by Durnford and Kimura (1971).

Insofar as the clinical studies are concerned, it is not clear what the relation is between disabilities in stereopsis and more real-life, or "ecologically valid," measures of depth perception. On the one hand, as Benton and Hécaen (1970) point out, those patients in their study who failed the random-letter stereoscopic task nevertheless performed adequately on a conventional test of stereoscopic vision (the Keystone slide) involving defined forms. Apparently, the stereogram task, in which monocular cues are excluded, is required to demonstrate the defect shown both in their study and in the Carmon and Bechtoldt (1969) study. On the other hand, the clinical literature contains numerous descriptions of the difficulty experienced by patients with right-hemisphere disease in estimating relative or absolute distance or size and the frequent mislocalization of objects in space (see Benton, 1969). Consequently, it is not possible to say that the human infant's demonstrated ability to detect the "deep" side of the visual cliff (Walk and Gibson, 1961), even well before he can locomote (Campos et al., 1970), constitutes evidence for right hemispheric specialization for depth discrimination of the kind implied in the studies reviewed above. The answer to this question must await further analysis of the particular skills or components of skills that comprise what we call "depth discrimination" (Harris, 1973b). For the time being, however, we can say that the available research is consistent with Durnford and Kimura's suggestion that the functional specialization of the right cerebral hemisphere for complex visuospatial functions "may be based on its predominance for fundamental visual processes" (1971, p. 395).

## AUDITION

The respective specializations of the left and right cerebral hemispheres for linguistic and nonlinguistic targets in the realm of vision are matched in audition. Speech sounds, such as spoken digits and other words, are heard more accurately by the left hemisphere, while nonspeech sounds, such as coughing, laughing, crying, or melodic patterns, are heard more accurately by the right hemisphere.

The method by which these auditory asymmetries have been demonstrated is the dichotic listening technique. This technique, devised by Broadbent (1954), usually involves simultaneous presentation of one target to one ear and a different target to the other. Several such pairs of targets are delivered in sequence during a trial and the subject then is asked to report what he has heard, in whatever order he likes.[6]

The value of this technique for the analysis of hemispheric specialization was discovered by Kimura (1961). She presented digits as the target sounds in a test with brain-damaged patients and found that patients with left-hemisphere damage in the temporal region reported fewer digits correctly than patients with right temporal-region damage. This was expected. But, fortuitously, she also found that patients, regardless of the region damaged, reported digits heard with their right ears more accurately than those heard with their left. Unimpaired people did the same.

Since the left and right ears do not have different basic capacities to detect sound, this right-ear superiority must be related to how the ears are connected to the brain. Here is where the principle of "contralateral innervation" referred to earlier is pertinent. Though the auditory system anatomically speaking is less crossed than the visual system or the tactual and motor systems, the crossed auditory connections are still stronger than the ipsilateral connections. The left hemisphere "prefers" to listen through the right, contralateral ear, and vice versa.[7] Since the left hemisphere is specialized for speech perception, it is predictable that speech sounds presented to the right ear would be perceived better. Vocal nonspeech sounds should show a left-ear superiority, suggesting that they are better processed by the right hemisphere.

The dichotic listening technique offers a means of tracing the chronologic development of hemispheric lateralization for both speech and nonspeech sounds. In the case of speech lateralization, one of the first studies with children was reported by Kimura (1963) with 120 normal-hearing children between four and nine years of age—all primary-grade children with above-average intelligence and with normal hearing. The test material consisted of spoken digits presented simultaneously to the two ears. The child was asked to report what he had heard, in any order he liked.

For each age group, digits arriving at the right ear proved to be better recognized than digits arriving at the left ear. The difference between ears actually decreased in the older children, probably because of their higher overall performance (ceiling effect). The right-ear advantage in children was corroborated by Knox and

Kimura (1970, Experiment 1) in a subsequent study with 80 five to eight-year-old children.

The use of a verbal method of report in these studies raises the question whether the right-ear advantage is more a reflection of left hemisphere specialization for verbal *expression* than for the reception of verbal signals. To test this possibility, Knox and Kimura (1970, Experiment 2) substituted a nonverbal method of report in a second experiment with 120 five to eight-year-old children. Each child heard a binaural voice saying "point to the . . .," followed by a dichotic pair of similar-sounding words. The members of each dichotic pair shared the same vowel sound but differed in either the initial or final consonant sound, e.g. "boys-toys." Then, for each trial, a card bearing four pictures (two depicting the dichotic words) was presented and the child was told to point to the picture of the word he had heard. The child also was asked to place one of six small toy objects (bell, cat, two rocks, car, bed, and box) on the appropriate picture in a book. The child heard a dichotic command, such as "Put the 'bell-bat' on the 'nail-pail', the first dichotic pair referring to the pictures in the book.

The results again indicated significant right-ear advantage for all age groups and for both the pointing and placing tasks.

Because the "placing" and "pointing" techniques make so little demand on language expression (the only linguistic demands placed on the child are those required by the $E$'s instructions), they seem an ideal means for tracing lateralization down to still younger children whose poorer articulation may prevent use of the usual verbal report method. Recently, these nonverbal techniques were used in a study by Ingram (1973), with 103 three to five-year-old children. The results corroborated both the earlier studies of Kimura (1963) and Knox and Kimura (1970). Words arriving at the right ear were responded to more accurately (59.3% correct) than words arriving at the left ear (37% correct) by all age groups. While there was no uniform increase in proficiency between the three and five-year-olds, the four and five-year-olds did significantly better than the three-year-olds.

Thus, as early as age three, spoken material arriving at the right ear is more accurately reported than spoken material arriving at the left ear, a result that suggests that left cerebral dominance for speech is established at least by the age of three. It would appear that children perhaps as young as twelve to fifteen months of age could be tested using this procedure, if stimulus materials are of objects familiar to the child.

If the evidence from the dichotic listening paradigm is that language becomes lateralized to the left hemisphere as early as three years of age, when are nonverbal abilities lateralized to the right hemisphere? With the dichotic listening technique, apparently the only reported attempt to answer this question was undertaken by Knox and Kimura (1970) with the same children who participated in the digit test described above. The earliest chronologic tracing of right-hemisphere functions with the dichotic technique is, therefore, to five years of age.

In Experiment 1, with eighty children, a variety of pairs of nonverbal, environmental sounds were presented, including a phone dialing—clock ticking; children playing—car starting; water pouring—yawning; coughing—brushing teeth, and several others. The two members of each dichotic pair were judged to be roughly comparable in ease of recognition, pitch, and rhythm. In Experiment 2, with 120 more children, the same pairs of environmental sounds were presented, plus a variety of animal sounds. For the environmental sounds, recognition was better by the left ear at *every* age level, just as digits had been better recognized by the right ear. For the animal sounds, the results were almost as clear: recognition was more accurate by the left ear for all groups except the eight-year-old boys and the seven-year-old girls.

It remains to be seen whether studies using the dichotic presentation with still younger children will disclose different *rates* of lateralization for language and nonlanguage stimuli. This is a research question clearly ripe for further study.

## HEMISPHERIC SPECIALIZATION IN HAPTIC PERCEPTION: LEFT-HAND SUPERIORITY FOR SPATIAL DISCRIMINATION

Although most of the evidence for hemispheric specialization comes from studies of auditory and visual perception, a few studies have provided evidence for the specialization of tactual perception as well. If the input from hand to cerebral hemisphere occurs contralaterally and if the right hemisphere specialization for visual-spatial perception holds for tactual perception, then in tasks requiring spatial discrimination, we should expect *better* performance by the *nondominant* hand (for most people, being right-handed, this would be the left hand). This is contrary to our usual expectations about differences in skill between the dominant and nondominant hands but it is precisely what the available research tends to show.

Perhaps the first such demonstrations were reported some forty-five years ago in the context of debate about the most efficient methods of instructing the blind in Braille-reading. Among the questions debated were the following: was one hand better than the other? Were two hands better than one? One opinion (Heller, 1904; cited by Smith, 1929, p. 220) held that both hands must be better than one. Heller speculated that in reading there is a division of labor between the two hands with a special function for each, the left hand being used chiefly for keeping the line and for slow, analyzing exploration, while the right hand would furnish the picture of the whole word or phrase. Later, Smith (1929), in a monograph entitled, "Which hand is the eye of the blind?", observed that this characterization would be necessitated by our practice of reading from left to right—a practice shared in Braille reading. Thus she writes: "The truth underlying Heller's statement seems to rest on the fact that *all normal reading* by a skilled reader becomes '*skimming*,' and that this in the blind is assumed by the right hand because its progress is never obstructed by the other hand (while reading from left to right)" (p. 220).

The question was put to test. Grasemann (cited in Smith, 1929; no reference given) had blind students read a text first with both hands, then with each hand alone. Based on reading time and number of errors, almost half of the subjects relied more on the left hand, while the remainder divided their preference. On the average, 153 seconds were used for two-hand reading, 89 additional seconds for left hand reading alone, and 108 additional seconds for right hand reading alone. Grasemann concluded that ". . . the right index finger can by no means be regarded as the proper reading finger, but rather the left" (cited by Smith, p. 221; no reference given).

Similar tests by Bürklen (1924; cited by Smith, 1929, p. 222) and

Hartmann (cited by Smith, 1929, p. 222, no reference given) yielded similar findings. Smith herself repeated these tests in a careful study, adding a comparison of left-to-right direction with right-to-left direction. Her results supported the previous findings. They also indicated that the left hand was superior regardless of the direction of scan.[8]

These results recently have been corroborated by Hermelin and O'Connor (1971a, 1971b). Interestingly, what stimulated their studies was a chance observation of a right-handed blind child who had hurt his left hand—which he called his "reading hand." The child claimed to be unable to read with the fingers of his uninjured right hand and indeed could not do so.

In one experiment (Experiment 1, 1971a; 1971b), sixteen children between eight and ten years of age, all blind from birth, were tested. Fourteen of the children were right-handed and two were apparently bidextrous. Twelve children read spontaneously with the index finger of each hand held close together, while the four remaining children used mainly the index finger of the left hand. The children were tested for reading speed with the index finger and with the middle finger separately for each hand. For the group as a whole, left hand scores were significantly faster than right hand scores in the reading of simple sentences. Only two children, both right-handers, read faster with their right-hand fingers.

When the measure was number of errors, the different scores were not significant, though marginally significant for the middle-finger, perhaps because it was the less-practiced finger. For at least some children, the difference in accuracy was striking: the authors report that some children, though fluent with left-hand reading, could only produce gibberish when required to read with their right. One wonders whether the difficulty at least partly stemmed from a confusion in direction of scan similar to that reported earlier by Smith (1929).

In a second experiment (1971a), Hermelin and O'Connor tested fifteen totally blind adults, twenty-five to sixty-five years of age. Nine had been blind from birth, while six had lost their sight later in life. Of these six persons, two had lost their sight only three years before the experiment. Most of the younger adults had been formally instructed in Braille, while most of the older ones had taught themselves.

This time the subjects were tested on repeated different orderings of the twenty-six individual Braille letters of the alphabet. The letters were arranged vertically and read from top to bottom to control for possible motoric scanning bias from left to right which might have favored the left hand (Smith's study, described earlier, had found such a bias). This time, number of errors but not speed (that is, total number of letters read) discriminated the two hands, the left hand making significantly fewer errors than the right.

The results of these studies may seem paradoxical, since one would expect that Braille characters, being symbols of letters of the alphabet, would be better discriminated by the *right*, not left hand (by the left, linguistic, hemisphere). However, Braille symbols consist of varying numbers of dots in different arrangements. Sighted subjects perceive similar dot patterns more efficiently when projected to the left visual field (right cerebral hemisphere) (Kimura, 1969), consistent with the notion that spatial arrays are better detected by the right hemisphere. Of course, the dot patterns in this case were not symbols of letters. Even so, the possibility occurs that, for the blind person, Braille symbols are first encoded as spatial configurations and only then processed as meaningful patterns (O'Connor and Hermelin, 1971a). We therefore might expect that subjects ignorant of the meaning of the Braille patterns would show even stronger left hand superiority in the course of learning the Braille patterns.

Parenthetically, it is interesting to note that some of Hermelin and O'Connor's subjects reported that they spontaneously had switched their Braille wrist watches from the left wrist, where it is normally worn by right-handed persons, to the right wrist. The numerals on Braille watches are expressed as combinations of raised dots. The subjects explained that they discovered that they could tell time more accurately with the left hand than with the right (personal communication from B. Hermelin).

The subjects in Hermelin and O'Connor's work, as well as in Smith's earlier study, were experienced Braille readers and, as Hermelin and O'Connor point out, usually read with their left hand when copying with their right. That is, since the right-handed blind person writes with his right hand, he must feel the letters to be copied with his left hand. The hand asymmetries in Braille reading therefore might be a result of this experience. Recently, however, an experiment with sighted children has been reported (Rudel et al., 1974), and while, as we shall see, it does not entirely resolve the question of prior experience, it does suggest (along with other studies to be described) that it probably should be judged secondary to an explanation stressing hemisphere specialization.

The subjects were eighty children ranging in age from seven to fourteen years. All were right-handed as defined by handwriting, and by the child's own and the teacher's designation. The children were average for grade placement and achievement. Each child had to learn six Braille letters with one hand, and six different letters with the other hand, in a paired associates procedure. Half the children were trained first with the left hand, then the right; for the remaining children the sequence was reversed.

The results were somewhat equivocal. Though average performance by the left hand was generally better, its superiority was significant only among the oldest children. For the youngest children, right-hand performance was better. One suspects that for sighted children, required to learn verbal labels to novel spatial configurations, language is involved to a substantially greater degree, and perhaps in fundamentally different ways, than would be the case with blind subjects tested on what is for them a familiar task. It may be that left hand superiority for younger sighted subjects might appear only late in training, as a "performance" difference well after the verbal associations themselves are learned.

Left-hand superiority in haptic discrimination has also been reported in two other recent studies with children. Ingram, in the same study described earlier (1973), gave 103 normal, right-handed boys and girls a variety of simple tasks:

For a test of "hand positioning," the child had to copy various hand positions from the deaf alphabet demonstrated by the examiner. For "finger spacing," the child had to copy the examiner's hand by grouping his fingers with spaces between them. For both tasks, the examiner sat beside the child. For "finger lifting," the child placed both hands palm down on a piece of paper, and then raised a single finger as it was touched by the examiner. For a test of "joint position," the child placed his hands flat on the table; then with his eyes open, he had to indicate the direction of movement as one of his fingers was raised or lowered by the examiner from a starting position just above the table. For "finger tapping," the child tapped a telegraph key with his index finger as quickly as he could. Finally, "hand strength" was measured with a dynamometer.

For these right-handed children, the right hand expectedly was significantly stronger than and tapped faster than the left hand. But on the hand-positioning, finger spacing, and joint position tasks, the left hand was superior. On the finger-lifting task, there were no hand differences. A spatial component of the hand positioning and finger spacing tasks seems, therefore, to have accounted for the hand differences, since both tasks required the fingers to be arranged in spatial configuration with reference to each other.[9]

A somewhat different procedure for assessing hemisphere specialization for tactual perception was used by Witelson (1973). She presented both nonlinguistic stimuli (unfamiliar meaningless four to eight sided shapes) and cut-outs of English letters in a tactual variation of the dichotic technique. Thus on any one trial, the child, for ten seconds, either felt two nonsense forms or two letter forms, and was simply told to identify the forms he had felt by pointing to a visual display. The subjects were forty-seven right-handed boys, ranging in age from six to fourteen years. Nonsense shapes presented to the left hand were more accurately recognized than those presented to the right hand.

Unlike the Rudel et al. (1973) findings with Braille reading, the hand asymmetry in Witelson's results was apparent throughout the age range, including the six-year-olds. Thus at least by six years of age, in right-handed boys, the right hemisphere appears to be specialized for the processing of nonlinguistic spatial information in the tactual perceptual system. It may be objected that Witelson's results simply indicate greater left-hand tactual sensitivity and thus have little to do with right-hemisphere spatial specialization *per se*. Witelson rejects this possibility on the grounds that what research that has shown differential hand sensitivity (e.g. Ghent, 1961) finds it only by eleven years of age in right-handed boys.

While Witelson's results indicate left hand superiority for *spa-*

*tial* perception, the expected greater right-hand (left hemisphere) accuracy for the dichotomous presentation of pairs of letters was not found. Instead there were no significant differences between the hands. Witelson observes that even if both hemispheres were equally able to process these simple linguistic stimuli (as the absence of hemispheric differences would appear to imply), requiring the child to name the letters would have necessitated left (speech) hemisphere participation at least at this point. Therefore letters presented to the right hand should, it seems, have enjoyed at least this advantage. If anything, however, the findings suggested a trend toward better left-hand perception, leading Witelson to suggest that ". . . at least in the initial processing of somesthetic linguistic stimuli the right hemisphere has a more important role. Although tactual letters are linguistic symbols, they are also spatial stimuli and to this extent may be dependent on right hemisphere functioning for spatial analysis" (Witelson, 1973).

## HAND DIFFERENCES: A FUNCTION OF STYLE
## OF HAPTIC EXPLORATION?

To account for left-hand superiority in these various tasks in terms of right hemisphere specialization for spatial perception is not completely satisfying inasmuch as it remains incomplete. For instance, Witelson's tasks were tasks of *haptic* discrimination, requiring the active tactual exploration of an object. As a result, was the left hand superiority partly or wholly due to a different and more adequate style of exploration? Some evidence to support this possibility comes from an earlier study by Levy-Agresti and Sperry (1968) of "split-brain" patients.[10]

The patients had to match three-dimensional forms, held in the left or right hand, with their unfolded shapes drawn as expanded patterns on cards and presented visually. The test, in the authors' characterization, assessed the patients' ability to think three-dimensionally. The results showed that the right hemisphere was superior to the left in that haptic sensitivity was greater for the left than for the right hand. Levy-Agresti observed that "while the left hemisphere seemed to analyze the stimulus properties, the right hemisphere seemed immediately to abstract the stimulus Gestalt—that is, as an integrated whole. It was as if the speaking hemisphere processed stimulus information in such a way that the stimulus could be described in language. Gestalt appreciation seemed to be actively counteracted by a strong analytic propensity in the language hemisphere . . ." (Levy [Levy-Agresti], 1969, p. 614).

Unfortunately, neither Levy nor Witelson provide descriptions of their subjects' actual behavior. Presumably Levy's references to style of analysis of each hemisphere (or hand) have to do with how her patients actually moved their hands over the surface of the three-dimensional objects placed in each hand. The implication may be that left-hand exploration was more far-ranging, with the fingers moving simultaneously, as though to gain some overall haptic picture of the object; while right-hand exploration was more piecemeal, covering the various facets of the object one at a time, in an orderly, "linear" fashion—as though (picking up Levy's suggestion, quoted earlier, that the ". . . speaking hemisphere processed stimulus information in such a way that the stimulus could be described in language") the patient thereby could say to himself, "Now here's a sharp point, then a flat side rather long, then another point, then a somewhat shorter flat side . . .," and so forth.

These speculations may be consistent both with a suggestion by Kimura and Vanderwolf (1970) that the preferred hand is characterized by "synergistic" rather than discrete patterns of movement and with findings that the preferred hand is characterized by a more consistent temporal pattern of movement than the non-preferred hand (Provins, 1956, 1958).

While frame-by-frame examinations of video-tape recordings of haptic exploration will help determine whether such hand differences exist, such differences, if observed, will not tell the whole story by themselves. There still appears to be a basic sensitivity difference over and beyond any possible differences in style of exploration. This conclusion is suggested in a recent study of "passive" stimulation by Benton et al. (in press).

The instrument used to present the tactile stimuli was an electro-mechanical stimulator (Carmon and Dyson, 1967)—a linear array of three stainless steel rods positioned above the subject's palm which were capable of being delivered to the palm in various directions guided by radial lines printed on a grid stamped upon the palms before testing. The apparatus thus permitted control of force, area of stimulation, duration of application, and direction of stimulation. The subject's view of his hand was, of course, obstructed throughout testing. The subjects (right-handed university students) were shown a card displaying the four directions and were told to point to the direction that was the same as the directional stimulation they felt each time they were touched. Of twenty-four subjects, accuracy of identification was significantly higher for the left hand than for the right in seventeen subjects, five showed the reverse effect, and the remaining two showed equal accuracy in the two hands.

The procedures used in these various studies can be easily extended to a variety of special research populations. The procedures, however, are complicated by the fact that one must take into account the nature of the subject's response. In Witelson's study, as the author points out, the extent to which the right hemisphere *can* process linguistic tactual stimuli is obscured, since the only response used involved speech (in the case of the letters).

As for age differences, as we have seen, there was no indication in Witelson's data of any differences in the strength of the effect across the age range studied (six to fourteen years). How far down in age, then, could these differential sensitivities between hands be traced? Ingram's findings suggest that such sensitivity is to be found among young children and perhaps even infants. In which hand, for instance, is the infant most likely to recognize his familiar rattle? Although the limited research on the early development of hand preferences (e.g. Gesell and Ames, 1947) appears to indicate a good deal of shifting about in usage—from the ultimately non-preferred to the ultimately preferred hand, with stages of bilateral usage included —it still may be that sensitivity differences are involved from the very onset. These different sensitivities might *not* be reflected in different hand usage *per se*, but only in such finer tests as could be presented and assessed in careful psychological analysis (e.g. Benton, 1962).

## THE MEANING OF "HAND DOMINANCE"

The research described here underscores the question, what do we mean by the familiar term "dominant hand" or, more generally, by the term "dominant hemisphere"? The "dominant" hand may be the quicker and the stronger, and for these reasons, to be favored for certain tasks; but the "nondominant" hand can no longer be considered merely a weaker, less skillful version of the other, no more than the right hemisphere can be called merely a weaker version of the left hemisphere. Rather it can be judged the "dominant" hand for certain spatial skills. Its newly rediscovered functions, furthermore, must be taken into account in the analysis of the development of handedness itself. For example, Gesell and Ames (1947) found that many children settle on one hand as the preferred hand only by three or four years of age, or even later. This is after language comes in strongly, though it is approximately when the child begins to use language to direct and control nonverbal (motor) behavior (Luria, 1969). Before this time, there are periods of preference for the hand that is ultimately to be the nondominant hand. Could these periods be expressions of greater sensitivity by the nondominant hand for the haptic exploration of the environment, and for the nonlinear, nonanalytic manner of exploration for which the spatial hemisphere apparently is better suited?

The role of the nondominant hand must also be considered in the analysis of the development of cognitive-spatial skills. For example, we usually attribute the different "haptic strategies" employed by children of different ages in the exploration of objects (e.g. in haptic-haptic or haptic-visual matching tasks) to the emergence of more and more sophisticated "cognitive" strategies. Now perhaps we have some reason to interpret "cognitive strategy" in terms of neurological specialization of each hand. Consider a specific instance. In a developmental study of haptic discrimination of forms, the usual procedure is to have the child feel the form with his preferred hand. Then most children, being right-handed, will be exploring the stimulus with the "linguistic" rather than the "spatial" hand. This fact suggests, for one thing, that most scores probably will be depressed. According to Witelson's data, this effect should be enhanced when the forms are nonsense forms (as they are in numerous studies of haptic discrimination) and may be present, though less strongly, for linguistic stimuli too.

But more critically, the research findings reviewed here suggest that in a developmental study of haptic discrimination, finding an age effect might be grossly misleading in a theoretical sense. Suppose most children use the right (preferred) hand and there are only small age differences in accuracy. This result could stem from greater functional lateralization for older children; that is, it could be that right-hand discrimination of nonsense stimuli is relatively more difficult for older children than for younger children. For older children, in other words, the left hemisphere is more nearly specialized for linguistic processes. With respect to developmental investigations of haptic discrimination, the point should be made that these findings must be considered not merely to add a small measure of control to the basic developmental design. Rather, to ignore the different statuses of the two hands is to risk gross distortion of one's results.

I have discussed asymmetries in the performance of haptic and visual discriminations separately primarily for the sake of convenience in organization. But there is a risk here, for separate discussion encourages the notion that the two perceptual modalities are more separable than they are, and that we therefore are dealing with two different and independent perceptual systems. At least with sighted subjects, or subjects with some history of vision, and particularly in the case of a haptic discrimination task, the likelihood is that just the reverse is the case. One's hands, like every part of one's body, are represented in a visual space, that is, one has a good idea (mental picture, or image) of where one's hands are. This is part of what is meant by "body image." Thus, in all the haptic discrimination tasks reviewed here, the subject, though unable to see his hands during the task, nevertheless can be assumed to represent his hands in visual space. The extent to which this visual representation intrudes on haptic perception is easily demonstrated in the familiar game whereby one crosses one's wrists, brings the palms together, interlocks the fingers, rotates the wrists in the vertical plane, and then, with the wrists covered so that the fingers cannot be visually traced down to their respective hands, tries to wriggle individual fingers as each is designated by another person. A finger on one's left side is easily mistaken for a finger belonging to one's left hand.

The extent to which being sighted influences this visual "mapping," or representing, of one's limbs is powerfully and cleverly demonstrated, in a different task, by McKinney (1964).[11]

## STRUCTURAL FACTORS UNDERLYING HEMISPHERIC SPECIALIZATION

It seems reasonable to assume that such striking asymmetries in function between the twin hemispheres must be associated with similarly striking asymmetries in structure. The search for such structural differences has been under way for more than a century.

### Morphological differences

Physical asymmetry of the hemispheres of the brain is only one of numerous morphological asymmetries in the human body. As many physiologists have noted, the asymmetries of paired organs are more the rule than the exception. For example, in most humans the right arm is slightly longer than the left; the left leg is slightly longer than the right; and the left clavicle is longer than the right (Martin 1957-1960). Woo (1931), in a study of the individual bones of the skull, found that in the frontal and parietal region, the right bone was consistently the larger one. There are many other such examples. As von Bonin (1962) observed, however, in summarizing the major lines of evidence as of 1961, attempts to find physical asymmetries in the brain itself have met with much less success. For instance, Boyd published brain weights in 1861, finding left hemispheres to be heavier than right hemispheres by about five grams. But subsequent investigations found the right hemisphere to be heavier. In 1866, Bastien determined the specific gravity of the gray matter and found the left side somewhat heavier. The differences do not inspire confidence: for the left frontal area, 1.0291; for the right, 1.0276; for the left parietal area, 1.0300; for the right, 1.0296; for the left occipital area, 1.0320; for the right, 1.0316. As von Bonin pointed out, either the left hemisphere has a higher concentration of cells in its cortex or the errors of Bastien's determination are of the order of .004. Von Bonin prefers the latter explanation—surely a prudent choice.

After reviewing some two dozen other studies, von Bonin concluded that all reported differences in hemispheric symmetry were quite small and the problem remained to correlate them with the remarkable differences in function. This, von Bonin wrote, ". . . is an entirely different question, and one that I am unable to answer" (p.

6). Jung (1962), after reviewing all of the negative evidence, suggested an answer: ". . . it may be inferred that—in spite of some innate factors for the function of cortical speech areas—the hemispheric difference is mainly acquired by learning, and the species difference is mainly a functional one" (p. 270).[12]

It is interesting to note the responses of other conference members to von Bonin's largely negative conclusion. One suggested that those who seek anatomical correlates of unilateral hemispheric dominance may be up against the possibility that the anatomy of the hemispheres is totally irrelevant to the problem. Instead, quantitative analysis of internal structure is called for on the cellular level (Bodian, 1962, pp. 25-26). Still another, however, observed that the situation—the mirror-image structure of functionally different organs—is not unique to neurology. Pasteur had found a similar problem when he investigated chemical substances that are optical isomers (Pribram, 1962, p. 110).

### Recent evidence

Since von Bonin's 1962 summary, Geschwind and Levitsky (1970) have reported what appears to be a convincing anatomical difference, a difference which, ironically, is gross-anatomical, not fine, as the discussants of von Bonin's paper had supposed it would have to be.

Geschwind and Levitsky studied one hundred adult brains, obtained at postmortum, and free of significant pathology. The researchers divided the hemispheres and then exposed the upper surface of the temporal lobe (supratemporal plane) on each side by cutting into the plane of the Sylvian fissures, the fissures separating the anterior and middle lobes of the cerebrum. (They thus exposed the top of the temporal lobes to full view. The area they studied would not have been visible in the intact brain because it lies within the depths of the Sylvian fissure.) Here they found that the "planum temporale," or temporal plane—a particular portion of the temporal lobe in the area behind Heschl's gyrus—was larger on the left in about 65 percent of the brains, equal in 24 percent, and larger on the right in about 11 percent. In absolute terms, the left planum was nine millimeters longer on the average than the right planum. In relative terms, it was one third longer than the right.

This newly-discovered enlarged part of the brain is in an area constituting part of the temporal speech cortex (an extension of Wernicke's area). This latter was identified one hundred years ago (1874) as being intimately involved in the higher analysis of speech sounds. The most critical area is the hindmost—the parieto-temporal area. Damage to this area usually results in serious aphasia.

The handedness of the persons from whom these brains were taken was not known, but presumably, since about 96 percent of the population (mixing left and right-handers) are left-brained for speech, these one hundred cases would have to have consisted of approximately this proportion of left-brain-dominant subjects. In a later paper Geschwind (1970, p. 944) mentions confirmation of these results by Wada (1969).

Structural differences between the hemispheres consistent with Geschwind and Levitsky's (1965) findings have been observed in living persons through the method of arteriography. LeMay and Culebras (1972) studied the carotid arteriograms of forty-four patients with bilateral arches and without any large intracranial lesions to distort the pattern of vessels.[13] The arches formed by the branches of the middle cerebral arteries as they left the posterior part of the Sylvian fissures were clearly narrower on the left than on the right in thirty-eight of forty-four patients. The implication is that the parietal operculum[14] was larger on the left than on the right in these thirty-eight patients. In other words, the arches formed by the middle cerebral artery as it turns to escape from the Sylvian fossa were more sharply angulated on the left side. This finding, the authors point out, confirms many earlier observations (Cunningham, 1892) that the right Sylvian fissure angles upward more than the fissure on the left.

LeMay and Culebras then went on to study the relative positions of the Sylvian points in dissected brains. The point on the left was lower than that on the right in fourteen of eighteen brains, consistent with the arteriographic findings of greater development of the parietal operculum on the left in living persons.

Thus a morphological factor would seem to underlie left-hemisphere specialization for language. What of the right hemisphere? Does it owe its apparent specialization for visuospatial functions merely by default, that is, to its having a less-developed linguistic structure? Or is there also some area specialized for spatial processing that is enlarged, or better developed, on the right side? The evidence on this question is thin, but at least one possibly relevant difference has been reported in the parietal occipital area (McCrae et al., 1968). For many years it has been known that there is an asymmetry of the occipital horns of the lateral ventricles and that the left occipital horn is usually larger (Penfield, 1925; cited in McCrae et al., 1968). If the occipital horn is larger or longer, this means that the corresponding part of the cortex will be smaller. It also is known that unilateral cerebral atrophy may lead to widening of the occipital horn, and even to lengthening in the case of pronounced atrophy (McCrae et al., 1968).

McCrae et al. (1968) assessed the degree of correlation between handedness and the incidence of a larger occipital horn in the left hemisphere (or, *indirectly*, the relation between handedness and the size of the occipital cortex in the *right* hemisphere). To do this, they scored one hundred pneumoencephalograms and ventriculograms for occipital horn type and length. The records were from hospitalized neurological and neurosurgical patients. Of the eighty-seven right-handed patients in this sample, fifty-seven showed a longer left occipital horn, thirteen showed a longer right occipital horn, and thirty showed occipital horns of equal length. A longer left occipital horn thus correlated moderately well with right-handedness. The number of left-handers and ambidextrous subjects was too small for analysis, but a longer right horn was found more often in the left-handed patients than chance would indicate. The authors consider these findings as evidence that the "dominant cerebral hemisphere may be slightly smaller, at least posteriorly, than the non-dominant one" (p. 98).

From Geschwind and Levitsky's work, we know that a certain part of the temporal lobe is larger in the left hemisphere, and from McCrae and other's work, we have at least indirect and suggestive evidence that the parieto-occipital lobe is larger on the right. Since in the great majority of individuals, speech is subserved by the left temporal (and frontal) lobe, and spatial visual perception in the right parieto-occipital region, the results of these two studies agree with results of the dichotic listening, tachistoscopic, and haptic discrimination studies reported earlier.

Geschwind (1972, p. 194) also mentions preliminary studies by Sheremata and Geschwind suggesting a high correlation between a longer left occipital horn and a larger left planum. If a longer left occipital horn means a smaller occipital cortex, and if the occipital cortex is important in visuospatial perception, then this correlation suggests that the left hemisphere both possesses special language capacity and lacks visuospatial capacity. Presuming that the reverse relation holds for the right side, we may infer that the right hemisphere possesses special visuospatial capacity while lacking linguistic capacity.

Whatever the eventual status of the neuroanatomical evidence, these conclusions cannot be accepted unqualifiedly. There are at least two reasons. One is that in the normal person, the right hemisphere has language capacity, though, as Jackson pointed out over a century ago (1868), it is of a different kind than that subserved by the left hemisphere. "I think the facts of cases of loss of speech from damage to but one—the left—half, show conclusively that as regards the use of words the brain is double in function. But the very same cases show that the two hemispheres are not mere duplicates in this function. Both halves are alike in so far as each contains processes for words. They are unlike in that the left alone is for the use of words in speech" (Jackson, 1915, p. 81).

Those forms of language organized bilaterally were, according to Jackson, the more "primitive" or automatic forms, such as emotional utterances, and to a somewhat lesser extent, comprehension. Dominance, then, was a matter of degree; and damage to the "leading" hemisphere (Jackson himself, according to Head, 1926, never used the term "dominant") would affect above all the most complex and least automatic aspects of psychological functioning. Recent experimental and clinical evidence has borne out Jackson's views.

A second reason is that the right hemisphere seems to be capable of taking over even the more complex language functions when the left hemisphere sustains *early* injury, such as in infancy or early childhood. Broca, in 1861, had made just this surmise. As Zangwill (1964) said of Broca, "His inspired guess has been brilliantly vindicated" (1964, p. 107). A review of case histories is offered by Basser (1962).

## HEMISPHERIC DIFFERENCES IN INFANCY

From the developmental standpoint, all these differences still leave unanswered the question of origins. Are these anatomical differences a product of our genetic endowment or are they somehow a product of acculturation? The data most relevant to these questions have been obtained from studies of human infants. Several studies have been reported recently.

### *Asymmetry in size of anatomic structures*

The same asymmetry described by Geschwind and Levitsky (1968) in the planum temporale has been found in newborn infants. Witelson and Pallie (1973) measured the brains of eleven infants ranging in age from one to twenty-one days, three infants ranging in age from one to three months, and also sixteen adults. As in the Geschwind and Levitsky study, all brains were free from neurological pathology; the causes of death were identified for the neonates as cardiovascular, respiratory, and gastrointestinal diseases. The results corroborated Geschwind and Levitsky's: the left planum was significantly larger by about two/thirds than the comparable area on the right side in both infants and adults.[15] Similar differences in fetal brains are reported to have been found by Wada (1969; cited by Geschwind, 1970). Lemay and Culebras (1972), in the same study described earlier, also found asymmetries resembling those of adult brains in the Sylvian fissures of ten fetal brains.

### *Postural position in early infancy as an indication of early hemispheric specialization and preferred usage*

Is there any other evidence for very early hemispheric specialization? Consider, for example, some observations on infants' head-orientation preferences. It has been observed that the young infant shows a marked preference for lying with his head turned to the right. Gesell and Ames reported this preference in 1947, and Turkewitz, Gordon, and Birch confirmed this observation in 1965. In one series of observations, Turkewitz et al. (1965) made systematic sample observations of the head positions of one hundred infants ranging in age from several minutes to slightly over one hundred hours and found that on more than three thousand observations during which the infants were observed while lying on their backs, their heads were turned to the right of body midline during 88.0 percent of them. The heads were in midline position during only 2.8 percent of the observations and to the left of body midline during only 9.2 percent of the observations. Furthermore, not only did the infants, while in the supine position, spend about ten times as much time with their heads turned to the right as to the left, but most individual infants spent over 90 percent of the time with their head maintained in a position to the right of body midline. Not a single infant was found to have his head turned to left of midline more frequently than to the right, though some of the infants kept their heads turned to the right more regularly than did other infants.

Turkewitz et al. (1965) first suspected that the extremely high incidence of head right posture was the result of some systematic bias on the part of the nursing staff and, thus, was unrelated to the infants' preferences. To explore this possibility, they studied the *spontaneous* position preferences of two and three-day-old infants by placing the infant's head in midline position, releasing it and then by continuously noting its position during the next fifteen minutes. Under this condition, the infants were found to keep their heads turned to the right for about 75 percent of the test period. The authors concluded that in these two-day-old babies, asymmetrical placement (if such *is* hospital practice; the evidence is that it is not) is *not* required to produce a systematic preference for the head right posture.

Entus (personal communication) has found similar preference for the head-right posture in sixty-two orphanage children between six days and eleven months of age. Of forty-seven infants whose spontaneous posture was observed, forty-one lay supine, thirty-six with head right, five with head left. The remaining six infants lay prone, three with head left, three with head right. The orphanage staff's reported practice was to prop, systematically, the babies' heads to the left and the right during alternate periods of the day.[16]

Turkewitz and Birch (1971) speculate that this first appearance of lateral differentiation of behavior provides a possible basis for the subsequent development of more far-reaching and more functionally significant differences. For example, they suggest that the early lateralization of responsiveness may result in the establishment of a leading side of the body in dealing with the environment, which may lead either directly or indirectly, through some kind of learning process, to the increasing permanence of lateral preference.

I would like to speculate, however, that these lateral differences may indeed *be* the *first* manifestation of hemispheric differentiation, if we begin with the question, why does the infant prefer the head-to-right posture in the first place? Is this an indication of left-ear preference? Since in the case of audition, the contralateral connections are better than the ipsilateral connections, this means that the infants are getting better "input" to the right cerebral hemisphere. Is this evidence that the right hemisphere is, even in earliest infancy, better for detecting environmental (nonlinguistic) auditory stimuli, with this superiority, in turn, leading to the left-ear preference (right head turn)?[17]

Support for this interpretation is provided in a recent and convincing demonstration by Molfese (1972). Molfese (1972) obtained auditory evoked responses (AER) recorded from Wernicke's Area, in the left hemisphere, and from a corresponding area in the right hemisphere, to verbal and nonverbal stimuli, for three groups of subjects—ten infants ranging in age from one week to ten months, eleven children (four to eleven years of age), and ten adults (twenty-three to twenty-nine years). Six sounds were presented: two nonmeaningful speech syllables (/ba/ and /dae/); two mechanically-produced sounds (a C-major piano chord and a speech noise burst); and two meaningful words ("boy" and "dog" spoken by an adult male).

The adults, in general, responded to all verbal stimuli with greater AER activity in the left hemisphere and greater AER activity to the mechanically-produced stimuli in the right hemisphere. The children's responses were substantially similar to the adults. These results might be expected, considering past work with the dichotic listening technique. But the same results were found for the infants. Of the ten infants, nine responded to the noise stimulus with greater right-hemisphere AER activity and all ten infants responded to the musical chord stimulus with greater right-hemisphere activity. Moreover, all ten infants responded with greater left-hemisphere AER activity to the speech syllables, with nine of the ten showing greater left hemisphere AER activity, to one of the word stimuli, and eight to ten to the other. The results, of course, do not mean that the infants "understood" the words— rather that the left hemisphere may be peculiarly sensitive to certain structural features of speech sounds well before the semantic components are learned.

So Molfese's findings suggest that even before the first year of life, the brain is specialized to such an extent that the left cerebral hemisphere subserves language functions, while the right hemisphere subserves nonlanguage functions (in this case, nonmeaningful environmental sounds).

### Hemispheric differences in "strength" and "activity"

We have already mentioned how the right hemisphere, in keeping with its presumed status as the "nondominant" hemisphere, was once considered merely a "weaker" version of the "dominant" left hemisphere. It also was once believed that these presumed differences could be explained as a result of asymmetries in blood supply. It had long been known that the blood supply to the two hemispheres of the human brain was markedly asymmetric. The right cerebral hemisphere is supplied from a vascular trunk which it shares with the right upper extremity, while the left hemisphere is supplied directly from the aortic arch. According to Blau, in his historical monograph, *The Master Hand* (1946), this inequality of blood supply was first advanced as an explanation of sidedness by Lueddeckens (1900), by Lombroso (1903), and by Judd (1911). They contended that because of the asymmetrical arterial system, the blood supply of the cerebral hemispheres was unequal and that handedness would depend on the hemisphere receiving the greater supply. Blau points out how, at the time, careful measurements of the carotid arteries which supply the brain had not yet been made. Thus the assumption of larger carotid arteries to the "dominant" left hemisphere could not be refuted. Blau goes on to mention how the measurements were finally made by Cunningham (1902), who failed to find the alleged difference.

Recent studies using more sensitive techniques, however, have lent new support for the "blood supply" hypothesis, but not in the way expected. One procedure—the so-called "Oldendorf" technique (Oldendorf and Crandal, 1961)—involves injection of hippuran labeled with radioactive iodine into the vein of the arm and released abruptly. Two scintilators placed over the two hemispheres record gamma irradiation and two curves are obtained, one for each hemisphere. (The radioactive isotope disappears from the blood very quickly and is excreted in the first urination. The amount of irradiation is less than 1 Rad., about what is produced by a single X-ray picture.) The curves give a measure of the transit time of the isotope through each hemisphere. Shorter transit time means better flow. The peak and area of the curves which designate blood volume in each hemisphere are also measured.

With this technique, Oldendorf and Crandal (1961) and Thompson (1964) found that irradiations after Iodine 131 injections in adult subjects were usually higher over the *right* hemisphere. Since in a random sample, the great majority of subjects would be expected to be "left-brained" for language, these results appear to indicate greater blood volume and, by implication, greater oxygenation in the "nondominant" hemisphere.

The Oldendorf technique was used also in a recent study by Carmon et al. (1972) which, unlike the previous studies, sought to determine directly whether asymmetries in cerebral blood supply are correlated with asymmetries of hemispheric function. The subjects were eighty-five healthy fifteen to twenty-three year olds. The behavioral measures of dominance were hand preference as measured in terms of responses to a questionnaire, and performance on a dichotic listening test with verbal stimuli.

The results for transit time were negative. Nearly equal proportions of left and right-handed subjects (about 40%) exhibited slightly shorter transit times over the right hemisphere. The results for differences in hemispheric blood volume were positive. Right hand preference or a right ear advantage in the dichotic task were associated with larger blood volume in the *right* hemisphere. Left handedness or left ear advantage were associated with larger blood volume in the *left* hemisphere. When the two measures of cerebral lateralization were combined, the associations were stronger. Once again, then, the evidence suggests greater blood supply to the "nonthan the left hemisphere.

Possibly consistent with these findings are reports of differential prevalence of bioelectrical cerebral pathology in the two hemispheres. Paoluzzi and Bravaccio (1967; cited in Subirana, 1969) examined over four thousand EEG records of patients with diagnosed exclusive or prevalent localized pathology in a single hemisphere and found evidence of more frequent pathology in the *left* hemisphere by a ratio of 7:3. Paoluzzi and Bravaccio conclude that the left hemisphere is more vulnerable. (Presumably, the great majority of Paoluzzi and Bravaccio's EEG records were from right-handed patients.)

Unfortunately, we do not know whether Paoluzzi and Bravaccio took account of the age at which the patients in their study were known to have developed the pathological condition. Some findings by Taylor (1969) suggest that this would be important to know. Taylor determined the incidence of occurrence of epileptic lesion produced through febrile convulsion (i.e. a convulsion resulting from a fever) in each cerebral hemisphere in children of different ages. The results suggested that before children became two years of age, the left cerebral hemisphere appeared to be more at risk than the right, but this differential risk was reversed after two years of age. Taylor interprets both the hemisphere difference and the age crossover as indicating that the lesion tends to occur in whichever cerebral hemisphere was functionally the less active. Therefore, the left hemisphere was more at risk in early years, the right hemisphere less at risk, because before the establishment of language at about two years of age, the left and right hemispheres were, respectively, less and more active. These results appear to support the notion that the *right* hemisphere is more active earlier than the left hemisphere.[18]

Finally, we might note a recent report by Crowell et al. (1973). These investigators obtained EEG's from ninety-seven clinically normal, full-term babies. Recordings were made from right and left occipital areas. The babies were stimulated by repetitive light flashes. EEG changes ("driving") were present in thirty-six infants, sixteen of whom showed significantly greater activity on the right side, two on the left side only, and eighteen on both sides. So eighteen of the thirty-six infants (or about 18 of the total 97) had "unilateral" driving, in sixteen of whom the EEG activity was confined almost exclusively to the right hemisphere.

As Crowell et al, point out, the visual stimulus used in their study produced a diffusely illuminated visual field which they assumed—reasonably, it seems—would stimulate both retinae. But even had the visual input been unilateral rather than bilateral, the partial crossing of the optic pathways would have ensured transmission to both occipital hemispheres. For these reasons, the authors interpret their results to mean that the visual cortical matrix of the left hemisphere is slower to mature and to respond.

## THE RIGHT HEMISPHERE: DIFFUSE ORGANIZATION AND SPATIAL PERCEPTION

The evidence, thus far, indicates that there are neural bases for hemispheric specialization (though we should add that the neuroanatomic factor has been more clearly identified for the left hemisphere and language specialization—the enlarged planum temporale —than for the right hemisphere and spatial specialization). It even indicates, in the case of the left hemisphere, that this specialization is present at birth or before birth. Finally, there is evidence which at least suggests the possibility that the right hemisphere may be stronger, and more active early in life. But we still lack a model for understanding why these neuroanatomic differences play the role they do.

Semmes (1968) has offered a provocative explanation based on some unexpected results of research with war veterans who had suffered penetrating brain injuries in either the left or right hemiphere (Semmes et al., 1960). The purpose of the research was to uncover correlates of astereognosis. The researchers gave the patients a variety of tests, the most revelatory being three "cutaneous" tests: touch-pressure threshold, two-point discrimination, and point localization.

The surprising results were asymmetries on the three tests in both contralateral and ipsilateral sensorimotor processes. In the case of contralateral processes, the incidence and severity of deficits for the right hand was maximal after lesions of the left sensorimotor region. But for the left hand, the deficits were *not* clearly related to lesions of the right sensorimotor region. In other words, they failed to find significant regional localization in the right hemisphere for these tests—a failure, Semmes suggests, deriving in part from the seeming greater effectiveness of the right than the left nonsensorimotor lesion and in part from the lesser apparent effectiveness of right sensorimotor lesions. Therefore, there seemed to be an asymmetry between the hemispheres in contralateral representation in such an elementary function as somatic sensation. Similar asymmetries were found for motor reactions and for reflex functions.

In the case of ipsilateral processes, left-hemisphere lesions proved to be more likely than right-hemisphere lesions to produce ipsilateral deficits. This asymmetry has also been demonstrated in a study by Wyke (1966; cited by Semmes, 1968), who found, in a test requiring the subject to maintain his arms in certain positions without the aid of vision, that left-sided lesions produced significant (though not equal) impairment in both arms, while right-sided lesions impaired only the *contralateral* arm. Semmes concluded that the left-hemisphere thus seems to exhibit "dominance" with respect to the bilaterality of its role in sensation and movement.

From these findings, Semmes proposes a major theoretical assumption: if the hemispheres differ in the principle of representation of *elementary* functions, then might this difference be the basis for true hemispheric dominance at higher levels? The more complex coordinations characteristic of the higher centers might be brought about by convergence of lower-level centers. Sensorimotor integrations involving a set of *similar* functional units presumably would be favored by the anatomic concentration of these units within a small area, that is, by focal representation of elementary functions. "Where there is a higher concentration of units representing a particular part at one level, the convergence of these units upon those of the next level would bring about a more precise coding of the input and would thus make possible a more finely modulated control of the output. This finer control could be based not only on concentration of similar input elements, but also on an analogous concentration of similar output elements. The development of such precise control of the articulatory apparatus may provide an optimal substrate for speech representation in the left hemisphere" (p. 22).

Semmes goes on to suggest that if focal representation is the basis of left hemisphere dominance for language, then qualities that particularly distinguish animals from man—capacity for language and symbolic thought—are "ultimately based on the phylogenetic trend toward increased localization of function and that the left hemisphere has proceeded farther than the right in this direction" (p. 23).

If the left hemisphere's specialization for language is based upon focal representation of sensorimotor functions, then what would be the basis for the specialization of function shown by the right hemisphere? Semmes suggests that the diffuse organization of the right hemisphere may actually be advantageous for spatial abilities. Localization of function has proceeded further in humans than in other animals, yet other animals still might equal or surpass humans in topographical orientation. Semmes suggests that this may be no coincidence. "The proximity of unlike functional elements in a diffusely-organized hemisphere would be expected to lead to a different type of integration from that characterizing a focally-organized hemisphere: *unlike* units would more frequently converge, and therefore one might predict heteromodal integration to an extent surpassing that possible in a focally-organized hemisphere." (Semmes, 1968, p. 23.) Thus, compared with functions that may depend on a high degree of convergence of *like* elements, spatial function might depend instead on the convergence of *unlike* elements—visual, kinesthetic, vestibular, and others—"combining in such a way as to create through experience a single supramodal space" (Semmes, 1968, p. 24).[19]

How, more abstractly, then, might the different roles of the two hemispheres be characterized? We could say that the left hemisphere—the "language hemisphere"—analyzes stimulus information input sequentially, abstracting out the relevant details to which it attaches verbal labels. The right hemisphere, however, is more concerned with the overall stimulus configuration and organizes and processes information in terms of wholes.

We have already alluded to a similar characterization offered by Levy. She and Sperry (Levy-Agresti and Sperry, 1969) wrote, of the same findings reviewed earlier (Levy, 1969), "The data indicate that the mute, minor hemisphere is specialized for Gestalt perception, being primarily a synthesist in dealing with information input. The speaking, major hemisphere, in contrast, seems to operate in a more logical, analytic, computer-like fashion. Its language is inadequate for the rapid complex syntheses achieved by the minor hemisphere" (p. 1151).

Several other investigators have offered similar characterizations on the basis of studies of various perceptual deficits characteristic of unilateral brain lesions in man (e.g. Zangwill, 1961; Bogen, 1969; De-Renzi, Scotti, and Spinnler, 1969).

This characterization seems to square with observations of such complex behaviors as spatial orientation (e.g. either a human being or an animal finding its way home from a strange place). Consider such a remarkable and complex behavior as the navigation of birds over hundreds or even thousands of miles, from one hemisphere of earth to another. Kenyon and Rice (1958; cited in Gibson, 1969, p. 265) describe eighteen albatrosses taken from their nests at Midway atoll in the Pacific and then released from widely spaced points. Fourteen of the birds returned to the nest. The bird released at the greatest distance, over four thousand miles, returned in thirty-two days. How did the birds guide their flight? They might have determined direction by correcting for the sun's daily azimuth displacement; or they might have determined latitude and longitude from the sun's altitude, while determining time by an internal (biological) clock; finally at night they could have used the stars to determine fixed compass direction and to derive information from temporal shifts of the constellations. The available evidence supports all three possibilities (Meyer, 1964; cited by Gibson, 1969, p. 265). But the point, as Gibson brings out, is that ". . . the stimulus information for bird navigation is not simple, nor is the ability integrated by association" (Gibson, 1969, p. 265).

In the case of human behavior, it is worth noting that the kind of skill served by the diffusely organized right hemisphere is frequently most resistant to "linear," or focal, definition. In other words, it is most resistant to precise verbal description, or encoding. Consider, for instance, the perception of part-whole relations. Since this requires a conceptualization of the total stimulus configuration from fragmentary information that is not easily verbally encoded, it ought to be a task on which the right hemisphere excels. This expectation is supported in a demonstration by Nebes (1971), in commissurotimized patients, showing superior capacity by the right hemisphere to judge, from a given arc, the size of the complete circle to which it corresponds.

Consider, for another example, the recognition of faces. Human beings possess an extraordinary ability to recognize faces. Despite this ability, most persons would be hard put to describe, in words (a left

hemisphere activity), those specific characteristics that make an individual face unique and recognizable. Imagine your own face—or
the face of someone you know intimately—a parent, your child, or
spouse. You have seen this face innumerable times and presumably
you would recognize it anywhere. In a complicated group picture,
you usually are able to pick it out almost immediately. Yet even your
carefully thought out verbal description is not likely to go beyond
such characteristics as color of hair and eyes, and general facial contours. Certainly your characterization would be most unlikely to
permit someone else—someone unfamiliar with the face—to identify
it from among a group of merely similar faces. Facial learning is
"configurational," multi-dimensional, and "diffuse," requiring coordination of all the particular and verbalizable features into an un-
verbalizable whole. In other words, the process of face learning and
recognition would seem to be parallel, or Gestalt, rather than serial
(feature by feature), the latter being the kind of processing more
amenable to verbal encoding.

Facial recognition, therefore, should be more accurately subserved
by the right than by the left cerebral hemisphere. Several lines of
evidence bear out this view. For example, with tachistoscopic projection, faces are better recognized in the left than in the right visual
field (Levy et al., 1972). Even more dramatic is the phenomenon of
"prosopagnosia," or "facial agnosia"—an impaired ability to recognize faces—which has been associated with right-hemisphere disease
(e.g. De Renzi and Spinnler, 1966; Gloning et al., 1967; Hécaen
and Angelergues, 1962; Yin, 1970). Sometimes the patient cannot
recognize even his own face in the mirror or the faces of his most
intimate acquaintances.

From this line of reasoning on the relation between language and
"configurational" discrimination, we also might speculate that in
some circumstances, language might not merely fail to aid discrimination but could actively hinder it. Some very interesting evidence
bearing on this speculation is provided in a study by Wallace (1972).
Wallace found that deaf children ten to twenty years of age were
significantly less able than were hearing children fourteen to sixteen
years of age to recall visually presented *letters*, but were significantly
more able to recall faces. In the case of the letters, the optimal strategy probably would be to recode the items by an articulatory or

acoustic code for later serial verbal recall. The hearing children could do this. The deaf children could not. Those deaf children trained in oral communication tried to recode the letters by an articulatory or acoustic dimension but they were restricted because of their hearing loss. Those deaf children trained in manual communication (signing) tried a kinesthetic code based on finger spelling or tried some other manual code but without great success either. On the faces, then, the hearing children may have had worse recall because they continued to use an articulatory or acoustic code, but in this case—for not easily labelable targets—a strategy thus actively interfering with recall. Wallace reports, for example, that the hearing subjects overtly rehearsed salient characteristics (e.g. big nose, pointed chin) of the faces, often with expressly bad effects. Thus in one inspection series, one male face was wearing glasses, while in the test series, this face appeared with two other totally dissimilar faces, also with glasses. Some hearing children said during the test series that one of the faces had been wearing glasses and then, looking for only that attribute, chose the wrong bespectacled face in the test series.

Wallace suggests another possible explanation. Because faces are not easily labelable targets, the deaf and hearing children were on more nearly equal ground to start with. The advantage actually may have shifted to the deaf children because the deaf attach particular significance to facial expression as an additional means of communication. Consequently the deaf children may have scrutinized the faces more thoroughly during the inspection series. Whichever interpretation is to be preferred, the results show that the deaf subjects used visual coding more extensively and more efficiently than the hearing subjects did. Wallace is careful to point out that the results do *not* thereby resolve the question whether the deaf possessed a better "visual memory" or whether they merely used more efficient visual strategies. That is, there was nothing in the results to suggest that hearing subjects could not be trained to successfully suppress their normal tendency to verbally code faces.

It remains for some other essay to discuss the implications of this line of argument for the more general question of the importance of language in concept-learning—a question currently of some dispute. On the one hand, there are psychologists such as Vygotsky (1962) and Luria (1969), who argue that language is the *sina qua non* of thought. On the other hand, there are psychologists who regard language as separate or different from thought, and who argue that children acquire many concepts before they acquire language—a view represented best by Piaget (see Carroll, 1964). The evidence presented in this essay would be toward the latter view or some middle ground view (e.g. Bruner et al., 1966).

By this time we should have recognized that the skills under discussion—the kind most difficult to characterize verbally—are, of course, those that are "perceptually learned" (Gibson, 1969). In other words, these are skills that typically are *not* taught by example, much less by explicit and verbal instruction. Rather, they are skills learned in the course of normal interaction with one's environment —skills not only defying verbal description but quite irrelevant to, and even separate from, verbal intelligence. Incidentally, recognition of this difference between verbal and nonverbal intelligence should help us better appreciate the methodological principle that a subject's verbal justification should *not* be the *sina qua non* for establishing whether the subject—child or even adult—has mastered a particular spatial skill or concept.

## CEREBRAL DOMINANCE REEXAMINED

We earlier reviewed several studies suggesting earlier and greater activity, better blood supply, and greater resistance to disease in the "nondominant" hemisphere. If we can accept the results of these studies at their face value, we should see implications for our traditional beliefs about cerebral dominance. One implication surely is that the very labels "dominant," or major, and "nondominant," minor, imply value judgments more than scientific judgments and reflect the much greater value placed on language and on the "analytic" cognitive style by the academic and scientific culture. In our evolutionary history, however, articulate "propositional" speech is probably a relatively recent development, perhaps appearing—were the history of our existence compressed into a single hour—only in the last few minutes or even seconds. Given the sorts of environmental challenges posed to us throughout our history, it is not unreasonable to suppose that for the much greater time we were predominantly "spatial" creatures, that is, that our thinking and problem solving were of the style that we could now characterize as appropriate to the right hemisphere. Of course, insofar as ontogenetic development is concerned, we must be careful with this proposition, since we do not want to be led into a simplistic "ontogeny recapitulates phylogeny" argument. But at the very least, the proposition suggests some basis for the notion that in the individual human child, spatial skill *ought* to be precocious and ought *not* to depend on the prior development of language skills. Recent studies strongly bear out this view.

It has been said that developmental psychologists, especially in this decade, have "rediscovered" the infant and have rescued him from the doldrums of cognitive inactivity. Now, thanks in large measure to the efforts of Piaget and many other researchers, we have reason to believe that infancy is not only a period of substantial cognitive growth but that the infant has quite impressive skills perhaps from the very beginning. What is the nature of this very early development in cognitive ability? It is what could well be called the development of spatial knowledge—a knowledge of the layout of the world.

Let us consider some examples. One indication of very early spatial knowledge is the appearance, within the first few months of life, of head and eye orientation to a sound source in the peripheral visual field, which Piaget (1953) has interpreted as evidence for early coordination of auditory and visual space. Even at birth, some psychomotor coordination is apparently present. Wertheimer (1961) reports noting a crude form of auditory localization in his own child within a half-hour after her birth and in a second child within ten minutes of birth. In the latter case, a toy "cricket" was clicked next to the left or right ear of the baby who was lying on her back. As soon as the first click was made, the baby, who had been crying with her eyes closed, opened her eyes and turned them in the direction of the click. On fifty-two successive trials, there was eye movement on twenty-two trials, eighteen in the direction of the click and four in a direction opposite to the click. Apparently, within only a few minutes after birth, a rudimentary form of directional auditory localization and directional oculomotor response is possible. Wertheimer suggests, too, that at least on a reflex level, there might be ". . . a rough coordination between auditory space and visual (motor) space. . ."—a finding not compatible with the belief that space perception, in particular cross-modal spatial coordination, is based on long, arduous learning (Wertheimer, 1961, p. 1692).

More recently, Aronson and Rosenbloom (1971) reported a dramatic demonstration of spatial perceptual ability in infants between thirty and fifty-five days of age. Each infant watched his mother, located directly in front of him, while she spoke to him. Her voice, however, was audible only through a stereo speaker system. By changing the balance of this system, her voice could be shifted from straight ahead to ninety degrees left or right. As long as the mother's voice came from straight ahead (where she was located), the babies remained calm. But when the voice was shifted to either side, they became extremely upset, struggling vigorously, grimacing and sticking out their tongues, all the while continuing to look at their mothers.

To ensure that the infant's reaction was the result of the auditory-visual discrepancy and not to the shift in the location of the voice *per se*, the authors repeated the same procedure with other infants for whom the mother was not visible while she spoke to her infant. This time, lateral displacement of the mother's voice produced little visible reaction in the infants. When the original procedure was repeated with additional infants tested with strangers, the effect was the same as with the infants' mothers.

These investigators suggest that the spatial dislocation apparently violates the young infant's perceptual world in which speaker and voice commonly share the same spatial position. Because the infants' responses are so consistent, Aronson and Rosenbloom think it unlikely that this capacity is developed in the first few weeks of life. "The expectation that voice and speaker are a spatial unit is presumably learned but the learning would require the prior existence of a perceptual system that has access to and reliably coordinates information from separate modes" (p. 1163).

They go on to say that the infant, if he does not initially perceive the spatial integrity of such information, at least must register the temporal correspondence between modes and somehow must begin to spatially coordinate this intermodal temporal unit. He must do this at a time in his life when, the *received view* has it, his processing capacities are very undeveloped. If learning does underlie this auditory-visual-spatial coordination, it must necessarily be *very* rapid and *very* efficient.

Another complex spatiotemporal skill which even very young

human infants appear to possess is accurate detection of an approaching object plus the knowledge that visual variables have tactile consequences. A dramatic demonstration of this skill has been reported by Ball and Tronick (1971). The authors' characterization of the likely stimulus components of this skill well illustrates the complexity of this spatiotemporal event. An object's displacement is specified optically by the transformation of a bounded segment of the optic array; the solidity and shape of the object are specified by its closed contour and by transformations of it that produce kinetic depth; the approach path is specified by the symmetrics or asymmetrics of an expanding bounded segment, while withdrawal is specified by its minification; finally, collision is specified when the bounded segment fills 180° of the frontal visual field. Thus, the psychophysics of the infant's capacities requires assessment of its responses to these higher-order event-specifying stimuli (Ball and Tronick, 1971, p. 819).

Ball and Tronick simulated an approaching object with a shadow caster—a device which, by shifting a point of light on a projection screen, produces a growing shadow that appears, according to how the point of light is shifted, either to be coming toward an observer on a "hit path" (symmetrical growth), or to be moving on a "miss" path (asymmetrical growth). Moving the cube away from the point source after an approach appears, to an adult observer, to be an object moving away from the observer. Twenty-four infants ranging in age from two to eleven weeks were tested. The results were dramatic. During a "hit" sequence, the infant moved his head back and away from the screen and brought his arms toward his face. He would move his head back toward the screen usually only after the shadow had begun to fill the field but never before the transformation began. The person holding the infant often reported that the infant's body "stiffened" during looming phases and then relaxed during the recession phase. Responses on the miss trials were sharply different. Usually, the infant merely turned his head and eyes slowly along the path of the shadow or object. The arms tended to come up, but the head did not come back nor did the infant stiffen. Visitors with no knowledge of the stimulus conditions, who observed video tapes of the babies' responses, commented that the baby seemed to be either avoiding or following something in the respective conditions (Ball and Tronick, 1971, p. 820).

Oxford Brookes University

**Customer ID: ****8394**

Title: Theorizing a new agenda for
architecture : an anthology of
architectural the
ID: 0085045103
**Due: 24/10/2011 23:59**

Total items: 1
15/10/2011 16:19

Thank you for using Oxford Brookes
library Self Service

Both these qualitative as well as quantitative results indicate that these babies could detect object qualities of direction and relative depth of approach and collision for both real objects and their optical equivalent. Since there was no difference between the two-week-olds and the eleven-week-olds, the babies' responses cannot easily be explained in learning terms. It would be very interesting to test infants on either Aronson and Rosenbloom's (1971) test of visuospatial coordination or on Ball and Tronick's (1971) test of detection of an approaching object, comparing infants according to strength of left-ear preference and strength of right-hemisphere unilateral driving during the first thirty days of life. Would infants with a strong left-ear preference show earlier and stronger evidence of detecting the spatial mismatch between a person's face and voice?

Finally, research indicates very early shape and size constancy and distance perception (Bower, 1966) and remarkably early discovery of the object concept (Bower, 1971). Even babies as young as twenty days of age seem to know, for instance, that an object that moves out of sight behind another object does not cease to exist.

We have already discussed evidence from studies of both normal and brain-damaged adults, of the critical role of the right cerebral hemisphere for the recognition of faces as well as other spatial-configurational targets. Therefore, still another indication of early right-hemisphere functioning, and of early visuospatial ability, would seem to be the precocious nature of facial learning in the human child. Infants respond differentially very early to faces and face-like targets (e.g. Ahrens, 1954; Kaila, 1932; Kagan, 1965; Spitz and Wolf, 1946) and discriminate between individual faces (the mother's or caretaker's faces and unfamiliar faces) as early as twenty weeks of age (Ambrose, 1961, 1963; Fitzgerald, 1968). We can appreciate how face recognition would be an important skill for human babies to master. The baby's response to the familiar face of its mother is to smile and coo—delightful behaviors even to the most crotchety. The baby's response, therefore, would seem to be critical to the establishing of the mother-infant social bond. A baby's smile and vocalizations, and later reaching, both strengthen the bond and at the same time solicit care and suppress expressions of aggression. Unsmiling babies are not pleasant to care for, as most parents know.

It does not seem unreasonable to conclude, from such studies as have been cited here, that the acquisition of such critical perceptual skills should be subserved by a part of the brain that is active early and is well-oxygenated. In other words, we might conclude that the human infant is neuroanatomically disposed to effective spatial learning.

These are just some of the lines of evidence for the role of neurological factors in the development of visuospatial skills. There are, of course, other kinds of evidence, some of it in studies already reviewed, which for reasons of length I have not discussed. In particular, some studies suggest differential employment of linguistic and visuospatial "strategies" (i.e. of left and right-hemisphere participation) by males and females in the solving of spatial problems. Several studies suggest weaker lateralization of linguistic and visuospatial functions in left-handers than in right-handers. Consideration of these findings may eventually help us to better understand the often-demonstrated superior spatial abilities of the male, and the apparently greater capacity of the left-hander to recover from left-hemisphere injury. These questions are taken up in other papers (Gur, Gur, and Harris, 1974; Harris, 1973a; Harris, in preparation).

The search for the neuropsychological underpinnings of spatial skill is really just beginning. Despite a long history of interest in the problem, I expect that the next ten years will see important discoveries, with perhaps many of our fondest ideas about human development facing stiff challenge. Finally, with respect to this chapter, I must point out that my charge was to review only *one* research orientation—the neuropsychological—in the analysis of spatial development, with other research orientations left to other contributors to this volume. Thus my emphasis on neuropsychological factors obviously does not mean that the analysis of spatial development is complete when and if the underlying neurological structures are identified or that I believe that environmental and genetic factors play insignificant roles. Understanding the neurological factors provides us with only a starting point for psychological analysis. Since psychological analysis must always, I believe, be sensitive to the biological foundations of behavior, it is a starting point that cannot be ignored.

## REFERENCES

1. Electrophysiological studies clearly show that the qualifier "mainly" should not be forgotten. Sensory and motor processes of each side of the body are represented in the ipsilateral as well as in the contralateral hemisphere (e.g. Woolsey and Fairman, 1946; Adey and Kerr, 1954; Nakahama, 1958; Malis, Pribram, and Kruger, 1953; Patton and Kennedy, 1962; Korn, Wendt, and Albe-Fessard, 1966; Evarts, 1966; all cited by Semmes, 1968).

2. Broca was a surgeon at the Bicêtre Hospital in Paris. His discovery was made during a postmortem examination of a man who had shown severe loss of speech for several years before his death. The term "aphasia" is from the Greek, meaning "speechlessness." Broca's patient had suffered from "motor aphasia"—an inability to speak and to organize the movements of speaking, though the organs of speech are not themselves paralyzed. Two major categories are recognized: manual aphasia ("agraphia"), an inability or difficulty in writing language; and speech aphasia, an inability or difficulty in expressing language vocally, or to think in terms of language. Henry Head (1920) distinguished four kinds of speech aphasia: Verbal: "defective power of forming words, whether for external or internal use"; Syntactical: "lack of that perfect balance and rhythm necessary to make the sounds uttered easily comprehensible" (the person tends to drop or slur articles and prepositions); Nominal: "the inability to use words as names, and a failure to appreciate the nominal character of words"; Semantic: "disturbances of the connected sequence of verbal or written expression."

These motor, or expressive aphasias can be distinguished from the sensory aphasias: auditory aphasia (word deafness): difficulty in understanding the meaning of words and language as heard; and visual aphasia (word blindness, or "alexia"): disturbances of perception of the meaning of language as written. The area primarily responsible for these aspects of linguistic skill lies within the first convolution of the *temporal* lobe, rather than the frontal lobe as is the case for the motor, or "expressive," aspects of language. The area is called "Wernicke's area," after its discoverer (1874).

3. Throughout, as we attempt to characterize the functions of the two cerebral hemispheres, we shall be talking only about right-handed persons. The reason is that the functional differences between the hemispheres are somewhat different in left-handers. It has been estimated that approximately 95 percent of right-handers are "left-brained" for language, compared with only 65 percent of left-handers. (Branch et al., 1964)

4. An agnosia is an inability to recognize the import of sensory stimuli. Astereognosis is a difficulty in recognizing objects or forms by touch. Auditory agnosia is a "psychic" deafness for noises and music (the latter called "amusia").

Visual agnosia refers to disorders of visual recognition of objects or pictures; impaired recognition of color, not the same as color blindness—rather, difficulty in understanding color as qualities of objects, a faulty color concept, an inability to evoke color images (Head, 1920); and finally, to disorders in orienting one's body in space.

"Apraxia (or "dyspraxia") refers to disturbances of the memory of movements. Head (1920) distinguishes four varieties: limbkinetic: the patient "appreciates the nature of the movement but cannot carry it out with ordinary skill" (believed to involve a loss of innervatory memories for complex forms of movement); ideokinetic: "a loss of memory of how to make movements"; ideational: "impaired conception of a whole movement. The patient, for example, does not "know how" to use a simple familiar tool; Constructive: "In typical cases the patient experiences difficulty in laying out sticks to copy a given design, in building with blocks, in drawing." This latter has been studied frequently and constitutes what often is meant by a spatial disorder.

5. Benton (1972) recounts that some thirty years after Jackson's papers appeared, Rieger, a German neurologist, in all likelihood unaware of Jackson's papers, made a very similar proposal. In 1909 he postulated the existence of what he called two distinct, interacting "apparatuses" in the brain, one serving verbal-conceptual functions, the other, spatial-practical functions. Rieger's student, Reichardt (1923), went on to conclude, from observations of brain-injured patients, that the spatial "apparatus" was located in the posterior right hemisphere.

6. Broadbent's purpose was to study the limits of immediate memory on two separated channels, in particular to test the possibility that listeners can hear two spatially separated signals successively rather than simultaneously. He found that correct responses to bi-aural lists of spoken digits were reported in such an order that all digits presented to one ear were reported before any presented to the other ear.

7. The experiments most frequently cited as providing the neurophysiological basis for this generalization are studies by Tunturi (1946) with cats and by Rosenzweig (1951) with dogs. In the latter case the procedure was as follows: An electrode was placed on the dura mater (the outermost membrane of the brain) or the pia mater (the innermost membrane that envelops the brain and spinal cord) over the auditory area of the cortex. The size of cortical responses then were measured when first one ear was stimulated and then the other. The implitude of the response was used as a rough measure of the number of cortical units that have been excited. To test whether each ear is more strongly represented at its contralateral hemisphere, Rosenzweig recorded the response of each ear at both hemispheres. This is critical: recording from only one hemisphere, a difference in the response of the two ears could be attributed to a difference in ear sensitivity; recording from both hemispheres but stimulating only one ear, a difference in the responses of the two hemispheres could be attributed to asymmetry of the electrode locations or to a difference in responsiveness of the hemispheres.

The results indicated that the response of each ear (i.e. the cortical response elicited by stimulation of each ear) was larger at the contralateral hemisphere. That is, at the left hemisphere, the response of the right ear was the larger; at the right hemisphere, the response of the left ear was the larger.

Rosenzweig concluded that at the auditory cortex of each cerebral hemisphere, each ear is represented by a population of cortical units. The population representing the contralateral ear is larger than the population representing the ipsilateral ear. The two populations overlap, so that some units belong to both populations.

8. Smith's explanation of her results, described earlier, nicely anticipates the contemporary interpretation in terms of hemispheric specialization. Essentially, Smith used her findings to argue for a distinction between sensory and motor functions of the hands, with the left hand better at sensory functions and the right hand better at motor functions. In support, she also cites a study by Bowman (1928), who, speaking of the operation of "pegging," wrote:

"It is interesting to note that in most of the right-handed *Ss* the left hand was much more skillful in 'feeding'" (p. 120). Smith goes on to explain, "An analysis of the phrase, 'skillful in feeding' should make clear that it is the equivalent of 'skillful as a sensory organ.' In the operation of pegging, the work is so divided that while the right hand is doing the actual pegging on the board—motor activity—the left hand is holding the pegs and handing them to the right hand just where they are needed—sensory activity. The fact that in the 'feeding' movement the left hand of the right-handed person is, according to Miss Bowman, more skillful than the right hand, indicates that the left hand is naturally more readily used for sensory activity, the right hand being needed for the motor activity of the real pegging, which is *controlled by the visual sense*" (Smith, 1928, p. 244, emphasis hers).

9. Ingram cites two kinds of evidence in support of the interpretation that the fine movements of the left hand are controlled primarily by the right (spatial) hemisphere. Individual finger movements of one hand are controlled primarily by the contralateral hemisphere in split-brain monkeys (Brinkman and Kuypers, 1972); and motor control in the human hemiplegic is primarily contralateral. Thus Ingram suggests that fine movements of the left hand would be controlled primarily by the right (spatial) hemisphere.

There are, however, other interpretations of the results. For example, Ingram suggests that differentially greater motor innervation to the left hand could facilitate the execution of individual finger movements. In support, Ingram cites studies showing a higher proportion of ipsimanual motor and sensory deficits in left-lesion patients than right-lesion patients (Vaughan and Costa, 1962); that patients with left-cerebral lesions show bilateral impairment of arm movements, while patients with right-sided lesions show only contralateral impairment (Wyke, 1967, 1968, 1971); and finally showing, through nonverbal testing of commissurotomized patients, greatest impairment of finger movement when the right hemisphere is required to control posture-like movements of the right hand, while the left hemisphere can direct such movement reasonably well in both hands (Gazzaniga, Bogem, and Sperry, 1967).

Second, Ingram cites evidence that the left hand also has a greater bilateral somastosensory cortical representation than the right hand (e.g. Semmes et al., 1960).

10. These were patients with uncontrollable epilepsy who had undergone a "split-brain" operation (severance of corpus callosum) in hopes at least of confining seizures to one hemisphere. In the case of the patients in Levy-Agresti and Sperry's study, only the forebrain commissures were divided; in other patients, hind-brain commissures have been divided as well. "Split-brain" operations frequently have proven to be more successful than expected: seizures have not merely been confined to one hemisphere but have tended to be nearly totally eliminated, almost as though they had been facilitated by the intact callosum.

Since the corpus callosum facilitates inter-hemispheric communication, the "split-brain" patients provide a better opportunity for studying the independent functioning of the two hemispheres than is afforded by other procedures. The reason is that after commissurotomy, the left side of the body is *directly* controlled by the right hemisphere rather than being mediated, via the corpus callosum, by the left hemisphere. The obverse is also the case (see Gazzaniga, 1970, for a review of clinical and experimental studies).

11. In haptic discrimination tasks, it would be useful to use control conditions in which, for example, the two hands are reversed so that the right hand appears in the left part of the represented visual field, the left hand in the right field. Any attenuation of usual left-hand superiority with this rearrangement might index the extent to which the hand effects are purely *intra*-modal.

It is even possible to suggest a particular mechanism that would precipitate the participation of visual representation in the haptic task, either facilitatory, in the case of the usual hand position or disruptive, in the case of the reversed arrangement described above. The suggestion builds on a new model outlined by Kinsbourne (1970) for the analysis of laterality effects in tachistoscopic recognition. The visual field differences typically found, viz., better left-field discrimination for visuospatial targets, better right-field discrimination for linguistic, symbolic targets, are usually explained as direct manifestations of better discrimination of linguistic and nonlinguistic stimuli by the left and right hemispheres, respectively. Kinsbourne suggests, instead, that the effect is an indirect product of postexposural conjugate lateral movements of the eyes in a direction contralateral to the hemisphere activated in solution of the problem—thus to the left when a spatial target has been presented and to the right for linguistic problems. Thus linguistic material is recognized better in the right side of the visual field and nonlinguistic material, better in the left field, because the subject's attention is biased to the appropriate side in each case.

This model can be applied to the case of haptic perception. When the hands are in the usual position, simultaneous presentation of spatial targets forces eye movement to the left, thus focusing attention on the left side and resulting in better left-hand discrimination. With the hands crossed, however, leftward eye movement would focus attention to the *right* hand and would be expected therefore to attenuate the usual left-hand superiority.

12. By "species difference," Jung was making reference to the absence at that time of any evidence for hemispheric specialization in nonhuman animals. But see Webster, 1972, for a recent demonstration of hemispheric specialization in cats.

13. The patients are not otherwise described. Arteriography is roentgenography or photography by roentgen rays of the arteries. In a carotid arteriogram, the artery under study is the carotid—either of the two major arteries in the neck that carry blood to the brain.

14. The operculum is that part of the cerebrum lying above the island of Reil—an isolated part of the cerebral cortex in the fissure of Sylvius.

15. Witelson and Pallie improved methodologically on the Geschwind and Levitsky study. Preliminary inspection of adult brains indicated that the shape of the planum temporale varies considerably, thus making it possible that area measurement might be a more valid indicator of left-right asymmetries than the linear measurement used by Geschwind and Levitsky. As it turned out, the correlations between linear and area measurements for the two hemispheres were quite high (approximately .80 or above).

16. Turkewitz et al. also studied the head-turning response to laterally applied somesthetic stimulation of the perioral region in normal infants between 24 and 72 hours of age. Though the response typically elicited by stimulation of either side is a turn in the direction of stimulation (Prechtl, 1958), Turkewitz et al. (1965) instead found such ipsilateral responses to be elicited more readily by stimulation of the infant's right side than by stimulation of his left side. They also found that contralateral responses, though made infrequently to stimuli applied either to the left or right side, were significantly more common when the stimulus was applied to the infant's left side.

Turkewitz et al.'s interest in the early instance of lateralization seems to be mostly for its predictive value: infants in poor condition at birth (low Apgar scores) made head turns as frequently as normal infants did but they showed differences in lateral organization of these responses. Infants whose Apgar scores were either intermediate or high made significantly more responses to stimulation at the right than at the left, whereas infants with low Apgar scores showed no such lateral difference and in fact were slightly more responsive to stimulation at the left.

This very early lateral differentiation thus is not restricted to audition. The human newborn has been shown to be more responsive to tactile (Siqueland and Lipsitt, 1966;

Turkewitz et al., 1965), and visual (Wickelgren, 1967) stimuli presented at the right than at the left side.

At least in the case of tactile and auditory stimulation, it appears that it is the infant's prior maintenance of the head right posture that, at least partly, determines the lateral difference in responsiveness. The idea here is that when the infant lies with his head turned to the right, the right ear is occluded and the ambient level of stimulation therefore is lower at the right than at the left ear. An experimental test (Turkewitz et al., 1966) supported this interpretation. It is harder to see, though, how the same interpretation could be applied in the case of lateralization of responsiveness to visual stimulation (Wickelgren, 1967).

17. In connection with these speculations about left-ear superiority for detection of environmental sounds, we can mention recent findings by Salk (1973) that babies, and even dolls, are ordinarily held by the left arm with the baby's head in the crook of the left elbow. The preference apparently is unrelated to handedness, since both left and right-handed women have the same strong preference for this posture. Salk's explanation is that the mother unconsciously holds her baby in her left arm (and generalizes this unconsciously-determined preference even to dolls) so that the baby's head is closer to the left side of her body where her heart beat is stronger (even though the heart is really located more nearly at body midline). The assumption, borne out in some experimental studies, is that the heart-beat has a soothing effect on the baby.

The posture would tend to bring the right ear closer to the maternal chest and heartbeat but would, like the baby's head-to-right posture while lying supine, leave the left ear more exposed to other environmental sounds. Recently, in a letter to *Scientific American*, Moore (1973) speculated that this practice could be related to asymmetry obtained in the dichotic-listening studies. The evidence, surely, is against this notion in its stronger form, namely, that the maternal practice *causes* the ear-asymmetry. But it is conceivable that the initial asymmetry, present at birth or shortly thereafter and due, apparently, to anatomical hemispheric asymmetries (Witelson and Pallie, 1973; Wada, 1969) is augmented, or strengthened, by this maternal practice.

It would be most interesting to find out whether as a result of this practice, heart-beat, unlike other environmental stimuli, is detected better by the *right* than by the left ear.

18. Taylor's results, however, seem to conflict with Paoluzzi and Bravaccio's (1967) findings of significantly more frequent left-sided than right-sided pathology, though Taylor himself suggests that his results are consistent with a similar study (Rey et al., 1949) which found a greater proportion of left-sided than right-sided epilepsies. But it seems as though Taylor's hypothesis instead would have predicted more frequent *right*-sided pathology, since the right hemisphere—at least after about two years of age —would be the functionally less active hemisphere and therefore would be *less* resistant to disease or injury.

One wonders, then, whether there were any selection factors in Paoluzzi and Bravaccio's data that biased the evidence in the direction of their findings. Left-hemisphere damage would have resulted in aphasic symptoms, which are both more dramatic and generally considered more important than are the kinds of symptoms resulting from right-hemisphere damage. Might more left-hemisphere-damaged persons select themselves into the hospital?

Another ambiguity in Taylor's (1969) report is that *after* language becomes established (and therefore is presumed to become lateralized into the left hemisphere) the left hemisphere is presumed to be more active than it was before. But the hypothesis apparently depends on the assumption that it is now functionally more active than the right hemisphere. The hypothesis thereby supposes that older human beings (the transition age presumably being about two years) are more "verbal" than they are "visuospatial," in some quantitative, measurable sense: the left hemisphere is more involved in day-to-day activities than is the right hemisphere.

19. It must be noted that Semmes' view that tactile functions are represented focally in the left hemisphere and diffusely in the right, has not been consistently supported. Benton (1972) recently has reviewed a number of the negative studies. For example, severe somatosensory defect has been found to be associated only with lesions of the postcentral gyrus of *either* hemisphere (Corkin, Milner, and Rasmussen, 1964); and no differences have been found between left-hemisphere and right-hemisphere lesion patients in the effect of intra-hemispheric locus of lesion on frequency of tactile deficits (Carmon and Benton, 1969).

Still another conclusion that would seem to follow from Semmes' hypothesis is that tactile deficits should be more closely interrelated on the right than on the left hand. Vaughan and Costa (1962) found a substantial correlation of .52 between pressure sensitivity and two-point discrimination for the contralateral (right) hand in patients with left-hemisphere disease, but an even higher correlation of .87 for the contralateral (left) hand of patients with right-hemisphere disease.

Finally, Carmon and Benton (1969a), in the study cited above, failed to find substantial differences in the strength of relation among performances on various tactile tasks in patients with left and right-hemisphere lesions. The correlations among levels of tactile sensitivity on both the contralateral and ipsilateral hands were not higher in patients with right-hemisphere lesions.

It is not clear why these results should have failed to confirm those of Semmes et al. (1960). But until these discrepancies are resolved by further analysis, the characterizations of the neuroanatomical organizations of the left and right hemispheres as "focal" and "diffuse," respectively, probably should be regarded as only an hypothesis.

# Chapter 2

# SOURCES OF VARIANCE IN PERFORMANCE OF SPATIAL TESTS

S. G. VANDENBERG

ALTHOUGH I have been charged with the task of reviewing the status of studies concerning hereditary influences on children's spatial development, I would rather discuss the urgent need for spatial tests which are appropriate for young children. This decision is prompted by the fact that a lack of suitable spatial tests presents a major obstacle to further research efforts, regardless of orientation. It is also prompted by the fact that a summary of research on hereditary influences has already been published elsewhere (Vandenberg, 1966, 1967, 1969).

The purpose of this chapter, then, is to consider briefly the development of spatial tests, the several sources of variance with respect to performance on those tests and the development of a new test of spatial reasoning which is appropriate for children. The chapter begins with some observations about the evolution of spatial tests.

A subtest called "Block Counting" was included in the Army Beta Test developed during World War I. Ever since Thorndike (1921) showed that performance on this task did not correlate highly with "general intelligence," there has been a theoretical interest in, but a practical neglect of, what came to be called "spatial" tests. The history of such tests, the concept behind them and the evidence for its importance, has been reviewed in a book by McFarlane Smith (1964). In the United Kingdom, such tests are variously named "practical," "concrete" or "spatial," and are usually described as measures of a factor 'k' since El Koussy's study of the visual perception of space (1920).

The precise nature and limits of the hypothesized spatial ability are still not clearly understood, in part because some authors have used the term "spatial" to describe features of tests which use geometric figures but which only require a minimal degree of visualization and mental manipulation of two or three dimensional objects. Examples of such tests which sometimes have—perhaps improperly —been called spatial are the Progressive Matrices of Raven (1962), various wooden or paper-and-pencil form boards, mazes and the Kohs blocks. Actually, the latter test may have a "spatial" component, because it requires two-dimensional rotation of individual blocks. However, to the extent that the Kohs designs can be copied by trial and error, this test may be confounded by verbal reasoning and form perception.

There may be several distinguishable spatial abilities. French (1951) reviewed several factor analytic studies and concluded that two factors existed which could be described as spatial orientation and spatial visualization. Spatial orientation he defined as the aptitude to remain unconfused by the changing orientations in which a spatial configuration may be presented. Spatial visualization was defined as the aptitude to comprehend imaginary movement of objects in three-dimensional space.

Somewhat later, Guilford and his associates also proposed two spatial factors with the same names but with slightly different definitions. They defined the first factor as spatial orientation and described it as an ability to appreciate spatial relations with reference to the body of the observer. In contrast, they defined the second factor, spatial visualization, as an ability to imagine movements, transformations and other changes in visual objects. (Michael et al., 1951, 1957; Guilford and Zimmerman, 1956).

Although the names of these two spatial abilities are identical, it is clear that the definitions proposed by French and by Guilford are somewhat different. The difference is underscored by the fact that each used a different pair of tests to measure the two spatial abilities. On the one hand, French (1962) selected a test of Thurstone's called "Identical Blocks" to measure spatial orientation. In this test, subjects are required to decide whether two cubes in different orientations are identical or not, according to symbols shown on the faces of the cubes. French selected another of Thurstone's tests called "Paper Folding" to test visualization. Here the subject is asked to imagine folding and unfolding a piece of paper in order to decide where holes punched in the folded paper will show in the unfolded paper. This was an item in Binet's scale.

On the other hand, Guilford and Zimmerman (1956) developed a spatial orientation test which required the subject to examine carefully five pictures which show the prow of the boat and to select one picture which matches a schematic drawing of a line and a dot representing the horizon and the point of the prow. For spatial visualization, Guilford and Zimmerman constructed a test requiring the subject to visualize or imagine rotating an alarm clock in order to match the clock face with one of five pictures which shows the clock's orientation after it has been moved as shown by an arrow.

Borich and Bauman (1972) obtained correlations between these

TABLE 2-I

CORRELATIONS BETWEEN FOUR MEASURES OF SPATIAL ABILITIES
(Borich & Bauman, 1972)

|  | Guilford-Zimmerman Spatial | | French Spatial | |
|  | *Orientation* | *Visualization* | *Orientation* | *Visualization* |
|---|---|---|---|---|
| GZ S.O. | (.88)* | | | |
| S.V. | .67 | (.93)* | | |
| Fr. S.O. | .48 | .53 | (.66)* | |
| S.V. | .34 | .44 | .55 | (.51)* |

*Reliability reported by test authors.

four tests when they applied the Campbell and Fiske (1959) multitrait-multimethod model to the test scores of forty college students. Although the sample size was rather small, their results indicate that the two abilities measured by tests of the same author correlate higher than do tests of the same ability constructed by the two different authors. In the past decade there have been other tests developed with the intention of measuring these and other closely related spatial abilities. Not all, unfortunately, are appropriate for children when developed or adopted for children, it is interesting that performance on spatial tests is less correlated with social class differences than is performance on vocabulary tests or on tests of general intelligence. For example, Figure 2-1 shows the percentage of children from five socioeconomic groups who obtained a score in the top

10 percent on four ability tests, one of which was a spatial test. It can be seen that on the spatial test, the bottom two classes accounted for a higher number of cases than for the other three tests. These results were obtained by Nuttin (1965) in Belgium, but similar findings have been reported from many other countries. For a more detailed review, see Vandenberg (1974). The absence of large social class differences in spatial ability could be due to a variety of reasons: (1) there may be smaller differences between classes in relevant experience leading to the development of this ability, (2) spatial ability is more universal, (3) spatial ability is less determined by social class related hereditary differences or (4) there is less of an hereditary

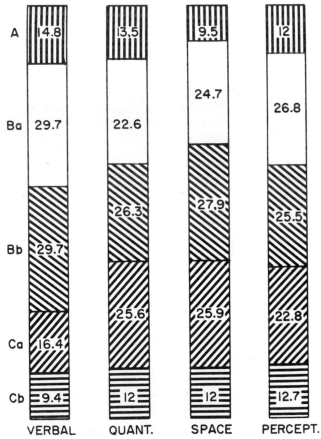

Figure 2-1. Contribution of 5 socioeconomic groups (A Sa etc.) to the top 10 percent of children for 4 ability factors (after Nuttin 1965).

factor in spatial ability due to an absence of assortative making. Of course, all or only some of these reasons may be valid. However, the second explanation has little merit because individual differences in spatial ability are as large or larger than for other abilities.

There have been many reports that women perform less well than men on spatial tests compared to other tests (Maccoby, 1966; Sherman, 1967; Garron, 1970). In 1943, O'Connor suggested that this highly specific sex difference has an hereditary basis. Support for this hypothesis has come from several sources:

1. R. E. Stafford (1963) obtained a pattern of father-son, father-daughter, mother-son and mother-daughter correlations suggestive of sex linkage. Similar results have been reported by Hartlage (1970) and by Bock and Kolakowski (1973). Table 2-II shows a summary of these findings.

TABLE 2-II
CORRELATIONS BETWEEN SPATIAL TEST SCORES OF
PARENTS AND CHILDREN IN THREE STUDIES

| | | Correlations between | | | | |
| | | Father and | | Mother and | | Father and |
| *Author* | N | Son | Dau. | Son | Dau. | Mother |
|---|---|---|---|---|---|---|
| Stafford (1963) | 104 | 02 | 31 | 31 | 12 | 03 |
| Hartlage (1970) | 25 | 18 | 34 | 39 | 25 | — |
| Bock and Kolakowski (1973) | 167 | 15 | 25 | 20 | 12 | 26 |

Although Stafford and Hartlage each used a different test, Bock and Kolakowski employed both tests and added a third. Bock and Kolakowski results generally confirmed the findings from the two earlier studies. Indeed, Bock and Kolakowski concluded that the evidence provided support for the hypothesis that spatial ability depends on a recessive gene on the x-chromosome with a frequency of approximately .5 in U. S. whites. Although their hypothesis would seem to imply that the dominant gene inhibits the development of spatial ability in the heterozygote, it is not clear how this might occur. Could it be that the development of verbal ability tends to inhibit spatial visualization? We will return to this question later in this essay.

2. The results of several twin studies indicate that spatial ability has a considerable genetic component in each of the samples studied (Vandenberg, 1966, 1967). In a recent study, it was also found that the genetic component varied considerably from one test to the next (Vandenberg, 1969). In this latter study an attempt was made to determine whether different spatial visualization tasks, including those

requiring the comparison of two dimensional drawings, the mental rotation of three dimensional representations or the perception of perspective and comparison of static forms, i.e. figures in the same orientation (perceptual speed and accuracy), are under hereditary control to the same degree. No clear relationship was found between the different tasks or with respect to the hereditary component. (Vandenberg, 1969).

3. The genetic component in spatial test scores seems to be largely independent from the genetic component in other ability test scores. (Vandenberg, 1965; Bock and Vandenberg, 1968).

Money and his associates have reported that phenotypic females with only one sex chromosome, the so-called Turner syndrome or XO aneuploidies, performed less well on the nonverbal or "performance" subtests of the Wechsler than on the verbal subtests. Money has suggested that this difference in performance was due to a specific impairment of mental functioning which he labelled visual agnosia. He related the difference to the earlier reports of a sex-difference in spatial ability and then hypothesized that it is this spatial ability which is impaired in Turner's Syndrome. To test this hypothesis, Money constructed a special road map test of directions which he thought would measure spatial ability. It remains unclear, however, how scores on Money's test (or other measures requiring one to find one's way around) relate either to the clarity with which one can visualize objects (mental imagery) or to the ease with which one can manipulate them mentally.

Actually it is not obvious either how the impaired performance of Turner's Syndrome cases fits into the sex linkage hypothesis, since XO individuals should be more similar to normal males (XY) than to normal females (XX) if spatial ability is located on the X chromosome.

In fact, the usual frequencies for males and females in a sex linked trait seem to be reversed. This will be clearer if we review the situation which obtains in tritanopia, one of the more common types of anomalous color vision. Tritanopia has a frequency of about 4 percent in males, but of only $(.04)^2 = 16$ per ten thousand in women, because in a woman *both* X's have to carry the abnormal gene for her to be affected. If we took a low spatial test score to be a parallel to color blindness, we would expect women to have a lower frequency of low scores than men, so that their mean score would be higher. It turns out that the mean for women is lower than the mean score for males.

Either we will have to consider good spatial visualization to be the recessive trait and *poor* ability the *dominant* or we will have to look for another genetically dominant trait which has the curious attribute that possessing it (or more of it) inhibits or depresses spatial visualization. As mentioned before, perhaps the frequently reported earlier development of verbal ability in women meets these qualifications. Possibly this earlier language development is due to an earlier lateralization of functions in the left and right hemispheres in women compared to men. There remain a number of rather loose connections in this chain of reasoning.

More recently Money (1970) has reported that persons with Turner's Syndrome also have certain personality characteristics. He claims these characteristics are, at least in part, due to the fact that such persons are usually "infantilized" by their parents, i.e. they are given less than the normal amount of responsibility and are treated as if they were younger than they really are. It may be that such infantization contributes to their poorer performance on nonverbal or spatial tests.

Such a psychological explanation, which makes the effects not a direct genetic one but one secondary to the delayed physical development, is reminiscent of recent proposals that the increased incidence of XYY in violent criminals is due to their increased height and to their earlier growth. This combination of height and growth provoke more fighting during adolescence, because such individuals have a greater chance of winning than their shorter age mates.

All of these genetic concerns, however, will remain unexplored until we possess better tests for measuring spatial ability. Indeed, until we develop such tests, we will remain ignorant as to how early it is possible to test children's spatial ability. To my knowledge, little has been learned from the usual paper and pencil tests, although studies of Piaget and others on the development of spatial concepts may provide us with new tests as well as information about certain "performance" tests such as mazes or Kohs Blocks.

Recently Shepard and Metzler (1971) developed a set of drawings showing combinations of ten blocks in various orientations.

They asked subjects to judge whether or not two such drawings showed the *same* set of blocks but in *different* spatial orientations. They gave the name "mental rotation" to the ability required for this task. Because this seemed to me to capture the essence of three-dimensional spatial visualization, I constructed a paper and pencil test from some of their drawings. In a trial with forty-six college students, a KR 20 reliability of .88 was obtained. A copy of this new test may be obtained by writing the author.

## EFFECTS OF TRAINING ON SPATIAL SCORES

At the time of this writing, I have administered this test to children in the sixth grade. My interest is to ascertain the effects of model building using blocks from some of the models shown in this test, upon their subsequent performance on the spatial test. I am also interested to see what the size of the sex difference is at different ages.

There have been few attempts to improve the performance on spatial tests by practice or relevant training. Brinkman (1966) compared the performance of two groups of eighth grade students on the DAT spatial relations test. Both groups were tested twice, but only one group received a self-instructional program intended to increase their understanding of selected concepts in geometry. The "trained" group scored very much higher (p $<$.001) than the control group: the mean for the "trained" group increased by eighteen points while the mean for the control group increased by only three points. Brinkman contrasts his findings with the negative results from three unpublished studies of the effect of regular courses in geometry or mechanical drawing upon spatial ability test scores.

In an earlier study, Blade & Watson (1955) found significant increases in spatial test scores after a year of engineering courses. Students in other curricula obtained much smaller gains. Incidentally, they also reported that performance in the upper third on the spatial test was as good a predictor of success in engineering school as scoring in the upper third of a mathematics test. It could, however, be argued that students taking engineering courses are, to some extent, a self-selected sample with more motivation and perhaps more latent spatial ability. Of course, random assignment of subjects would obviate such criticism.

I have only some preliminary data to report on my efforts to study the effects of training. These come from a group of twenty-two male and thirty female sixth graders. Figure 2-2 shows the results of that pilot study. The test-re-test correlations are .845 for the boys and .635 for the girls. This was only a small effect of the model building. The means changed from 27.36 to 30.09 for the boys and from 24.97 to 28.31 for the girls. Using a one tailed t-test for matched samples, we obtained $t = 1.4222$ (n.s.) for boys and $t = 3.7165$ (p $<.005$) for girls.

Before concluding, I should like to point out that increasing test scores on spatial tests through training does not invalidate conclu-

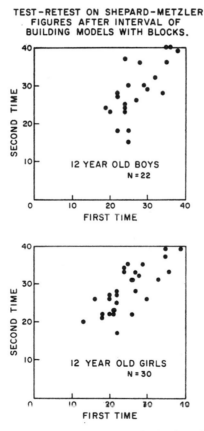

TEST-RETEST ON SHEPARD-METZLER
FIGURES AFTER INTERVAL OF
BUILDING MODELS WITH BLOCKS.

Figure 2-2. Test-retest scores on Shepard-Metzler figures after interval spent building models with blocks.

sions about the hereditary components which might influence such test scores. Estimates of genetic variance are based on, *and limited to*, the conditions under which the data were obtained and do not permit one to predict genetic variance under different conditions.

In summary, the present evidence suggests that there is an important hereditary component in the observed variance on spatial tests. Although the evidence of family studies fits a model of recessive sex linkage, the poor performance of Turner's Syndrome patients does not seem to fit this hypothesis. Some of the discrepancy may be due to the use of different psychological tests which do not necessarily measure exactly the same ability.

# Chapter 3

# ON THE RELATIONS BETWEEN SPATIAL AND LINGUISTIC PROCESSES

### David R. Olson

SOME FACTS can be represented in more than one way; pictures and sentences may provide complementary evidence in a court of law or in a biology textbook. But while the surface structure of pictures and other visual representations (including print) is primarily spatially organized and that of spoken language is temporally organized, the meanings underlying these surface differences and the mental processes involved in extracting and processing those meanings may or may not be different. This chapter is concerned with examining some of the ways in which spatial and linguistic processes are related and with showing some of the ways in which the underlying cognitive processes reflect these surface structure differences. An important and largely ignored domain for examining this problem is through the linguistic representation of spatial relations. Hence, we shall consider some aspects of the language of space, how children acquire that language and how the language of space is related to a direct spatial perception.

But let us begin with some characterization of these temporal auditory "linguistic" processes and the spatial visual "pictorial" processes. Consider the following tasks:
Competence on these sorts of tasks has traditionally been called verbal ability.

> What is a miser?
> How are apple and peach alike?
> Day is to night as summer is to *winter*.

67

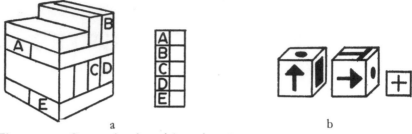

Figure 3-1. Conventional spatial test items.
  a) How many blocks touch each of the lettered blocks?
  b) Are these two objects the same?

Competence in these sorts of tasks has traditionally been called "spatial ability."

At a more molecular level: Are these two letters the same?

Spatial Aa    No (Physical match)
Linguistic Aa    Yes (Name match)

Such verbal and spatial tasks presumably require different processes for their solution. This conclusion seems inescapable in view of the repeated findings over half a century, that people skilled at one of these types of problems are not necessarily skilled at the other. L. L. Thurstone (1938) was among the first to report a space factor in his studies of primary-mental abilities. Thurstone's tests involved the presentation of a pair of objects—figures, cards or flags—with the two members of the pairs being in different positions. Subjects had to decide if the pictures could be rotated (within the plane) to match each other. While these tests correlate highly with each other, thereby specifying a common spatial factor, they correlate little with such verbal tests as vocabulary, opposites, synonyms, proverbs and the like which specify a verbal factor.

Interestingly enough verbal analogies such as:

foot:shoe—hand:—————————

were closely related to the verbal factor while syllogisms:

Jones is younger than Brown
Brown is younger than Smith
Therefore Smith is younger than Jones

were closely related to the spatial factor.

Later studies by Thurstone and Thurstone (1941) in which letters were substituted for the names in comparable syllogisms resulted in the assignment of this test to a number factor with low positive correlations remaining with spatial tests. More analytic studies of the relations among those skills have been carried out by Guilford (1967, 1971); those relations will be treated elsewhere in this volume.

More recent evidence from another tradition has tended to reinforce the distinction between spatial, pictorial processes and linguistic ones. Sperry (1964), Bogen (1969), Milner (1971) and Ornstein (1973) have provided considerable evidence that these types of tasks are solved by different cerebral hemispheres. Illustrative of this finding is Bogen's report that "split-brain" subjects with a severed corpus collosum were able to write English with their right hand (left hemisphere) as well as they were before, but who could no longer draw. A square may be copied as four corners stacked together; the nominal attributes of the object were preserved but their spatial interrelations were lost. With the left hand, (right hemisphere) the same subjects could copy the square, but not written English. Kimura (1973) has recently reported that the tasks of locating an object in space either in a plane or in depth was performed better by the right hemisphere than by the left. Hence, there is some evidence that these processes are differentiated both at a psychological and at a neurological level.

Another line of evidence comes from the studies of Ruth Day (1973) who made the interesting finding that people with different patterns of ability not only excel at different problems (something we knew from the old IQ studies) but that they solve the same problems in quite different ways. Typical of this latter point is the fact that people with a verbal bias (high verbal abilities and low spatial abilities) show the classical serial position effect in digit recall; people with high spatial, low verbal ability show a relatively flat recall curve.

I have recently come upon a task that appears to be soluble in two quite different ways. The task (Meuris, 1973) is offered as a spatial task but a closer look indicates it can be solved on a spatial or a linguistic basis. Some adults faced with this task (see figure 3-2) solve it linguistically as follows:

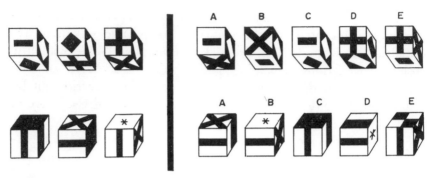

Figure 3-2. Which of the lettered alternatives continues the series begun on the left?

1. The central section is altered from picture to picture so in the solution that section will be different from any of the preceding ones.

2. The right section is constant so in the solution that must be the same.

3. The lower surface is altered from picture to picture so the solution will be different again.

Other adults faced with this display see it as a cube which they rotate 90° in their heads and then look for a corresponding display.

Although we have not yet done any studies to prove that these types of solutions call upon different abilities; following Day's results, it would seem likely that they do.

But, assuming these processes are different, carried out perhaps in different parts of the brain and distributed differentially in people, how are these abilities, skills or mental activities to be characterized and further, how are they related? Before I try to give them any formal characterization (as in Goodman's (1968) theory of symbols), let us consider some of the evidence on how some of these problems are solved.

## LINGUISTIC MENTAL PROCESSES

Some important studies have recently been conducted which yield considerable promise of unravelling some of the processes in the processing of linguistic information, some in comprehension and verification studies, some in logical thinking. A representative study is that of Clark and Chase (1972) who reported a series of studies in which subjects were to decide the truth or falsity of such sentences as:

A star is above a plus.

A plus is below a star.

against a picture which either conformed to the statement or violated it. Subjects' decision times were recorded.

On the basis of these reaction times, Clark could provide a model of the process of verifying a sentence. The model essentially consisted of the following mental operations:

1. Set up a featural representation of the sentence, that is a deep structure coding of the sentence.

2. Code the picture in an equivalent format.

3. Carry out a series of comparison or matching operations over each feature of the coding while keeping track of the "truth index." Assume the sentence is true; upon detection of a mismatch change the "truth index" to false; for the second change it back to true and so on.

4. Make a response.

This model is shown in Figure 3-3.

Contemporaneously, Trabasso, Rollins, and Shaugnessy (1971) offered essentially the same model for the comprehension of negation.

Following their leads, Olson and Filby (1972) offered a comparable model for the verification of active and passive sentences. These models are identical in that they consist of a set of sequential, binary matching operations each of which adds a component to the reaction time. Similarly, each mismatch which results in a change of the truth index adds an additional increment to processing time. Some more recent research (Garrod, 1972 and Anderson, in preparation) have shown that when the information being processed is retrieved from memory rather than from the immediate input (or from STM), the "representation" is different in that it involves the deep structure relations (actor-patient) rather than surface structure (Subject-Object) relations. Yet, the nature of the model is the same; the process still consists of a set of binary matching operations applied sequentially to yield a decision.

Comprehension and verification of sentences may not be a paradigmatic example of verbal thinking, yet these same processes have

Model A and Its Consequences for Eight Types of Sentences

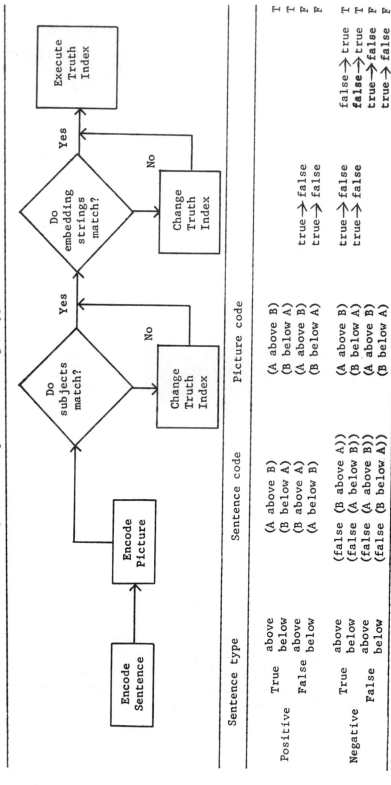

Figure 3-3. A model for sentence verification (from Clark & Chase).

been found to be operative in solving ordering syllogisms or three-term series problems such as:

> Harry is taller than Sam.
> Bill is shorter than Sam.
> Who is tallest?

The primary feature of the explanation is again the nature of the relational terms in the premises and in the question. And again, the difficulties which subjects have with these problems reflect the number of mismatches they detect in arriving at the congruity of the premises among themselves and with the question. Clark (in press) has recently generalized this model to account for a wide range of linguistic processes: following instructions, verifying sentences, answering questions and so on.

Notice that such processes consisting of a series of matching operations depend upon a representation that has an essentially binary structure in which one representation may be translated into the other by means of a set of transformations, thus:

> A is above B → B is below A
> John hit Mary → Mary was hit by John
> A has more than B → B has less than A

Such structures appear to be somewhat unique to the logical uses of ordinary language and formal languages and, secondly, they appear somewhat late in children's intellectual development. That is, young children fail to realize the implications of their utterances (Olson, 1972); for example, they do not realize that if John has more than Mary, Mary has less than John (Pike, 1973). I have described these linguistic binary, matching operations in some detail so they can serve as a contrast to the spatial mental processes I shall now describe.

## SPATIAL MENTAL PROCESSES

While it has been known for decades that the ability to imagine orientation and transformations of objects in space is a distinctive and valuable mental skill, it is only recently that some of the distinguishing characteristics of these processes have been determined. A paradigmatic case of spatial thinking, that of comparing different pictorial representations of the same physical three-dimensional object, has recently been examined in an ingenious study by Shepard and

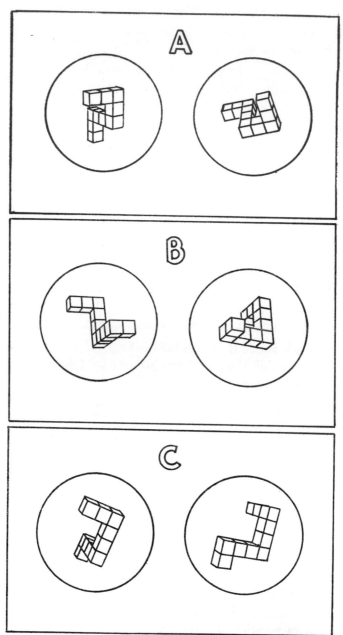

Figure 3-4. Examples of pairs of perspective line drawings presented to the subjects. (A) A "same" pair differing by an 80° rotation in the picture plane, (B) a "same" pair differing by an 80° rotation in depth, and (C) a "different" pair, which cannot be brought into congruence by *any* rotation. Taken from Shepard and Metzler, 1971.

Metzler (1971). They timed adult subjects while they made same-different judgments as to the identity of objects represented in drawings similar to those shown in Figure 3-4.

The critical feature of this study is that the degree of rotation between the two stimuli varied on each trial from as little as 20° to as much as 180° by 20° intervals. The time which subjects required to judge the identity of the two block drawings was found to be a linear function of the degrees of rotation separating the two blocks (see fig. 3-5). Furthermore, the slope of the obtained function corresponds to an average rate of mental rotation of about 60° per second.

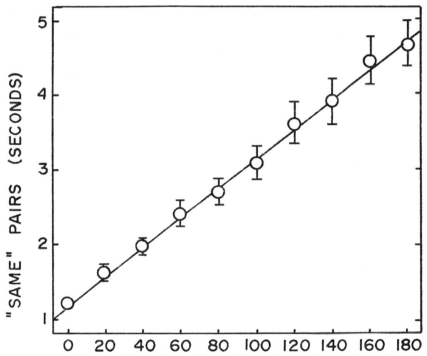

Figure 3-5. Mean time to respond that two perspective line drawings portray objects of the same three-dimensional shape plotted as a function of angular difference in portrayed orientation. Taken from Shepard and Metzler, 1971.

Two important features of the processes which subjects use in solving such problems emerge from this study. First, the transformations are continuous rather than a series of binary match-mismatch operations. Secondly, this process was called upon when the problem could not be assigned a simpler, featural structure as Shepard and Metzler pointed out.

What then makes a problem a spatial one? This question defies a simple answer. It is reasonable to argue, however, that what makes a problem spatial is not its surface properties but rather the structure of the symbol system or mental representation employed in obtaining the solution. Nelson Goodman (1970) and Gardner, Perkins, and Howard (1974) argue that these symbol systems are basically of two sorts: notational (linguistic) and non-notational (pictorial, spatial). The primary distinguishing feature of these systems is that the first is contrastive, often binary; the latter is continuous such that for any two positions there is a further point between them. Either of these may be called upon depending on the structure of the tasks, their complexity, the thinker's purpose and above all, his knowledge of or compliance with the relevent symbolic systems. The continuous spatial transformations found by Shepard and Metzler are appropriate only to certain types of tasks and for particular purposes.

Some evidence as to the conditions under which a stimulus will be treated notationally (linguistically) and when it will be treated non-notationally (spatially) can be gleaned from the research literature on serial versus parallel processing. A number of studies have indicated that when stimulus events are matched in terms of their common category or name (*A* and *a* share the same name, "a"), the matching process is serial; the more letters in the array, the longer it takes to compare them. However, when the stimulus events can be matched on the basis of their physical properties or appearance, the matching processes could be carried on in parallel; adding more letters to the array does not add to the time required to compare them. (Neisser and Beller, 1965; Beller, 1970). Like the spatial and verbal processes we contrasted earlier, these parallel and serial processes have been shown to be related to hemispheric functions. Cohen (1972, 1973) showed that the left hemisphere was relatively better at name or category matches while the right hemisphere was better at physical matches. Furthermore, she was able to provide some evidence that when a set of letters were judged as same (all identical) or different (one item differing from the rest), left hemisphere judgments increased with the number of items in the set while right hemisphere judgments did not. That is, there appears to be a serial versus parallel distinction between the left and right hemispheres of the brain.

This claim should not strike us as startling if it is kept in mind that the decision sometimes called a "physical match" may be equally well designated as a spatial match. That is, even a letter of the alphabet may be treated in terms of its name or meaning, that is its notational properties or as a spatial pictorial pattern in terms of its spatial properties. If it is treated as a name or a linguistic category, it is treated notationally by processes that are serial set of match-mismatch operations. If it is treated as a spatial pattern, its processing would be comparable to that for any other spatial array such as those of pictures, maps or the spatial representations employed by Shepard and Metzler.

Not only can verbal stimuli be treated either as notational categories or as spatial displays, but spatial arrays may also be processed either in terms of the spatial, continuous transformations (in parallel) described above or in terms of notational, propositional categories. Consider the pairs of triangles in Figure 3-6.

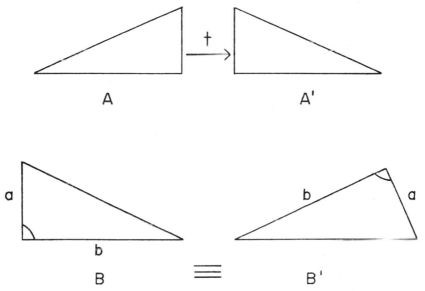

Figure 3-6.   Are these triangles equivalent?

The triangles A and A′ could be judged equivalent by continuous spatial means, namely, by imagining a transformation (t) of a 90° clockwise rotation, which could be applied to A to yield A′. Such mental operations would not, however, prove the triangles equivalent or congruent. By means of different mental operations, those represented by formal geometry, B could be shown to be identical to B′. Euclidean geometry is the translation of spatial intuitions into true statements; it is a language of space and as such is linguistic or notational. The two triangles are not congruent by virtue of the claims that your manipulated mental images appear to coincide as in the Shepard and Metzler task but rather by means of a series of essentially linguistic stages.

Notice too that there is more than one notational representation of space. Descartes' contribution to this problem was to show that there was an algebraic solution to every geometric problem—both of these types of solutions, however, are notational, not spatial or pictorial. Yet how these systems are related has been the ground of controversy between the intuitionist and the formalist mathematicians for decades, (Poincaré) and promises to be an important area of study for cognitive psychologists.

As to the more specific question as to how spatial and linguistic or notational processes are related to the solution of the tasks that have been studied psychologically at least two suggestions may be made. The more popular suggestion was mentioned earlier, namely, that spatial and linguistic modes of processing information are alternative minds represented in the left and right hemispheres. Alternatively, these systems may be hierarchically organized such that the output from one system serves as the input to the other. How this proceeds may be suggested by reference back to Figure 3-3. Notice that the first step of even a notational process following the reading of a sentence or the viewing of a picture consists of setting up a representation of those events—casting the information into notational terms. That process may be a spatial one at least in some cases as we shall see in the next section.

## SPATIAL ASPECTS OF LINGUISTIC THINKING

To this point I have argued that people can use a strategy of spatial transformation for solving some types of problems at least in some circumstances. Are those problems only visual-spatial ones?

A current controversy revolves around the possibility that the solution of some linguistic problems are solved by means of spatial strategies in which statements are "spatialized" or translated into a common spatial framework from which answers can subsequently be retrieved. The typical task used to demonstrate these processes is the one we discussed earlier as paradigmatic of linguistic processes in general, namely, logical transitivity or three-term-series problems:

If A > B

B > C

Which is greatest?

Studies by DeSoto, London and Handel (1965) indicated that subjects solve verbal, logical problems of this sort by constructing mental spatial arrays with the positive member of a comparative adjective at the top of the array and the negative member at the bottom. Huttenlocker (1968, 1970) has importantly extended this argument by showing that subjects comprehend these sentences as if they were following instructions to construct actual physical arrays of objects. This link between comprehending and doing was clearly shown in the fact that such sentences as "The blue block is above the red block" were more easily obeyed if the grammatical subject is the block in hand and the grammatical object is in a given, fixed location. (Further studies with active and passive sentences showed that it is the logical or deep structure subject that must correspond to the moveable object to make the sentence easy to comply with). She then extended her findings to the three-term-series problems. It is as if subjects have to place three counters in an ordered, spatial arrangement (as in following instructions) and then read off the queried information. The relative difficulty of the problem is determined by the same factors that account for the difficulties in arranging physical objects except in this case they are constructing imaginary arrays (in DeSoto's terms) "a spatial paralogic."

Considerable controversy revolves around these claims (Clark, 1969 a and b, 1972, Jones, 1970; Johnson-Laird, 1972). Subjects introspectively report that they are doing as Huttenlocker claims, yet the data appear to be accounted for as well or better in terms of the principles of linguistic representations, lexical marking, and match-mismatch testing for congruence which we described earlier.

Notice, however, two facets of this controversy. One is the fact that while Huttenlocker administers her problems in oral form, Clark (1969 a and b) and Jones (1970) give their's via print. This could be expected to contribute to contested differences in two ways. First, Clark's subjects have less of a memory load as the critical features of the task are visually present in the text. Subjects can, therefore, as Clark admits, discard information keeping in mind only the extreme member of the contrasted pair as they continue their analysis, a technique inconceivable in speech when you have no indication of what is to follow. In print you can, in fact, read up and down: you can compare the relational terms, the object of sentence 1 with the subject of sentence 2 and so on, yielding the truncated decisional patterns found by Clark. Huttenlocker's subjects, however, have to hold all information in memory. Most subjects, under such conditions, respond by casting some of this information into a spatial format. There is too much information to rehearse it and to make the match-mismatch operations all in short term memory. Thus, Clark's subjects have a "technological" memory, print; while Huttenlocker's subjects are forced to construct a spatial memory. Once constructed, both groups of subjects presumably then compare the remembered structure with the structure of the question in a series of match-mismatch operations to yield the answer.

If this analysis is true, then it would enable us to predict, for example, that if Clark's propositions were presented to a subject and removed, prior to the presentation of the question rather than being printed all together, subjects would resort to spatial strategies as a means of preserving ordered information (See Schultz, in preparation). Clearly, if the problems involve more than two propositions, subjects would have to resort to some spatial means in order to store comparative or spatial information. Indeed, some recent evidence on a seriation task by Karlins and Trabasso suggests that this is the case. Wood (1969) and Johnson-Laird (1972) suggest that the choice of strategy depends upon a subject's experience with the tasks, the linguistic strategy being a wasteful but faster strategy; familiarity may have the same effect as print medium, namely, selective attention to a few contrastive or critical features.

Another line of evidence shows that spatial processes may be involved when otherwise linguistic or notational processes are inappropriate in some way. Recall that in Thurstone's (1938) data, verbal analogies on IQ tests, such as:

Horse is to rider as violin is to ——————————
Cat is to kitten as dog is to ——————————

correlate highly with verbal abilities but not with spatial abilities. Yet Rummelhart and Abrahamson (1970) have been able to show that verbal analogies such as:

Rat is to pig as Rabbit is to (chimpanzee, *cow*, rabbit, sheep) are solved using the three-dimensional semantic space earlier described for the semantic representation of animals by Nancy Henle (1969). The impressive fact, to me, is that subjects were able to select answers on the basis of the similarity of a known animal to each of the three-dimensional properties of the abstract representation. That is, if no animal fit the requirements, subjects performed as if they could search the three continuous dimensions until they hit a semantic space for which they knew an animal.

A comparable semantic "space" has repeatedly been isolated by Osgood (1957, 1971) in his studies of the connotative or affects aspects of meaning. In twenty-five different cultures, Osgood has continued to find that there is a remarkable congruence in the judgment of the qualifiers appropriate to such nouns as house, girl, defeat, love. These qualifiers fall into a common space marked by the primary dimensions of evaluation (good-bad), potency (strong-weak) and activity (active-passive). It is possible that subjects could solve analogies in such a semantic space. Two qualifications of this model are that first, the theory deals with affective aspects of meaning rather than denotative features (those usually marked in a dictionary) and secondly, the dimensions or features are assumed to be continuous rather than discrete. It is possible, however, that it is the qualifiers, largely adjectives, that create the continuous semantic space, not the nouns themselves as Osgood has assumed. Comparison is, after all, the primary function of adjectives.

My conjecture is that spatial processes are called upon in solving verbal problems whenever either the information involved exceeds the limitations of short-term memory, and whenever the "semantic system" under consideration is not sufficiently structured in terms of a finite set of alternatives which are contrastively organized around a basic set of features. Where our semantic system is so organized, the solutions appear to be simply notational:

Cat is to kitten as dog is to _____

The three-dimensional space found by Rummelhart and Abrahamson and by Osgood is constructed because a simpler contrastive, binary system is lacking. Spatial representation is, thus, a means for organizing information which fails to comply with the requirements of a notational representation.

Perhaps most of our ordinary language fails to exhibit the contrastive, binary features of a notational system. Aspects of language which are compatible with such a notational organization may be restricted to those of formal, logical languages, to those few noun systems such as kinship which are organized around binary features and to the large number of qualifiers including adjectives which represent continuous dimensions by means of contrastive, binary features. It is important to notice that even spatial terms can be treated as notational, as they are in Clark's and Chase's task.

★    ★
The star is above the plus.   A+   B+

A continuous "spatial" representation, such as the drawing of a display would preserve both the distance and the directionality of the relation; in that case A and B would not be considered equivalent. For purposes of Clark's and Chase's task, A and B are considered equivalent; spatial distance information is lost or traded off for some logical advantages. It appears, then, that the language of space is notational and represented in terms of a set of formal, binary features which can be compared in a series of match-mismatch operations.

Even these notational aspects of spatial language may remain tied to spatial representations. Luria (1966) has provided convincing evidence that damage to the parietal-occipital divisions of the left hemisphere (and to a lesser extent, the right) disturbs spatial orientation not only in regard to visual perception and activity but also in regard to the comprehension and production of *spatial and logical language*. Thus, subjects with damage to this area of the brain may be unable not only to find their way around the hospital and to distinguish symmetrical positions of the hands of a clock (ten minutes to six from ten minutes after six, but also to handle such logico-grammatical relations in such spatial terms as "above-below" or such comparative relations as "lighter than," "before"; all of which seem to involve a spatial component. Perhaps Arnheim (1969, p. 226) is correct in his assertion that "thoughts need shape."

To summarize, one cannot simply contrast linguistic with spatial processes; some linguistic problems are treated spatially, and some are treated notationally. Reciprocally, some spatial problems are represented spatially (as in pictures, maps, graphs) and some notationally (as in Clark's and Chase's problems). The operations employed by a subject in solving such problems will depend upon the nature of the task, its complexity and the subject's competence in translating the task into one symbolic system or another.

Brooks (1970) has conducted a series of studies which show the complementary nature of linguistic and spatial processes. In his studies subjects were shown an outline drawing of an ★F and then were asked to decide from memory if each of the corners beginning at the ★ were at the top or bottom (yes) or in the middle (no). On other trials, they were given a sentence and then asked to decide, from memory, if each word of a sentence was a noun. He found that for a spatial pattern it was very difficult for subjects to respond spatially by circling a Y(Yes) or an N(No) for each decision point but relatively easy to respond verbally by saying Yes or No. On the other hand, when the sentence was held in memory, he found it was difficult for subjects to signal verbally their decision about nounness by saying Yes or No, while it was easy to circle the Yes or No printed on a sheet of paper. Similarly, it was easier to count verbally the corners of the F but more difficult to count the words of the sentence verbally.

Even more impressive is a more recent experiment by Brooks in which the following sentences were read to subjects who either read along with the speaker or listened only:

In the starting square put a 1
In the next square to the left put a 2
In the next square down put a 3
In the next square to the right put a 4
In the next square down put a 5
In the next square down to the right put a 6

In the next square up put a 7
In the next square up to the right put an 8

Empirically, he found that reading along while listening diminished a subject's recall performance. He argued that the message is a spatial one requiring visualization or spatialization; print is a spatial medium, hence reading interferes with spatialization. When the spatial terms were replaced by nonspatial words, the effect was reversed and reading while listening facilitated recall over simple listening. Even more interesting is Brooks' observation that in the course of reading such spatial messages, subjects diverted their gaze from the text at the end of each sentence. This point provides a more secure footing for the hypothesis made earlier about Clark's task. Ironically, recall that Clark's linguistic account assumes a spatial medium, print!

In general, then, Brooks has shown that spatial and verbal systems play complementary roles as the cognitive processes. On one hand, interference occurs when the same system is used for both internal processing and external responding. On the other hand, facilitation occurs when the problem can be divided between the two systems—either between the internal and external processes as in Brooks' tasks or between different parts of the internal processes as in the Huttenlocker and Rummelhart tasks.

Some further analysis of the spatial aspects of printed language is required. Even if both spoken and written language are notational or contrastively structured, only written language is a spatial, visual medium. The invention of writing systems and the development of reading skills in children may have a more profound effect on intellectual development than most theories of child development imply. It would be interesting to see, for example, if reading tended to suppress visual spatialization and spatial abilities generally. The only evidence I know of is ambiguous; girls read more than boys and they also have lower spatial abilities. If such a relationship was found, we would at last know what price, if any, we pay for our emphasis on literacy.

## THE LANGUAGE OF SPACE

To this point we have contrasted continuous, spatial processes with verbal, linguistic "notational" ones and examined some of the ways in which they serve complementary roles in performing an activity when one system is overloaded. A more precise conception of the relation between language and space may be obtained from an examination of ordinary language. There is a language of space, the structure of which has been examined by Bierwisch (1967), Teller (1969) and Leech (1970). Clark (1971) has written an important summary article which specifies some of the psychological and developmental implications of these linguistic structures.

The most interesting property of the language of space is the fact that to understand the meaning of such terms you must know something about space. The question is: does the linguistic structure learned by every speaker of the language determine how he "codes," "organizes," or "perceives" space, a Whorfian notion, or is the causal relation operative in the opposite direction—the structure of perception of space determines the subsequent structure of the language of space. Even the "deep structure theorists" such as Bierwisch (1967) and Clark (1971) opt for the latter—perhaps because of their interest in linguistic *universals* rather than linguistic *relativity* (Olson and Hildyard, in preparation).

English has a fairly large number of spatial terms that fall into the form classes of adverbials: here/there: prepositions: up/down; on the left/on the right; at the front of/at the back of; in/on; by; above/below; adjectives: big/small; long/short; wide/narrow; thick/thin; deep/shallow; and nouns: top/bottom; left/right; front/back; side/end. These spatial terms have several common properties. Firstly, they all assume a point of reference—the speaker or some other object. Secondly, they are organized around particular dimensions such as verticality or length. Thirdly, these terms usually come in contrastive polar pairs specifying the dimension as in the following:

| Dimension | Contrastive Pair |
|---|---|
| where: | here/there |
| vertical: | up/down; high/low; above/below |
| horizontal: | right/left |
| frontal: | front/back |
| length: | long/short |
| distance: | far/near |
| height: | tall/short |
| width: | wide/narrow |
| depth: | deep/shallow |
| thickness: | thick/thin |

Finally, these contrastive pairs have the property of "marking." The "unmarked" number of the pair normally occurs in the neutral question form, "How high is the airplane?" and it is generally the positive form. The marked form is generally defined in terms of the negation of the unmarked number, e.g. short → not long, while the converse does not hold.

Clark, Carpenter and Just (1973) have sought to show that the structure of language (L-space) reflects in a precise way perceptual space (P-space) both in the choice of reference plane, in dimensions, and in positive-negative directions along those dimensions. In particular, he has suggested that gravity specifies the natural dimension of verticality and the ground level specifies the first natural reference plane to which that dimension would be related. Because the direction above the ground is visible while that below is not, he suggests upward is naturally positive and downward is negative. Lexically this dimension is specified by such terms as up/down; above/below; high/low; top/bottom, and the like. The second natural direction is specified by the orientation of our perceptual apparatus to yield a horizontal dimension extending on either side of a vertical "frontal" plane separating the front from the back of our bodies. Again the front would be positive and the back negative directions. Lexically this would appear as front/back; ahead/behind; to/from and so on.

Both of the planes and directions mentioned thus far are asymmetrical. The third direction is also horizontal and specified in terms of the vertical "lateral" plane dividing left from right. Because of the bilateral symmetry of the human body, the directions from this reference plane are symmetrical. Lexically this dimension is specified by the terms left/right and beside.

The perceptual asymmetries of the directions from the first two reference planes, namely, up/down and front/back would account for the lexical marking of the negative number of the pair. Lexical marking has been found to be closely related to ease of comprehension and verification. A spatial term that is the marked number of the pair, e.g. *below* in the pair *above/below* is in fact more difficult to comprehend and to verify against a perceived event or picture (Clark and Chase, 1972).

However, there are at least two major obstacles to simply identifying P-space and L-space. The first is that P-space is, it would appear, continuous while L-space is notational or binary—properties, directions and distances are represented by simple binary contrasts such as open/closed, front/back, up/down and so on. Perhaps a better way to state this point is that P-space is as well represented by drawings as by sentences; it is, therefore, just as continuous (nonnotational or spatial in our early terms) as it is binary, discrete or "notational."

Secondly, the identification of P-space and L-space involves what William James called the "psychological fallacy," attributing to the world and its perception the end product of one's cognition. In regard to three-dimensional Euclidean space, Piaget concludes:

> It would be a complete mistake to imagine that human beings have some innate or psychological precocious knowledge of the spatial surround organized in a two or three-dimensional reference frame. . . Far from constituting the starting point of spatial awareness, the frame of reference is in fact the culminating point of the entire psychological development of Euclidean space (p. 416).

Piaget and Inhelder (1956) provided evidence for this claim by showing that children cannot estimate spatial position or spatial orientation in terms of horizontal or vertical dimensions until approximately nine years of age. Rather these positions and orientations are represented in terms of their relationship to each other (adjacency and order) or the frame of reference present in the visual field. Hence, when children are shown a bottle of water and asked to anticipate the water level when the bottle is tilted, they represent it in terms of its being perpendicular to the walls of the container (or parallel to its base) and not in terms of a true horizontal. Similarly when presented with a sand "mountain" and asked to mount telephone poles "straight up" in the sand, they insert them perpendicular to the surface of the hill and not in terms of a true vertical. Children's drawings show the same features; trees stand perpendicular to the hill instead of vertically. Clearly then, children represent spatial dimensions in terms of the visually salient properties of the visual field and *not* in terms of invariant Euclidean dimensions with vertical and horizontal axes. It may be added that even adults have difficulty with objective verticality and horizontality. As late as the eighteenth century, Hogarth's (1697-1764) drawing of the reflection of vertically oriented windows, reflected in an obliquely oriented bottle, are drawn in terms of the axes of the bottle, that is parallel to the side of the bottle and oblique to the primary axes of Euclidean space (Pirienne, 1970).

Both Bierwisch and Clark's claim is that Euclidean dimensions form the *a priori* basis of spatial perception and linguistic structure; Piaget's claim is that far from being *a priori*, the Euclidean dimensions constitute a late developing solution to the problem of representing continuous space.

It remains to be seen if these two apparently contradictory views can be reconciled or at least brought to empirical test. One possible way in which this important problem could be attacked is through the study of a child's acquisition of spatial terms.

## ASPECTS OF THE ACQUISITION OF THE LANGUAGE OF SPACE

The two major factors which may be expected to influence the order of acquisition of children's spatial terms are the nature and development of the child's conception of space, and the complexity of the structure of the lexical items "representing" that space.

In regard to the first factor, there is considerable evidence available to show that a child's early perception of space is egocentric, and that the earliest spatial relations between objects are coded in terms of such topological features as proximity and enclosure. Only later are spatial relations coded in terms of dimensionalized space. Hence, lexical items specifying these topological relations should be among the earliest acquired (Parisi and Antinucci, 1970).

As we have noted, it is not clear how the egocentric perception of space is related to the language of space. On the whole, as Clark has shown, the child's perceptual space maps on to his linguistic space in a remarkably economical manner; the orientations and directions specified in organizing our perceptual world are well represented in our ordinary language. Perception and language diverge, however, in regard to the effects of egocentrism. There is some evidence to show that a child's conception of space is organized egocentrically as, for example, in Piaget's famous mountain task in which a child has difficulty imagining how an arrangement would look from a different point of view. If a child's conception of space is egocentric, then spatial terms that rely upon this egocentrism such as *here/there* or *come/go* should be acquired earlier than ones that do not such as *big/small* or *long/short*. Such a conclusion, however logical, would not be justified because language is by nature a social instrument; it maps most directly on to features of the environment that are invariant *across* speakers. Hence, lexical invariants are incompatible with egocentrism. This is most clearly seen in the child's acquisition of proper names and pronouns. Inasmuch as the child's own name, *Billy*, is shared by both the adults and the child, it is acquired before the personal pronouns *I* and *me* which change with the speaker. Pronouns, in other words, are not invariant across speakers and although one of the first perceptual distinctions made by a child is the egocentric one between self not-self, it is one of the later linguistic ones. Thus egocentrism has some explanatory power for perception of space but little for the language of space. To generalize this to the Piaget-Vygotsky controversy, language is not simply the replica or copy of knowledge, including spatial knowledge, but rather, to borrow a metaphor from the visual arts, the restructuring of that knowledge in terms of the requirements of a given medium of representation whether ordinary language or drawing (see Olson, 1970; Olson, 1974).

In regard to the second factor that may be expected to influence children's acquisition of spatial terms, namely the complexity of the lexical items themselves, Fillmore (1971) has pointed out that the spatial preposition *on* implies a two-dimensional noun object while *in* requires a three-dimensional noun object—for example, we would say *on the wall* but we would say *in the room*. Similarly, positionals; *at*, *on*, and *in* are simpler than directionals; *to*, *into*, *onto*, *into*, *across* and *through*, in that directionals imply positionals and add a motion component. Moreover, some spatial terms such as *by*, indicate proximity in a horizontal plane without indicating any particular direction, while others such as *beside* and *in front of* maintain that horizontal proximity relation while adding a particular direction. In all these cases, it is reasonable to assume that spatial terms which specify more features or which satisfy more complex "conditions of application" (Clark, 1973) would be acquired later than those which satisfy fewer. Alternatively, more complex spatial terms may be used by children as if they were synonyms for the simpler terms. Indeed, even adults frequently use *in* when they mean *into*, e.g. "Put the eggs in the fridge."

In addition to their semantic complexity, spatial terms differ in their syntactic properties. Why are some spatial terms nouns while others are adjectives, prepositions or adverbs? As we shall see, some of these form class differences and relate in an interesting way to the "criteriality" or definingness of these spatial features for the objects referred to.

Applying this argument to spatial terms, children may be expected to learn spatial terms that are invariant across speakers, that is to spatial relations between objects, before they learn to use spatial terms that vary with the speaker. Within the set of spatial terms that are invariant across speakers there are some that relate to the ego as well, such as up and down (*to the left* or *in front of* are not invariant across speakers) and this coincidence may facilitate the learning of these spatial terms.

Having indicated these general parameters relating to the child's acquisition of spatial terms, let us attempt in a preliminary way to specify how these parameters may interact in the acquisition of children's spatial terms.

One set of spatial terms that pertain to directions of movement of ego without specifying a goal are the adverbials:

1. up/down
2. forward/backward
3. left/right

These may appear in such sentences as: Up! Jump up! Pick me up! Put me down! Go up!, etc. In that these terms involve the child's primary activity in space, they may be thought to be primary. However, only in the first of these pairs is there congruence between the actual or absolute direction of movement between the speaker and the listener. Hence (1) should be the first acquired. Further, following Clark et al. (in press) given that (1) is asymmetric in that gravitational cues utilized in maintaining vertical orientation are asymmetric and (2) in that front/back distinction is asymmetric given the position of our perceptual apparatus while (3) is symmetric given bilateral symmetry, (3) should be the last to be acquired.

Within each of these pairs, Clark, on the basis of the visibility of the first member and the nonvisibility of the second, has suggested that we may expect the first mentioned member of the pair to be the positive unmarked member, while the second is the negative or marked member. There is no obvious basis for predicting for (3) that either right or left to be the positive member of the pair, yet G. Olson and Laxar (in press) have recently provided evidence that the fragment *right* is more easily verified against a drawing than is the fragment *left*.

Although I know of no clear evidence on the acquisition of these spatial terms, considerable evidence exists as to the primacy of the vertical dimension underlying (1) and the lateness of that underlying (3). Infants, for example, avoid the visual cliff (Walk and Gibson, 1961); many species and children find left/right discriminations difficult. This difficulty has been attributed both to the bilateral symmetry of the body and to the fact that left/right differences are not invariant driven locomotion in a horizontal plane (Rudel and Teuber, 1963; Sutherland, 1960; Lashley, 1951; Olson, 1970). It would be interesting to know if rats could learn to run a maze organized in a vertical plane, that is one whose choice points involved up/down, more easily than the classical mazes organized in a horizontal plane with its left/right choice points; comparable data with children would also be of interest.

A second set of spatial terms pertain to positions of objects relative to some specified referent object:

4. here/there (where)
5. by, next to, beside
6. near/far
7. above/below; over/under
8. in front of/in back of; ahead/behind
9. on the left/on the right

Most of these terms can take ego as one of the two objects being related. Indeed, (4) is an adverbial that is exclusively related to ego and should perhaps be treated separately. The fact that *there* has an existential use (*There* are seven days in a week) as well as a locational one, has led some writers, including Clark (1971) and Kuroda (1968) to conclude that *there* is the unmarked form. While *here* is the more egocentric term and hence may be perceptually salient, its usage is not congruent across speakers—*here* for the ego as speaker is not the same as *here* for ego as listener while in most cases, *there* is the same for both. Hence, *there* may be more readily acquired. For adults, however, *there* would seem to be the more complex in that it can be defined as the negative of here. Both of these terms are used diectically, that is in terms of the perceptually specified spatial-temporal context in which they are uttered.

The remainder of these terms (5-9) are prepositions specifying position relative to the object of the preposition. Consider the differing nature of these relations. Proximity relations are marked by (5) and (6). These are the relations which Piaget and Inhelder (1956) and Olson (1970) found to be so critical in a child's attempts to copy a pattern. Note that these proximity terms are undifferentiated as to the particular direction in space that the relation holds. Thus *next to* could be applied either vertically or horizontally; *by* appears restricted to horizontal proximate relations but is undifferentiated as to *in front of* and *beside*. (7), (8) and (9) preserve these proximity relations but are more complex in that they specify, in addition, a direction of application—(7) applies vertically, (8) frontally and (9) laterally. Why (8) takes *in* while (9) takes *on* is interesting but unclear. These prepositional phrases generated by (5) through (9) like the following ones may be thought of as elaborated forms of the diectic *there*.

A third set of spatial terms are prepositions that are specified not by their direction of application but rather by the spatial properties of the objects to which they relate.

10. at, on, in
11. to/from
12. onto/off
13. into/out of
14. via, across, through

Both Fillmore (1971) and Clark (1971) have pointed out that while *at, on* and *in* specify locations in the same way, they presuppose one, two and three- dimensional space respectively. Hence one may say *The deer is on the grass* but not *The deer is on the forest*, Clark (1971). He summarized these positional terms and their related "directional terms" as follows:

TABLE 3-I
PREPOSITIONS OF LOCATION AND OF LOCATION—DIRECTION

| *Number of dimensions* | *Position* | *Positive Direction* | *Negative Direction* | *Path* |
|---|---|---|---|---|
| 1 | at | to | from | via |
| 2 | on | onto | off of | across |
| 3 | in | into | out of | through |

Clark has further pointed out that the complexity of these prepositions increases as you read both down and across this table, and the ordering of these prepositions may predict the order of acquisition of these terms by children. It is interesting to note that in French, both *on* and *onto* are represented by the single lexical item *sur*; while both *in* and *into* are represented by the word *dans*. Which of their meanings is acquired first would be important evidence for this hypothesis. Further, some preliminary observations with young children indicate that they use a spatial preposition "from" in the place of the nonspatial "of" in such sentences as "You know the picture *from* me."

An important set of spatial terms are adjectives that refer explicitly to the spatial properties of the objects they modify:

15. big/small
16. tall/short
17. long/short
18. wide/narrow
19. thick/thin
20. deep/shallow

While (15) assumes a nondimensionalized space, (16) to (20) assume a dimensionalized space of at least one dimension for (16) and (17), at least two dimensions for (18) and at least three dimensions for (19) and (20). These adjectives differ then in what Clark (1971) calls their "conditions of application." Furthermore, as Bierwisch (1967), Teller (1969) and Clark (1971) have all pointed out, the first member of each pair is the unmarked form in that they could serve in the neutral question, "How long is the box?" Furthermore, (16) through (20) could all take measurement expressions. It is reasonable to suggest that (16) to (20) imply as Euclidean conception of dimensionalized space. Young children's conception of space, as we suggested earlier, is primarily topological and nondimensionalized. Hence, it is reasonable to expect that big/small terms will be learned before any of the dimensional terms and that the acquisition of the latter will reflect in a consistent manner the elaboration of a continuous Euclidean space compatible with measurement. Further, it would not be at all surprising to find that non-western cultures (non-Euclidean cultures) did not have lexical equivalents of (17), (18) and (19). Indeed, Wales and Campbell (1970) report a decrease in the use of "big" in three to four year old children. They also report the beginnings of dimensionalized adjectives, and have provided some recent evidence that three-year-old children, when asked to choose the *big* one from two rectangles, one of which has a larger surface area and the other of which is taller, will select the larger one. By four years of age, however, they select the taller one, thereby indicating the beginnings of dimensionalized spatial conceptions. The first and most salient of these dimensions is length, as indicated by the linguistic analysis above, namely, length requires at least one-dimensional space while width requires at least two-dimensional space and so on. Hence a pattern of complexity similar to that for *at, on* and *in* may be found in studies of children's acquisition of spatial terms.

A similar explanation may be offered for children's quantity judgments over the age range 2.4 to 4.7 (Mehler and Bever, 1967; Mehler, 1971). When the longer array actually has the smaller number, both the youngest and the oldest children make the most accurate judgments of quantity with the poorest performance being given by the children in the middle of the age range (3.8-3.11 years). This decline in performance with development appears to reflect the same factors that were suggested for the concept of size and for spatial representations generally; namely, the development from a nondimensionalized conception of magnitude to a dimensionalized one of which length (height) is the primary dimension.

Finally, it is interesting to notice that there are some spatial terms which occur as nouns:

21. top/bottom
22. front/back
23. left/right
24. side, end, etc.

Elsewhere, we have argued (Bialystok and Olson, in preparation) that nouns may be differentiated from adjectives on the basis that nouns refer to objects and their criterial attributes. Attributes are intrinsic to the object, while adjectives refer to the noncriterial attributes of objects, that is, features that are not invariant to an object. Consider, for example, a car that has wheels, is blue, and is small. Wheels, being criterial, are marked in language by a noun; blue and small, being not criterial to the object identity, are marked by adjectives.

When this postulated difference between nouns and adjectives is applied to spatial terms, it leads to the observation that spatial adjectives refer to nonintrinsic or noncriterial features of objects—a flag pole remains a flag pole regardless of whether it is long or short. On the other hand, the intrinsic or criterial parts of objects are also spatially distributed, and this spatial distribution is designated by the somewhat comparable spatial terms; top, bottom, front, back and so on. But being intrinsic to objects, they are represented in language by nouns. The original assignment of these nouns depends upon the normal or canonical "anomical" orientation of the object, as Clark pointed out, and/or the basis of analogy with human orientation. The critical point to notice, however, is that spatial features that are critical to objects are nouns. Moreover, they are invariant to the object despite the object's location. If the object is moveable, as the object moves the parts move and alter the spatial location; the invariant parts of the object are described by the same nouns regardless of location in space. Thus, a person's back or front remains his back or front regardless of his location in space. Hence, your back can be on the floor if you lie down and your top can be at the bottom if you stand on your head; similarly a horse's back is on top! Although the *front* as a noun can occur in any spatial position depending on the position of the object as a whole and still remain the *front*, these same terms are used as part of a preposition, e.g. *at the front of*. The usual spatial position is not intrinsic to the object and is not an invariant feature of the object. As nouns are generally acquired before adjectives, it is possible to predict that these spatial terms will be used first as critical attributes independent of their actual spatial location, that is, as nouns and only later as adjectives and prepositions.

The study of the child's comprehension and production of these spatial terms promises to throw important new light upon not only the child's spatial representation of himself and his world but also upon the structure of human language. Although some work on various aspects of this problem has already begun, (Parisi and Antinucci, 1970; Wales and Campbell, 1970; Amidon and Carey, in press; Clark, 1972) much more needs to be undertaken.

## THE LANGUAGE OF SPACE AND SPATIAL PERCEPTION

The remainder of this chapter will focus on one aspect of the relationship between what is perceived and what is represented in the lexicon, namely, the perception and lexical representation of oblique lines.

In the concluding chapter of my book, *Cognitive development: The child's acquisition of diagonality*, I pointed out that children's difficulty in constructing a diagonal pattern was mirrored by a lacunae in English for such spatial terms. That lacunae is shown in Figure 3-7.

The important point here is that horizontal and vertical lines have distinctive lexical representation and further, they may be differentiated into specific directions each of which again has a corresponding lexical representation. Not so for obliques. There is no lexical item in English for differentiating the opposite obliques nor are there any lexical items for the four directions which result from adding directional cues. When these orientations are to be described, we use compound descriptions derived from the horizontal-vertical system, such as "up to the right."

In terms of our earlier discussion, obliques constitute the particular case of spatial representation where an orientation lies between the primary dimensions of lexical space—front/back, up/down, left/right. They are therefore, a promising territory for determining how language and perception relate. In principle, they lie outside linguistic space and yet our language can be "applied" to them. The question is, is this linguistic lacunae related to perception of orientation?

The first point to notice is that the lacunae in language maps on, rather directly, to the difficulty experienced by children in differentiating opposite obliques. Rudel and Teuber (1963), for example, found that children under age five are unable to discriminate opposite obliques. Similarly, Bryant (1969) has shown that if abso-

FEATURES

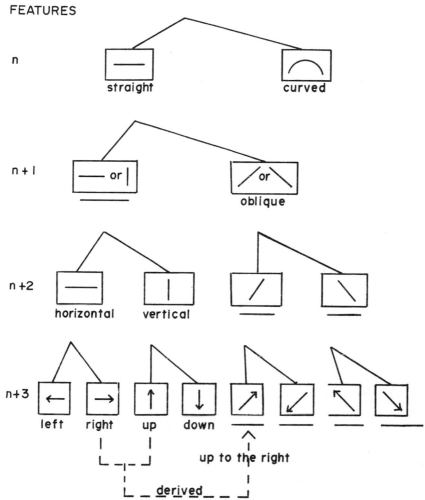

Figure 3-7. The orientation of line and its lexical representation (from Olson, D. R., *Cognitive Development: The child's acquisition of diagonality*. New York, Academic Press, 1970).

lute position cues are removed, even children of seven years cannot discriminate obliques. More recently, Olson (1970) found that young children cannot reconstruct oblique patterns. However, not only do young children have difficulty in discriminating opposite obliques and in constructing obliques, many other species have the same difficulty—octopi, rats, goldfish—virtually all animal species excluding pigeons, according to a recent review by Appelle (1972).

Hence, children's difficulty cannot be explained in Whorfian terms; what is there about the structure of English that would predict the difficulties experienced by octopi? Rather the difficulty would have to be described in terms of a perceptual universal—a bias in the whole species towards one way of perceiving and representing the world, a bias which subsequently appears as a linguistic *universal*. I have examined this problem in detail elsewhere. (Olson and Hildyard, in preparation)

The second observation has to do with the fact that perception and reconstruction of obliques may be done on quite a different basis. In an earlier experiment, for example, I reported (Olson, 1970) that by modifying the task to admit such topological cues as adjacency or proximity, the diagonal could be changed from a complex problem solved by five year olds to a simple problem solved by three year olds. This task did not, however, demand that the child keep track of the orientation of opposite obliques. Even when the task is superficially one of discrimination of orientation, it may be solved in more than one way. Bryant (1969) showed that in the sequential discrimination of opposite obliques, a task that was solved by Rudel and Teuber's seven year olds, when "absolute position cues" were removed, even seven year olds could not make the discrimination. That is, if an oblique was shown in one part of the visual field and the matching stimulus in a different part of the visual field, seven year olds were *unable* to discriminate them; they failed to discriminate on the basis of orientation cues exclusively. Young children apparently notice and recall the absolute layout of the line representation including, for example, that there is something in the upper right hand corner. To succeed on Bryant's task, they must treat the orientation as invariant regardless of its position. What happens between age seven and adulthood which makes this task soluable? How are these orientation cues "represented" and processed mentally?

Angela Hildyard and I (Olson & Hildyard, in preparation) have conducted a series of experiments on the perception of orientation in adults which may help answer these questions. Our original conjecture was that the perception and mental representation of obliques was more complex than that of horiontal and vertical lines. We tested this conjecture in two ways.

In the first, following upon a pilot experiment by Greg Finlayson and David Ireland, Angela Hildyard timed subjects, age approximately 14 years, as they searched through sheets of arrows for the exemplars of the one particular direction indicated at the top of the sheet. Each sheet consisted of 80 arrows, 10 bearing each of the 8 directions of the compass. To examine the effects of the direction of search, subjects were required to search the sheet in four different directions—up, down, to the left, to the right. All of these factors were counterbalanced. Search times for lines of various orientations with the four directions of search are shown in Figure 3-8.

The main point to notice is that, as predicted, search times are much longer for oblique lines; the direction of search, while it interacts with orientation, does not appear to be a plausible explanation for the poor performance on the recognition obliques. Some evidence from the pilot study indicated that while the differences between obliques, horizontals and verticals increased with practice, the effects of this practice should be determined more precisely.

Our second means of testing the hypothesis that the mental representation of obliques is more complex involved a digit-span test of memory for lines in various directions. We constructed arrays of line segments varying from two to five segments per array. The array was shown to the subject from two to five seconds, depending on the number of lines in the array. It was then removed and replaced by two alternatives from which the subject had to select the matching alternative. The nonmatching alternative differed from the correct alternative by a single line segment which was transformed either 90° or 180°. A sample item is shown in Figure 3-9. Again, all these factors were counterbalanced. This digit span test was administered individually to children in the eighth grade who were approximately fourteen years of age. Again the results generally showed that the more oblique lines in the array, the less of the array the Subject could remember. This pattern is shown in Figure 3-10.

The number of errors was a function of the number of obliques in the array. As an aside, it would be interesting to see if this digit span, being a spatial task, is related to ordinary digit span which is a verbal task. It is possible, on the other hand, that they both meas-

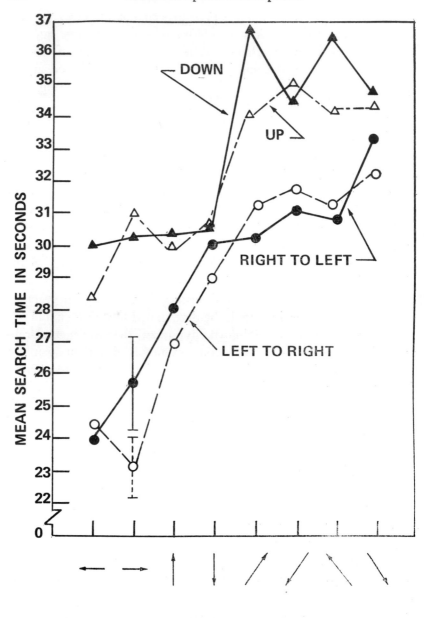

ORIENTATION

Figure 3-8.   Search times for lines of various orientations for 4 directions of search.

## SHEET I

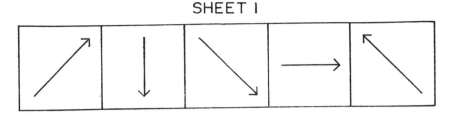

## SHEET 2

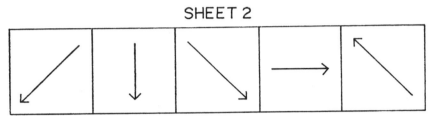

Figure 3-9. A sample item from the test for memory for lines in various orientations.

ure the same ability; subjects may give the line segments either notational or linguistic descriptions and then remember these descriptions. This possibility can be assessed by looking at the pattern of confusions which are presented in Figure 3-11. These confusions support the contention that this memory task relies on featural, notational descriptions. If an error is made on an oblique, it is most likely to be confused with a line rotated 90°. However, if an error is made on a horizontal or vertical line, it is most likely confused with a line rotated 180°. These confusions make it possible to discover some of the features of the underlying representations. "Up" was confused with "down," with a 180° transform suggesting a common feature of "verticality." Similarly, the "up to the left" oblique was confused with "up to the right" oblique, a 90° transform, suggesting that the feature "oblique" plus the feature "up" had been retained. The more complex representation of features required for obliques would, in addition, account for the lower memory span for obliques. It may be concluded that such memory tasks are handled in the linguistic or notational manner we discussed above. But what about the *perception* of orientations as opposed to the *memory* for orientation?

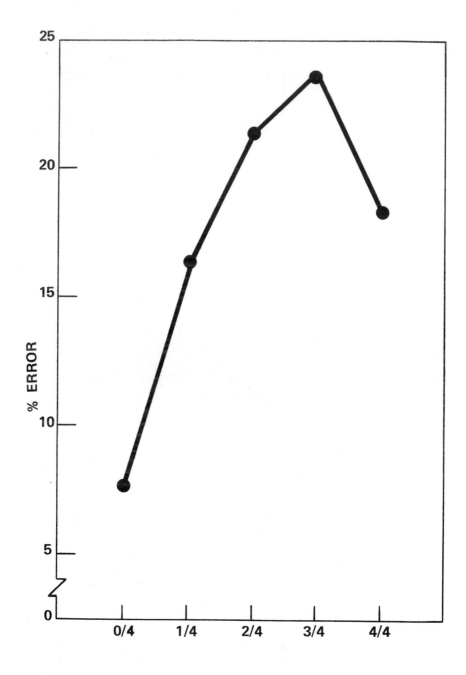

Figure 3-10. Test of memory for lines: Percentage of errors as function of the number of obliques in the array.

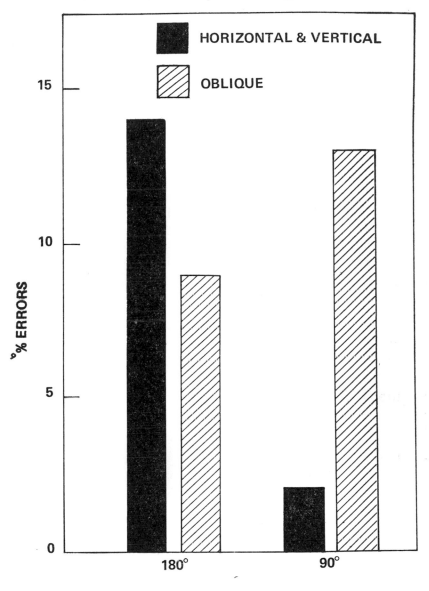

Figure 3-11. Percentage of errors in test of memory for lines. Nonmatching alternative differed from correct alternative by 90° or 180° transformation.

We have recently completed two recognition experiments with adults in which one oriented line is exposed for approximately ½ second, a delay of four seconds ensues, then the second oriented line appears. At the onset of this second line, a clock is activated which, in turn, is stopped when the subjects press one of two telegraph keys; one for "Same," and the other for "Different."

In the first of these experiments, a line segment bearing one of four orientations, horizontal, vertical and the opposite obliques (without the directional arrow heads) appeared in the center of a square screen. The matching stimulus appeared four seconds later in one of the four corners of the display. Recognition times for the oblique orientations as a function of the position of the second line segment is shown in Figure 3-12.

The most obvious fact is that, even after this delay, there is a strong interaction of orientation with absolute positions such that

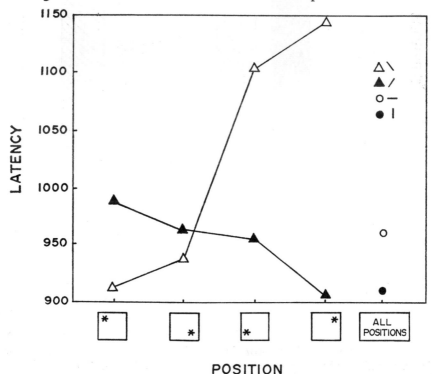

POSITION

Figure 3-12. Recognition times for oblique orientations and function of the position of the second line segment.

an oblique appearing in either of the corners specified (or pointed towards) by the original oblique is recognized very easily; the same oblique in the other positions is recognized with considerable difficulty. This suggests that even adult subjects give a prior coding of obliques in terms of absolute position, that is, in terms of the corners of the display. Subjects also give the oblique a secondary coding in terms of orientation which is called upon if the positional coding is inappropriate. To generalize, spatial information pertaining to position and to orientation is processed separately; with positional information being much simpler to process than orientation information.

When these absolute position match trials are removed, we do indeed find that recognition times are somewhat slower for obliques than for horizontal and vertical lines, thereby giving somewhat vague support to the theory that the perceptual processing of oblique orientations is more complex than that for horizontals and verticals. (V-908 msec; H-959 msec; /-975 msec; \\-1060 msec.) But the strong interaction between orientation and position makes the comparisons somewhat suspect, hence we repeated the experiment with some basic modifications.

Our fourth and most recent study is superficially much the same as the preceding one except that we replaced the square screen with a round one. Moreover, we balanced the possible positions of the second line by projecting it in any of eight positions around the periphery of the screen rather than at the four corners as in the preceding experiment. Recognition times for both a match and a mismatch conditions for the four orientations are shown in Figure 3-13. As predicted, match times for obliques were considerably slower than for horizontal and vertical lines with the "grave" oblique (\\) being dramatically slower than the "acute" (/). All of these differences are highly significant. Unlike the preceding experiment, almost all the reaction time is accounted for by the second stimulus. The match-mismatch effect has almost completely disappeared. There is a small interaction between the compared orientations when the second orientation is an oblique. In this case, mismatch time for the opposite oblique is slightly longer than for horizontals and verticals. This difference is significant only when that second oblique is the "grave" (\\). Generally, however, an

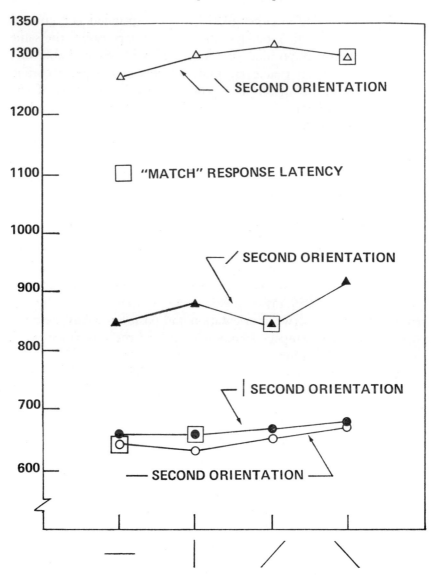

**ORIGINAL ORIENTATION**

Figure 3-13. Recognition times for 4 orientations of $S_2$ as a function of the orientation of $S_1$ (round screen).

oblique is almost as difficult to recognize if it follows a horizontal or vertical as if it follows another oblique.

Notice further that the absence of the square frame had no adverse effect upon the recognition times of the horizontal and vertical lines; if anything, they are recognized even more quickly than in the preceding experiment. Because this comparison is across experiments, it cannot be stated with certainty. Obliques, on the other hand, are consistently more difficult to recognize than horizontal and vertical lines.

I would advance two conclusions based upon these data: the first conclusion refers to the argument about the relation between language and perception of space; the second conclusion bears on the nature of spatial perception generally and upon the perception of orientation specifically.

In regard to language and perception, the difficulty which adult subjects have with the perception of obliques relative to the perception of the orientation of horizontals and verticals, confirms the relationship between our perception and lexical representation of space. This relationship, however, is not congruent with the Whorfian conception in that other species have comparable difficulties. Contrary to the Whorfian notion, it seems more reasonable to argue that the structure or organization of our perception of space in terms of horizontal and vertical axes underlies or determines the structure of our language. Our perceptual biases, then, account for our linguistic biases. As this bias in our perception is common to our species (perhaps to all terrestrial animals), we should expect to find a common bias in all the languages in the world; such a bias would constitute a linguistic universal. The origins of this universal lie, not in an inherited linguistic structure, but rather in shared perception of space. Whether this perceptual bias is genetic or acquired is open to question (Ganz; Ganz and Spinelli).

In regard to the second conclusion, the nature of spatial perception, it appears to be the case that spatial position is processed more directly than spatial orientation; hence the presence of absolute position cues both radically simplified the matching task in Experiment 3 and provided the basis for Bryant's (1969) five year olds to make the discrimination. Positional information, in general, must underlie all aspects of pattern recognition. Perception of orientation, on the other hand, is complicated in that while perceived space may be completely symmetrical, the symmetrical space must be represented by asymmetrical lateralized systems such as: up/down, left/right and front/back. Spatial perception ordinarily does not preserve such information. Adults do not normally remember if the line drawing of a face depicted a left profile or a right profile. Children are notorious both for looking at pictures up-side-down and for "mirror writing." Rather, ordinary perception preserves the spatial relations among the constituents or units of the array in terms of such properties as symmetry, adjacency, curvature and so on. The preservation of orientation information is achieved, not by simple memory of the visual array, but rather by the application of one of our asymmetrical representations of space to the display—we notice that it is "on the left" or "at the top," thereby applying to symmetrical space the asymmetry of our own bodies and its corresponding lexical system. The assignment of these asymmetric representations to symmetric space is both lately acquired by children and time-consuming for adults. Children may give the appearance of handling space asymmetrically—up/down, left/right—when in fact they have preserved only order and proximity relations. Thus "down" and "near the ground" may yield similar behavior, but only the former indicates the presence of an asymmetrical spatial axis. Furthermore, the assignment of a specific orientation to an oblique line can only be achieved by the coordinated representation of both of these up/down and left/right asymmetries. In children, this shows up in the fact that children succeed in discriminating opposite oblique orientations (in the absence of positional cues) about nine years of age and about the same time, they develop an elementary conception of abstract dimensionalized Euclidean space, succeeding for the first time on such tasks as Piaget's water level task and his telephone pole task. For adults, the assignment of these two dimensions to the detected orientation would account for the long latencies to the oblique stimuli. It is the construction of that spatial representation which consumes time. Once it is constructed, the comparison processes are relatively simple. This interpretation is supported by the additional finding that the recognition times for obliques is a function of the position of the second oblique. The primary position effects are as follows: up < down < right < left, all of which are significantly easier than the four intervening positions. When the representation of the position corresponds to the representation of the orientation (e.g. "up to the right"), the perceptual matching of that oblique is facilitated. Oblique orientation is represented in terms of position!

This explanation is complex; it should be advanced only when simpler explanations are ruled out. The simplest explanation of difficulty with obliques is that of visual acuity, the fact that the resolving power of the eye is less for obliques than for horizontals and verticals. While lack of acuity would explain some effects, it would not explain the effects reported in this paper. For one thing, acuity would not explain the strong positional effects obtained in this experiment. Secondly, it would not account for the fact that obliques are processed quickly when the visual field is square (as in the third experiment). Moreover, we have recently tested two subjects on a simple reaction time task measuring response to lines of various orientations. These subjects observed the same displays presented in Experiment 4, but were provided only one response key. They were instructed to press the key whenever any line segment occurred on the screen. The range of mean reaction times for each of the four orientations was only 31 msec. Neither subject gave any indication that the oblique lines were more difficult to detect than the horizontal and vertical lines.

Having exhausted these alternative explanations, we are left with our more complex theory of the representation of orientation in space. Two other features of the data deserve comment. Firstly, it appears to be the case that these dimensional assignments are given sequentially; assignment of two dimensions takes longer than either horizontal *or* vertical assignments alone. Secondly, it appears to be the case that the left oblique ($\diagdown$) is more difficult to match than the right oblique ($\diagup$). If the dimensionalized representations are asymmetrical, one pole may be positive and the other negative which may give rise to such differences. Handedness may also provide a basis for the left-right asymmetry; Leonardo da Vinci, an eminent left-hander, is known to have shaded his work with a left oblique.

An important aspect of spatial development, then, is the mastery of an asymmetrical lexical system for representing space. That is not to imply that the non-notational or continuous spatial systems fail to develop with age as well. That some development occurs is shown by the simple fact that the norms for children's performance on spatial ability tests increase with age. Some more analytic studies of the nature of this development have been begun by Joanne Rovet, a student of mine. Employing spatial transformation tasks of the type studied by Shepard and Metzler, Rovet gave eight to twelve-year-old children drawings of three-dimensional figures rotated 30°, 60° or 90° and asked for their same-different judgments. The interesting finding was that while the younger children succeeded with the 30° tasks, they tended to find the 60° and 90° transformations both too difficult. In contrast, the older children tended to find both the 30° and 60° tasks soluable, but performed just as poorly as the younger children on the 90° tasks. It appears from such data that children's ability to make such transformations develop systematically with age.

Some studies are also underway which examine the extent to which instruction can influence the development of these spatial skills. Studies by Salomon (in preparation), Feldman and Snyder (in preparation) as well as that by Joanne Rovet, have tended to show that these skills are amenable to instruction but that the effects of instruction depend importantly upon the existing competencies of the learners.

In summary the study of the development of spatial perception, spatial concepts, spatial language and spatial skills is not only becoming an exciting area for research, but also promises to play a critical role in our understanding of human cognition.

# Chapter 4

# ON THE COMPONENTS OF SPATIAL REPRESENTATION

GEORGE E. FORMAN

## DIFFERENT CONCEPTIONS OF SPACE

FOR YET ANOTHER TIME, man has found himself underestimating the fundamental nature of space. First Newton demonstrated the limitations of Aristotle, then Einstein showed the limitations of Newton. The possibility of a third, comprehensive revision in cosmology has caused us to doubt the reliability of the observer. The study of the cosmos becomes as well a study of the thinking process. In the history of science, the thinker has taken principles as true in a narrow sense, and has implicitly accepted them as true in a larger context; Aristotle's physical medium the ether, Newton's straight lines in space. To understand space, we must first understand the thinker, how he is or is not being geocentric, conventional and arbitrary. If we can cultivate this self-awareness, the risk of taking a convenient fiction as an immutable fact is greatly reduced.

This self-awareness typically has been fostered by critical thinking about thinking, the role of the epistemologist. These critiques have usually been applied *post hoc* to the theories of science. An alternative method for assessing the validity of scientific theories is to compare the formation of that theory with the beginning acts of the infant. To study the development of spatial concepts in the child is to study the limitations placed upon the adult when that adult attempts to grasp the nature of the cosmos. Although the study of thinking processes has been the subject of empirical psychologists since Wundt, the study of children to understand the origins of science has been explicated first by Baldwin and more recently Piaget, a pursuit termed genetic epistemology.

111

The purpose of this chapter will be to establish the significance of research in spatial development by defining the relation between research and epistemology. The limitations of early theories of space will be related to similar conclusions made by modern children in their development of spatial concepts.

According to accepted tenets of genetic epistemology, concepceptions of space, time and causality are constructed through commerce with the environment. The child gradually learns that what he cannot touch, he cannot move; only gradually he learns that change of position cannot be instantly propagated. Presumably, the child builds a system of relations between position and movement in order to deal effectively with his terrestrial world. The question considered here is how the influence of this constructed system of terrestrial mechanics affects our assumptions about cosmological and microcosmological space, spaces which cannot be touched and which often cannot be seen directly.

On the one hand, it is not necessary to think that the children of ancient Greece had systems of practical, everyday spatial relations which were less perfect in any sense than the systems of children of Newton's day, nor that children in Newton's day were less practical than children in the twentieth century. On the other hand, the study of the development of this practical system can disclose the *ad hoc* quality of our first premises about space, and how these intuitions influence our representation and measurements of space. The scientist is forever trying to transcend this narrowness as he extends the context of his laws.

### Aristotle's Space

As was the case for others before him, Aristotle faced the riddle of planetary motion. What keeps the planets aloft? If they are suspended by a medium, how can they then move? What determines the shape of the orbits? Aristotle proposed answers to these questions which have their influence today.

According to Aristotle, the idea of space as a vacuum was impossible. Instead, the planets required the support of a space with substance, a highly viscous substance which would allow movement at the slow planetary speeds, similar to the speed which a weighted wire sinks through a paraffin block. The elements of fire, air, water, and earth all had a natural position toward which they moved. For example, the flames of fire moved away from earth toward its natural position somewhere between the earth and the boundary of space. Similarly, iron moved toward the earth because its natural position was the earth. In both cases, space was an instrumental agent in the propagation of this movement. Aristotle argued that an object hurled continues to move even after leaving contact with the hand because, as the object changes positions, the space being replaced behind the moving object exerts pressure in a forward direction, like the wind coming in the rear window of a car. In each of these cases, space was endowed both with a causality which we now recognize as anthropomorphic, and with a direction we now understand to be geocentric. Aristotle, in short, applied the terrestrial mechanics of solids and fluids to outer space (Toulmin and Goodfield, 1961).

For the purpose of relating science to psychology, consider the child before he learns about the constant direction of space, i.e. gravity. The child places a block on the pinnacle of a resting triangle. When his block meets with physical resistance from the triangle below, the child releases his grip in full anticipation that the new block will remain on the stack. The physical resistance is sufficient to cue his release. The block falls and the child is surprised: he tries again; same results, same surprise (Forman, 1971b). Although physical resistance usually has been sufficient to cue release, in this case the child has overgeneralized. Gradually he learns that space possesses direction which must be counteracted in order to stack objects.

The Greek adult extended the same reasoning to more complex problems. Aristotle's practical experience taught him that objects need support, and that this support must be used in a certain (geocentric) direction. He generalized this experience to the planets. Thus, both child and the Greek adult have used their knowledge of familiar events to assimilate new events. The child did not consider directions in space; only support. The Greek adult did not consider the relativity of direction (relative to mass); only a single direction plus support. Both were treating a special case as if it were a general rule. As we shall see, the progress of science has been a continual spiral of successive decentrations away from those perspectives most immediate to man and earth.

## Newton's Space

Copernicus developed, with great detail, a system which placed the sun at the center of planetary motion. This system was itself a remarkable example of decentering from the more immediate and personal perspective (see Kuhn, 1957). Moreover, Galileo helped to free the moving planets from the Aristotlean spheres. However, Galileo did not manage to explain the order of planetary motion, which is, in a sense, a question about the composition of space.

If the planets were not attached to spheres, were they supported by whirling vortices as Descartes believed? How did Newton account for planetary orbits? What kept the planets aloft? Newton changed the question to "Why don't the planets fly out into space," as a ball does when it is spun round on a string and let loose. Now, unlike the ball on the string, Newton decided that the motion of the planets themselves was already there, not continually propelled by some externally applied force. The planets' motion simply *is*, and the only force exists in an intrinsic sense, the *vis insita*, or innate force or power which resists change. By themselves, Newton held that the planets would move in a straight line forever. The deflection of that motion conjures intuitive notions of force such as pull and push. Gravity, the attraction between large masses, continually deflects the planets from the would-be straight line. Newton concluded that the planets are not held aloft; they are held aground. This conclusion can be taken as a clear case of Newton decentering from his schoolboy intuitions of falling objects.

Newton understood that the difficulty in explaining planetary motion was, in part, due to the receptivity of his audience. Too often, explanations are rejected or ignored because they do not provide a physical cause for the event to be explained. Newton made no attempt in his *Mathematical Principles* to explain how the attraction between large masses is mediated through space.

> Whether that cause be some central body (such as is the magnet in the centre of the magnetic force, or the earth in the centre of the gravitating force) or anything else, that does not yet appear. For I here design only to give a mathematical notion of those forces, without considering their physical causes and seats. (Newton, 1686, p. 7).

Force has its effects, but we may never know its physical nature. Force, then, was to Newton, a "hypothetical construct" (MacCorquodale and Meehl, 1948) like the word *pi* in geometry. Nonetheless, Newton did not spend his genius searching for its source. Instead, he simply assumed that "it exists," and then spent his talents describing what he took to be its effects, motion. In this stroke, Newton helped to emancipate science from the scholastic compulsion to deduce knowledge from self-evident givens (personal intuitions). This was most definitely an advance, but the idea of force as cause was still embedded in science, an idea which general relativity theory makes unnecessary.

The everyday intuitions of force take the form of an imagined push or pull, of some agent acting on a target object. Newton's concept of *vis insita* was difficult to assimilate. In Newton's system, even a resting object has force, i.e. its resistance to movement. It may now be asked, what has discussion of force and motion to do with concepts of space?

If for Newton inertia is the resistance to change, it is change in reference to what? That reference is space, absolute space. Not all objects at rest will have resistance. That is, because objects are not truly at rest; they are only at rest relatively. Imagine two objects which never change positions relative to each other in the void of space. If they are both actually moving in absolute space at the same speed and direction, a thread stretched from one to the other could not be made taut. The slightest tug on one end would cause the other to move in that direction *without resistance*. However, if these two objects were not only at rest with respect to each other, but also with respect to absolute space, the thread could be made taut. One object would resist the tug from the other. Newton believed that his laws of inertia lead to the inevitable conclusion that there is an absolute space, unchanging and immovable, through which objects pass.

Another consequence of Newton's theory was the removal of direction from space at large. Direction was made relevant to mass and not to some intrinsic property of space, as was implicit in Aristotle's theory. Objects in space could move in any direction whatsoever beyond the effects of other masses. There were no privileged positions intrinsic to space, which was empty in Newtonian thought.

To summarize, Newton extended our thought beyond the geocentric view that objects will stay aloft only if continually pushed up. His genius was to think that objects in space must be continually pulled down. This means that space has no direction intrinsic to itself. Force sometimes was active resistance, not just push or pull. The pull of gravity was propagated through space in straight lines.

Does this mean that the new concepts of seventeenth century space were a regression to the precausal notions of the child? Is the action at a distance similar to Piaget's child kicking her feet in expectation that mother will reappear? One obvious difference lies in the levels of awareness between the infant and the adult. The child makes these mistakes in causality because he fails to differentiate his wish-as-cause from contact-as-cause. Perhaps it took so long for a Newton to think of earthly gravitation effecting planets because culturally it was difficult to make the same differentiation. Despite the fact that most children learn that movement requires contact, Newton still related earthly gravity to the planets, a bold speculation in his time. He was fully aware of his dilemma of action at a distance, but decided other facts made this hypothesis inescapable, despite its violation of our intuitions. To be led completely by his keen observations was Newton's contribution to the further decentration from everyday intuitions of space.

Newton went about as far as he could go. As we shall see upon discussing relativity, even the hypothetical pull of gravity across space is rendered unnecessary. Newton belonged to what Poincaré (1952) terms the Thread School of thought, and this model is not consonant with the twentieth century concepts of field theory and relativity.

### Einstein's Space

The space represented in the General Theory of Relativity is perhaps the most advanced theory to date. It will be impossible to discover how it may be constrained by the limits of our spatial intuitions until we pass into a post-Einsteinian era. Nor can the fish discover water until a bold one leaves his aqueous environment and *returns*! However, we can use relativity theory to understand the limitations of previous theories about space.

Little of what will be said in this section can be understood on an intuitive level, no more than Newton's action at a distance can be grasped intuitively. What is to be understood is that action at a distance is an unnecessary model to represent space. By adding the dimension of time to the three dimensions of space, Einstein was able to deduce that gravitational "attraction" was a fictitious force, the result of thinking that straight lines were curved (Rogers, 1960, p. 499). For all practical purposes, Einstein reduced the mysterious action at a distance to a new type of geometry (Eddington, 1920).

Einstein, like Newton before him, was not preoccupied by first and efficient causes of universal motion through space. Like Newton, Einstein asked what keeps the planets in orbit, but he changed the question to read: "What creates the circular path of moon around the earth." When asked in this form, an appeal to attraction or force is not necessary for an answer.

Recall that Newton considered the natural, undisturbed motion of planets to be a tangent to the orbit they maintained, a straight path rather than the visible curve resulting from centripetal force. Rather than focus upon the nature of the forces, Einstein concentrated on the nature of the paths. He knew that all objects, regardless of their mass, assumed the same path. This meant that more "force," if such existed, would be dispensed through space more for one object than another. Sensing a contradiction, Einstein began to study the geometry used to measure the paths. In his attempts to find a geometry which accounted for all types of paths, he developed a geometry which carried a startling premise; namely, that the space-time manifold was curved in the vicinity of large masses.

To relate the bulge in space-time to gravity, follow this fantasy. Imagine a large mass, A, traveling in a straight line through space. The direction of travel is North from South. This mass is surrounded by a huge glass sphere etched with circles parallel to each other and perpendicular to the line of travel, like a giant Christmas tree ornament. There exists a second mass, B, in contact with the glass sphere at one of the etched circles. B's contact with the sphere is at some point below the largest circle which is the middle circle. Both mass A and B are traveling in the same direction. As A and B continue their motion, B will be continually displaced along the etched circle which is the point of contact with the sphere. The etched circle is the path of least resistance. Going over the bulge would be more difficult. This displacement is not the result of some force or attraction from mass A, but rather the result of the shape of space through which B is traveling.

Since B is continually displaced, it is actually tracing a spiral path through space-time, time being the North bound movement. Yet this path, when viewed from someone on mass A from inside the glass sphere, appears to be a circle, not a spiral. Remember that A and B are traveling together in the same time-slice. Some distant omnipresent observer who could see time would see A moving straight with B spiralling around it. To repeat Einstein's original question, "what creates the circular path of the moon around the earth," the answer is "the natural movement of the moon in a straight line through curved space-time."

It is acknowledged that this homey example of the mass-on-the-glass gives the appearance of substituting one type of force for another, the force of repelling for the force of attracting. The example should not be taken so literally that the bulge is conceived as some sort of physical medium which offers resistance. Such a conception would return us to the Newtonian concept of force. Instead, it should be understood that the deflection of mass B is a result of a change in the *field* through which it travels, rather than the result of straight line vectors as imagined by Newton. Further, it should be appreciated that the apparent circularity of orbits depends on the perspective of the observer. A more complete explanation of general relativity theory can be found in Sir Arthur Eddington's fine book *Space, Time, and Gravitation*.

What were Einstein's special contributions to our understanding of universal space? Taking advantage of advances in mathematics, particularly non-Euclidean geometry, Einstein was able to show that the shape of motion depends on the perspective of the viewer. This thinking clearly exemplifies decentering on Einstein's part. The shift from thinking in terms of *force* to terms of *course* is another example of objectifying the universe beyond intuitive notions. Thinking in the four dimensions of space-time rather than the more immediately perceptible three dimensions of space also represents a discovery of how previous theories made arbitrary presupposition, e.g. the independence of space and time.

Perhaps the most important contribution Einstein made was his method. To understand the natural phenomena of time and space, he turned first to mathematics. He asked what sort of equations were necessary to "predict" what is known about planetary movements and about the path of light through the universe. In the process of fitting these equations, he realized that space-time was not flat. With this realization, Einstein reversed the role of mathematics. He changed its role from that of summarizing empirical data to that of discovering empirical data; a change which prompted scientists to ask questions which would not have been considered before. The mysterious "force" of gravity disappeared with the more suitable form of geometry to study the great distances across space (Rogers, 1960).

The preceding, simplified review of three stages in scientific conceptions of space reflects changes in children's conceptions. At each stage, the conceptions of space departed more and more from practical spatial concepts learned as a child, but each stage was itself limited by other spatial intuitions. It will be useful for several reasons now to review what is known about the development of spatial concepts across age. First, one careful study of development may tell us why either the shifts in history were so long coming or what sorts of "unlearning" were required for a Newton or Einstein to emerge. Second, in the interest of teaching relativity theory to adults, it is important to know quite explicitly the origins of spatial concepts. The novice to relativity theory repeatedly and unconsciously translates the four-dimensions of space-time into the more familiar, more easily visualized three-dimensions of space. In short, we need to know exactly how spatial concepts develop.

## THE DEVELOPMENT OF SPATIAL CONCEPTS

### Changes in Position and State

The genetic epistemologist seeks to answer both the questions "What do we know?" and "How do we come by this knowledge?" Consider the *what* question first. Comments regarding *how* the what comes about will be delayed until later.

When the child learns that a third-dimension extends beyond his own body, he is able to make certain critical distinctions about his surroundings. His development can be described in terms of these distinctions.

An early critical distinction is between an apparent change in state and a real change in position. As an object recedes in the distance, its retinal image grows smaller. The child learns early in life to (or can already) apprehend that changes in size are only apparent, but that change in position is real. As he grows older and accumulates experience, the child remains unconfused by an apparent change of position by a real change in state. For example, a stationary circle may change its diameter when projected on a screen at varying distances. Again, Bower (1966) has shown that the six-week-old infant can distinguish between changes of position and apparent changes of state, i.e. size constancy, when motion parallax is present. The distinction between an apparent change of position and a real change in state is more difficult, as indicated by the fright children show when a two-dimensional circle shows rapid expansion. Evidently this apparent change in position is treated as quite real by the viewing infant (Bower, 1971).

### Real Changes in Existential Object

Knowledge of an external space is also involved in conserving the identity of a given object. An object changing positions is still, existentially, one and the same object in both positions. Similarly, the existential identity of the object does not change with a real change in its state (shape). Both distinctions must be learned.

In the early months of life, an object seems to have permanence even though it has disappeared from sight. The earliest manifestation of this inferred permanence is in the visual tracking of the object. When an object moves behind a screen, the infant not yet sixteen weeks, will look to the other side in anticipation of its emergence (Bower, Broughton, and Moore, 1971). The object continues its existence and its motion even though visual contact has been eliminated. Just what is conserved? The object *qua* object, as a distinct shape or perhaps just something that moves? Until the age of sixteen weeks, the child does not show surprise reactions to a toy elephant emerging when it was a toy clown that disappeared. It is inferred that the child was aware of the change of position, but not aware of the change of object.

Now consider a slight modification of Bower's research. This modification deals less with object permanence and more with the coordination of changes in position, state and object. Substitute a translucent screen for the one Bower used, so that in this case, the object will never be really out of sight. Again, the infant is presented a toy clown which moves from left to right at a steady, slow speed. In the course of this movement, it passes behind the translucent screen which clouds its shape but not its continued shadowy existence. While the toy clown is passing behind the translucent screen, rotate it slowly so that now a toy elephant faces the screen. Thus, although the child cannot discern any change in the amorphous image on the screen, when the object emerges it will be an elephant.

If the infant shows surprise when the elephant emerges, we can conclude that the child is aware that a change of position, continually viewed, usually does not entail a change of the object. If he shows no surprise, we can conclude that the change in object was masked by the continuity of position change. Presumably, it is reasonable to expect the child to discriminate a clown from an elephant when both are presented simultaneously (see Fantz, 1961).

At first glance this example might be interpreted as requiring an accurate coordination of change in position with change in state. Compare the earlier example involving a circle. A circle passing in full view from left to right would change its state toward the end of the path, and would look elliptical. The child's lack of surprise in the second example would only be evidence for shape constancy. The emerging object in the second example, however, was totally different; an elephant rather than a clown. Changes in state of this magnitude usually signal a change in object.

Of course, there are changes in state of this magnitude which are not confused with changes in the material substance, regardless of changes in the categorical identity. If the child watches the experimenter take a ball of clay and reshape that clay into a doughnut, he may understand that this change in state does not mean that the clay itself has been exchanged. The ball is not still somewhere else. However, if the experimenter shows the child the ball of clay, remolds it under the table out of the child's sight, and then shows the doughnut, the child has no way of knowing if the doughnut is the same clay as that in the ball. The ball could still be under the table. These distinctions of within-object versus between-object variations are basic to the conservation tasks (see Elkind, 1969).

Consider next, a situation where the object which emerges from behind a screen is in no way different in state from the object that disappeared, but the child knows that the emerging object is not existentially identical with the first. In such a situation, the change of object is cued by a discontinuous change of position. For example, imagine a toy animal moving behind the left side of screen A. Visualize an identical toy animal emerging from the right side of screen B which is several inches separated from screen A, a few seconds later. The timing of disappearance and emergence would constitute a single continuous movement. Does the child look behind screen A for an object, or does he think that the object emerging from B is existentially the same as the object disappearing behind A? If he does look behind A, he has used discontinuity of movement, or the absence of visual continuity in spite of temporal continuity, to make the inference regarding the existence of the toy animal. In other words, the child has learned that an apparent change in the position of one object can be distinguished from a real change of objects.

To summarize, some changes in state indicate a change in objects, if the change across position is discontinuous (objects exchanged). Some changes in position indicate a change of object, even if the state remains the same, as in the above example, when the change of position is discontinuous (see Moore, 1973).

### Apparent Changes in Existential Object

In both of the above examples, the change in the object was real and the child was deluded by an assumed change of position or assumed constancy in position. In the example with two separated screens, the change of position from A to B was assumed. In the example of the translucent screen, the absence of a change in position (the concealed rotation of the clown) was assumed. There are cases, however, where the child treats a real change in position as if it were a change in the object. Presumably, this confusion must constitute a rather primitive level of development.

If a child sees an object at position A and later at position B, he has no way of knowing whether he has seen the same object twice or two physically identical objects once each. If he sees an object at A and at the same time at B, he most likely concludes that these are two existentially different objects. The same object is not usually in two places at the same time. Moreover, it takes time for objects to pass from A to B and it takes time for one object to change positions. The child, in short, does not usually confuse two objects at one time with one object at two times. Or does he?

When an infant recognizes his mother's face, can he distinguish if from the face of his mother's twin sister? Such a distinction functionally may not be critical; he would probably smile at the sister. But epistemologically the difference *is* important. If he knew that there was only one mother's face, he should show some surprise at seeing two faces of Mom at two places at the same time. Bower (1971) found that few children show surprise at seeing multiple images of the mother occurring at the same time but in different places. From Bower's data, therefore, we can infer that the child cannot distinguish change of position from change of object. The infant who does not show surprise has not yet discovered the relativity between object and time.

At perhaps a more complex level, this failure to distinguish time, space and object underlies the problem encountered by Jacqueline in Piaget's poignant anecdote about the slugs.

> J. (2:7) "There it is!" (the slug) on seeing one, and when we saw another ten yards further on, she said: "There's the slug again." I answered: "But isn't it another one?" J. then went back to see the first one. "Is it the same one?"—"Yes"—"Another slug?"—"Yes."—"Another or the same?"— . . . The question obviously had no meaning for J. (Piaget, 1951, p. 225).

Jean Piaget knew enough about the proverbial slowness of the snail to conclude, without looking back, that the second sighting was indeed a different, but similar snail. More important is the fact that he also knew to include the rate of change of position between points in his judgment of one twice vs. two once. Jacqueline, for several possible reasons, could not distinguish between that which was physically similar and that which was existentially different, at least verbally. The fact that she went back to check the first slug, however, indicates her nonverbal awareness that two slugs existed. She was only seeing if their physical similarity was sufficient to use the word same, as in the phrase "exactly the same." It was in terms of her mental representations that she could not grasp the contrast between one-and-the-same versus two-identical objects separated in space. According to Piaget, to have grasped these differences, she would have had to use internalized movement; but that is getting into the question of *how*.

Sometimes the child must cope with changes in state which do not signal an existential change in the object. Although mother-in-a-new-hat is the same person as mother-without-a-hat, baby frets to the hatted object and coos to the hatless object. If he coos to both, is he indicating a knowledge of existential identity between the two cases? Such a knowledge is unlikely; rather the infant may be generalizing the stimuli between two configurations which are identical in most respects (the common face).

To make a case for conservation of existential identity, a change in state need be complete. Consider a smiling father standing at the window looking out while his small son is looking in. Father lowers the shade and stretches a silk stocking over his head. When he raises the shade, son begins to cry and to shriek. Responding to the intensity of his son's reaction, the stretched-face monster opens the window to comfort the boy, whereupon the son hits new octaves in shrieking. Obviously, to the small boy this is not father-in-a-mask but an existentially different being.

Now perform the same exercise without the shade. Smiling father holds the stocking in his hand and then gradually pulls it over his head. The child grimaces, he may even cry; but his response does not continue beyond surprise and uneasiness. (see Charlesworth, 1969). Does this second exercise provide evidence for the conservation of existential identity, or is it another case of response transfer to a gradually changing stimulus; something pigeons can do without error (Terrance, 1963)?

The difference between the stocking task presented the child and the pigeon in Terrance's work seems sufficient to conclude that more occurs than just stimulus generalization. In studies where a fading procedure is used in operant responding, each subtle change is usually followed by an opportunity to confirm its association with reward. Put another way, the pigeon pecks and is reinforced. In the case of the child, each change in the stimulus, as the stocking lowers, is not followed by an opportunity to confirm its association with the father. Indeed, the child would most likely react to this completely new stimulus in the same manner (e.g. says "daddy," smiles at it, etc.). The analogy for the pigeon would be for the animal to peck at a square after only watching, but not responding, to its gradual change from a circle, the original stimulus. Unlike the pigeon, the child is not generalizing between successive stimuli. He is dissociating change in state from existential change in object.

The stocking task for the child is even more complex than noting continuity of change. If smiling father held no stocking, and if his nose and ears gradually began to flatten, even mother would probably shriek. The child may roar and shriek when father covers his face behind the shade, or he may only cry and grimace when the father puts on the stocking, depending on the child's ability to distinguish extrinsic (and reversible) changes from intrinsic (and probably irreversible) changes. If the child only grimaces, he has not probably distinguished the drawn stocking from the drawn face.

In summary, one object changing is distinguished from two different objects by following a trajectory of change through time and space. An abrupt change in state is commonly judged to be a change in objects. A gradual and continuous change does not usually alter the existential identity of the object.

In the course of this discussion, an important distinction must be underscored between confusing one change for another versus not being aware of one change. In the case of the infant seeing multiple images of his mother, it is equally possible that the infant does not know that simultaneous images occur in different places. His attention may be so centered that while viewing one image, he is not aware of the other. In other words, the images appear to come at him successively in time, as he shifts his gaze. Hence, he is not confusing change of position with change of object. He is simply unaware of any difference in the successive and simultaneous positioning. The images appear to him singularly, but neither simultaneously nor successively because he does not possess the perceptual mechanisms to make that distinction (Piaget, 1969, p. 110). In order to make such a distinction, Poincaré (1946) tells us that the child must identify and coordinate changes in the position of his own receptors with changes in the position of external objects.

What, then, is the most basic distinction the child must learn? Perhaps the most elementary *what* is the difference between objects as independent entities and oneself. Once such a distinction is learned, the child has discovered something about space; namely, that objects which do not invariably move when self moves are not part of self. Later the object itself is conserved across variations in its physical existence. The object which disappears behind the screen is still in existence. Object permanence does not demand conservation of the unique identity of a single object, because the child only knows that some object is behind the screen. As he begins to coordinate changes of position and state within the limitations of time, the unique object can be conserved even in the face of physical similarity between objects.

## ORIGINS OF SPATIAL KNOWLEDGE

### *Mind, Senses, or Activity*

Is knowledge of space derived from the senses; is it a given intuition of the mind; is it the result of internalized action? Kant (1781) insists that space is not a concept abstracted from experience. Our awareness that external objects are indeed external, that they rest "in space" and that they are bounded is *a priori*, is temporally prior to any sensory registration of the object. The child could not sense the object qua object unless he could first know that it was separate and in space.

> Space is not an empirical conception which can be abstracted from external experiences. For in order that certain sensations may be related to something external to me (that is, to something in a part of space different from that in which I am), and similarly, in order that I may represent them as outside of and next to each other, and consequently as not merely different from each other, but also as in different places, the representation of space must already be there as a basis. Consequently, the representation of space cannot be borrowed from external appearances through experience; but, on the contrary, that external experience is itself first of all possible solely through the said representation. (cited in Garnett, 1939, p. 166).

Kant contends that the distinction between state and position is given to the human mind. Piaget, in *The Child's Construction of Reality*, traces the development of the object concept as it results from activity. The child learns to distinguish changes of state from changes of position by comparing changes which can be reversed by self-generated movement (changes of position) with changes which can not be thereby reversed (changes of state). The ball hidden behind a screen is not absorbed by the screen (change of state), but is only *behind* the screen (change of position). In this instance, Piaget disagrees with the *a priorism* of Kant.

Berkeley, in his treatise, *Concerning the Principles of Human Knowledge* (1710), takes a view contrary to Kant. According to Berkeley, the general concept of space is gradually formed by pooling many experiences with the extension of physical objects.

> The mind having observed that in the particular extensions perceived by sense there is something common and alike in all, and some other things peculiar, . . . it considers apart or singles out by itself that which is common, making therefore a most abstract idea of extension, which is an idea entirely precinded from all these. (p. 404).

The extension of conceptual space, vacant space, was for Berkeley an extrapolation of experience with palpable objects. By contrast, Kant maintained that the very extension of physical objects which Berkeley gives full blown to the senses is not possible without the intuition of space. Extension is a limitation on the infinitude of space, and presupposes knowledge of that infinitude. Space, to Kant, is metaphysically given, intuitive, nonempirical and both logically necessary and temporally prior to sensing the object.

Piaget accepts Berkeley's empirism no more than Kant's *a priorism*. Piaget distinguishes between two types of abstraction, only one of which is similar to that referred to by Berkeley. This one type of abstraction is called *extracting*.

> "This abstraction reduces to dissociating one newly discovered property from the others and disregarding the latter. Thus it is physical experience that allows the child to discover weight while disregarding an object's color, etc." (Piaget, 1970, p. 721).

A second type of abstraction is called logicomathematical or reflecting abstraction.

> "The knowledge derived from it is not based on the physical properties of these objects but on properties of the actions that are exerted on them, . . . properties introduced by actions which did not belong to the object before these actions."

The knowledge of space is largely of this second type of knowledge, neither a knowledge about objects, as Berkeley would have it, nor a knowledge which comes fully developed, as Kant would have it. Piaget is Kantian to the extent that he posits knowledge is not to be found in the world of objects. He is Berkelean to the extent that he speaks of gradual development rather than *a priori* development.

This controversy between Kant and Berkeley has more than historical significance. In particular, the importance of activity, as a form of interiorized knowledge, has been contested by Olson (1970). Activity, or the performatory act in Olson's scheme, is regarded as important because it brings the perceiving organ into contact with alternatives which are important to the guidance of that performance. What is later retrieved from memory is not an action schema, but rather the correct choices made conspicuous by the child's confrontation with decisions in the process of activity. Activity is only one of several such means; instruction is another (Olson, 1970, p. 197).

Piaget and Inhelder (1967) hold a position similar to Olson's. They contend, for example, that

> "it might be suggested that the idea of space ceases to depend upon action and only involves recalling to mind the results of actual or potential action through signs and symbols rather than evoking the action itself as a memory image." (p. 452).

They argue, in the next several pages of their book, that spatial concepts are interiorized actions per se. Specifically their reasons hinge upon a premise, one with which Olson evidently does not agree, that spatial relations cannot be detected; they must be constructed. Piaget and Inhelder contend that spatial relations are not something which can be *contacted* by activity, but rather are *constructed* from activity.

The difference between these two epistemologies can best be drawn by using a single exemplary task for both. Suppose a child is shown a knot, and then asked to tie a similar knot with another piece of string. After he successfully ties the knot, the strings are removed and he is asked to draw a picture of the knot which he tied. Olson would say that the act of tying the knot directed the child's attention to a set of alternatives, only some of which were correct. The child notes the effects of his actions, what goes where, and remembers these effects when asked to draw the knot.

Piaget and Inhelder would possibly agree with Olson in the

specifics of the task. Piaget, a contemporary of Montessori, has never denied that hand actions bring into focus specific content useful to the solution of a specific task. But Piaget is asking a broader question, "How is the child able to represent the spatial order of any task?" By contrast, Olson is asking, "How does the child remember that loop A goes over, and not under, loop B?" The difference between these two questions is in their level of generality. Piaget is asking: how is *order* processed; Olson is asking: how is a *particular* order remembered. For Piaget, the important question is not how the child eliminates incorrect alternatives, but how the child constructs information which exists nowhere in the world of palpable objects.

The order of the parts of the knot is not something on which sight can make contact. Spatial order, certainly its graphic representation, is an active arrangement of static images across time. Seeing loop A and seeing loop B is not sufficient for placing them in their correct temporal relation. The child's ability to reproduce the order of any series comes from an interiorized action schema of placing, displacing, and reversing objects. These interiorized schema are not retrieved in the usual sense of a content-filled memory. To refer to the storage of specific action information, like the first loop A, then loop B, Piaget chose the term *internalization. Interiorized* actions are content-free which explains their generality (see Furth, 1968).

The notion of content-free operations makes Piaget's epistemology controversial, as in Kantian epistemology. Piaget differs from Kant in that the concept of content-free mental operations that emerges is dependent upon the child's earlier sensori-motor activity.

It should be said here, parenthetically, that Piaget's emphasis on interiorized activity resembles space-time relativity at least in the sense that our knowledge of space can never exist without motion. Motion is space in time; the one depends upon the other. Theories which hold that spatial relations are not constructed, but rather are perceived, also hold, by logical extension of their reasoning, that space and time in the child's knowledge can be independently formed. The interdependence of space and time concepts in the child's development will be discussed further.

### The Receptors

The work of Hubel and Wiesel (1962) can be interpreted by some as evidence that spatial relations are detected as static features. Hubel and Wiesel found that certain single brain cells respond to specific patterns at the eye. Some cells responded to movement in one direction, some to movement in another direction; some to a resting line in one orientation, others to a resting line in a different orientation.

Does this finding mean that detection of orientation in space can exist without actions on objects? First of all, the cells studied were in the occipital cortex of adult cats. These cells could have developed their sensitivity to orientation as a result of earlier experience. Secondly, the detection of orientation of a line is not the same thing as detection of position in space. Firing retinal cell one and four versus retinal cell two and three distinguishes two patterns but places neither in space. The frame of reference is the retinal matrix itself, and not an external spatial reference. Thirdly, all of these distinctions can be made without the added distinction of depth. Even Piaget suggests that the topological features of proximity, continuity, separateness and enclosure are quite possibly perceptual givens (Piaget and Inhelder, 1967).

To relate the findings of Hubel and Wiesel to Piaget's theory of spatial development, consider the retina as if it were a two-by-two matrix of receptors with receptors numbered left to right, beginning upper left. This matrix projects to the occipital cortex in such a manner that the position of the receptors is coded.[1] The order of firing is also coded. If receptors one and four (diagonal corners) fire simultaneously, a particular cortical cell spikes. This cortical cell is a diagonal detector. The cortex can also distinguish retinal receptor one firing before two versus two firing before one, i.e. direction of movement.

The question is, what are the limitations of this system? First, this system is not sufficient to distinguish movement of head from movement of an object in space. Second, it is not sufficient to distinguish a horizontal line on the retina from a horizontal line as referenced

1. This example does not suggest that the retinal-cortical projection is a point-to-point isomorphism. Nor does it limit the number of such matrices that can act as a unit in various retinal position (see Pribram, 1971, p. 125).

externally. Third, this system is not sufficient to distinguish near from far. What it can do is make elementary two-dimensional distinctions such as the topological distinctions of proximity, separateness, order, continuity and enclosure. The information from the retina alone is sufficient to distinguish order in the sense of object A before object B, but is insufficient to separate order due to accidental movement of the receptors versus real movement of the objects. (It is in this second sense that order is constructed and does not inhere in objects.)

What about evidence for early depth perception? Thomas Bower (1966) demonstrated that the six-week-old infant could discriminate between changes in size and changes in depth (size constancy). An apparent change in the state of an object was not confused with a real change in position. Does this mean that activity on the object is not important? Such a conclusion might follow if head movements and the resultant parallax could be ruled out. Since Bower's infants could discriminate depth only when objects moved or when depth cues were available for the parallax effect, it is unlikely that depth can be directly seen (Walk and Dodge, 1962). Motion is important.

The basic distinction between self-regulated displacements and external displacements (Poincaré, 1946) requires the object to be in space, separate from the ego. The coodination of rates of displacements, either self-regulated or externally regulated, place several objects in relative depth via the parallax so created. Object permanence is something else again.

Evidence for early depth perception is not tantamount to evidence for object permanence. In object permanence, space not only has depth, but also has discontinuous planes in the continuum of depth. The object interposed between ego and target has a limited third dimension, such that the target object is not absorbed but is behind and discontinuous with the interposing object. Consonant with the greater complexity of object permanence, Piaget reasons that more complex placements and displacements must be coordinated to effectuate its development.

The fact that Bower's infants were still neonates might suggest to some that depth perception is innate. Piaget, a biologist by training, would agree that the infant is born with many biological structures which facilitate the organization of experience (Piaget, 1971). Yet Piaget is neither wholly nativist nor empiricist. He insists that activity is necessary for cognitive development. The biological structures assist in organizing that activity, which is the "aliment to development" (Piaget, 1963). The empiricists are committed to the view that if experience is not organized, neither will be the mind. Piaget argues that experience can be jumbled; the biological structures assist by constructing invariances.

If the visual system of the infant is innately prepared to register the kind of information given by motion parallax, what sort of mechanism could handle this information? Pribram (1971) suggests an interesting model. He likens the visual system to a holograph, a type of photography which uses two beams of coherent light, one light reflected from the subject, the other a reference beam. The two rays of light set up interference patterns which are recorded upon a photographic plate. When coherent light passes through any part of the developed film, the interference patterns are organized into a virtual image in three dimensions. Pribram offers evidence that the synaptic junctures act on basis of interference patterns of visual input. What better mechanism exists for processing motion parallax than something analogous to holography?

## SPACE AS RELATED TO OTHER KNOWLEDGE

Research on spatial development is important because the child uses his knowledge of space as a means of understanding many other systems of knowledge. Quite often, the spatial relations which help the child visualize some ostensibly nonspatial knowledge goes underground, becomes implicit, but nonetheless exerts its influence. When these implicit metaphors are rediscovered and explicated by the researcher, more is learned about the system and about how the child learns the system. For example, although it was known that children naturally use correspondence in dealing with numbers, no attempt was made to explicate correspondence *per se* before Cantor (Bogartz, 1973). Beyond what is learned about the child, the limitations of the system are exposed by careful inspection of the "givens," which are often spatial intuitions. An example, already offered, is the judging of lines to be straight and the assuming that parallels do not meet. Both are givens in Euclidean geometry.

Euclidean geometry has now lost its absolute status and has been placed among other geometries, equally consistent within their own premises. The evolution of relativity theory is an example *par excellent* of making explicit spatial intuitions which have gone underground.

## Causality

Precausal concepts are evident when the child makes a movement and then expects correlated movement from an object out of reach or contact. The expectations arise more from a lack of differentiation between self and objects than from any magico-phenomonalistic ideas about action between self and object (Piaget, 1969). After making this distinction between object and self, the child's ideas of force are closely related to personal will. Something moves "because it wants to." The child assimilates all spontaneous motion to his knowledge about living beings. For example, the book falls off the shelf "because it is tired."

When the child begins to use contact as a source of force, it is often poorly localized. The horse draws the cart, but the road makes the horse move, or the people in the row boat make the river flow downhill. Force is endowed with aim, just as each movement the child himself makes has some purpose. The clouds move to get away from the sun. (How different was Aristotle's theory that the fire rises because the sky is its natural place?) As the child grows older, this animism is minimized, contact is properly located, and a gross acceptance of inertia occurs. The acceptance of inertia is not complete, because the child (and Newton's contemporary adults) assimilate gravitational force as being something transmitted by an invisible medium, a variation on the theme of contact between acting agent and moving object.

This last point shows how difficult it is for man to accept as explanation something which he can not assimilate into his everyday spatial intuitions. For example, if the heavenly bodies are inanimate, then their motion can not easily be understood without referring to some sort of transmitted force. To think otherwise, men reasoned, would be an indulgence in childish precausality.

As teleology was eliminated from Aristotle's theory of the planets, and as force vectors were eliminated from Newton's theory, what other facts will be exposed as only apparent? Heisenberg has already set limits to our knowledge of speed and mass in his position, and Eddington has set limits of speed and position in his principle of uncertainty. Eddington has likewise set limits to our knowledge of causation in his concept of the Absolute Elsewhere (Eddington, 1959). The Absolute Elsewhere is that never-never land where world points in the space-time manifold can never meet. Hence, they neither precede nor follow each other, but only exist. Is the idea that one object can be in only one place at a time an immutable fact? If science advances to the point where inertial mass can be exceeded, this bedrock fact will become another whispy fiction.

Michotte (1963) undertook a comprehensive program of research with children to ascertain which types of positional change would be seen as cause and effect relations. The child watched two spots move horizontally across a projection screen. When A bumped into B while B was at rest, B would continue while A remained at the point of contact. The child usually said that B's movement was caused by A. But if A overtook a more slowly moving B, and if, upon contact, B accelerated away from A quickly, the child would attribute part of B's velocity to the B itself, as if B had been frightened by A. To make judgments about causation and source of causation, the child not only used change of position but also contact and rate of change.

Interestingly enough, Michotte discovered that the child would tolerate a large amount of separation between the spots at their point of "contact." This still gave the illusion of causation from A to B. The faster the speed of A, the larger the gap had to be before the illusion disappeared. The usual justification for this separation was to invent some invisible jell or glass wall.

The direction of movements and the timing of stopping A and starting B were primary in causing the illusion of efficient force. If A moves to B, and stops there, and then 150 milliseconds later B moves away from A, the illusion does not occur. When the motion is continuous, the child perceives that A's force is transferred to B, which had no force of its own. When the motions are discontinuous, the child concludes that A moves because of its intrinsic force, and B moves because of its intrinsic force which is different from that of A's. The illusion may be due solely to temporal continuity rather than spatial continuity. The importance of spatial continuity is seen when A approached B in a line slightly above B, made contact with B at its northernmost point, and B left in a continuous motion at the instant of contact. The children reported that B's movement was intrinsic to B and was not imparted to it by A. Thus both spatial and temporal continuity are necessary to create the illusion of causality.

Here again the role of continuity plays an important role in whether the child perceives one and the same or two different somethings. It is *force* in the current example. It was the existential identity of the object in the earlier example. Certainly the continuity-discontinuity continuum represents an intriguing dimension of cognitive development.

### Time

The hands on the clock indicate the time of day by their position. If position is a spatial property, then time can be reduced to space. Unfortunately life is not that simple. Two objects may simultaneously depart from the same point but arrive at the same distant point in different times (traveling at different velocities). Does space then reduce to time? Is time motion through space or is space a still of time? Can differences in velocity be directly perceived?

According to Bergson (1912), when the viewer follows the movement of the hands on the clock, he is counting simultaneities. The sweeping second hand is now at position one, now at two, etc. Bergson is careful to explain that this sort of perceived simultaneity is not temporal, but rather is spatial: two events at the same position. These simultaneities are singular, mutually exclusive positions; and this is all they are without the mind's contribution of duration. Yet, in the absence of the discrete divisions on the clock, there would never be more than an experience of pure duration, thoughts which endure but which have no order, no homogeneous flow in one direction. Order implies sequence; sequence implies elements; elements imply the division of space into discrete parts. But the division of space is not itself a succession, only a division. In "pure" space, there are mutually exclusive positions but no succession. "Pure" duration is less than order; pure space is less than order. Order is the result of the mind combining its knowledge of pure space (division) with its intrinsic property of duration, which is not a derivative of spatial knowledge, but is given. Duration is the very essence of existence. To exist means to endure, to change. Existence is time (duration) itself (Bergson, 1911).

Piaget accepts Bergson's thesis that time, as an object of consciousness, is an act of superimposing space upon duration. But Piaget also emphasizes objective relations (cause and effect) and personal actions, e.g. directed movements (Piaget, 1969a). There seems to be no basic disagreement between Piaget and Bergson. Bergson begins his analysis with a definition of the living system; Piaget begins later, with an analysis of how this living system orders events in time, first by using space, then by dissociating time from space.

Piaget (1969a) writes that time to the infant is not a conceptualized, homogeneous flow within which all events can be ordered. Temporal relations to the infant are certain practical recurrences and delays, like bottle before milk, and when will relief come. The elementary notions of succession and duration are bound to actions in space, isolated from each other, not placed in unidirectional change. Succession is so inextricably tied to position that the infant will expect an object to reappear at its usual location regardless of the velocity which would be required for the return of that object.

According to Piaget, the child eventually dissociates time from space. It takes the child awhile before this dissociation is complete. At first, he confuses space and time. Temporal succession is confused with the spatial position at journey's end. Temporal duration is confused with the distance of the journey. A faster object may be judged slow if it does not spatially overtake the slower object.

Piaget states that the child has not completely grasped time as a system independent of space until the child can judge the equality between successive durations at different velocities. Simultaneous durations can be compared by reliance upon spatial factors alone. If X and Y travel parallel paths leaving at the same instant, the duration of X relative to Y can be judged by coordinating simultaneities. If X is still changing position while Y has stopped, the duration of X is longer. Comparing durations which begin simultaneously requires no more than the qualitative logic of classes.

The comparison of successive durations, according to Piaget

(Piaget, 1969a), requires the achievement of a quantitative logic of metrics. At some point, the child learns to use a standard velocity, one which he knows both to be constant from day to day, and one which he can recall at will. The psychological velocity of rapidity or effort has to be corrected by some neutral constant, nonpsychological, portable velocity.

At first, the child cannot judge the uniformity of movement from one minute to the next. If his work rate increases, he assumes the sand drains faster through the hour-glass. Later, he learns that the sand falls through the glass at the same rate regardless of his own work rate. The child has at this latter point separated psychological time from physical, but more than this is necessary to equate two successive durations, as Piaget explains.

Once the idea of uniform motion has been grasped, the child readily proceeds to the equalization of two successive durations corresponding to equal distances traversed successively by one and the same uniformly moving object. The child knows that since X moves with an unchanging velocity across space, if path AB is the same length as BC, then the duration AB is equal to the duration BC. This equating of successive intervals is defined by Piaget as isochronism, of which continuous intervals of equal velocity is a special case. Judging the equality of durations which are both discontinuous and of different velocities requires both the separation of duration from velocity and the quantitative operation of unit iteration.

To test for more discontinuous judgments, Piaget asked a child to perform some rhythmical work, transfering objects to the beat of a metronome. The child continued until the sand from a nearby hour-glass had completely drained. Then he was shown a stopwatch which registered from zero to thirty while again the sand completely drained (synchronous durations between clock and sand). The child easily understood that the duration of his work was equal to the sand, and that the duration of the clock was equal to the sand. These each were synchronous pairs and could be judged directly. But then the child was asked to compare the two discontinuous durations of unequal velocity: his work compared to the duration of the clock. When asked if he would get as much work done in the duration of the clock as he had by the duration of the sand,

the child responded, "I will get less work done by the clock because the clock moves faster." The clock does move faster, but
the durations are equal between clock and sandglass.

Once again the child is confused by velocity; although when
presented with synchronous durations, he has learned how not to
be confused by the velocity of his own work. He can equate single
synchronisms, continuous isochronisms, but not discontinuous isochronisms. It is likely that the child reverts to some form of spatial
imagery to handle the discontinuous isochronism.

The equal duration of stopwatch and sand are perceived as requiring equal spatial intervals. The child, however, perceives that
the clock moves faster than the sand. He concludes that the fast
clock speeding across the same imaginary distance as the slow sandglass will leave him less time to work. It is by imagining an equal
distance for different velocities that duration is made to vary with
velocity. The spatial factors conquered in synchronous intervals
reappear to confuse him in discontinuous, isochronous intervals.

Piaget claims that the only way the child can separate apparent
changes in duration from real changes in velocity across discontinuous comparisons is to use a quantitative logic, the operation of
unit iteration. By use of the transitive operation, he eventually can
conclude that durations each equal to a common duration are equal
to each other. He reiterates the common duration from one interval to the other, and he makes the generalization that if $A = B$ and
$C = B$, then $A = C$.

Piaget admits to an intriguing vicious circle contained in his explanation of the development of quantitative time. While the quantitative measurement of time rests on uniform velocity, independent
of effort, uniform velocity rests on the fact that two equal distances
are covered in two equal durations. Hence, how is it possible to
establish that a given motion is uniform if we lack the very unit of
time being developed (p. 272)? In other words, quantitative time defined as $A = B$, $C = B$, therefore $A = C$, presupposes that the child
has already equated B when compared to A, and B when compared
to C. How does he know that B equals B at two different times?

Piaget answers that this problem illustrates the operational organization of thought, a sort of boot-strapping emergence. At the same
time the child discovers the conservation of uniform motion, he dis-

covers how to measure durations by using identical operations (Piaget, 1969a, p. 272). By conservation of uniform motion, Piaget evidently means the judgment between two discontinuous, but equal velocities.

Whitehead maintains that the uniformity of continuous motion is directly perceived (Grunbaum, 1963, p. 51). A point moving uniformly can be distinguished from a decelerating or accelerating motion. If this is so, then the equality of durations for a single uniform motion through equal, contiguous segments does not require quantitative operations. The equality of durations in the continuous case is almost as palpable as the congruence of two equal line segments simultaneously compared.

The intriguing question is how the child generalizes what he knows about continuous segments to what he is asked about discontinuous segments. How does he know that a change in the occasion for the second measurement has not also been followed by a change in his standard velocity or his standard distance? Piaget acknowledges that this same question has been asked by modern physicists, but he does not venture an answer.

The only answer which this author can venture is that the child does not know, he presumes. He does not know, nor can he check, that his clock runs at the same speed from day to day. He assumes that it does, and this assumption is the foundation for equating successive durations of unequal velocities. This assumption is an extension of what he perceives to be uniform motion when it is continuous. He makes this generalization because, after all, it is still the same clock existentially. Furthermore, both teacher and parent have told him that it is the same clock. The generalization to discontinuous velocities might be a type of rote knowledge that Piaget calls social, rather than logico-mathematical.

For a brief moment, reflect back to the discussion about the development of the object and the development of causality. In both cases, the importance of continuity being extended to discontinuity was emphasized. The child distinguishes change in state from change in existential object only when he can see the transformation through time-space continuity. Later he extends this to discontinuous changes of state when position has remained constant, and still later when some psychological dimension remains constant. In the case of causality, continuity of motion was critical to the impression of causation between moving objects. This continuity has to be in both time and space. Too long a pause at contact destroyed the illusion. Contact from above rather than at the side destroyed the illusion. The transfer to discontinuous situations of cause and effect was seen when the spots traveled fast but did not touch before A launched B. The assumption that discontinuity was an extension of continuity was indicated by the child's use of some invisible gell to justify the "action at a distance."

In the case of time, continuity again is extended to discontinuous situations. The isochronism of successive intervals within the uniform motion of a single object is transferred to isochronisms of discontinuous movements of that same object. How is this accomplished? It is accomplished in the same manner as described under the formation of the object, and under the concepts of causality. Change of positions, changes of objects and changes of state are co-ordinated. The sweep of the second hand from numeral one to two, then from two to three is directly perceived as possessing no change in state, but only a change in position; as having no change in object, but only a change in position; as having no change in motion (rate), but only change in position. The sweep of the second hand from numeral one to two, then eleven to twelve (discontinuity) is more difficult. To accomplish this, the child must reason that because there was no change in object (same clock), because there was no change in state (same distances between one and two as between eleven and twelve); there was only a change in position. If the object remains the same and if the distances are the same, the child concludes that the motions must be the same. Thus, the uniformity of motion is mediated by an awareness that the object is existentially the same as that seen when motions were spatially continuous (between numeral one to two, then two to three). If some discontinuous velocities, embodied in a single object, are felt to be equivalent, then the child used this standard to register discontinuous durations, each with different velocities.

The point of this discussion is that man must make a leap of faith to the discontinuous. Such a leap may be the point where man is most likely to make his most profound mistakes. Relativity theory has already shown us one case where this faith in the isomorphism between contiguous and discontiguous events is not warranted.

What does relativity theory have to say about the continuity between time and space? Does it imply that the child was correct all along in thinking that duration depends on velocity? No, the child's mistake results from an imposition of space on time. Relativity theory describes the interaction between space and time. The child imposes a unit distance on unequal velocities, and concludes that the successive durations are necessarily unequal. In special relativity theory, all the coordinations of Piaget's quantitative, operational time are preserved. Time is still measured by the colligation of a standard, but it is understood that the standard unit will be different for the observers moving at different velocities, when the velocity is near the speed of light. The child is confused by the different velocities of two objects lasting for equal durations. In relativity theory, it is not the velocity of the two objects which is important, but rather the velocity of the observer himself relative to those two velocities. Two rates which appear equal to one observer, at relative rest to those movements, will appear different to an observer speeding away from those two rates. Duration is relative to the velocity of observer, but not to the velocity of the object within a given duration. (See Rogers, 1960, for a clear account of how speeding observers would see asynchrony in each other's clocks but not in their own.)

### Classification

The taxonomic system of *genus* and *specie*, while used rigidly in biology, is used casually in daily conversation. *Genus* defines the attributes that a group of elements have in common, as in "we are all brave." The *specie* defines differences within the *genus*, as in "some will succeed, some will fail." In reference to any single element, the *genus* and the *specie* combined define how that element is both similar to, yet different from, other elements. If a *genus* has but two *species* within it, the one *specie* is complementary to the other since they both together compose the whole *genus*. For example, hardbound books is the complementary class of soft-bound books, within the larger class books.

These relationships are determined by the qualitative features for each element and are not determined by the spatial contiguity between elements. The logical group is neither constrained nor determined by parts which must physically fit, like children joining hands to form a circle. The class *children* refers to elements with a particular set of attributes, not a particular spatial configuration. Yet in learning the rules of classification, the child passes through stages where elements are included into a "class" because they complete some spatial configuration of the collection of elements.

Inhelder and Piaget (1969) define classification as the coordination of intension and extension. Intension is the basis for the class as a whole, the defining rule. Consider, for example, the command to "sort out the wood from the metal." Thus, while intension is a general definition applicable to all instances of the class, extension is the basis for placing a single element into the group. Intension and extension are usually, but not always coordinated. Intension is concerned with the rules of similarity and difference which define the class composition; extension is concerned with the rules of relating element to class or part to whole.

When the child can classify discrete objects, he mentally stores the intensive content (wood vs. metal) and then, at the point of placing a chosen element, he remembers that content, looks at both piles, and places that element according to the intensive rule in storage. If extension is coordinated with intension, he will use the "wood vs. metal" contrast to identify a new object. At an early age, the child has difficulty applying rules generally. For example, at the moment of classifying an object, the very act of putting objects together calls his attention to the spatial configuration of the collection. For the young subject, putting-together are acts of creating spatial continuity between elements physically placed, not acts of creating categories.

At this stage, what Inhelder and Piaget describe as the stage of graphic collections, the child classifies objects according to definite spatial properties. For example, the child might create a bridge of metal and wood, or a bridge of only wood, or perhaps a group with pleasing symmetry. Extension is less a type of class inclusion determined by the intensive rules of similarity generally applied, and is more a relation of spatial part to spatial whole; specifically applied. The emerging configuration is the whole; the individual piece, the part. The piece is not similar, it is not even related to each and every member of the group, but is a physical part of the collection as a whole. Metaphorically speaking, the child is unable to "see" an infinite extension of specific elements contained within a single element. That is, the single element is not a "representative" of its class. The concept of a representative instance is much more than a simple one for one matching of objects based upon their physical similarities, and it is even more than a child creating a group of similar objects by successively relating one element to another in a chaining process. When extension is coordinated with intension, the child "sees" the many in the one, which is more than seeing one as similar to one other (see Vygotsky, 1962).

It is tempting to say that when the child begins to classify an object in order to create a configuration, he has simply changed the class intension. The point is that when the elements are added in this fashion, there can be no class. In classification, each member within the group is equivalent to every other member in spite of the fact that each member is physically separate. Each member is equivalent to all other members because each member possesses the intensive content. Each member can be identified as a class member without reference to a single, other, physically present, second member of the class. In the spatial configuration, each element maintains its distinctiveness and has no definition independent of the physical presence of other elements, since the configuration of the several determines the placement of the one. In the graphic collection, the child is not using a rule that can be applied uniformly to all members, but at best, a rule which gives some members privileges, and a rule which does not carry the implication of an infinite extension. As soon as the configuration is complete (the circle closed, or the symmetry established), no other elements will be added to that collection. The true class is never closed but is always open as long as there are new instances of the class intension. In this sense, true classes exceed the limits of space.

Here again we see the recurrent theme, the problem of continuity vs. discontinuity. When asked to classify, the child is being asked to superimpose categorical continuity upon elements which are physically discontinuous. In the stage of graphic collections, the child possesses only one way to consider continuity, and that way is to perceive physical continuity, the configuration. In the true class, continuity transcends space and becomes categorical. In true classes, continuity means seeing the many in the one, not seeing one as part of a whole. In the true class, the discrete and discontinuous nature of the elements has been coordinated with the continuity of class intension. In the graphic collection, the child can only consider discontinuity and continuity in a successive fashion, the concept of *part-to-whole*. In classification, he can consider discontinuity and continuity in a simultaneous fashion, the concept of *one-of-many*.

Another problem exists when the child is asked to work with sets and sub-sets. This requires that he coordinate similarities and differences within intension, and complementarity and inclusion within extension, and all four with each other. For the purpose of illustrating how spatial concepts affect the child's development, the last set of relations will be discussed.

Specifically, the child is asked to decide if he has more cowboys than people in his set of eight cowboys and five Indians. For convenience, the cowboys will be labeled A, the Indians A′ and the people B. The child answers that he has more cowboys. He has been asked to compare A and B, but he obviously is comparing A and A′. According to Piaget, the difficulty is not due simply to perceptual conspicuousness, the greater bulk of the cowboys compared to the Indians. Instead, the problem is the child's inability to separate himself from actions, actions which can be performed in time and space (Lunzer, 1969).

If an adult were asked to sort cowboys from people, he would probably just laugh. Cowboys cannot be placed physically in a cowboy group and a people group at the same time. However, the child can conceive of including the cowboys in two groups because he thinks in terms of virtual actions or virtual spatial arrangements. The A to B comparison carries an implicit operation. A must be compared to $A + A'$ (or B). To solve the problem, he must think that any one cowboy is, at the same time, both an A and a B.

In operative classification, the relation $A + A' = B$ necessarily leads to the relation $A = B - A'$. A and A′ are two complementary classes included in the class B. By the rule of inversion, A is necessarily smaller than B since something has to be subtracted from B before it equals A; $A < A + A'$. To work with these relations, the child has to transcend the figurative, spatial nature of knowledge. These operations call for thinking about relations, themselves nonspatial. The evolution of these structures are necessarily preceded by actions in space. These actions, according to Piaget's theory of development, are part of a spiraling exchange between assimilation and accommodation.

The crux of the class inclusion task is the simultaneous coordination of both intensive contrasts; i.e. this element is both similar to some elements, yet different from other elements in the superclass B. If actions are important to the formation of this coordination, how might those actions gradually transform themselves to the more operational mode of thought. The sensorimotor origins of this coordination of similar-yet-different was the concern of a study by Forman (1973).

The act of picking up one block, followed by the act of picking up a second block identical to the first, may be considered an obvious example of a case of responding to the similarities of the two blocks. Forman noticed that when two-year-olds picked up the second identical block, they almost invariably banged the blocks together at the midline. The banging was often modulated with an alternation between bringing blocks together and drawing them apart. This bilateral banging seldom occurred when two different blocks were held. The two-year-olds showed such conspicuous delight with their achievement that the experimenters searched for variation of this response in video tapes of these same children taken over a two year period of time. The observed transformations tell an interesting story about how action gets translated into figurative products, with the entire process facilitating the coordination of similar yet different.

Three categories occurred, ordered developmentally as follows: bilateral banging of identical blocks, bilateral placement on table with the identical blocks touching, and lastly, around age 3 ½, bilateral placing on table with a deliberate space made between identical blocks. The assumption was made that the child, in bilateral banging, was intrigued with the physical identity yet physical separateness of the two blocks. In previous research (Forman, 1971a), it was found that in placing jigsaw pieces, children about this age become intrigued with the alternate manner in which a piece can be separate from its recess, and then apparently disappear into its recess. They would alternately insert and remove the same piece.

When placing the two blocks together, the children even tried to "stick" blocks together, as if the blocks were broken parts of the same whole. Then they would draw the blocks apart and smile as if the separateness was even the more intriguing because block boundaries were a moment before completely superimposed. It is not too far to speculate that these children were creating (or testing) similarities when the blocks were pressed together, and were creating (testing) differences when drawing the blocks apart. The difference tested in this case, of course, is existential difference, not categorical difference. This means that the contrast *similar* (superimposed) was occurring temporally close to the contrast *different* (drawn apart) during the alternation in bilateral banging. In fact, these contrasts were being made as close as actual movements in space can allow. In operative coordination, these contrasts occur simultaneously (A is similar to A' in *genus*, but different in *specie*).

The other two response patterns seem to represent a transformation from action-based expression of similar-yet-different to a product-based expression. Two identical cylinders adjacently placed are similar, as expressed by their adjacency, yet different, as expressed by their distinct boundaries. Had the two blocks been stacked, their differences would have been less obvious, their boundaries more continuous. Two blocks placed near, but not touching, represent even more clearly the simultaneous contrasting of similar (near) yet existentially different (deliberately spaced rather than touching).

The product, the spatial arrangement, has become an embodiment of the real actions. To complete this line of thought in both directions, Forman speculated that the anatomical and neurological structure of the human body, particularly its bilateral symmetry, either imposes constraints on movement patterns or predisposes the child to make certain movement patterns (see Gesell, 1946). These actions in turn, when reaching their limits in time and space, are transformed into spatial arrangements which literally stand for those actions, and thereby exceed the limits of pure movement. These spatial arrangements later become the content of thought (figurative knowledge) as we discussed. Finally, figurative knowledge is replaced by operative knowledge which exceeds the limits of virtual actions and products. Thus the growth of logic proceeds from the biological givens of neurological and anatomical structure, to action patterns, to real spatial arrangements, to virtual actions and arrangements, to non-spatial operative thinking.

## DIRECTIONS FOR FUTURE RESEARCH

The foregoing speculation constitutes a somewhat disjunctive comparison of the development of spatial concepts in child and man. Parallels have been drawn to accentuate the fact that laboratory research with the child has relevance to both the philosophy of science and to the philosophy of knowledge. It is possible that close analysis of the child can bring into relief the formation of "root metaphors" (Pepper, 1942) which aid, but also restrict our understanding of the systems of life and the universe.

The development of science has been portrayed in terms of ideas based upon successive intuitions and discoveries, which become too constraining and too overgeneralized. Just as Aristotle's geocentric view of absolute direction and privileged positions in space was replaced by Newton's concept of constant mass, absolute space and gravitational force, so these latter ideas have been replaced by the principles of relativity. First Newton decentered from the position of the observer; then Einstein decentered from the position change of the observer.

The child, too, progresses through his own sets of decentrations, first discovering the object independent of himself, then discovering himself as occupying position in space, and finally when he develops a system of reference, discovering that position itself has position. Position is arbitrary and completely relative to the orientation and origin of the Cartesian coordinates.

It is not profound to say that the child can progress further as a result of the development of science. But can science progress as a result of the child's development, or better stated, by a more complete understanding of child development? Perhaps the most important insights in science, the paradigm shift (Kuhn, 1962), result from just this type of study. The scientist introspects on his first premises and asks the important question, how did I first learn the truth of this premise? Newton's answer was "through personal experience with objects falling toward the earth." When Newton took the attitude that movement toward the earth may be no more than a special case, he was ready for the discovery of free "falling" movement away from the earth. The implication here is that science cannot advance while working within its own paradigms; instead, it must continually reflect upon the paradigms themselves. Can the developmental psychologist assist in the analysis of these paradigms?

## Limitations of the Spatial Metaphor

Piaget's distinction between figurative and operative knowing is at once an indictment against the completeness of a knowledge spatially represented. In the discussion of classification, spatial representations or the graphic collections are incomplete. Even classification as movement through space is inadequate as a solution for the class inclusion problem.

Research in the development of spatial concepts is even more important today considering the demands made on the modern mind to think in nonspatial terms. Research on the transition from spatial to nonspatial knowledge could well disclose areas where the transition is incomplete as well as disclose where the spatial metaphor is completely inappropriate as a model for the new knowledge. Euler's circles give a convenient spatial symbol for the logic of classes, but space soon reaches its limits as a reference.

How difficult it is for the Euclidean mind to grasp the four dimensions of space-time. Popular, nonalgebraic accounts of relativity theory only seem to confuse the student by drawing spirals and elongated people on the two-dimensional page. Man has only recently learned to portray the third dimension into the flat surface of a painting (Arnheim, 1969). The ordinary picture is not too difficult because the three-dimensional object itself can be seen. The picture has a concrete referent in objective space. However, the popular artists of space-time want the viewer to "see" four dimensions. Such perception requires two dimensions more than are contained on the page, and one dimension more than can be seen in our daily lives.

Descartes brought science somewhat closer to seeing the fourth dimension in the calculus, represented by a point tracing a trajectory across the page. Still, the plotted trajectory on the coordinates of space $\times$ time loses some dimensions when trying to represent others. The horizontal axis is time; the vertical axis is vertical distance. The point itself has only a single dimension for its representation; space does not have its usual second (height) and third (depth) dimension. Now the common picture conjured to handle plotted trajectories is to imagine that the horizontal axis is the ground line. Take the profile of a tennis court as an example. Then the trajectory plotted on paper is no more than the path of the ball as we see it being lobbed across the net. Right away we have made a mistake. The graph actually traces the movement of an object that is thrown upward and returns to *the same spot* on the ground. It takes a while for the high school student to "see" time as pure change, not change in position.

What if the tennis ball passes from one side of the court to the other in the course of its ascent and descent? This would require three coordinates, one for time, height, and horizontal distance. This can be represented as a three dimensional model with a line curved from the front left corner of a cube to the back right corner. The axis from front to back represents the distance across the court within a single vertical plane. This model serves well for free falling objects, since most trajectories do stay within a single vertical plane. The model breaks down when depth is added.

What if a tennis ball is lobbed over the net but the wind catches it and displaces the movement from a single vertical plane. (Recall the mass on the glass analogy.) The line in the cube can be used to show the change in height and change in distance the length of the court. How will the change in distance the width of the court be represented? We have run out of dimensions in the model. Spatial representation of time breaks down in this situation, even with three dimensional representations.

Change of position cannot be accurately represented as a line in space, unless the change is confined to one plane. To think that change can be completely represented spatially is to forget the lesson of relativity; that space is time and time is space. One cannot stand in for the other! The viewer continually and unconsciously flattens space or freezes time in his attempts to represent their complete interaction.

The developmental psychologist can help by studying just how and where these inappropriate translations occur. Piaget has done this in his studies on geometry and number. Once the nature of the problem is delimited, educators can build from errors. Better models can be created to teach the newer concepts of science. Holography, time-lapse photography, video-tape and the oscilloscope all have their special dynamic features for teaching time-space concepts. Motion must be added to the newer models.

### Research Tasks

Basic contemporary research by and large has been limited to the psychology of static features, rather than change; and limited to the psychology of choice, rather than transformation. Time needs to be added to studies of space.

Studies in spatial development most commonly ask the question, what spatial cues are perceptible? Can the child see the difference between an asymmetrical object and its mirror image? The more important question, from an epistemological perspective, is, can the child see which object is a 180 degree change of the standard object, i.e. can he distinguish a change in position from a change in state? Or, if the change is discontinuous, what strategies does the child use to distinguish change of position from change in state. Of particular importance is the question exactly how does the child learn to handle discontinuous change as an extension of continuous change, a problem which plays a leading role in the development of number, geometry, time, classification, and causality.

To know that the child can make these distinctions is not necessarily to know how he makes them. Even knowing what features he can or cannot use to make these distinctions tells us nothing about how the features are used, how they are combined and coordinated. The shift of focus from features to coordination of input and action is the message of Poincaré and Piaget. Why is it that the older child can use features that are useless to the younger child? What does the older child do? One way to study how the child copes with transformations of the stimulus is to observe him in the act of putting stimuli through various transformations. Give him more than a two choice situation. More will be said about this in the section on the need for open-ended response measures.

The newer studies in "spatial visualization" are certainly a step toward a time-space combination. The child is asked to mentally rotate some spatial arrangement, either an object or a scene. The change is through a single axis of rotation. To create tasks more analogous to the problem of space-time, the rotation should also be rotated. Granted a child might be able to predict that a spot on a plexiglass sphere will be to his right, having been on his left before the sphere was rotated 180 degrees around its vertical axis. But could he predict that the spot would be to his upper right and rear if the sphere were simultaneously rotated on both its vertical and horizontal axes? Assume that the sphere has no pivots set running from North-East to South-West, etc. This is adding the third dimension to Olson's (1970) "representative anecdote," the acquisition of diagonality. Then, to test the limits, at least the limits as we now know them, could the child make predictions about the spot by moving the entire sphere through space while at the same time rotating it on both axes simultaneously? Should the child attempt such a prediction, he would have to note how several objects simultaneously move through space. To make the prediction, in other words, the child would have to coordinate change in the four dimensions of time-space. There is some danger, of course, that the experiment, if taken as a didactic, might lead the child to think of time as passage through some absolute, container space, in absolute rest. He might translate the reference points of the experimenter's room into a Euclidean model of general space. The task of the psychologist and teacher combined would be to avoid as much misinformation and over-simplification as possible.

### A New Research Language

Research in cognitive development is now asking questions of such refinement that the channel capacity of the reader will soon be exceeded. The recent research on the subskills involved in variations on the object permanence task is a good example. Researchers frequently debate the precursory skills to a certain task only to discover later that their respective reference tasks were not equivalent.

Cognitive development can be viewed conveniently as a series of computer subroutines that are differentiated and then coordinated into a more comprehensive computer program. Khlar and Wallace (1972) have shown the elegance of computer language to keep classification tasks clearly defined. Simon (1962) has made interesting suggestions for using information processing theory as a model of intellectual development. A noteworthy recent arrival is Cunningham's

(1972) flow chart model for changes across the sensori-motor period of development.

The Artificial Intelligence Lab at M.I.T. is doing exciting work directly relevant to spatial visualization, although their work is not currently focused on questions of development. Marvin Minsky and his staff have developed computer programs that can make complex spatial distinctions. These distinctions include the points of articulation within an arrangement of blocks, as well as the distinction of shadow from object (Minsky and Papert, 1972). They have developed a lengthy dictionary of subroutines: functional argument, memory protection, indirect address, conditional breakpoint, look-ahead, etc. These concepts should be useful to developmental research.

The advantage of the computer program as a model intelligence is that it places the functioning intelligence in real time. Cognitive processing in this system is more than a list of component tasks that must be mastered, but also is a complex system of coursing through these tasks, making decisions at junctures created by previous decisions, all in real time. Herein lies a sophisticated method of adding individual differences to the more typical stage-analysis of Piagetian research. That is, the task analysis characteristic of Piagetian research could be complemented by the decision analysis characteristic of computer programming.

Of course, one needs to be cautious in the application of sophisticated computer programs as a model of human intelligence. (This venture is more the concern of the Carnegie-Mellon group than of the M.I.T. group and carries the label "computer simulation" rather than "artificial intelligence"). Even a computer program which prints out "behavior" identical to that of the child, including the child's typical errors, may contain subroutines beyond the competence of the child. This problem is most likely to occur when the researcher begins to fill in gaps in his program based on what he knows about computers rather than what he knows about children. For example, response to the simple instruction: *build a bridge with three blocks*, may be written as follows: place block 1 near, but not touching, block 2; then place block 3 over the space. Although it might be noted that children can build the three block bridge, a close analysis shows that the child places the top block first and then scoots the second supporting block under the eave of the top block. Perhaps this is a mere difference in order of placement, but it may be an important difference. Specifically, it may mean that the child, unlike the computer, cannot judge vacant distances, only filled distances. The computer routine assumes this knowledge. One form of preventive medicine might well be the microanalysis of the child's actual behavior. Microanalysis could prevent the researcher from assuming that the child has knowledge routines which the child, in fact, does not possess. Put another way, it may be that the function microanalysis might serve is to fill in the apparent discontinuities which occur in cognitive development. This is not to suggest, as is often misunderstood, that cognitive development is continuous in the sense that later functions can be reduced to a combination of earlier functions. Rather, the suggestion is to employ microanalysis to discover more explicitly the nature of the interactions which create the emergent functions.

Microanalysis has the further advantage of putting focus back on the child rather than on the task alone. It is not enough to know which tasks can be solved in what developmental order according to what scalogram analysis. Until the experimenter actually watches and records and codes and analyses the process of task solution, he is left with an inadequate and indirect interpretation. His interpretation is derived from his own reasoning of what is logically required to solve task X and what is logically missing if the child cannot solve the next task in the progression. Why not look at the child? For example, it has been reasoned that the child can distinguish a two-dimensional "concavity" from a two dimensional "convexity" by using the convention stated as "shadows come from above" (Yonas, 1973). Another reader could object and point to different features of the task which might have been the actual cues for the response. If researchers would take a closer look at the child, using high-speed photography, they may find something in the nature of the reach which would strengthen interpretation. For example, what if the child extended a single finger toward the "concavity," as if to place his finger "inside," but when approaching the "convexity" he maintained an infantile thumb-forefinger opposition as if to pinch at the "protrusion." Microanalysis of these behaviors could add much to our understanding of spatial development, as already exemplified by the microanalysis of visual scanning patterns (Vurpillot, 1968).

## The Need for Open-ended Responses

As stated earlier in this discussion, psychology has been by and large the psychology of choice, and not the psychology of transformations. One of Piaget's messages to psychology has been that the child learns by making transformation on objects and, moreover, that he learns from these self-generated transformations.

"In manipulating, the child, besides learning something about the object in the course of such an experiment, also learns something of the way his actions are coordinated and how one determines the other" (Piaget, 1967, p. 454).

Regardless of Piaget's contribution, the dominating method for research in child development consists of successive presentations of stimuli controlled by the experimenter. Trial n + 1 follows trial n and so on. The nature of what follows is determined by the need to counterbalance independent variables to prevent the ubiquitious confounding which, it might be added, is always there awaiting discovery. What Piaget says is that we must allow the child to determine his own trial n + 1. How can a child exhibit a self-regulated pattern if he is not allowed to self-regulate? This question underscores the whole of the new structuralist approach.

Does this mean we have to sacrifice precision of psychological observation? If input variables occur at the whim of the child, how will we ever know what causes what? The answer to this question depends on what one will accept as a definition of explanation. If it is efficient causality, a question of what are the antecedents, then the new structuralism will seem archaic. If one will accept the legitimate claim that formal causality has to the role of an explanation, the new structuralism will be the answer. Microanalysis of behavior, computer programs of continuous decision-making, open-ended responses all require a shift in our basic paradigms of thought, from the mechanistic models of Skinner and Hull to the organismic models of Werner, Levi-Strauss and Piaget.

This shift is more than a shift from a linear model to a cybernetic model. Both of these models are mechanistic, the latter is only more complex. Both seek to answer the questions "what for" and "from what." The new structuralism seeks to ask the question "what and then what." A complete and comprehensive description of change *is* an explanation. These shifts are difficult for the researcher to make, mainly because he is often unaware of the model which he implicitly adopts (see Reese and Overton, 1970). Along with the shift to structuralism will come new languages, methods and technology, and hopefully new understanding of man.

# PART II

# ABSTRACTS

# Chapter 5

# ABSTRACTS OF
# SELECTED JOURNAL ARTICLES

Neil J. Salkind

John Eliot

## PURPOSE

ONE OF THE MANY DIFFICULTIES attending research in any discipline is the overwhelming amount of published as well as unpublished material which must be located and examined. The adage that "more people are writing than are reading" might very well be applicable to this situation. With respect to the area of children's spatial abilities, the abundance of literature both experimental and nonexperimental is readily apparent due as much to the diversity of research approaches as to the differing traditions of disciplines which are involved. Most researchers at one time or another need a "starting point" for their research. It is the purpose of the extended bibliography of this book as well as the abstractions of selected journal articles to help provide all researchers with a selection of "starting point" studies in the area of children's spatial abilities.

How were studies selected for abstraction or inclusion into the extended bibliography? For the most part, the extended bibliography is a combination of references from both primary and secondary sources (such as other shorter bibliographies). A wide range of sources, including computerized literature searches were examined for the bibliography, and as some references are the result of secondary or tertiary sources, errors in some references may be present. The authors, of course, take full responsibility for these errors.

The forty abstracts in this part of the book represent summaries of diverse studies in the general area of children's spatial abilities and

159

their development. The summaries are thought to be fairly representative of the numerous areas being investigated by those interested in the development of such behaviors in children. In selecting the studies, an attempt was made not to overemphasize any one trend of thought or topic, but instead, to sample the contents of the bibliography. The topic area of each reference is thought to be representative of a much larger body of references.

Specifically, the authors employed two criteria for the selection of studies to be abstracted. First, the sample employed in all studies was limited to subjects under twenty years of age. Second, since the purpose of this book is to suggest relevant issues to the interested researcher, studies were chosen which clearly posed a question.

Following each abstract is a list of references to other studies which either may lead off to different topics or are concerned with the same topic. This listing is not extensive for many reasons; one of which was the availability of materials (unpublished manuscripts and dissertations were not always readily available). The references, however, should provide a temporary focus for those whose interest has been caught by a particular topic.

Each abstract is divided into five sections: purpose, sample, methodology, results and discussion. The *purpose* section of each study presents the research question or issue posed by the author(s). The research hypothesis(es) per se may or may not be included in the abstract. The *subject* section contains as complete a description as necessary of the children who were used as participants in the study. Unless otherwise stated, age is expressed in chronological, not mental years. The *methodology* section details the research procedure and test instruments employed in the experiment. The *results* section contains a specification of the independent and/or dependent variables, information about scoring procedures and a statement of the main results of the analysis. Often information contained in the results section went beyond the primary purpose of the experiment. This information was not included. The experimental design, method of analysis, test statistic, as well as level of significance are presented when available. Critical and obtained values of the test statistic are not presented and, due to limitations of length, tabular data is also not presented. The *conclusion* section contains the conclusions or main points emphasized by the original author(s). Due to the complexity of some of the research, these statements were sometimes reproduced verbatim to preserve as clearly as possible their intended meaning.

It is clear that more efficient methods of disseminating information regarding research in any discipline must be developed. The use of abstracts in this book might help to alleviate some of the material burden placed on the prospective researcher. It is hoped that the combination of abstracts and bibliography will stimulate further research activity on a number of topics related to children's spatial development.

## ABSTRACTS

Alvy, K.: Relation of age to children's egocentric and cooperative communication. *Journal of Genetic Psychology, 112*:275-286, 1968.

*Purpose:* To investigate cooperative communication among children by creating a situation that requires one child to assume another's viewpoint in order to cooperate successfully over a commonly shared task.

*Subjects:* N = 96, 16 male/16 female at 6, 8, and 11 years of age.

*Methodology:* Following training on an identification task while physically separated by a screen, subjects were required to identify and verbally communicate to each other which object was chosen.

*Results:* The dependent variables were the percent of total pictures matched, the percent of children who used ambiguous speech, and the number of questioning responses from the other partner. The percent of total pictures matched by the subjects increased with age (z test, p < .01), with no difference in performance by sex. There was also an inverse relationship between the percent of speakers using ambiguous descriptions by age (p < .01), and the percent of listeners asking for more information by age (p < .01).

*Conclusions:* Egocentric communication decreases with age. Successful completion of the task varies inversely with the amount of egocentric communications. It was also shown how the child's level of cognitive development has predictable effects on his interpersonal behaviors.

**Further References:**

Cowan, P.A.: Cognitive egocentrism and social interaction in children. *APA Proceedings*, 1966.

Kingsley, P.: Relationship between egocentrism and children's communication. Paper read at SRCD Convention, 1971.

Rubin, K.: Egocentric communication and popularity. *Developmental Psychology*, 7:364, 1972.

Towler, J.: Egocentrism: A key to map-reading ability. *Social Education*, 35:893-898, 1971.

Ames, L.B. and Learned, J.: The development of verbalized space in the young child. *Journal of Genetic Psychology*, 72:63-84, 1948.

**Purpose:** To examine the developmental trends apparent in the verbalization of space by children.

**Subjects:** $N = 115$; 20 children at 24 months, 25 children at 30, 36 and 42 months, and 20 children at 48 months.

**Methodology:** Children were observed for one school year (from September to June), and all spontaneous verbalizations involving or implying space were recorded from behind a one way screen. Children were also asked questions about various aspects of space.

**Results:** The dependent variables were the percentage of children answering correctly and the frequency of certain words at the specified age levels. Consistent trends in the development of verbalized space in children were found. A table of the most commonly presented space words, as well as responses to the questions posed to the children, presented by the author.

**Conclusions:** The sequence of word usage as well as word frequency was found to be consistent between children as well as for each child.

**Further References:**

Asso and Wyke: Visual discrimination and verbal comprehension of spatial relations by young children. *British Journal of Psychology*, 61:99-107, 1970.

Court, S.R.A.: Numbers, time, and space in the first five years of life. *Pedogical Seminary*, 27:71-89, 1920.

Frandsen and Holder: Spatial visualization in solving complex verbal problems. *Journal of Psychology*, 73:229-233, 1969.

Guardo, C.J.: Personal space for children. *Child Development, 40*:
143-151, 1969.

Johnson and Beck: Development of space perception. *Journal of Genetic Psychology, 58*:247-254, 1941.


Ayres, A.J.: Patterns of perceptual-motor disfunction in children: a factor-analytic study. *Perceptual and Motor Skills, 20*:335-365, 1965.

**Purpose:** To determine the relationship between the different kinds of sensory perception, motor activity, laterality, and selected areas of cognitive function.

**Subjects:** N = 150; 69 male/31 female with suspected perceptual dysfunctions, and a control group of 50 children, matched on M.A., sex, and parental occupation.

**Methodology:** R and Q factor analysis was conducted on a series of measures.

**Conclusions:** For the group suspected of perceptual dysfunction, 23 factors were identified. For the control group, the major factors identified were not comparable to the first group.

**Further References:**

Ayres, A.J.: Interrelations among perceptual-motor functions in children. *American Journal of Occupational Therapy, 20*:68-71, 1966.

Ayres, A.J.: Characteristics of types of sensory integrative dysfunction. *American Journal of Occupational Therapy, 25*:329-334, 1971.

Ayres, A.J.: Types of sensory integrative dysfunction among disabled learners. *American Journal of Occupational Therapy, 26*: 13-18, 1972.


Beilin, H., Kagan, J. and Rabinowitz, R.: Effects of verbal and perceptual training on water-level representation. *Child Development, 37*:317-322, 1966.

**Purpose:** To determine if language and perceptual experience can play a significant role in symbolic imagery.

**Subjects:** N = 180, mean age 7 years-6 months.

**Methodology:** A total of nine treatment groups was employed, dependent on whether or not perceptual training was administered, type of verbal training (four groups), and three control groups. The pretest and posttest measures consisted of eight trials requiring the identification of the water level in a covered gallon jar tilted at different angles. The transfer task was identical except that the container was shaped differently.

*Results:* The dependent variable was the number of correct predictions as to the position of the water in the jar. One dimensional ANOVA yielded no differences in pretest performance or in transfer skills, but difficulties on posttest performance (p. < .01).

*Conclusions:* The results of the training suggest that water level representation is more dependent upon nonverbal than verbal mediated processes.

**Further References:**

Bannatyne, A.D.: A comparison of visuospatial and visuomotor memory for designs and their relationship to other sensorimotor psycholinguistic variables. *Journal of Learning Disabilities, 2:* 451-466, 1969.

Smedslund, J.: Effect of observation on children's representation of water surface. *Journal of Genetic Psychology, 102:* 195-201, 1963.

Berry, J.W.: Temne and Eskimo perceptual skills. *International Journal of Psychology, 1:* 207-229, 1966.

*Purpose:* To examine the relationship between the cultural and ecological characteristics of a society, as well as the perceptual skills of members of that society.

*Subjects:* N = 90; a group of traditional, isolated, rural Eskimo Indians, and a group of Westernized, urban Temne Indians.

*Methodology:* A test of visual discrimination (where a series of forms presented tachistoscopically were to be reproduced), and four tests of spatial skills (Kohs' Block Design, Witkin Embedded Figures, Morrisby Shapes, and Raven Matrices) were administered to all subjects.

*Results:* The transitional sample for both cultures scored higher than the traditional sample on all tests but shapes. Eskimos scored higher than Temne, and spatial scores were found to be highly related to level of education. In discrimination skills, Eskimos performed better than Temnes.

**Conclusions:** A racial explanation for differences between cultures in differing societies was found not to be acceptable by the author(s). Furthermore the data lends credence to the contention that a culture-free or culture-fair test is unattainable since peoples with different cultures and ecologies develop and maintain different skills.

**Further References:**

Cowley and Murray: Some aspects of the development of spatial concepts in Zulu children. *Journal of Social Research*, *13*:1-18, 1962.

Hudson, W.: Study of pictorial perception among unacculturated groups. *International Journal of Psychology*, 2:90-107, 1967.

MacArthur, R.S.: Some cognitive abilities of Eskimo, white and Indian-metis pupils ages nine to twelve years. *Canadian Journal of Behavioral Society*, *1*:50-59, 1969.

Serpell, R.: Discrimination of orientation by Zambian Children. *Journal of Comparative Physiology and Psychology*, 75:312-318, 1971.

Vernon, P.E.: Education and intellectual development among Canadian Indians and Eskimos. *Educational Review*, *18*:79-91, 1966.

Bowden, E.A.F.: Perceptual abilities of African and European children educated together. *Journal of Social Psychology*, 79:149-154, 1969.

**Purpose:** To determine if any "residual" advantage exists in Europeans over Africans in perceptual ability tests when education and other environmental factors are controlled.

**Subjects:** N = 200; 9 through 16 years of age.

**Methodology:** A nine item test was devised which involved comparing two different stimuli with reference to a standard for each item. The subjects' task was to select which of the two test stimuli was most like the standard.

**Results:** Analysis of covariance, with age as the covariate, yielded significant main effects for ethnicity ($p < .06$, with Europeans scoring higher than Africans), and sex ($p < .01$, with males scoring higher than females).

**Conclusions:** The educational and cultural backgrounds of the two different ethnic groups of subjects are responsible for the differences in perceptual abilities.

**Further References:**

DeLemos, M.: Development of the concept of conservation in Australian Aborigine children. *International Journal of Educational Psychology*, 4:255-269, 1969.

Hudson, W.: Pictorial depth perception in subcultural groups in Africa. *Journal of Social Psychology*, 52:183-208, 1960.

Morgan, P.: Observations and findings on the 7-squares test with literate and illiterate black groups in Southern Africa. *Journal of National Institute and Personnel Research*, 8:44-47, 1959.


Bradley, L.: Responses of retarded children on $3^d$ and $2^d$ visual tasks. *Exceptional Chidren*, 36:165-170, 1969.

**Purpose:** To examine the performance of two groups of mentally retarded children on tasks employing three-dimensional objects and two-dimensional colored pictures; and to determine if children classified as having a severe visual motor handicap (SVMH) have more difficulty responding to three-dimensional objects than those children having a minimal visual motor handicap (MVMH).

**Subjects:** $N = 30$; mentally retarded children, mean CA 15 years-8 months, matched on CA, MA, and IQ.

**Methodology:** The subjects were presented 90, three-dimensional objects categorized as tools, animals, furniture, transportation items, clothes or items relating to work or play. They were also presented 90 two-dimensional colored pictures. Subjects were asked "What is this?" "What do you call it?". Each subject was given sixty seconds to reply.

**Results:** The dependent variable was the number of correct responses. A t test between scores yielded no significant difference between the identification of two-dimensional and three-dimensional stimuli for SVMH, a significant difference between SVMH and MVMH on identification of three-dimensional objects (SVMH lowes), and a significant difference ($p < .01$) between the identification of three-dimensional and two-dimensional stimuli for MVMH (superior on objects).

**Conclusions:** Perception of the third dimension is lacking or poorly developed in the visually motor handicapped child, and there is a need for differentiation of teaching materials in accord with the individual learning handicap of the child.

**Further References:**

Halpin, V.G.: Rotation errors made by brain-injured children on the Goldstein-Scheerer Tests. *American Journal of Mental Deficiency, 59*:485-489, 1955.

Hartlage, L: Measuring spatial aptitudes of retardates. *Perceptual and Motor Skills, 33*:1107-1110, 1971.


Brown, L.B.: The reconstruction of a two-dimensional visual display. *Journal of Genetic Psychology, 115*:257-262, 1969.

**Purpose:** To examine children's perception of depth in a two-dimensional display.

**Subjects:** N = 70; 3.5 through 9 years of age.

**Methodology:** Subjects were presented with three photographs of five objects, and were required to reconstruct the photographic scene from a set of toy farm objects.

**Results:** The dependent variable was the differences in arrangement between what was presented to the child, and the actual stimulus array. Scoring was in terms of the arrangement being random, reversal, rough, relational, or systematic.

**Conclusions:** Five stages of development were isolated by the author passing from the random placing of objects to the 1:1 correspondence with the photograph. The latter was achieved by the subjects around the age of 8 to 9 years old.

**Further References:**

Uhlaner, J.E.: Relationship between two-dimensional and three-dimensional spatial-relations aptitude. Unpublished Ph.D.: Thesis, New York University, 1946.


Caldwell and Hall: The influence of concept training on letter discrimination. *Child Development, 40*:63-72, 1969.

**Purpose:** To determine the influence of concept learning upon a discrimination task, and to investigate how incomplete task analysis might be a source of false positives in research with children.

**Subjects:** N = 72 kindergarten children.

**Methodology:** Children were randomly assigned to one of three groups, and were provided with warm-up tasks requiring the overlaying or matching of standards until identical shapes were found. Children in group 1 were not allowed to rotate the plastic overlay of the standard in the matching attempt. Children in group 2 were not allowed to rotate the overlay in any way. Children in group 3 were given no information (orientation was irrelevant as a cue for matching the standard and the transformation). While group 1 was required to attend to shape and orientation, group 2 was required to attend to shape alone. After the warm-up task, each child was administered a test similar to the Davidson Letter Perception Test, which required them to discriminate between letters such as b and d, and p and q.

**Results:** The dependent variable was the percentage of correct responses for each child on all trials of the test. One dimensional ANOVA for differences between the three groups was significant (p < .01). Scheffé procedures showed group 1 performing better than group 3, and group 3 performing better than group 2.

**Conclusions:** Group differences were found to be a function of the different procedures employed, and the degree of attention required during the warm up process. The authors conclude that although attention is an important factor in discrimination learning, in the present experiment attention per se does not account for the group differences. It is the manipulated variable, group membership (or concept learning) which is responsible.

**Further References:**
Caldwell and Hall: Concept learning in discrimination tasks. *Developmental Psychology*, 2:41-48, 1970.
Davidson, H.P.: A study of the confusing letters, B, D, P, and Q. *Journal of Genetic Psychology*, 47:458-468, 1935.
Laubengayer, N.C.: The effects of training on the spatial egocentrism of preschoolers. Unpublished master's thesis, University of Minnesota, 1965.
Lovell, Healey and Rowland: Growth of some geometrical concepts. *Child Development*, 33:751-761, 1962.
Melametsa, L.: Influence of training upon level of test performance and the factor structure of intelligence tests. *Scandinavian Journal of Psychology*, 6:19-25, 1965.
Schubert, J.: Effect of training on the performance of the Wiscon-

sin block design subtest. *British Journal of Social and Clinical Psychology, 6:*144-149, 1967.

Smith, I.D.: Effects of training procedures upon the acquisition of conservation. *Child Development, 39:*515-526, 1968.

Worsencroft, R.R.: Effects of training on spatial visualizing ability of engineering students. *Journal of Engineering Drawing,* 1954.

Corsini, D.A.: Kindergarten children's use of spatial-positional, verbal, and nonverbal cues for memory. *Journal of Educational Psychology, 63:*353-357, 1972.

*Purpose:* To explore the ability of kindergarten children to utilize memory codes dependent upon the spatial properties of objects.

*Subjects:* N = 66; 33 male/33 female in kindergarten.

*Methodology:* Subjects in one of six conditions received instructions and were required to perform four different manipulative tasks of increasing difficulty. The six conditions were dependent upon whether questions were presented verbally or nonverbally, and upon the successful completion of the task at each respective level of

*Results:* The dependent variable was the number of points based upon the type of objects used.

difficulty. A two dimensional ANOVA (condition x difficulty) yielded significant main effects for condition ($p < .001$), and level ($p < .025$).

*Conclusion:* One of the ways which children comprehend verbal information is by pairing the information with a concrete referent. Kindergarten children remember best under conditions in which both verbal and nonverbal stimuli are available.

*Further References:*

Braine, L.G.: A developmental analysis of the effect of stimulus orientation on recognition. *American Journal of Psychology, 85:* 157-187, 1972.

Deleon, Raskin and Aruen: Shape perception in preschool children. *Developmental Psychology, 3:*358-362, 1970.

*Purpose:* To determine the relative roles of touch and vision in shape perception by children.

*Subjects:* N = 48; two groups of twenty-four subjects, ages 36 to 42 months, and 48 to 54 months, with equal number of boys and girls in each group.

**Methodology:** After a period of pretraining, each child performed discrimination tasks under all four of the following conditions: (1) visual, (2) tactual, (3) tactual and visual, and (4) tactual and visual, tactual. The basic procedure for all conditions was the presentation of a stimulus in the respective sensory mode, and the requirement to match that stimulus to its counterpart.

**Results:** The dependent variables were the number of correct identifications and the average response time. A four-dimension, repeated measures ANOVA (sex x age x sensory modality x order of presentation) was performed, where the main effects of age ($p < .01$), and modality ($p < .001$) was found to be significant. For the dependent variable response time, the main effect of modality ($p < .01$) was found to be significant. More correct responses were made under the visual, tactual-visual than tactual conditional.

**Conclusions:** The findings are consistent with other studies where visual discrimination in young children was found to be superior to tactual discrimination, but the data does not support the contention that tactual cues are a necessary component of visual discrimination in young children.

**Further References:**

Abravanel, E.: Development of intersensory patterning with regards to selected spatial dimensions. *SRCD Monograph*, *13*:118, 1968.

Denner and Cashdan: Sensory processing and the recognition of forms in nursery children. *British Journal of Psychology*, *58*:101, 1967.

Graham, Berman and Ernhart: Development in preschool children of ability to copy forms. *Child Development*, *31*:339-359, 1960.

Hermelin and O'Connor: Spatial coding in normal, autistic and blind normal children. *Perceptual and Motor Skills*, *33*:127-132, 1971.

Krauthamer, G.: Form perception across sensory modalities. *American Psychologist*, *14*:396, 1959.

Langdon, J.: Role of spatial stimuli in the perception of shape, part 2. *Quarterly Journal of Experimental Psychology*, 7:28, 1955.

Wohlwill and Winer: Discrimination of form orientation in young children. *Child Development*, *35*:1113-1125, 1964.

Elkind, D.: Children's conceptions of right and left: Piaget replication study IV. *The Journal of Genetic Psychology, 99*:269-276, 1961.

**Purpose:** To replicate Piaget's study, and to compare Piaget's results using Swiss children with those results obtained using American children.

**Subjects:** N = 210; 30 children at 5, 6, 7, 8, 9, 10 and 11 years of age.

**Methodology:** Tests 4 and 6 (suggested by Piaget but not used) replaced two tests that Piaget found to have low discrimination ability. The tests consist of affirmative statements which increase in difficulty, where the child is required to perform a task.

**Results/Conclusions:** Results of the original and the replication study were in agreement regarding the age levels at which particular tests were passed; stage one (7-8); child has a nondifferentiated conception of right and left, stage two (9-10); concretely differentiated conception of left and right, stage three (10-11); fully differentiated or complete conception of right and left.

**Further References:**

Belmont and Birch: Lateral dominance, lateral awareness and reading disability. *Child Development, 36*:57-71, 1965.

Boone and Prescott: Development of left-right discrimination in normal children. *Perceptual and Motor Skills, 26*:267-274, 1968.

Chamberlain, H.D.: The inheritance of left-handedness. *Journal of Heredity. 19*:557-559, 1928.


Emerson, L.L.: The effect of bodily orientation upon the young child's memory for position of objects. *Child Development, 2*: 125-142, 1931.

**Purpose:** To determine the effect of bodily orientation upon memory for spatial placements of wooden rings on an easel, and to investigate the factors which appear to influence the ability to make successful placements.

**Subjects:** N = 32; 18 female/14 male, 2 through 5 years of age.

**Methodology:** Each child was required to place a ring on an easel in a position similar to that of the ring on the experimental board. The relationship between the child's and experimenter's easels was manipulated to produce 9 different relationships (two easels parallel, two easels at right angles, etc.). Twenty placements at each position were required.

*Results:* The dependent variable was the number of correct placements for each of the nine positions. The easiest position was found to be the one where the child was required to place his ring over that of the experimenter's on the same board. The most difficult situation was where the child was required to place his ring on the reverse side of the examiner's easel. A general increase with age in the total number of correct placements was noted ($r = .77$).

*Conclusion:* The more change in the child's bodily position, the greater the difficulty in making an accurate placement. Thus, bodily movement has a distinct influence upon memory for placement.

*Further References:*
Fisher, S.: Sex differences in bodily perception. *Psychological Monographs*, 78:591, 1966.


Gaddes, Mckenzie and Barnsley: Psychometric intelligence and spatial imagery in two Northwest Indian and two white groups of children. *Journal of Social Psychology*, 75:35-42, 1968.

*Purpose:* To compare the perceptual abilities of two cultural subgroups.

*Subjects:* N = 124; 69 male/55 female, ranging in age from 6 years two months to 14 years 1 month; 68 white children and 56 Indian children (Salish and Kwakuitl tribe).

*Methodology:* Each child was administered four tests; Block Design (WISC), Cattell Culture Fair Test, Goodenough Draw a Man, and Porteus Maze Test.

*Results:* One dimensional ANOVAS were conducted for all four dependent variables and yielded the following significant main effects: Cattell ($p<.01$), Block Design ($p<.05$), and Porteus ($p<.01$). ANCOVA was also performed using the Block Design and the Porteus Maze scores as the criterion, and the Draw a Man and Cattell scores as covariates, yielding insignificant results.

*Conclusions:* No differences were found in spatial imagery skills between the Indian and the white children.

*Further References:*
Aveling, F.: The relevance of visual imagery in the process of thinking, II. *British Journal of Psychology*, 18:15-22, 1927.

Barratt, P.E.: Imagery and thinking. *Australian Journal of Psychology*, *5*:154-164, 1953.

Drummond: Nature of images. *British Journal of Psychology*, *17*: 10, 1926.

Fernald, M.R.: The diagnosis of mental imagery. *Psychology Review*, Monograph Supplement, *14*:58, 1912.

Goldschmid, M.L. and Bentter, P.M.: Dimensions and measurement of conservation. *Child Development*, *39*:787-802, 1968.

***Purpose:*** To evaluate a number of tasks previously employed as measures of conservation, and from these tasks construct a conservation scale with sound psychometric properties.

***Subjects:*** $N = 142$; grades K, 1, 2.

***Methodology:*** Each child was individually administered tests of conservation in the following ten areas: substance, weight, continuous quantity, discontinuous quantity, number, area, distance, length, and both two- and three-dimensional space. The children were required to compare the relative weight, length, etc. of two objects after the shape or form of the objects had been changed by some manipulation.

***Results:*** The dependent variable was the number of correct responses and, if subsequent explanation by the child indicated a comprehension of the type of conservation under examination, another point was awarded. There was a total of 44 tasks, with differing numbers of tasks within each of the ten tests. KR 20 was high enough to consider tasks reliable. The results of a multidimensional scaling technique demonstrated consistency across large numbers of items. Scales A, B, and C were created with A and B being parallel forms.

### CROSS VALIDATION

***Subjects:*** $N = 107$; grades K, 1, 2.

***Methodology:*** Scales A and C were first given to all S's, followed 2 weeks later by Scale B and again C.

***Results:*** Coefficients of reliability (KR 20) were computed and found to be .98, .99, .97, and .97.

***Conclusion:*** The introduction of psychometrically sound scales as developed in this study could influence the direction of research based on Piaget's theory.

**Further References:**

Braine and Shanks: Development conservation of size. *Journal of Verbal Learning and Verbal Behavior,* 4:227-242, 1965.

Braine, M.D.S.: Conservation of shape property. *Canadian Journal of Psychology, 19*:197-207, 1965.

Cahoon, O.W.: Group training on conservation tasks. Unpublished dissertation, Pennsylvania State University, 1970.

Gaudia, G.: Conservation on Piaget's tasks. *Developmental Psychology, 6*:158-165, 1972.

Griffiths, Shantz and Siegel: A methodological problem in conservation studies: The use of relational terms. *Child Development, 38*:841-848, 1967.

Mermelstein and Shulman: Lack of formal conservation. *Child Development, 38*:39-52, 1967.

Moynahan and Glick: Identity and equivalence conservation. *Developmental Psychology, 6*:247-251, 1972.

Piaget and Inhelder: *The Child's Conception of Space.* New York; Humanities Press, 1956.

Siegel and Goldstein: Conservation of number: recency versus relational strategies. *Developmental Psychology, 2*:128-130, 1969.

Stephens, McLaughlin and Miller: Factorial structure of selected psychometric-educational measures and Piaget reasoning assessments, *Developmental Psychology, 6*:343-348, 1972.

Sweetland, R.C.: The use of mental imagery among young children in the acquisition of Piaget's principles of conservation. *Dissertation Abstracts, 29*:69-1088, 1969.

Tuddenham, R.: Piagetian tests of cognitive development. In Dochell, (ed) *On Intelligence,* Methuen, 1970.

Whiteman and Piesach: Perceptual and sensorimotor supports for conservation tasks. *Developmental Psychology, 2*:247-249, 1970.


Guardo and Meisels: Factor structure of children's personal space schemata. *Child Development, 42*:1307-1312, 1971.

**Purpose:** To identify the factor structure of children's personal space schemata.

**Subjects:** N = 431; grades 3 through 10.

**Methodology:** Each child was required to make 20 interpersonal distance settings, based upon the silhouettes of single peers of the same and opposite sex, and groups of peers of the same and opposite sex.

**Results:** The correlational matrices for each sex age group were analyzed using the principal components solution followed by varimax rotations. For females grade 3-6, seven factors accounted for 66.3% of the variance. For females grade 7-10, six factors accounting for 64.7% of the variance were extracted. For males grade 3-6, eight factors accounting for 67.2% of the variance, and males grade 7-10 seven factors accounting for 66.4% of the variance were extracted.

**Conclusions:** The more identifiable factors in the older range and the identification of the causal interaction factors for the older group suggest an increase in the use of social space with age. Also, spatial patterning tendencies develop in a consistent, identifiable manner. This patterning takes place later for boys than girls.

Harrell, W.: A factor analysis of mechanical ability tests. *Psychometrika,* 5:17-33, 1940.

**Purpose:** To identify preference for color, form, borders, lines and dots for preschool children and adults.

**Subjects:** N — 25; preschoolers, mean CA 4 years 9 months and adults, mean CA 26 years 3 months.

**Methodology:** Sets of stimulus patterns differing in color (red/green), form (triangle/circle), borders (presence/absence), interior lines (presence/absence), and dots (presence/absence) were presented to each subject. Adults were tested in a group, while children were tested separately.

**Results:** The dependent variable was the number of summed choices for dimension over each subject. Age x problem analysis showed that preschoolers preferred form over other stimuli, while adults preferred borders.

**Conclusion:** The present research supports the hypotheses that a child's preferences for various dimensions are different from those of an adult, and that learning tasks should be designed to utilize preferred dimensions efficiently.

**Further References:**
Bates, Wallace and Henderson: A statistical study of four mechanical ability tests. *Proc. Ia. Acad. Sci.,* 50:130-134, 1943.

Beard, R. M.: The structure of perception: a factorial study. *British Journal of Educational Psychology*, *35*:210-222, 1965.

Divesta, Ingersoll and Sunshine: A factor analysis of imagery tests. *Journal of Verbal Learning and Verbal Behavior*, *1*:83-90, 1971.

El-Koussy, A.H.: *Trends in research in spatial abilities*. International Colloquium on Factor Analysis, Paris, 1955.

Harris, L.: Discrimination of left-right directionality and development of the logic of relations. Paper presented at the Biennial Meeting of the Society for Research in Child Development, Santa Monica, California, March, 1969.

*Purpose:* To examine the problem of why performance on left-right tasks of discrimination lags behind other similar conceptual or relational tasks such as up/down.

*Subjects:* $N = 200$; 4 through 12 years of age.

*Methodology:* An array of objects was presented to subjects, using responses to Piaget's six questions as the dependent variable. The array was also rotated to an up and down situation.

*Results:* A two-dimensional ANOVA yielded age ($p<.001$ and test situation ($p<.005$) differences.

*Conclusions:* Young children can pass relational tests so long as the relations are up/down or front/back rather than right/left.

*Further References:*

Belmont and Birch: Lateral dominance and right-left awareness in normal children. *Child Development*, *34*:257-270, 1963.

Benton, A.L.: Right-left discrimination. *Pediatric Clinics of North America*, *15*:747-758, 1968.

Blackman, T.O.: Reading Disability and right-left discrimination. *Dissertation Abstract*, *27*:67-2026, 1967.

Boone and Lates: Left-right discrimination problems in neurologically impaired children. *University of Kansas Bulletin in Education*, *21*:12-18, 1966.

Bryden, M.P.: Left-right differences in tachistoscopic recognition: directional scanning or cerebral dominance? *Perceptual and Motor Skills*, *23*:1127-1134, 1966.

Enstrom, D.C.: Reading help for lefties. *The Reading Teacher*, *25*:41-44, 1971.

Fisher, S.: Developmental sex differences in right-left perceptual directionality. *Child Development*, *33*:463-468, 1962.

Wapner and Cirillo: Imitation of a model's hand movements: age changes in transposition of left-right relations. *Child Development, 39*:887-894, 1968.

Hartlage, L.C.: Verbal reports of spatial conceptualization. *Journal of Experimental Psychology, 80*:180-182, 1969.

**Purpose:** To determine the degree to which responses to spatial questions is dependent upon being exposed to visual stimulation.

**Subjects:** N = 20; 10 blind, grades 2, 3, 5, 7 and 12 matched with sighted counterparts.

**Methodology:** An ordering of syllogisms containing 16 space and 16 nonspace questions was administered to each subject.

**Results:** The dependent variable was the number of correct responses. A two dimensional ANOVA yielded the following significant main and interaction effects; grade ($p < .005$), space/nonspace ($p < .05$), interaction ($p < .005$), with no difference between the blind and the sighted children.

**Conclusion:** The data supports the prediction that blind children performed significantly less well than sighted on space questions. Moreover, the presence or absence of vision is a critical factor with regard to responses to questions involving space.

**Further References:**

Furby, L.: The role of spatial visualization in verbal problem solving. *Journal of Genetic Psychology, 85*:149-150, 1971.

Mackinnon, A.J.: *Spatial and verbal intelligence in visualizers and nonvisualizers.* Conference for Postgraduate Psychologists, University of Cardiff, Wales, July 1968.

Houssiadas, L. and Brown, L.: Coordination of perspectives by mentally defective children. *Journal of Genetic Psychology, 110*: 211-215, 1967.

**Purpose:** To investigate how mentally defective children perceive space: particularly their ability to interrelate their own point of view with that of other observers.

**Subjects:** N = 40; 8-9, 10-11, 12-13, and 14-15 years of age.

**Methodology:**

*Experiment 1*—Using a stimulus situation consisting of four objects (a church, a toy car, a hedge and a telegraph pole) placed in a specific location on a table, each subject was required to select one of the four full-sized photographs which best represented the view from the position the subject was occupying. Subjects were shown a doll which they were told had taken the pictures from three different positions. They were then asked to identify the picture "taken from each position."

*Results*: The dependent variable was the position chosen; either correct, egocentric (choosing a photograph of objects from subjects viewpoint when presented other board arrangements); and incorrect.

*Experiment 2*—Using the same objects plus two model houses, the subjects were required to arrange the objects in order corresponding to that shown in the different pictures.

*Results*: The dependent variable was a judgment made as to the type of error made in the arrangement; either gross or correct.

**Conclusions:** Although overlapping of the stages of development made it difficult to identify specific age groups, the trend in development of egocentrism was found to be in the same direction as the trend for normal children.

**Further References:**

Barragy, Sister: The effect of varying object number and type of arrangement on children's ability to coordinate perspectives. Unpublished dissertation, 1970, George Peabody College for Teachers.

Benton, A.L.: Disorders of spatial orientation. *Handbook for Clinical Neurology, Vol. 3*, P.J. Vinken and G.W. Bruyn, Eds., 1969.

Blank, Weider and Bridges: Verbal deficiencies and abstract thinking in easy reading retardation. *American Journal of Orthopsychiatry, 38*: 823-834, 1968.

Ghent, L.: Effect of orientation on recognition of geometric forms by retarded children. *Child Development, 35*: 1127-1135, 1964.

Huttenlocker, J.: Children's ability to order and orient objects. *Child Development, 38*: 1169-1176, 1967.

**Purpose:** To investigate the parallels in children's ability to order and orient objects, and to determine if these parallels reflect the same underlying developmental processes.

### Experiment 1 (Ordering objects)

*Subjects*: N = 24; males and females, four years of age.

*Methodology*: Children were required to copy the order of 24 sets of 2 or 3 blocks. Twelve sets were arranged in piles, and twelve sets were arranged horizontally left to right. Six of each set consisted of 2 blocks, and 6 of each set consisted of three blocks.

*Results*: The dependent variable was the mean number of errors made by the child while copying the vertical or horizontal arrays. A Wilcoxin Signed Ranks Test (p < .01) yielded a significant difference between the number of errors made, with fewer errors made when the blocks were in the vertical array.

### Experiment 2 (Orienting objects)

*Subjects*: N = 21; males and females, four years of age.

*Methodology*: Children were required to match the position of their "horseshoe" with one presented by the experimenter. Each child was given twenty-four trials, six of four different types, dependent upon whether the figure the child was to match opened up or down, left or right.

*Results*: The dependent variable was the number of correct positionings. Relative position as well as plane was found to be a significant factor.

**Conclusions:** Some common features of the child's relationship to his spatial environment may underlie ability to order sets of objects and to orient single objects. Plane (up/down-left/right) is a factor over and above relative position.

### Further References:

Becker, J.T.: Spatial orientation and visual discrimination. *Perceptual and Motor Skills, 31*:943-946, 1970.

Ghent, Bernstein and Goldweber: Preferences for orientation of form under varying conditions. *Perceptual and Motor Skills, 11*: 46, 1960.

Olson, D.R. and Baker, N.E.: Children's recall of spatial orientation of objects. *The Journal of Genetic Psychology, 114*:273-281, 1969.

Rothenberg, B.B.: Preschool children's understanding of the co-ordinated concepts of distance, movement, number and time. *Journal of Genetic Psychology, 115*:263-276, 1969.

Jennings, F.: Preferences of preschool children for specific geometric figures. *Child Development*, 7:227-235, 1936.

**Purpose:** To investigate the preferences of preschool children for geometric figures.

**Subjects:** N = 22; 31 through 59 months of age.

**Methodology:** Each child was presented three sets of five cards. The first set consisted of black and white pictures, while the second and third sets consisted of geometric figures cut out of black construction paper. The child was required to choose the card they preferred out of each of the three sets, and was required to do this three times.

**Results:** The criterion measure for consistency was three choices of the same card as well as the serial position of the card. On the three scales a total of ten children met the criterion in the three different sets. An increase in consistency as age increased was found, and children who chose according to specific cards tend to agree on the cards they prefer while children who chose according to position tend to prefer the middle and last position. Adults (earlier results) and children also tend to prefer the same forms.

**Conclusion:** The choice for position requires a longer time than the choice for card, but this difference does not seem to be reliable.

**Further References:**

Borich, G.: Preferences for color, form, borders, lines and dots by preschool children and adults. *Perceptual and Motor Skills, 31*: 811-817, 1970.

Braine, L.G.: Age changes in the mode of perceiving geometric forms. *Psychonomic Science*, 2:155-156, 1965.

Brain and Goodenough: The relative potency of color and form perception at various ages. *Journal of Experimental Psychology*, *12*:197-213, 1929.

Eisenman, R.: Creativity, birth order and preference for symmetry. *Journal of Consulting and Clinical Psychology*, *34*:271-280, 1970.

Estes, B.W.: Judgment of size in relation to geometric shape. *Child Development*, *32*:277-286, 1961.

Eysenck and Castle: Training in art as a factor in the determination of preference judgments for polygons. *British Journal of Psychology*, *61*:65-81, 1970.

Graham, Berman and Ernhart: Development in preschool children of ability to copy forms. *Child Development, 31*:339-359, 1960.

Karmel, B.Z.: Age, complexity and contour on pattern preference. *Journal of Experimental Psychology, 7*:339-354, 1969.

Rosenblith, J.F.: Judgments of simple geometric figures by children. *Perceptual and Motor Skills, 21*:947-999, 1965.

Kielgast, K.: Piaget's concept of spatial egocentrism: a reevaluation. *Scandinavian Journal of Psychology, 12*:179-191, 1972.

***Purpose:*** To retest and evaluate the world-field assumption in an experimental setting.

***Subjects:*** N = 36; ages 6 through 8 years of age.

***Methodology:*** Four objects (tree, house, church, and tower) were photographed from 8 different positions with approximately 45 degrees between each position. Each child learned to describe their own perspective from all 8 positions and each child was randomly assigned to one of two groups differing in verbal terms used to describe the perspective. One group (R group) learned to describe the relations between the 4 objects ("Tell me what is in front and what is behind when you stand here.") The second group (I group) learned to describe the iconic features where the child described how each object looked as seen from their own position ("Tell me what you can see fully and what you can see only partly.")

***Results:*** The dependent variable was the number of correct responses.

***Conclusion:*** The children in this sample did not appear as egocentric or as self-centered as in Piaget's description, but these children were more exclusively centered on the world of objects around them. Success in the task appeared to be a question of perceptual differentiation.

***Further References:***

Lovell, K.: A followup of some aspects of the work of Piaget and Inhelder on the child's conception of space. *British Journal of Educational Psychology, 29*:107-117, 1959.

Peel, E.A.: Experimental examination of some of Piaget's schemata concerning children's perception and thinking. *British Journal of Educational Psychology, 29*:89-104, 1959.

Stephens, McLaughlin and Miller: Factorial structure of selected psychometric-educational measures and Piaget reasoning assessments. *Developmental Psychology*, 6:343-348, 1972.

Kraunak, A.R. and Raskin, L.M.: The influence of age and stimulus dimensionality on form perception by preschool children. *Developmental Psychology*, 4:389-393, 1971.

*Purpose:* To determine the influence of stimulus dimensionality, age, and sex, upon perception and discrimination of two and three-dimensional geometrical forms.

*Subjects:* N = 64; two groups of children, mean ages for group 1: 38 months; for group 2: 54 months.

*Methodology:* Sixteen children from each of the two age groups were randomly assigned to either the two- or three-dimensional condition. After a pretraining session, the experimental session began where the child was required to match a two or three-dimensional stimulus (two-dimensional forms are drawn on white cards, three-dimensional forms are a cube, pyramid, or polyhedron). A total of 15 trials was administered.

*Results:* The dependent variable, number of correct responses was examined using a two-dimensional ANOVA design. The effects of age ($p < .01$, older children performing at a higher rate than younger children), and age x condition ($p < .05$) were found to be significant.

*Conclusions:* The older children in the three-dimensional condition made more correct responses than the other group, indicating that these children were able to use effectively the additional information provided by the discussion of depth, while the younger children cannot.

*Further References:*
Golomb, C.: Evolution of human figure in three-dimensional medium. *Developmental Psychology*, 6:385-391, 1972.

Kuezansky, P.E., Rebelsky, F. and Dorman, L.: A developmental study of size constancy for $2^d$ and $3^d$ stimuli. *Child Development*, 42:633-635, 1971.

*Purpose:* To examine the development of size constancy perception of both two and three-dimensional stimuli in children.

*Subjects:* N = 64, 8 male/8 female at 3, 4, 5 and 6 years of age.

*Methodology:* Children were required to select one of two stimuli (two or three dimension/near or far) with respect to a standard stimulus.

*Results:* The dependent variable was the number of errors, an error being a misjudgment on either side of the standard. The score was the sum of the positive and negative errors without regard to the magnitude. A three dimensional ANOVA for age, sex, and dimension yielded the following main and interaction effects; age (p < .05), dimension (p < .01), and age x sex x dimension (p < .01). Errors were found to decrease with age, and more errors were made with $2^d$ than with $3^d$ objects.

*Conclusion:* The three-dimensional stimuli induce greater constancy. Possibly the number of cues present influences judgments about constancy. Constancy is also enriched with additional information.

*Further References:*

Bower, T.G.R.: Slant perception and shape constancy in infants. *Science, 151*:832-834, 1966.

Renshaw, T.: *A factorial study of two and three-dimensional space tests.* Ph.D. Thesis, University of Edinburgh, 1950.

Lord, F.E.: A study of spatial orientation of children. *Journal of Educational Research, 34*:481-505, 1941.

*Purpose:* To study the spatial orientation ability of children in the later elementary school grades.

*Subjects:* N = 317; 173 male/144 female, grades 5 through 8.

*Methodology:* Four major tests of orientation were administered to each subject; a test of orientation with reference to direction, a test of orientation with reference to cities in space, a test of orientation in the community, and a test of the ability to maintain orientation during travel.

*Results:* For all four tests, an improvement as grade increased was noted. Males scored higher than females on all tests but orientation in the community, where performance was equal.

*Conclusions:* The authors note marked individual differences with males superior.

**Further References:**

Bisov, S.A.: A test for investigating space orientation. *Sovetsk Psikhotekh, 3*:254-257, 1933.

Harris and Schaller: Preference for orientation vs. identification of upright two-dimensional forms by young children. Paper read at SRCD Convention, 1971.

Kershner, J.: Ethnic differences in children's ability to reproduce direction and orientation. *Journal of Social Psychology*, 1972, in press.

McGurk, H.: The role of object orientation in infant perception. *Journal of Experimental Child Psychology, 9*:363-373, 1970.

**Purpose:** To determine through three experiments whether infants perceive differences between different object orientations.

**Subjects:** N = 18; 3 groups of six children, ages 6-12 weeks, 13-19 weeks, and 20-26 weeks.

### Experiment 1

*Methodology*: A pair of objects, two identical faces and two funnel shaped drawings were each presented with a member of the pair right side up (0 degrees), and the other member of the pair upside down (180 degrees). Half of the infants received faces followed by funnels, while the other half received the reverse order.

*Results*: The dependent variable was the total fixation time towards each orientation. Wilcoxin test yielded insignificant differences in orientation, and a Kruskal-Wallis analysis of variance procedure yielded insignificant differences in age.

### Experiment 2

*Methodology*: Infants were presented either six familiarization tasks of 20 seconds duration where a face was presented on four trials using the funnel. Following the last trial, the subject was presented the same object but in an orientation differing 180 degrees from the familiarization task. One half of the infants were exposed to the face first, followed by the funnel. This order was reversed for the other half. One half of the infants were familiarized in 0 degrees and the other half in 180 degrees.

*Results*: Using the Kruskal-Wallis procedure, differences in age were found not to be significant. Over the series of trials, there was a decline in fixation towards the object whether funnel or face.

### Experiment 3

*Methodology*: Infants were given an 80 second familiarization with pairs of identical objects presented in the same orientation (either 0 degrees or 180 degrees). Infants were then given post-familiarization episodes where the orientation of one member of the pair was altered 180 degrees.

*Results*: Using the Kruskal-Wallis procedure, differences in familiarization were found at the .05 level of significance.

**Conclusions:** The data supports the notion that very young infants are more sensitive to object orientation than previously thought. This is found to be especially so with respect to the differential responding to orientation over all age ranges.

### Further References:

Aronson and Tronick: Perceptual capacities in early infancy, in Eliot, J., *Human Development and Cognitive Processes*, Holt, Rinehart and Winston, 1971.

Bower, T.G.R.: The visual world of infants. *Scientific American*, *215*: 80-92, 1966.

Gibson and Robinson: Orientation in visual perception: the recognition of familiar plane forms in differing orientation. *Psychology Monograph*, *46*: 39, 1935.


Meyer, E.: Comprehension of spatial relations in preschool children. *Journal of Genetic Psychology*, *57*: 119-151, 1940.

**Subjects:** To investigate the evaluation of the notion of space in preschool children.

**Purpose:** N = 63; 33 male/30 female, 18 months to 5½ years of age.

**Methodology:** Through a series of exercises, comprehension of spatial relations between objects was studied (the fitting of forms together, and the comprehension of a moving object in relation to other objects). Also, comprehension of the individuals own shifts of position was studied through their coordination with a freely moveable object, and their coordination with an object whose movements were regulated.

***Results/Conclusions:*** Anecdotal summaries of behavior show a trend in development from a "practical" to a "subjective" to an "objective" level of space comprehension.

***Further References:***

Dodwell, P.C.: Children's understanding of spatial concepts. *Canadian Journal of Psychology, 17*:141-161, 1963.

Fishbein, Lewis and Keiffer: Children's understanding of spatial relations: coordination of perspectives. *Developmental Psychology, 7*:21-33, 1972.

Huttenlocker, J.: Constructing spatial images: A strategy in reasoning. *Psychological Review, 75*:550-560, 1971.


Neale, J.: Egocentricism in institutionalized and noninstitutionalized children. *Child Development, 37*:97-101, 1966.

***Purpose:*** To determine if emotionally disturbed children show a higher level of egocentrism than a control group of public school children.

***Subjects:*** N = 20; emotionally disturbed children from a hospital and public school children ages 8, 9, 10 and 11 years of age.

***Methodology:*** Each subject was administered a replication of Piaget and Inhelder's three-mountain task, employing nine different drawings. A plastic model of a man was used as the "viewer."

***Results:*** The dependent variable was the number of correct recognitions of the view from which the drawing was made, as well as the position of the mountains. Mann-Whitney U procedure yielded a significant difference between groups, with the nondisturbed sample showing less egocentrism.

***Conclusion:*** Emotionally disturbed children are more egocentric than normal children. Also Piaget's theory of the breakdown of egocentric behavior through interpersonal contacts is supported.

***Further References:***

Chandler, M.J.: Egocentricism and antisocial behavior. *Developmental Psychology, 9*:326, 1973.

Chandler, M.J.: Egocentricism in normal and pathological child development, in F. Monks, Hartup and DeWitt, *Determinants of Behavioral Development*, Academic Press, 1972.

Flavell, et al.: *Development of role-taking and communication skills in children*, Wiley, 1966.

Thompson, L.A.: Role Playing Ability and Social Adjustment in Children. Unpublished dissertation, University of Michigan, 1968.

Nerlove and Monroe: Environmental experience on spatial ability. *Journal of Social Psychology*, *84*: 3-10, 1971.

**Purpose:** To replicate an earlier study which found that children's physical distance from home was related to performance on an intelligence task requiring spatial ability.

**Subjects:** N = 26; 13 male/13 female, 5 through 8 years of age. The Gusii children of Southwestern Kenya were used in this study. Previously the Logoli children were used as subjects.

**Methodology:** Each subject was observed in the natural setting for a total of 20 times over a three-week period. Distance from home was converted into a five point scale from 0 to 500 feet by 100 foot measurements. Three tests of spatial ability were then administered (copying block patterns, copying geometric forms and the Arthur revision of Porteus Mazes).

**Results/Conclusion:** Children who were further away from home than their marked counterpart were also more skillful at the three spatial tasks. All tests of significance showed significant differences at the .05 level between both groups.

**Further References:**

French, J.W.: How important is spatial ability? *Contemporary Psychology*, *11*: 38, 1966.

Kearney, G.E.: Cognitive capacity among the Orokawa of New Guinea. *Research Bulletin*, *13*: 1-25, 1966.

Suchman, R.G.: Cultural differences in children's color and form preferences. *Journal of Social Psychology*, *70*: 3-10, 1966.

Osborne, R.T. et al.: Racial differences in heritability estimates for tests of spatial ability. *Perceptual and Motor Skills*, *27*: 735-739, 1968.

**Purpose:** To test the hypothesis that the American Negro is handicapped on tests of spatial ability because of an environmental disadvantage.

**Subjects:** N = 568; one hundred and seventy-two pairs of identical twins, and one hundred and twelve pairs of fraternal twins;

forty-three pairs of twins were Negro, and two hundred forty-one pairs Caucasian; ranging from 13 through 18 years of age.

*Methodology:* After zygosity and dizygosity of the subjects was established, each subject was administered the following tests: Cube Comparison Test, Surface Development Test, Object Aperture Test, Mazes Test, Paper Folding Test, Newcastle Spatial Test, and Identical Pictures Test.

*Results:* Four different heritability ratios were computed to determine intrapair similarity. Heredity and environment produce significantly greater differences in fraternal twins on tests of spatial visualization, perceptual speed, and spatial orientation than environmental influences alone produce in identical twins.

*Conclusion:* The hypothesis of a lower heritability ratio for Negro than Caucasian children is rejected, but differences in $h^2$ suggest more genetic or biological contributions for Negro children than Caucasian children on spatial test performance. Environment does not play a more significant role in the mental development of the spatial abilities of the Negro child, than in the Caucasian child.

*Further References:*

Lesser, Fifer and Clark: Mental abilities of children from different social and cultural groups, *SRCD Monograph, 102,* 1965.

Sigel, A.S.: Classification behavior of lower and middle class Negro preschool children. *Journal of Negro Education, 35*:218-229, 1966.


Radaker, L.D.: Imagery and academic performance. *Elementary School Journal, 63*:91-95, 1962.

*Purpose:* To test if children who consistently use imagery in school subjects have more vivid experiences than children who use imagery less consistently.

*Subjects:* $N = 60$; 29 male/31 female, 8 through 11 years of age.

*Methodology:* Three experimental groups, one control and two imagery practice groups (depending on the amount of training in imagery skills received) were formed. The following four newly developed measures of imagery were administered to each subject: the visual imagery index, the memory for designs test, the memory for objects test, and the memory for word forms test.

*Results:* ANCOVA using a pretest as a covariate yielded significant differences (p < .01) between groups. The groups receiving training in imagery performed higher than control.

**Conclusion:** The children shown to have more vivid experiences, consistently used imagery in school subjects.

**Further References:**

Hollenberg, C.: Functions of visual imagery. *Child Development,* *41*:1003-1016, 1970.

Riviore, J.L.: Development of reference systems in children. *Perceptual and Motor Skills, 15*:544, 1962.

**Purpose:** To determine if a series of ontogenetic developmental stages for the concept of space can be determined.

**Subjects:** N = 144.

**Methodology:** All subjects were administered the author(s) developed Form Development Test consisting of seven items each of four types of space; topological, affine, projective, and Euclidean. After each stimulus was presented for ten seconds, four possible figures were presented to the subject and it was the subject's task to select the response most similar to the stimulus.

**Results:** Analysis of variance showed significant differences between the types of space, items within types of space, and age levels, but no sex differences.

**Conclusion:** Results show that children developed the concept of topological space later than Piaget and Inhelder's sample reported in 1959. The concept of projective space developed earlier and affine relationships were well established by the age of six years. Euclidean reference systems developed later.

**Further References:**

Newhall, S.M.: Identification by young children of differently oriented visual forms. *Child Development, 8*:105-111, 1937.

Smith, W.F.: Direction orientation in children. *Journal of Genetic Psychology, 42*:154-166, 1933.

Stotland, E.: Exploratory investigations of empathy, in Berkowith (Ed.) *Advances in Experimental Social Psychology,* 1969.

Rubin, K.: Egocentricism in childhood: a unitary construct? *Child Development, 44*:102-110, 1973.

**Purpose:** To examine the nature of correlations among tasks purporting to measure communication, cognition, role taking and ego-centrism in children; and to identify constructs from a group of variables measuring egocentrism and conservation.

**Subjects:** $N = 20$; 10 male/10 female, grades K, 2, 4 and 6.

**Methodology:** Each subject was administered measures of the following: cognitive egocentrism, spatial egocentrism, and communicative egocentrism. Four other variables were also collected: chronological age, mental age (Peabody Picture Vocabulary Test), conservation, and a measure of popularity.

**Results:** Interrater as well as test/retest reliability coefficients ranged from .82 to .98. One dimensional ANOVA showed differences among grades on all four main dependent variables at the .01 level of significance. Factor analysis including chronological age, mental age, cognitive and spatial egocentrism, role taking, conservation, and popularity produced a factor accounting for 56.9 percent of the total variance identified as decentration.

**Conclusion:** An age related centration factor was determined which is felt to reflect the interrelationships between measures of interpersonal egocentrism and conservation.

**Further References:**

Borke, H.: Interpersonal perception of young children: egocentrism or empathy? *Developmental Psychology, 5*:263-269, 1971.

Elkind, D.: Egocentricity of adolescence. *Child Development, 38*: 1025, 1967.

Papalia, D.E.: Status of several conservation abilities across the life-span. *Human Development, 15*:229, 1972.

Piaget and Inhelder: *The Child's Conception of Space.* New York, Humanities Press, 1956.

Rubin, K.: Egocentricism in early and middle childhood. Unpublished dissertation, Pennsylvania State University, 1971.

Rubin, Attewell, Tierney and Tumolo: Development of spatial egocentricism and conservation across the life-span. *Developmental Psychology, 9*:432, 1973.

Shantz and Watson: Developmental study of egocentrism: violation of expectancies. *Psychonomic Science, 18*:93-94, 1970.

Welch, L.: Development of discrimination of form and area. *Journal of Psychology, 7*:37-54, 1939.

Shantz, C. and Smock, C.: Development of distance conservation and the spatial coordinate system. *Child Development, 37*:943-948, 1966.

***Purpose:*** To determine if children who employ the Euclidean coordinate system concept also employ conservation of distance, and if children who are not able to conserve distance are not able to employ the coordinate system.

***Subjects:*** N = 20; 10 male/10 female, ages 6 years 4 months to 7 years 10 months.

***Methodology:*** Five measures were used to test if distance remains constant whether space between two points is filled or empty, and that distance between two points remains identical regardless of the direction of travel. Tests of conservation and use of the coordinate systems included objects as well as drawings. All children received all the tests, one half pictures first, then objects and the reverse order for the second group of children.

***Results:*** The criterion measure for successful performance was passing four of five items for both concepts, conservation and use of the coordinate system. On the tasks using drawings, five children used both concepts and seven children used neither. No child who used the coordinate system did not show distance conservation. Eight children showed conservation of distance, but not the coordinate concept. The same general trends of data were found for subjects tested on objects.

***Conclusion:*** The data seem to support the hypothesis of the developmental priority of distance of conservation to the coordinate system.

***Further References:***

Bratfisch, O.: A further study of the relation between subjective distance and emotional involvement. *Acta Psychologica, 29*:244-255, 1969.

Kershner, J.R.: Conservation of multiple space relations by children: effects of perception and representation. *Journal of Learning Disabilities, 4*:6, 1971.

Kershner, J.R.: Conservation of vertical-horizontal space perception in trainable retarded children. *American Journal of Mental Deficiency*, in press, 1973.

Smith, O.: Judgments of size and distance in photographs. *American Journal of Psychology,* 71:529-538, 1958.

Vandeventer, M.: Development of distance conservation and the spatial coordinate system reconsidered. *Research Bulletin,* Educational Testing Service, 1968.

Yonas, J.: *Development of reference systems.* Paper read at SRCD convention, 1973.

Shantz, C.U., et al.: Spatial abilities and spatial egocentrism in the young child. *Child Development,* 42:171-181, 1971.

**Purpose:** To assess the child's ability to make specific predictions of the location of objects after the child has been moved to various positions in reference to those objects. The hypothesis is that the ability to correctly predict object locations after the child has moved is positively related to his ability to identify object arrangements from a doll's position.

**Subjects:** $N = 48$; 29 males/19 females, three groups of sixteen children, ages 44 months to 60 months, 60 to 71 months and 72 to 78 months.

**Methodology:** Each child was required to predict the location of three objects in a box and then check these predictions by lifting up three of the nine lids in the box top to verify these predictions. This procedure was repeated five times with three of the five trials "real" and two of the five trials "trick." Each child was also required to choose from a set of pictures (taken from different positions around the board), the photograph indicating which picture "shows what the doll sees from there."

**Results:** The dependent variables for the tasks were the number of errors made in predicting the location of the three objects employed, and the relevant verbal statements made by the child immediately following the lifting of each of the three doors. The dependent variable for the doll task was the number of trials failed. A chi-square test ($p < .02$) supports the hypothesis that a significant positive relationship exists between accuracy in predicting location of objects when the child is moved, and when the doll is moved.

**Conclusion:** The ability to predict the location of objects when the child moves is found to emerge prior to, is easier than, and is significantly related to the ability to make predictions from another's view point (in this case the doll's).

**Further References:**

Loofrand, C.: Egocentricism and social interaction in young and old adults. *Aging and Human Development*, 2:21-28, 1971.

Looft, W.R.: Egocentricism and social interaction across the life-span. *Psychological Bulletin*, 78:73-92, 1972.

Shantz and Watson: Assessment of spatial egocentricism through expectancy violation, *Psychonomic Science*, 18:93-94, 1970.

Stafford, R.E.: Sex differences in spatial visualization as evidence of sex linked inheritance. *Perceptual and Motor Skills*, 13:428, 1961.

**Purpose:** To determine the nature of parent-child relationships (father/son, father/daughter; mother/son, mother/daughter; mother/father) on a measure of spatial visualization.

**Subjects:** N = 104 fathers and mothers and their 58 teenage sons and 70 teenage daughters.

**Methodology:** Each subject was administered the Identical Blocks Test, with a conversion to standard scores partialing out age differences.

**Results/Conclusion:** For both parents as well as children performance by males averaged significantly higher. Pearson r's (attenuated) between family members supports the hypothesis that the aptitude for visualizing space has a hereditary component which is transmitted by a sex linked recessive gene located on the X chromosome.

**Further References:**

Bieri, Bradburn and Galinsky: Sex differences in perceptual behavior. *Journal of Personality*, 26:1-12, 1958.

Bock, R.D.: A family study of spatial visualizing ability. *American Psychological Association*, 1967.

Castore and Stafford: Effect of sex role on performance. *Journal of Psychology*, 74:175-180, 1970.

Dolan, II.K.: Further study of the inheritance of structural visualization. *Bulletin 651*, Human Engineering Laboratory, 1962.

Stafford, R.E.: Spatial visualization and quantitative reasoning. One gene or two? *Eastern Psychology Association*. Atlantic City, 1965.

Taylor, R.A.: Analysis of 39 children and their parents with respect to inheritance of structural visualization. *Bulletin*, Human Engineering Laboratory, 1969.

Swanson, R. and Benton, A.: Some aspects of the genetic development of right-left discrimination. *Child Development*, 26:123-133, 1955.

*Purpose:* To gather data and to investigate the use of a right-left discrimination test as a psychodiagnostic instrument in the evaluation of children suspected of suffering from cerebral dysfunction.

*Subjects:* N = 158; ages 5 years 6 months to 9 years 5 months.

*Methodology:* The dependent variables were "verbal symbol" (number of correct responses made) and "discrimination score" number of consistent discriminations disregarding the correctness of the responses with respect to the verbal symbols "right" and "left."

*Results:* The reliability coefficients of test were found to be .67 and .72. No difference in performance between sexes was noted.

*Conclusion:* Right-left discrimination ability has a progressive development through the ages of six through nine years, the growth of the skill beginning at about five years.

**Further References:**

Annenkov, N.I.: The spatial orientation system and its hereditary determination. *Zh Nevropat Psikhiat Korsakov* (Rus.), 69:1514, 1969.

Harris, L.: Children's discrimination of left-right and up-down mirror-images: the effects of stimulus alignment (unpublished paper, 1970).

Rife, D.C.: Heredity and handedness. *Science Monthly*, 73:188-191, 1951.

# PART III

# EXTENDED BIBLIOGRAPHY

# EXTENDED BIBLIOGRAPHY

JOHN ELIOT

NEIL J. SALKIND

## A

Abbe, M.: Temporal effect upon the perception of space. *Japanese Journal of Experimental Psychology,* 4:83-93, 1973.

Abbott, T. K.: *Sight and touch; an attempt to disprove the received (or Berkelian) theory of vision,* London; Longmans, Green, 1864.

Abel, Theodora M.: Tested mentality as related to success in skilled trade training. *Archives of Psychology,* p. 77, 1925.

Abravanel, E.: The development of intersensory patterning with regards to selected spatial dimensions. *Society for Research in Child Development Monography,* 33:118, 1968

Abravanel, E.: Choice for shape vs textural matching by young children. *Perceptual and Motor Skills,* 31:527-533, 1970.

Abravanel, E.: Short-term memory for shapes. *Perceptual and Motor Skills,* 35:419, 1972.

Acredolo and Pick: Intentional memory for spatial location. Paper presented at the SRCD convention, Philadelphia, March 1973.

Adcock, C.: A re-analysis of Slater's spatial judgment research. *Occupational Psychology,* 22:213, 1948.

Adcock and Webberley: Primary mental abilities. *Journal of Genetic Psychology,* 84:229-243, 1971.

Adey and Kerr: Cerebral representation of deep somatic sensibility. *Journal of Comparative Neurology, 100:* 597-625, 1954.

Adkins, C.J.: Verbal estimations of time at four spatial distances. *Perceptual and Motor Skills,* 35:411-8, Oct. 1972.

Aebli, H., Montada, L., and Shneider, U.: *Uber den Egozentrismus des kindes.* Stutgart; Klett, 1968.

Ahr and Youniss: Reasons for class inclusion failure. *Child Development,* 41:131-143, 1970.

Ahrens, R.: Beitrage zur Entwicklung des Physiognomie-und Mimikerkennes. *Zeitschrift fur Experimentelle und Angewandte Psychologie,* 2:412-454, 599-633, 1954. (cited in Gibson, 1969).

Akelaitis, A.J.: Studies on the corpus callosum. *Archives of Neurology and Psychiatry,* 45:788-796, 1941.

Albert and Hecaen: Relative movement perception following unilateral cerebral damage. *Trans American Neurological Association, 96*:200-202, 1971.

Alexander, W.P.: Intelligence: concrete and abstract. *British Journal Psychology Monograph Supplement, 19*:1-177, 1935.

Alexander and Money: Reading disability and the problem of direction sense. *Reading teacher, 20*:404-409, 1967.

Alexander and Money: Studies in direction sense. *Archives General Psychiatry, 10*:337-339, 1964.

Allen, M.: Training in spatial visualization: An examination of strategy change, ATT's, and the factor differentiation hypothesis. Unpublished dissertation, University of California, Berkeley, 1972.

Alley and Snider: Perceptual motor performance of mental retardates. *Developmental Psychology, 2*:110-114, 1970.

Alluisi, E.A.: On the use of information measures in studies of form perception. *Perceptual and Motor Skills, 11*:110-114, 1960.

Alluisi and Hall: Effects of a transphenomenal parameter on the visual perception of form. *Psychonomic Science, 3*:543-544, 1965.

Ambrose, J.A.: The development of the smiling response in early infancy. In B.M. Foss (Ed.), *Determinants of infant behavior*. New York; Wiley, 1961, pp. 179-196.

Ambrose, J.A.: The concept of a critical period for the development of social responsiveness in early human infancy. In B.M. Foss (Ed.), *Determinants of infant behavior, II*. New York; Wiley, 1963, pp. 201-225.

Amen, E.: Individual differences in responses of preschool children to pictures. *Genetic Psychology Monograph, 10*:319-385, 1941.

Amidon and Carey: Why can't five-year-olds understand *Before* and *After? Journal of Verbal Learning and Verbal Behavior*, in press.

Ananiev, B.G.: One basis of spatial discrimination. In B. Simon (Ed.) *Psychology in the Soviet Union*. Stanford University Press, 1957, 131-151.

Anderson, J.E.: The limitations of infant and preschool tests in the measurement of intelligence. *Journal of Psychology 8*:351-379, 1939.

Anderson, J.R.: Immediate and long-term memory for sentences. Stanford University, in preparation.

Anderson, L.D.: The Minnesota mechanical ability tests. *Personnel Journal, 6*, 473-478, 1928.

Anderson, Fruchter, Manuel, Worchel: Survey of research on spatial factors. *AFPTRC Bulletin*, 1954.

Andrew, D.M.: An analysis of the Minnesota vocational test for clerical workers, I, II. *Journal of Applied Psychology, 18*:139-172, 1937.

Andrews, D.H.: *The Conceptualization of Space in Peru*. (Presented at the 65th Annual Meeting of the American Anthropological Association, Pittsburgh, November 19, 1966).

Andrews, D.P.: Perception of contour orientation in the central fovea, Part I: Short Lines. *Vision Research, 7*:975-997, 1967.

Andrieur, C.: Contribution a' l'etude des differences entre hommes et femmes dans la perception spaciale, *l'année psychologique*, *55*:41-60, 1955.

Angell, J.R.: Methods for the determination of mental imagery. *Psychological Review, Monograph Supplement*, *53*:61-101, 1910.

Angell, J.R.: The determination of mental imagery. *Psychological Monograph*, *13*:61-107, 1910.

Angell, J.R.: *et al.*: Report of the committee of the American Psychological Association on the standardizing of procedure in experimental tests. *Psychological Monograph*, *13*: 1910.

Antelman, Olson, Orbach: Orientation-specific mechanisms in the human visual system. *Perceptual Psychology*, *6*:206-8, 1969.

Antonovsky and Ghent: Cross-cultural consistency of children's preferences for the orientation of figures. *American Journal of Psychology*, 77:295-297, 1964.

Appel, K.: Three Studies of Object Conceptualization. Unpublished dissertation, University of Houston, 1971.

Appelle and Goodnow: Haptic and visual judgments of proportion. *Journal of Experimental Psychology*, *84*:47-52, 1970.

Appelle, S.: Perception and discrimination as a function of stimulus orientation. *Psychological Bulletin*, 78:266-278, 1972.

Archibald, Wepman, and Jones: Performance on nonverbal cognitive tests following unilateral cortical injury to right and left hemisphere. *J Nervous and Mental Disabilities*, *145*:25-36, 1967.

Arciszewski, R.A.: Effects of visual perceptual training on Perception ability and reading achievement. Unpublished dissertation, Rutgers, 1968.

Argyle and Williams: Observer—observed, a reversible perspective person-perception. *Sociometry*, *32*:396-412, 1969.

Arnheim, R.: *Art and Visual Perception*. Berkeley, California; University of California Press, 1954.

Arnheim, R.: *Toward a Psychology of Art*. University of California Press, 1966.

Arnheim, R.: *Visual Thinking*. University of California Press, 1969.

Aronson and Rosenbloom: Space perception in early infancy: perception within a common auditory-visual space. *Science*, *172*:1161-1163, 1971.

Arps, G.: A marked case of double inversion. *American Journal of Psychology*, 27:203-216, 1916.

Arrigone and De Renzi: Constructional aproxia and the hemispheric locus lesion. *Cortex*, *1*:170-197, 1964.

Arseni, Voinesco, and Goldenberg: Considerations clinico-statistigues sur le syndrome parietal dan les tureurs cerebrales. *Revue Nuerologique* *99*:621 628, 1958.

Asch and Zimilies: Classification behavior in children of varying age and social class background. *Eastern Psychological Association*, 1969.

Asso and Wyke: Experimental study of the effect of letter reversals on reading. *American Journal of Psychology*, *58* (3 and 4):413-419, 1967.

Asso and Wyke, Discrimination of Spatially confusable letters by Young Children, *Journal of Experimental Child Psychology*, *11*:11-20, 1971.

Atkinson and Sheffrin: Human memory: A proposed system and its control processes. In Spence, *Psychology of Human Learning and Motivation*, Academic Press, 1968.

Attenborough and Farber: The relation between intelligence, mechanical ability, and manual dexterity in special school children. *British Journal of Educational Psychology*, 140-161, 1934.

Attneave, F.: Some informational aspects of visual perception. *Psychological Bulletin, 61*:183-194, 1954.

Attneave, F.: Symmetry, information, and memory for patterns. *American Journal of Psychology, 68*:209-222, 1955.

Attneave and Arnoult: The quantitative study of shape and pattern perception. *Psychological Bulletin, 53*:452-471, 1956.

Attneave, F.: Transfer of experience with a class-schema to identification learning with patterns and shapes. *Journal of Experimental Psychology, 54*:81-88, 1957.

Attneave and Olson: Discriminability of stimuli varying in physical and retinal orientation. *Journal of Experimental Psychology, 74*:149-157, 1967.

Attneave and Reid: Voluntary control of frame of reference and slope equivalence under head rotation. *Journal of Experimental Psychology, 78*:153-159, 1968.

Attneave, F.: Triangles as ambiguous figures. *American Journal of Psychology, 81*:447-453, 1968.

Attneave and Benson: Spatial coding of tactual stimulation. *Journal of Experimental Psychology, 81*:216-222, 1969.

Attneave and Frost: Determination of perceived tridimensional orientation. *Perception and Psychophysics, 6*:391-6, 1969.

Attneave, F.: Multistability in perception. *Scientific American, 225*:65-71, 1971.

Attneave, F.: Representation of physical space. In Melton and Martin, *Coding Processes in Human Memory*, V. H. Winston, 1972.

Attneave, F.: How do you know? *American Psychologist, 29*:493-499, 1974.

Atwood, G.: An experimental study of visual imagination and memory. *Cognitive of Psychology, 2*:290-299, 1971.

Ausubel, D.P.: Socioempathy as a function of sociometric status in an adolescent group. *Human Relations, 8*:75-84, 1955.

Avery and Day: Basis of the horizontal-vertical illusion. *Journal of Experimental Psychology, 81*:376-380, 1969.

Ayres and Harcum: Direction response-bias in reproducing brief visual patterns. *Perceptual and Motor Skills*, Southern University Press, *14*:155-165, 1962.

Ayres, L.P.: Psychological tests in vocational guidance. *Journal of Educational Psychology, 4*:232-237, 1913.

# B

Bagby, J.: Dominance in binocular rivalry in Mexico and the United States. *Journal of Abnormal Social Psychology, 4:*331-334, 1957.

Bagrash, Kerr and Thomas: Patterns of spatial integration in the detection of compound visual stimuli. *Vision Research, 11:*655-645, 1971.

Bagrash, Kerr and Thomas: *Spatial Interaction in Compound Visual Stimuli,* Los Angeles, Western Psychological Association, 1970.

Bahrick and Bahrick, P.: Independence of verbal and visual codes of the same stimuli. *Journal of Experimental Psychology, 91:*344-6, 1971.

Bailey, S.: *Review of Berkeley's Theory of Vision.* London; J. Ridway, 1842.

Bain, A.: *The Senses and the Intellect.* (4th Ed.) New York; Appleton, 1894.

Baird, J.C.: Area and distance estimation of single and multiple stimuli. *Vision Research, 5:*661-678, 1965.

Baird, J.C.: *Psychophysical Analysis of Visual Space.* Pergamon, 1970.

Baird, Romer and Stein: Test of a cognitive theory of psychopysics—size discrimination. *Perceptual and Motor Skills, 30:*495-501, 1970.

Bakan, P.: Resting EEG alpha and asymmetry of reflective lateral eye movements. *Nature, 223:*975-976, 1969.

Bakan and Shotland: Lateral eye movement, reading speed and visual attention. *Psychonomic Science, 15:*93-94, 1969.

Baker, Voelker and Crockett: *Detroit Mechanical Aptitudes Examination for Boys.* Bloomington, Ill.; Public School Publishing Company, 1928.

Baker and Wapner: *Effects of Degree of Stimulus Structure and Repeated Measurement Upon Space Localization.* San Francisco, American Psychological Association, 1968.

Balinski, B.: Analysis of mental factors of various age groups from nine to sixty. *Genetic Psychology, Monograph, 33:*191-234, 1941.

Ball and Tronick: Infant responses to impending collision: Optical and real. *Science, 171:*818-820, 1971.

Ballinger and Sundberg: *Drawings by Nepalese children: notes on content, symbolism, and spatial concepts.* Oregon; The Creative Education, Inc., 1969, 1-22.

Balter and Fogarty: Intra and intersensory matching by nursery school children. *Perceptual and Motor Skills, 33:* 467-72, 1971.

Banister and Smith: Vibration-induced white fingers and manipulative dexterity, *Journal of IND Medicin, 29:*264-7, July 1972.

Bannatyne and Wichiarajote: Hemispheric dominance, handedness, mirror imaging and auditory sequencing. *Exceptional Children, 36:*27-36, 1969.

Banta, T.J.: Tests for the evaluation of early childhood education: The Cincinnati autonomy test battery. In J. Hellmuth *Cognitive studies. Vol. 1.* New York; Brunner/Mazel, 1970, 424-490.

Barden, H.E.: The Stenquist mechanical aptitude test as a measure of mechanical ability. *Journal Juvenile Research, 17:*94-104, 1933.

Barlow, J.S.: Vestibular and nondominant parietal lobe disorders. *Disorders of the Nervous System, 31:*667-673, 1970.

Barratt, E.S.: An analysis of verbal reports of spatial-problem solving. Unpublished Ph.D. Thesis, University of Texas, 1952.

Barratt, E.S.: Space-visualization factors related to temperament traits. *Journal of Psychology, 39*:279-287, 1955.

Barratt, P.E.: Use of EEG in the study of imagery. *British Journal of Psychology, 47*:101-114, 1956.

Barratt and Fruchter: *Chair-Window Test*, 1953.

Barrett, T.C.: Visual discrimination tasks as predictors of first grade reading achievements. *Reading Teacher, 18*:276-282, 1965.

Barron: Psychology of imagination. *Scientific American, 199*:150-177, 1958.

Bartlett: The revelance of visual imagery in the process of thinking, III, *British Journal of Psychology, 18*:23-29, 1927.

Bartley and DeHardt: A further factor in determining nearness as a function of lateral orientation in pictures. *The Journal of Psychology, 50*:53-57, 1960.

Bartley and Thompson: A further study of horizontal asymmetry in the perception of pictures. *Perceptual and Motor Skills, 9*:135-138, 1959.

Barton, K.: Block manipulation by children as a function of social reinforcement, anxiety, arousal and ability pattern. *Child Development, 42*:817-826, 1971.

Barton, A.K.: Picture versus word and relevant value 'relatedness' in rule-learning problems. *Journal of Experimental Psychology, 96*:208-10, November 1972.

Barton, Goodglass and Shai: Differential recognition. *Perceptual and Motor Skills, 21*:431-437, 1965.

Bartsch, Nesselroade and Baltes: Cultural change and adolescent intellectual development. *1972 Second Conference on Research in Child Development*, Williamsburg, Va.

Bartz, B.S.: Maps in the classroom, *Journal of Geography, 69*:18-24, 1970.

Basser, L.S.: Hemiplegia of early onset and the faculty of speech with special reference to the effects of hemispherectomy. *Brain, 85*:427-460, 1962.

Bastien, H.C.: On the specific gravity of different parts of the human brain. *Journal of Mental Science, 56*:29, 1866.

Bayley, N.: Behavioral correlates of mental growth: birth to thirty-six years. *American Psychologist, 23*:1-17, 1968.

Bayley, N.: Development of mental abilities. In Mussen: *Carmichael's Manual of Child Psychology*, Wiley, 1970, 1163-1210.

Beach, C.K.: Selection of pupils in vocational-industrial schools. *Industrial Arts and Vocational Education, 32*:360-362, 1943.

Beamer, Edmonson and Strother: Improving the selection of linotype trainees. *Journal of Applied Psychology, 32*:130-134, 1948.

Bearison and Sigel: Hierarchical attributes for categorization. *Perceptual and Motor Skills, 27*:147-53, 1968.

Bearison, D.: Measurement in acquisition of conservation. *Developmental Psychology, 1*:653-660, 1969.

Bechinger, Kongehl and Kornhuber: Visual perception of length stimulus duration and information transmission. *Pfluegers Archives, 332*:R97, 1972.

Beck, J.: Perceptual grouping produced by changes in orientation and shape. *Science, 154*:538-540, 1966.

Beck, R.: *Spatial Meaning and the Properties of the Environment.* Research Paper, 109, Department of Geography, University of Chicago, 1967.

Bee and Walker: Experimental modification of lag between perceiving and performing. *Psychonometric Science, 11*:127-128, 1968.

Beery, K.E.: From reproduction as a function of complexity. *Perceptual and Motor Skills, 26(1)*:219-222, 1968.

Beery, K.E.: Geometric form reproduction: Relationship to chronogical and mental age. *Perceptual and Motor Skills, 26(1)*:247-250, 1968.

Begelman, D.A.: The role of retinal orientation in the egocentric organization of a visual stimulus. *The Journal of General Psychology, 79*:283-289, 1968.

Beilin and Franklin: Logical operations in area and length measurement. *Child Development, 33*:607-618, 1962.

Beilin, H.: Perceptual-cognitive conflict in the development of an invariant area concept. *Journal of Experimental Child Psychology, 1*:208-226, 1964.

Beilin, H.: Learning and operational convergence in logical thought development. *Journal of Experimental Child Psychology, 2*:317-339, 1965.

Beilin, H.: Feedback and infralogical strategies in invariant area conceptualization. *Journal of Experimental Child Psychology, 3*:267-278, 1966.

Beilin, H.: Development of physical concepts. In Mischel: *Cognitive Development and Epistemology,* Academic Press, 1971.

Beinhoff, W.: Technishces Verstandnis and Raumvorstellung (Technical understanding and space thinking). *Industrial Psychotechnology, 10*:16-22, 1933.

Bell, J.C.: Mechanical aptitude and intelligence. In J.C. Bell (Ed), *Contributions to Education, Vol. 1.* New York Society for the Experimental Study of Education, Yonkers; World Book Company, 1924.

Bell, J.R.: Prediction of Success in Industrial Drafting. Unpublished Master's Dissertation, Los Angeles, University of California, 1949.

Beller, H.K.: Parallel and serial stages in matching. *Journal of Experimental Psychology, 84*:213-219, 1970.

Bem, S.: Children's task comprehension. *Developmental Psychology, 22*:351-358, 1970.

Bender, L.: A visual motor Gestalt test and its clinical use. *Research Monograph of the American Orthopsychiatric Association,* 1938.

Bennett and Cruikshank: *A Summary of Manual and Mechanical Ability Tests.* New York. Psychological Corporation, 1942.

Bennett, G.K.: *Test of Mechanical Comprehension, Form AA. Manual.* New York; Psychological Corporation, 1951.

Bennett, G.K.: et al.: *Differential Aptitudes Test Manual,* 3d edition, New York, Psychological Corporation, 1959.

Bennett, Seashore, and Wesman: *Fifth Research Supplement to Differential Aptitude Test Manual.* Psychological Corporation, 1951.

Benson, D.F.: Graphic orientation disorders of left-handed children. *Journal of Learning Disabilities,* 3:126-131, 1970.

Benson and Geschwind: Developmental gerstmann syndrome. *Neurology,* 20:293-8, 1970.

Benton and Hutcheon: Arithmetic ability, finger-localization capacity and right-left discrimination in normal and defective children. *American Journal of Orthopsychiatry,* 21:756-766, 1951.

Benton, A.L.: *Right-left Discrimination and Finger Localization.* New York; Hoeber-Harper, Inc., 1959.

Benton and Kemble: Right-left orientation and reading disability. *Psychiatric et. Neurology* (Basel), 139:49, 1960.

Benton, A.L.: Clinical symptomatology in right and left hemisphere: discussion. In Mountcastle, V.B. (Ed) *Interhemispheric Relations and Cerebral Dominance,* Baltimore; The Johns Hopkins Press, 1962, 253-263.

Benton, A.L.: Hemispheric cerebral dominance. *Israel Journal of Medical Science,* 6:294-303, 1970.

Benton, A.L.: The 'minor' hemisphere. *Journal of the History of Medicine and Allied Science,* 27:5-14, 1972.

Benton, A.L.: *Hemispheric Participation in the Perception of Direction.* International Neuropsychological Society Convention, 1973.

Benton and Hecaen: Stereoscoptic vision in patients with unilateral cerebral disease. *Neurology, 1970,* 20:1084-1088, 1970.

Benton, Levin, and Varney: Tactile perception of direction in normal subjects: implications for hemispheric cerebral dominance. *Neurology,* in press.

Benton and McCann: Dyslexia and dominance. *Journal of Pediatric Ophthalmology,* 6:220, 1969.

Ben-Yishay, Diller and Mandleberg: Similarities and differences in block design performance between older normal and brain-injured persons: a task analysis, *Journal of Abnormal Psychology,* 78:17-25, 1971.

Ben-Yishay, Diller and Mandleberg: Similarities and differences in block design performance between older normal and brain-injured persons: a task analysis. *Journal of Abnormal Psychology,* 26:277-291, 1972.

Berdie and Sutter: Predicting success of engineering students. *Journal of Educational Psychology,* 41:184-190, 1950.

Berger, Cuilford and Christensen: A factor—analytic study of planning abilities. *Psychological Monograph,* 71(6):435, 1957.

Berger, Bernstein, Klein, Cohen and Lucas: Effects of aging and pathology on the factorial structure of intelligence. *Journal Consulting Psychology,* 199-207, 1964.

Bergson, H.: *Time and Free Will,* MacMillan, 1912.

Bergson, H.: *Creative Evolution,* MacMillan, 1960.

Berkeley, G.: *Essay Towards a New Theory of Vision and Other Select Philosophical Writings.* New York; E.P. Dutton, 1910.

Berkeley, G.: *Principles of Human Knowledge,* William Benton, 1952. (1710)

Berlyne, D.E.: Uniformity in varity-extension to three-element visual patterns and nonverbal measures, *Canadian Journal of Psychology,* 26:277-91, September 1972.

Berry, J.W.: Ecological and cultural factors in spatial perceptual development. *Canadian Journal of Behavioral Science,* 3:324-336, 1971.

Berzonsky, M.: Interdependence of Inhelder and Piaget's model of logical thinking. *Developmental Psychology,* 4(3):469-476, 1971.

Betak, J.: Two-dimensional syntax and visual cues in aerial photographs. *Remote Sensing Laboratory,* Northwestern University, 1969.

Bettman, Stern, Whitsell and Gofman: Cerebral dominance in developmental dyslexia. *Archives of Ophthalmology,* 1967.

Bever, Mehler and Epstein: What children do in spite of what they know. *Science, 162:*921-924, 1968.

Bialystok and Olson: Why are nouns acquired before adjectives? in preparation.

Bieri and Messerley: Differences in perceptual and cognitive behavior as a function of experience. *Journal Consulting Psychology,* 21:217-221, 1957.

Bierwisch, M.: Some semantic universals of German adjectivals. *Foundations of Language, 39:*1-13, 1967.

Bijou, S.W.: Studies in the experimental development of left-right concepts in retarded children using fading techniques. To be published in *International Review of Research in Mental Retardation, Vol. III,* 1968.

Bing, E.: Effect of childrearing practices on development of different cognitive abilities. *Child Development,* 34:631-648, 1963.

Binns, H.A.: Comparison between the judgments of individuals skilled in the textile trade and the natural judgments of untrained adults and children. *Journal Textile Institute,* 17:1615-1641, 1926.

Birch and Bitterman: Reinforcement and learning: The process of sensory integration. *Psychological Review,* 56:292-308, 1949.

Birch and Bitterman: Sensory integration and cognitive theory. *Psychological Review,* 58:355-361, 1951.

Birch and Lefford: Intersensory development in children. *Monographs of the Society for Research in Child Development,* 28:5, Serial No. 89, 1963.

Birch and Belmont: Auditory—visual integration in normal and retarded readers. *American Journal of Orthopsychiatry,* 34:852-861, 1964.

Birch and Belmont: Auditory—visual integration, intelligence and reading ability in school children. *Perceptual and Motor Skills,* 20:295 305, 1965.

Birch and Lefford: Visual differentiation, intersensory integration, and voluntary motor control. *Society* for *Research in Child Development Monograph,* 1967, 110.

Bird and Pechstein: General intelligence, machine shop work, and educational guidance in junior high school. *School Review, 24*:782-786, 1921.

Bird, V.A.: A study in the correlation of general intelligence and progress in learning machine shop work as related to the problem of educational guidance. *Industrial Education Magazine, 24*:67-69, 1922.

Bishop, Gayton and Bassett: An investigation of the efficacy of the Frostig program for the development of visual perception. *Pediatrics, 50*:154-7, July 1972.

Bishop, H.E.: Innateness and learning in the visual perception of direction. Unpublished dissertation, University of Chicago, 1959.

Blackwell, A.M.: A comparative investigation into the factors involved in mathematical ability in boys and girls. *British Journal of Educational Psychology, 10*:212-22, 1940.

Blade, M.: Experiment in visualization. *Journal of Engineering Drawing, 13*: 20-30, 1949.

Blade and Watson: Increase in spatial visualization test scores during engineering study. *Psychological Monographs, 69*:12, 1955.

Blair, H.: Some conceptions regarding egocentric visual location. *Archives Ophthalmology, 18*:415-427, 1937.

Blakemore and Campbell: On the existence of neurones in the human visual system selectively sensitive to the orientation and size of retinal images. *Journal of Physiology, 203*:237-260, 1969.

Blane, H.: Space perception among unilaterally paralyzed children and adolescents. Unpublished dissertation, University of Michigan, 1957.

Blane, H.: Space perception among unilaterally paralyzed children and adolescents. *Journal of Experimental Psychology, 63*:244-247, 1962.

Blank and Bridges: Cross-modal transfer in nursery school children. *Journal of Comparative Physiology and Psychology, 85*: 277-282, 1964.

Blau, A.: *The Master Hand: A Study of the Origin and Meaning of Right and Left Sidedness and its Relation to Personality and Language.* Research Monograph No. 5, New York; American Orthopsychiatric Association, Inc., 1946.

Blaut and Stea: *Place Perception Research Reports.* Clark University, 1969.

Blaut, McCleary and Blaut: Environmental mapping in young children, *Environment and Behavior, 2*:335-347, 1970.

Blom, E.C.: Mirror-Writing. *Psychological Bulletin, 25*:582-594, 1968.

Blood, E.T.: The language of space. *Journal of Social Issues, 13*:47-53, 1957.

Bock, R.D.: Family study of spatial visualization ability. *American Psychologist, 22*:571, 1967.

Bock and Vandenberg: Components of heritable variation in mental test scores. In S.G. Vandenberg, *Progress in Human Behavior Genetics,* Johns Hopkins Press, 1968.

Bock and Kolakowski: Further evidence of sex-linked major gene influence on human spatial visualization ability. *American Journal of Human Genetics, 25*:1-14, 1973.

Bodian, D.: Discussion, In V.B. Mountcastle, *Interhemispheric relations and Cerebral Dominance*, Johns Hopkins Press, 1962, pages 25-26.

Bodis-Wollner: Visual acuity and contrast sensitivity in patients with cerebral lesion. *Science, 178*:769-71, November 1972.

Boe, B.L.: Study of ability of secondary school pupils to perceive place sections of solids, *Mathematics Teacher*, April 1968.

Boehm, A.: Development of comparative concepts in primary school-children. Unpublished dissertation, Columbia University, 1966.

Bogartz, R.: Abstraction. Unpublished manuscript, University of Massachusetts, 1973.

Bogen, Fisher and Vogel: Cerebral commissurotomy: A second case report. *Journal of the American Medical Association, 194*:1328-1329, 1965.

Bogen, J. E.: The other side of the brain 11: an appositional mind. *Bulletin of The Los Angeles Neurological Societies, 34*:135-162, 1969.

Boguslavsky, G.W.: Psychological research in Soviet education. *Science, 125*:3254, May 1957.

Bond, C.L.: *The Auditory and Speech Characteristics of poor readers.* Teachers College Contributions to Education, 1935, p. 657.

Bonnardel, R.: Liaisons existant entre tests verbaux et tests de visualization. Etude portant sur de jeunes apprentis (Relations between verbal and spatial tests. A supporting study on young apprentices). *Travail hum, 9*: 195-200, 1946.

Book, H.M.: A psychophysiological analysis of sex differences. *Journal Social Psychology, 3*:434-461, 1932.

Book and Meadows: Sex differences in 5925 high school seniors in 10 psychological tests. *Journal of Applied Psychology, 12*:58-81, 1928.

Boone and Landes: Left-right discrimination in hemiplegic patients. *Archives of Physical Medicine and Rehabilitation, 49*, 1968.

Boos, R.W.: Dominance and control: relation to reading achievement. *Journal of Educational Research, 63*:466-470, 1970.

Borg, W.: Some factors relating to art school success. *Journal of Educational Research, 43*:376-384, 1950.

Borich and Bauman: Convergent and discriminant validation of the French and Guilford-Zimmerman spatial orientation and spatial visualization factors. *Educational and Psychological Measurement, 32*:1029-1033, 1972.

Boring, E.G.: *Sensation and perception in the history of experimental psychology.* New York; D. Appleton-Century, 1942.

Borke, H.: Chandler and Greenspan's, Ersatz Egocentrism, a rejoinder. *Developmental Psychology, 7*:107-109, 1972.

Borow, H.: Growth and present status of occupational testing. *Journal of Consulting Psychology, 8*:70-79, 1944.

Botzum, W.: Factorial study of reasoning and closure factors. *Psychometrica, 16*: 361-386, 1951.

Boulding, K.: *The Image.* University of Michigan Press, 1963.

Bowen, Hoehn and Yahr: Parkinsonism—alterations in spatial orientation as determined by a route-walking test. *Neuropsychologia, 10*:355-61, September 1972.

Bower, G.: Organizational factors in memory. *Cognitive Psychology, 1*:18-46, 1970.

Bower, G.: Analysis of a Mnemanic device. *American Scientist, 58*: 496-510, 1970.

Bower, T.G.R.: The visual world of infants. *Scientific American, 215*:80-92, 1966.

Bower, T.G.R.: The object in the world of the infant. *Scientific American, 225*:30-38, 1971.

Bower, T.G.R.: Stimulus variables determining spatial perception, *Science, 149*:88-89, 1965.

Bower and Paterson: Separation of place, movement, and object in the world of the infant. *Journal of Experimental Child Psychology, 15*:161-168, 1973.

Bower, Broughton and Moore (Harvard): Development of the object concept as manifested in changes in the tracking behavior of infants between 7 and 20 weeks of age. *Journal of Experimental Child Psychology, 11*: 182-193, 1971.

Bower, T.G.R.: *Development in Infancy*. Freeman, 1974.

Bower: The role of visual imaginery in reasoning. *Journal of Educational Psychology, 31*:436-446, 1948.

Bowers, H.: Factors influencing visual imagery for letter groups. *American Journal of Psychology, 44*:775-779, 1932.

Bowers, H.: Studies in visual imagery. *American Journal of Educational Psychology, 43*:216-239, 1931.

Bowers, H.: The role of visual imagery in reasoning. *British Journal cf Psychology, 25*:436-446, 1935.

Bowman, H.: The effect of practice on dextality types. *Journal of Psychology, 40*:117-120, 1928.

Boyd, R.: Tables of the weights of the human body and internal organs in the sane and insane of both sexes at various ages arranged from 2,114 post-mortum examinations, *Philosophical Transactions, 151*:241-262, 1861.

Boyd and Randle: Factor analysis of Frostig developmental test of visual perception. *Journal Learning Disabilities, 3*:253-255, 1970.

Bradbury, D.E.: An application of the Dexcoeudres performance tests to fifty-seven American-born four and five-year-old children. *Child Development, 4*:79-89, 1933.

Bradley, D.J.: The ability of black groups to produce recognizable patterns on the 7-square test. *Journal of National Institute Personnel Research, 8*:142-4, 1960.

Bradshaw and Wallace: Models for processing and identification of faces. *Perception and Psychological Physics, 9*:443-448, 1971.

Bradway and Robinson: Significant IQ changes in twenty-five years: A follow-up. *Journal Educational Psychology, 52*:74-79, 1961.

Brain, R.: Visual disorientation with special reference to lesions of the right cerebral hemisphere (from the Neurological Department, London Hospital) *Brain, 64*:244-272, 1941.

Braine, L.G.: Asymmetries of pattern perception observed in Israelis. *Neuropsychologia, 6*:73-88, 1968.

Braine, M.: The ontology of certain logical operations. *Psychological Monographs,* p. 475, 1959.

Brainerd, C.J.: Continuity and discontinuity hypotheses in studies of conservation. *Developmental Psychology, 3*:225-228, 1970.

Brainerd and Allen: Experimental inductions of the conservation of first-order quantitative invariants. *Psychological Bulletin, 75*:128-144, 1971.

Brainerd and Allen: Training and generalization of density conservation. *Child Development, 42*:693-704, 1971.

Brainerd, C.J.: Proportionality scheme in children and adults. *Developmental Psychology, 5*:469-476, 1971.

Brainerd, C.J.: Structures of thought in middle-childhood. *Annual Meeting on Structural Learning,* 1972.

Brand, J.: Classification without identification in visual search, *Journal of Experimental Psychology, 23*:178-186, 1971.

Braunstein, M.L.: Perception of rotation in figures with rectangular and trapezoidal features. *Journal of Experimental Psychology, 91*:25-29, 1971.

Brebner, Shephard and Cairney: Spatial relationships and S-R compatibility. *Acta Psychology (AMST), 36*:1-15, 1972.

Brewer, W.F.: Visual memory, verbal encoding and hemispheric localization. *Cortex, 5*:145-151, 1969.

Bridgman and Smith: Bilateral neural integration in visual perception after section of the corpus callosum. *Journal of Comparative Neurology, 83*: 57-68, 1945.

Brinkman, E.H.: Programmed instruction as a technique for improving spatial visualization. *Journal of Applied Psychology, 50*:179-184, 1966.

Brinkman and Kuypers: Splitbrain monkeys: cerebral control of ipsilateral and contralateral arm, hand, and finger movements. *Science, 176*:536-539, 1972.

Broadbent, D.E.: Role of auditory localization in attention and memory span. *Journal of Experimental Psychology, 47*:191-196, 1954.

Broadhurst, J.C.: Prediction of success in vocational technical courses. *Industrial Arts and Vocational Education, 35*:58-59, 1946.

Broadhurst, J.C.: *A Differential Prediction of Success in Vocational-Technical and Vocational-Industrial Courses in a Vocational High School.* Unpublished Doctor's Dissertation, New York University, 1949.

Broca, P.: Remarques sur le seige de la faculte du langage articule, suives d'une observation d'aphemie. *Bulletin of Society of Anatomy of Paris, 6*:330-357, 1861.

Brodzinski, Jackson and Overton: Effects of perceptual shielding in the development of spatial perspectives. *Child Development, 43*:1041-1046, 1972.

Brooks, L.: Suppression of visualization by reading. *Quarterly Journal of Experimental Psychology, 19*:289-299, 1967.

Brooks, L.: Spatial and verbal components of the act of recall. *Canadian Journal of Psychology, 22*:349-368, 1968.

Brooks, L.: An extension of the conflict between visualization and reading. *Quarterly Journal of Experimental Psychology, 22*:91-96, 1970.

Brooks, L.: Visual and verbal processes in internal representation, in Chase, W.G. *Human Information Processing,* Academic Press, 1973.

Broverman, Broverman, Vogel, Palmer and Klaiber: Automalization, cognitive style and physical development. *Child Development, 35*:1343-1359, 1964.

Broverman, Klaiber, Kobayaski, and Vogel: Role of activation and inhibition in sex differences in cognitive abilities. *Psychological Review, 75*: 23-50, 1968.

Brower, D.: Experimental study of imagery. *Journal of General Psychology, 38*:199-200, 1947.

Brown and Hopkins: Interaction of the auditory and visual modalities. *Journal of the Acoustical Society of America, 41*:1-7, 1967.

Brown and Campione: Recognition memory for perceptually similar pictures in preschool child. *Journal of Experimental Psychology, 95*:55-62, September 1972.

Brown and Ghiselli: The Relationship between the predictive power of tests for trainability and for job proficiency. *Journal of Applied Psychology, 36*:370-372, 1952.

Brown, F.: Effect of experimental course in geometry on ability to visualize in three-dimensions. Unpublished dissertation, University of Illinois, 1954.

Brown, Hitchcock and Michels: Quantitative studies in form perception: an evaluation of the role of selected stimulus parameters. *Perceptual and Motor Skills, 14*:519-529, 1962.

Brown and Owen: The metrics of visual form methodological dyspepsia. *Psychological Bulletin, 68*(4):243-259, 1967.

Brown, T.: *Lectures on the philosophy of human mind.* Andover; M. Newman, 1822.

Brown and Stephenson: A test of theory of two factors. *British Journal of Psychology, 23*:352-370, 1933.

Bruell and Peszcynski: Perception of verticality in hemiplegic patients in relation to rehabilitation. *Clinical Orthopaedics, 12*:124-130, 1958.

Brumbaugh, D.: Ability of children to associate a solid with its representation. *Arithmetic Teacher,* January 1971.

Bruner, Miller and Zimmerman: Discriminative skill and matching in perceptual recognition. *Journal of Experimental Psychology, 49*:187-192, 1955.

Bruner, Bresson, Morj and Piaget: Logique et perception. *Etudes d'Epistemologie Genetique*, 1958.

Bruner, J.S.: How we learn and how we remember. *Harvard Alumni Bulletin, 66*:166, 1963.

Bruner, J.S.: The course of cognitive growth. *American Psychology, 19*:1-15, 1965

Bruner, J.S.: *On Knowing*. Harvard University Press, 1965.

Bruner, J.S., Olver, R.R., and Greenfield, P.M., et al.: *Studies in cognitive growth*. New York; Wiley, 1966.

Bruner, J.: *Hand, eye and mind*. Paper read at Society for Research in Child Development meetings, New York, March 1967.

Brunswick, E.: Ratiomorphic models of perception and thinking. *In proceedings of the 14 International Congress of Psychology*, Montreal, 1954.

Brush, E.N.: Mechanical ability as a factor in engineering aptitude. *Journal of Applied Psychology, 25*:300-312, 1941.

Bryant, P.E.: Perception and memory of the orientation of visually presented lines by children. *Nature, 229*:1331-1332, 1969.

Bryden, M.: Tachistoscopic recognition, handedness and cerebral dominance. *Neuropsychologia, 3*:1-8, 1965.

Bryden, M.P.: Left-right differences in tachistoscopic recognition as a function of familiarity and pattern orientation. *Journal of Educational Psychology, 84*(1):120-122, 1970.

Bryden, M.P.: Auditory-visual and sequential-spatial matching in relation to reading ability. *Child Development, 43*:824-32, September 1972.

Buchsbaum and Fedio: Hemispheric differences in evoked potentials to verbal and nonverbal stimuli. *Psychology and Behavior, 5*:207-210, 1970.

Buckley, F.: Preliminary report on IQ. of patients with Turner's Syndrome. *British Journal of Psychiatry, 119*:513-4, 1971.

Bugelski, B.R.: Words and things and images. *American Psychologist, 25*:1002-1012, 1970.

Bunge, J.V.: IBM program for generating artificial stereograms. *Behavioral Science, 12*:344, 1967.

Burke, H.R.: Ravens progressive Matrices: Review and Critical Evaluation. *Journal Genetic Psychology, 93*:199-228, 1958.

Burklen, K.: *Blindenpsychologie*. Barth, 1924.

Burns and Cavey: Age differences in emphatic ability. *Canadian Journal of Psychology, 11*:227-230, 1957.

Burns, R.B.: Age and mental ability: Retesting with thirty-three years interval. *British Journal of Educational Psychology, 36*:116, 1966

Burt and John: A factorial analysis of Terman Binet tests. *British Journal of Educational Psychology, 12*:117 127, 156-161, 1942.

Burt, C.: The structure of the mind: A review of the results of factor analysis. *British Journal of Educational Psychology, 19*:176-199, 1949.

Burt C.: The genetic determination of differences in intelligence: a study of monozygotic twins reared together and apart. *British Journal Psychology, 57*:137-153, 1966.

Buswell, G.: *How People Look at Pictures.* University of Chicago Press, 1935.

Butler, J.: Visual discrimination of shape by humans. *Quarterly Journal of Experimental Psychology, 16*:272-276 1964.

Butt, A.S.: *The Differentiation of Reasoning Abilities at Adolescence.* Ph.D. Thesis, University of London, 1957.

Butters, Barton and Brody: Role of the right parietal lobe in the mediation of cross-model associations and reversible operations in space. *Cortex, 6*:174-190, 1970.

Butters, Samuels and Goodglass: Short-term visual and auditory memory disorders after parietal and frontal lobe damage. *Cortex, 6*:440-459, 1970.

Butters and Barton: Effect of parietal lobe damage on the performance of reversible operations in space. *Neuropsychologia, 8*:205-214, 1972.

Butters, Soeldner and Fedio: Comparison of parietal and frontal lobe spatial deficits in man: Extrapersonal vs. personal (Egocentric) space. *Perceptual and Motor Skills, 34*:27-34, 1972.

Buxton, C.: The application of multiple factorial methods to the study of motor abilities. *Psychometrika, 3*:85-93, 1938.

## C

Cairns and Steward: Young children's orientation of letters as a function of axis of symmetry and stimulus alignment. *Child Development, 41*:993-1002, 1970.

Caldwell, E.M.: *A Case of Spatial Inability in a Cerebral Palsied Child.* Published by the British Council for the Welfare of Spastics, 1956.

Cameron, P.: Introversion and ego-centricity among the aged. *Journal of Gerontology, 22*:465-468, 1967.

Campbell, A.: Some determinants of the difficulty of nonverbal classification items. *Educational and Psychological Measurement, 21*:899-913, 1961.

Campbell, Kruskal and Wallace: Seating aggregation as an index of attitude. *Sociometry, 29*, 1966.

Campbell and Green: Optical and retinal factors affecting visual resolution. *Journal of Physiology, 181*:576-593, 1965.

Campbell, Kulikowski and Levinson: The effect of orientation on the visual resolution of gratings. *Journal of Physiology, 187*:427-436, 1966.

Campbell and Kulikowski: Orientational selectivity of the human visual system. *Journal of Physiology, 187*:437-445, 1966.

Campbell, Carpenter and Levinson: Visibility of aperiodic patterns compared with that of sinusiodal gratings. *Journal of Physiology, 204*:283-298, 1969.

Campbell and Maffie: Electrophysiological evidence for the existence of orientation and size detectors in the human visual system. *Journal of Physiology, 207*:635-652, 1970.

Campbell, Nachmias and Jukes: Spatial-frequency discrimination in human vision. *Journal of the Optical Society of America, 60*:555-559, 1970.

Campbell, G.: Programmed learning in drawing. *Dissertation Abstracts, 30*(6):2354, 1969.

Campos, Langer, and Krowitz: Cardiac responses on the visual cliff in pre-locomotor infants. *Science, 170*:196-197, 1970.

Carbonneau, M.: Apprentissage de la notion de conservation de surface. Unpublished dissertation, University of Montreal, 1966.

Carey, N: Factors in the mental processes of school children. *British Journal of Psychology*, 7:453-490, 1915.

Carey, S.: Syntactic and Referential Aspects of Linguistic Encoding. Unpublished Honor's Thesis. Harvard University, 1964.

Carmon and Dyson: New instrumentation for research on tactile sensitivity and discrimination. *Cortex, 3*:406-418, 1967.

Carmon and Benton: Tactile perception of direction and number in patients with unilateral cerebral disease. *Neurology, 19*:525-532, 1969.

Carmon and Bechtoldt: Dominance of the right cerebral hemisphere for stereopsis. *Neuropsychologia*, 7:29-39, 1969.

Carmon, Harishanu, Lowinger, and Lavy: Asymmetries in hemispheric blood volume and cerebral dominance. *Behavioral Biology*, 7:853-859, 1972

Carr, H.: *An Introduction to Space Perception.* Longmans Green, 1935.

Carroll, J.B.: *Language and Thought.* Prentice-Hall, 1964.

Carterette, E.: *Brain Function: Speech, Language, and Communication.* University of California Press, Los Angeles, 1966.

Case and Ruch: *Survey of Spatial Relations Ability, Form A: Revised Manual.* Los Angeles, California Test Bureau, 1944.

Case, H.: Selection of aircraft engineering draftsmen and designers. *Journal of Applied Psychology, 31*:583-588, 1947.

Cashdan, S.: Visual and haptic form discrimination under conditions of successive stimulation. *Journal of Experimental Psychology*, 76:215-218, 1968.

Cassel, R.H.: The effect of mental age and etiology on two factors in form board performance. *Journal of Clinical Psychology*, 5:398-404, 1949.

Cassel, R.H.: Relation of design reproduction to the etiology of mental deficiency. *Journal of Consulting Psychology, 13*:421-428, 1949.

Cattell, J.: The time it takes to see and name objects. *Mind, 11*:63-65, 1886.

Cattell, R.: Some theoretical issues in adult intelligence. *Psychological Bulletin, 38*:592, 1941.

Cattell, R.: *I.P.A.T. Cultural Fair Intelligence Scales.* Institute for Personality and Ability Testing, 1957.

Cattell, R.: Theory of fluid and crystallized intelligence: A critical experiment. *Journal of Educational Psychology, 54*:1-22, 1963.

Cattell, R.: *Handbook of Multivariate Experimental Psychology.* Rand McNally, 1966.

Cattell, R.: Theory of fluid and crystallized intelligence at 5-6 years old. *British Journal of Educational Psychology*, 37:209-224, 1967.

Cattell and Butcher: *Prediction of Achievement and Creativity.* Bobbs Merrill, 1968.

Cattell, R.: *Abilities: Their Structure, Growth and Action.* Houghton Mifflin, 1971.

Cattell and Hakstian: A wider search for the structure of primary and higher order abilities, *Journal* (in press).

Cenac and Hecaen: Inversion systematique dans la designation droite-gauche chez certain enfants. *Annales Medico-Psychologiques, 96:*415-419, 1959.

Cernacek and Jagr: Hand and foot laterality in childhood. *Review of Neurology,* (Paris), *116:*683, 1967.

Chamberlain, H.D.: The inheritance of left-handedness. *Journal of Heredity, 19:557-559,* 1928.

Chamberlain, H.D.: A study of some factors entering into the determination of handedness. *Child Development, 6:*91, 1935.

Chapanis and McCleary: Interposition as a cue for the perception of relative distance. *Journal of General Psychology, 48:*113-132, 1953.

Chapman, R.L.: The MacQuarrie test for mechanical ability. *Psychometrika, 13:*175-179, 1948.

Chandler and Greenspan: Ersats egocentricism: A reply to H. Borke, *Developmental Psychology,* 7:104-106, 1972.

Charlesworth, W.R.: Role of surprise in cognitive development. In Elkind and Flavell (Eds.), *Studies in Cognitive Development.* Oxford University Press, 1969.

Chateau, J.: Le test de structuration spatiale. *Le travail Human,* 22:281-297, 1959.

Chatrian, Lettich and Miller: Pattern-sensitive epilepsy, I. an electrographic study of its mechanisms. *Epilepsia (AMST),* *11:*125-149, 1970.

Chein, I.: An empirical study of verbal, numerical and spatial factors in mental organization. *Psychological Records, 3:*71-94, 1933.

Chen, Podshadley and Shrock: Factorial study of psychological, vocational and ability variables as predictors of success in Dental School. *Journal of Applied Psychology, 51:*236-241, 1967.

Chhibber and Singh: Asymmetry in muscle weight and one-sided dominance in the human lower limbs. *Journal of Anatomy, 106:*553-556, May 1970.

Chissom and Thomas: Comparison of factor structures for Frostig developmental test of visual perception. *Perceptual and Motor Skills, 33:*1015-1019, 1971.

Chowdhury, K.R.: *An Experimental Study of Imagery and Its Relation to Abilities and Interests.* Ph.D. Thesis, University of London, 1956.

Chowhury and Vernon: Experimental study of imagery and its relation to abilities and interests. *British Journal of Psychology, 55:*355-364, 1964.

Christiansen and Stone: Visual imagery and level of mediator abstractness in induced mediation paradigms. *Perceptual and Motor Skills, 26:*775-779, 1968.

Chriswell, M.: Validity of a structural dexterity test. *Journal of Applied Psychology, 37:*13-15 (*5:*876), 1953. (See Burros 5 mm 877, too.)

Churchill, Curtis, Coombs and Hassell: Effect of engineer school training on the Surface Development Test. *Educational and Psychological Measurement*, 2:279-280, 1942.

Claparede, E.: L'Orientation Lointaine. *Nouveau Traité de Psychologie*, 7, 1943.

Clark, E.V.: Some perceptual factors in the acquisition of locative terms by young children. Papers from the eighth regional meeting of the Chicago Linguistic Society, 1972.

Clark, H.: Influence of language on solving three-term series problems. *Journal of Experimental Psychology*, 82:205-215, 1969.

Clark, H.: The primitive nature of children's relational concepts. In Hayes (Ed.) *Cognition and the Development of Language*. Wiley, 1969.

Clark, H.: Linguistic processes in deductive thinking. *Psychological Review*, 76:387-404, 1969.

Clark, H.: More about adjectives, comparatives, and syllogisms. *Psychological Review*, 78:505-514, 1971.

Clark, H.: On the evidence concerning Huttenlocker's and Higgins' theory of reasoning. *Psychological Review*, 79:428-432, 1972.

Clark and Chase: On the process of comparing sentences against pictures. *Cognitive Psychology*, 1972.

Clark, H.H.: Semantics and comprehension. In T.A. Sebeok, *Current Trends in Linguistics*, Vol. 12. Mounton, in press.

Clark and Carpenter: On the meeting of semantics and perception. In W.G. Chase, *Visual Information Processing*, Academic Press, 1973.

Clark, M.: Left-Handedness. London, University of London Press, *Scottish Council for Research in Education*, 1957.

Clark, M.P.: Changes in primary mental abilities with age. *Archives of Psychology*, 291, 1944.

Clark and Malone: *Relationship of Topological Orientation to Other Psychological Factors in Naval Aviation Cadets*, Report No. 001.059.01.32, U.S. Naval School of Aviation Medicine, 1952.

Clay, M.: An increasing effect of disorientation on the discrimination of print: a developmental study. *Journal of Experimental Psychology*, 9:297-306, 1970.

Cohen, G.: Hemispheric differences in a letter discrimination task. *Perception and Psychophysics*, 11:139-142, 1972.

Cohen, G.: Hemispheric differences in serial versus parallel learning. *Journal of Experimental Psychology*, 97:349-356, 1973.

Cohen, Hansel and Sylvester: Interdependence in judgments of space, time and movement. *Acta Psychologica*, 11:360-372, 1955.

Cohen and Klein: Referent communications in school age children. *Child Development*, 39:597-609, 1968.

Cohen, J.: The factorial structure of the W.A.I.S. between early adulthood and old age. *Journal of Consulting Psychology*, 21:283-290, 1957.

Cohen, J.: The factorial structure of the W.I.S.C. at ages 7.6, 10.6 and 13.6. *Journal of Consulting Psychology, 23*:285-299, 1959.

Cohen, L.: Interaction between limbs during bimanual voluntary activity. *Brain, 93*:259-272, 1970.

Coie and Dorval: Sex difference in the intellectual structure of social interaction skills. *Developmental Psychology, 8*:261-267, 1973.

Coie, Costanzo, and Farnill: Specific transitions in the development of spatial perspective-taking ability. *Developmental Psychology, 9*:167-177, 1973.

Cole, L.: Instruction in penmanship for the left-handed child. *Elementary School Journal, 39*:436-448, 1939.

Cole, Chorover and Ettlinger: Cross-modal transfer in man. *Nature, 191*: 1225-1226, 1961.

College Entrance Examination Board Special Aptitude Test in Spatial Relations. *Educational Testing Service*, Princeton, N.J., 1953.

Collins, J.K.: Isolation of the muscular component in a proprioceptive spatial aftereffect. *Journal of Experimental Psychology, 90*:297-299, October 1971.

Collins, R.L.: On the inheritance of handedness, II. Selection for sinistrality in mice. *Journal of Heredity, 60*:117-119, 1969.

Colonna and Faglioni: Performance of hemisphere-damaged patients on spatial intelligence tests. *Cortex, 2*:293-307, 1966.

Coltheart, M.: Visual feature-analyzers and aftereffects of tilt and curvature. *Psychological Review, 78*:114-121, 1971.

Colvin and Myers: The development of imagination in school children and the relation between ideational types and the retentivity of material appealing to various sense departments. *Psychological Monograph, 2*:85-126, 1909.

Connolly, K.: Some mechanisms involved in the development of motor skills. *Aspects of Education, 7*:82-100, 1968.

Connors, Schuette and Goldman: Informational analysis of intersensory communication. *Child Development, 38*:251-266, 1967.

Conrad, H.S.: *A statistical evaluation of the Basic Classification Test Battery (Form)*. (OSRD, 1945; Publ. Bd., No. 13294.) Washington, U.S. Department of Commerce, 1946.

Cooper, C.L.: Mechanical aptitude and school achievement of negro boys. *Journal of Applied Psychology, 20*:751-760, 1936.

Cooper and Shepard: The time required to prepare for a rotated stimulus. *Memory and Cognition*, in press.

Cooper and Shepard: Chronometric studies of the rotation of mental images. W.G. Chase (Ed.), *Visual Information Processing*, New York, Academic Press, 1973.

Cooper and Flavell: *Cognitive correlates of children's role-taking behavior.* Merrill-Palmer Quarterly, in press.

Corah and Gospadinoff: Colour-form and whole-part perception in children. *Child Development, 37*:837-842, 1966.

Corballis and Beale: Bilateral symmetry and behavior. *Psychological Review,* 5:451-464, 1970.

Coren, S.: Subjective contours and apparent depth. *Psychological Review,* 79:359-367, 1972.

Corkin, Milner and Rasmussen: Effects of different cortical excisions on sensory thresholds in man. *Transactions of the American Neurological Association,* 89:112, 1964.

Cornsweet and Teller: Relation of increment thresholds to brightness and luminance. *Journal of the Optical Society of America,* 55:1303-1308, 1965.

Cornwell, H.G.: Figure preference and personality. *Perceptual and Motor Skills,* 29:812-814, 1969.

Corsini, D.A.: Effect of nonverbal cues on the retention of kindergarten children. *Child Development,* 40:599-607, 1969.

Corsini, D.A.: Developmental changes in the effect of nonverbal cues on retention. *Developmental Psychology,* 1:425-435, 1969.

Corsini and Fassett: Intelligence and aging. *Journal of Genetic Psychology,* 83:249-264, 1953.

Costa, Vaughn, Horwitz and Retter: Patterns of behavioral deficit associated with visual spatial neglect. *Cortex,* 5:242-263, 1969.

Costello, C.G.,: The effects of prefontal leuctomy upon visual imagery and the ability to perform complex operations. *Journal of Mental Science,* 102:507-16, 1956.

Costello, C.G.: *Control of Visual Imagery in Mental Disorder.* M.Sc. Thesis, University of Durham, 1957.

Cote and Boersma: Reevaluation of role of reversibility in distance conservation. Paper read at *SRCD convention,* 1969.

Court, J.H.: *Researchers bibliography for Raven's Progressive Matrices and Mill Hill Vocabulary Scales.* Mimeographed volume, Flinders University, 1972.

Cousins and Abravanel: Some findings relevant to the hypothesis that topological spatial features are differentiated prior to euclidean features during growth. *British Journal of Psychology,* 62:475-479, 1971.

Cowan, P.A.: *Developmental study of logical transformations.* Unpublished dissertation, University of Toronto, 1963.

Cowan, P.A.: Link between cognitive structure and social structure in a two-child verbal interaction. *SRCD Convention,* New York, 1967.

Cowdery, K.M.: Measures of general intelligence as indices of success in trade learning. *Journal of Applied Psychology,* 6:311-330, 1922.

Cox, J.W.: *Mechanical Aptitude.* London. Methuen, 1928.

Cox, S.: Shape of subjective Space. *Nature,* 150:349,1942.

Crawford, J.E.: Spatial perception tests for determining drafting aptitude. *Industrial Arts and Vocational Education,* 31.10-12, 1942.

Crawford, J.E.: A test for tridimensional structural visualization: a new test for mechanical insight designed primarily to measure ability or aptitude in drafting. *Journal of Applied Psychology,* 24:482-491, 1940.

Critchley, M.: *The Dyslexic Child.* Springfield, Ill., Charles C Thomas, 1970.

Cromer, R.F.: The development of the ability to decenter in time. *British Journal of Psychology, 62:*353-365, 1971.

Cronin, V.: Mirror-image reversal discrimination in kindergarten and first-grade children. *Journal of Experimental Child Psychology, 2:*455-462, 1967.

Crowell, Jones, Kapuniai, and Nakagawa: Unilateral cortical activity in newborn humans. *Science, 180:*205-208, 1973.

Crown, S.: Psychological changes following prefrontal leucotomy. A review. *Journal of Mental Science, 97:*49-83, 1951.

Cruickshank, Bice and Wallen: *Perception and Cerebral Palsy. A Study in Figure Background Relationship.* Syracuse University Press, 1957.

Culbertson, J.: Temporal change in perceptual space. *Journal of Psychology, 21:*3-23, 1946.

Cullen, Harper and Kidera: Perceptual style differences. *Aerospace Medicine, 40:*407-408, 1969.

Culver and Dunham: Birth-order and spatial-perceptual ability. *Perceptual and Motor Skills, 28:*301-302, 1969.

Cunningham, D.J.: Contribution to the surface anatomy of the cerebral hemispheres. *Royal Irish Academy,* 131-136, 1892.

Cunningham, D.J.: Righthandedness and lefthandedness. *Journal of the Royal Anthropological Institute of Great Britain and Ireland, 32:*273, 1902.

**D**

Daehler, M.W.: Children's manipulation of illusory and ambiguous stimuli, discriminative performance, and implications for conceptual development. *Child Development, 41:*225-241, 1970.

Daehler, M.W.: Children's visual regard and manual activity in retention of information about spatial position. *Perceptual and Motor Skills, 33:*71-81, 1971.

Dailey, J.T.: The development of a comprehensive aptitude battery for Air Force technical specialties. Unpublished dissertation, University of Texas, 1949.

Dailey, J.F.: *The development of the Airman Classification Test Battery.* San Antonio, Texas, USAF Air Training Command Indoctrination Division 3309th Research and Development Group, Lackland Air Force Base, November 1948 (*Research Bulletin 48-4*).

Damon, W.: Relation of cognitive and moral development in children four to ten. Unpublished dissertation, University of California at Berkeley, 1973.

Danesteh, Morteza: (*Case Western Reserve*) A survey of spatial visualization and development of a test of visualization. *Dissertation Abstracts International, 32*(3-B):1819, September 1971.

Danko, D.: Perception and preference structures with respect to spatial choices. *Dissertation Abstracts International, 31*(9-B):5417, March 1971.

Dart and Pradhan: Cross-cultural teaching of science. *Science, 155*:649-56, 1967.

Dauterman, Shapiro and Suinn: Performance tests of intelligence for blind reviewed. *International Journal of Education Blind, 17*:8-16, 1967.

Davenport, Brooker and Munro: Factors in social perception: Seating position. *Perceptual and Motor Skills, 33*:747-752, 1971.

Davidson, H.P.: Study of reversals in young children. *Journal of Genetic Psychology, 45*:452-465, 1934.

Davidson and Whiteside: Human brightness perception near sharp contours. *Journal of the Optical Society of America, 61*:530-536, 1971 .

Davies, G.M.: Quantitative and qualitative aspects of memory for picture stimuli. *Journal of Experimental Child Psychology, 13*:382-93, April 1972.

Davis: Functional significance of imagery. *Journal of Experimental Psychology, 15*:630-660, 1932.

Davis, French and Lesser: *Identification of Classroom Behavior of Elementary-School Children Gifted in Five Different Mental Characteristics.* Hunter College, 1959 (Mimeographed).

Davol and Hastings: Effects of age, sex, reading ability, socioeconomic level and display position on a measure of spatial relations in children. *Perceptual and Motor Skills, 24*:375-387, 1967.

Davol and Quinn: Visual cues in tracking. *Perceptual and Motor Skills, 35*: 599-610, 1972.

Dawson, J.L.M.: Cultural and psychological influences upon spatial-perceptual processes in West Africa. *International Journal of Psychology, 2*: 115-125, 1967.

Dawson, J.L.M.: Cultural and physiological influences upon spatial-perceptual processes in West Africa, Part II. *International Journal of Psychology, 2*:171-185, 1967.

Day, R.H.: Visual spatial illusions: A general explanation. *Science 175:24*: 1335-1340, 1972.

Dee, H.L.: Visioconstructive and visioperceptive deficits in patients with unilateral cerebral lesions. Unpublished dissertation, University of Iowa, 1969.

Dee and Fontenot: Use of the nonpreferred hand in graphomotor performance—a methodological study. *Confinia Neurologica, 31*:273-280, 1969.

Degan, J.W.: A reanalysis of the AAF battery of mechanical tests. *Psychometric Monograph*, 58, 1950.

DeHaan and Wischner: Three dimensional objects versus projected color photographs of objects as stimuli in learning set formation by retarded children. *Journal of Comparative and Physiological Psychology, 56*:440-444, 1963.

Denis, P.M.: Perception des distances. *Aachives de l'sychologie, 37*:181-309, 1960.

Deregowski, J.B.: Difficulties in pictorial depth perception in Africa. *British Journal of Psychology, 59*:195-204, 1968.

Deregowski, J.B.: Pictorial recognition in subjects from a relatively picture-less environment. *African Social Research*, 5:356-364, 1968.

Deregowski, J.B.: On perception of depicted orientation. *International Journal of Psychology*, 3:149-156, 1968.

Deregowski, J.B.: Perception of 2-pronged trident by 2 and 3 dimensional perceivers. *Journal of Experimental Psychology*, 82:9-13, 1969.

Deregowski, J.B.: Symmetry, Gestalt and information theory. *Quarterly Journal of Experimental Psychology*, 23:381-385, November 1971.

Deregowski, J.B.: Orientation and perception of pictorial depth. *International Journal of Psychology*, 6, 1971.

Deregowski, J.B.: Responses mediating pictorial recognition. *Journal of Social Psychology*, 84:27-33, 1971.

Deregowski, J.B.: Reproduction of orientation of kohs-type figures: a cross-cultural study. *British Journal of Psychology*, 63:283-296, May 1972.

Deregowski, J.B.: A rejoinder to Symmetry, gestalt and information theory —a critique. *Quarterly Journal of Experimental Psychology*, 24:359-360, August 1972.

Deregowski, J.B.: Pictorial perception and culture. *Scientific American*, 82-88, November 1972.

DeRenzi and Spinnler: Influence of verbal and nonverbal defects on visual memory. *Cortex*, 2:332-336, 1966.

DeRenzi and Faglione: Relationship between visiospatial impairment and constructional apraxia. *Cortex*, 3(3):327-342, 1967.

DeRenzi and Scotti: The influence of spatial disorders in impairing tactual discrimination of shapes. *Cortex*, 5(1):53-62, 1969.

DeRenzi, Faglione and Scotti: Hemispheric contributions to exploration of space. *Cortex*, 6:191-203, 1970.

DeRenzi, Faglione and Scotti: Judgment of spatial orientation in patients with focal brain damage. *Journal of Neurology Neurosurg Psychiatry*, 34:489-495, 1971.

Derrick, E.: Visual-tactual dominance relationship as a function of accuracy of tactual judgment. *Perceptual and Motor Skills*, 31:935-939, 1970.

DeSilva, H.R.: A case of a boy possessing an automatic directional orientation. *Science*, 73:393-394, April 10, 1931.

DeSoto, C.B.: Predilection for single orderings. *Journal of Abnormal and Social Psychology*, 62:16-23, 1961.

DeSoto, London and Handel: Social reasoning and social paralogic. *Journal of Personality and Social Psychology*, 4:513-521, 1965.

Deutsch and Deutsch: Comments on Selective Attention: perception or response? *Quarterly Journal of Experimental Psychology*, 19:362-363, 1967.

DeVries, R.: The development of role taking as revealed by behavior of bright, average and retarded children in a social guessing game. *Child Development*, 41:759-770, 1970.

Dewing and Kennealy: Compositional structure in recall-in investigation of developmental differences. *Journal of Psychology*, 81:151-160, May, 1972.

Diamond and Gilinsky: Dark-adaptation luminance thresholds for the resolution of detail following different durations of light adaptation. *Journal of Experimental Psychology, 50*:134-143, 1955.

Dick and Dick: An analysis of hierarchical processing in visual perception. *Canadian Journal of Psychology, 23*:203-211, 1969.

Dick, Dick and Eliot: Development of Iconic Memory and Cognitive Operations. Unpublished paper, 1971. University of Rochester.

Dick, A.O.: Perception and informational processing: A stage analysis. In Eliot, J., *Human Development and Cognitive Processes*. Holt, Rinehart and Winston, 1971.

Dick, A.O.: Visual hierarchial feature processing: The relation of size, spatial position and identity. *Neuropsychologia, 10*:171-177, 1972.

Dick, A.O.: Parallel and serial processing in tachistoscopic recognition-two mechanisms. *Journal of Experimental Psychology, 96*:60-66, November 1972.

Dick, A.O.: Spatial Abilities, in Avakian-Whitaker and Witaker's *Current Trends in Neurolinguistics*, Hague Mouton Company, 1974.

Dimond, S.J.: Cerebral dominance of lateral preference in motor control. *Acta Psychology, 32*:196-198, 1970.

Dimond, S.J.: Hemisphere function and word registration. *Journal of Experimental Psychology, 87*:183-186, 1971.

Dockrell, W.B.: Cultural and educational influences upon the differentiation of ability. *Proceeding of 73rd Annual Convention of APA*, 1965.

Dodwell, P.C.: Visual orientation preferences in art. *The Quarterly Journal of Experimental Psychology, 13*:40-47, 1961.

Dodwell, P.C.: *Visual Pattern Recognition*. Holt, Rinehart and Winston, 1971.

Doehring: Visual spatial memory. *Journal of Speech and Hearing Research, 3*:138-149, 1960.

Doherty, W.J.: Rotational approach to psychological invariance. Unpublished dissertation, University of Southern California, 1973.

Dolan, H.K.: Study of inheritance of structural visualization. Human Engineering Laboratory, 1960, Report No. 649.

Dolphin and Cruickshank: Tactual motor perception of children with Cereral Palsy. *Journal of Personality, 20*:466-471, 1952.

Donaldson, M.: *A Study of Children's Thinking*. Tavistock, 1963.

Donaldson and Balfour: Less is more. *British Journal of Psychology, 59*:461-471, 1968.

Donaldson and Wales: On the acquisition of some relational terms. In Hayes (Ed.), *Cognition and the Development of Language*. Wiley, 1969.

Doorn, Koenderink and Douman: The influence of the retinal inhomogeneity on the perception of spatial patterns. *Kybernetik, 10*:223-230, April 1972.

Doppelt, J.E.: *The organization of mental abilities in the age range thirteen to seventeen*. Ph.D. Thesis, Columbia University, 1949.

Doppelt and Bennett: Longitudinal study of DAT. *Educational and Psychological Measurement, 11*:228-237, 1951.

Doppelt and Wallace: Standardization of the Wechsler Adult Intelligence Scale for older persons. *Journal of Abnormal and Social Psychology, 51*:312-330, 1955.

Dornbush and Winnick: Relative effectiveness of stereometric and pattern stimuli in discrimination learning. *Psychonomic Science, 5*:301-302, 1956.

Dorothy, R.E.: Motion paralax as a factor in the differential spatial abilities of young children. *Studies in Art Education, 14*:15-27, 1973.

Dosey and Meisel: Personal space and self-protection. *Journal of Personality, 11*:93-97, 1969.

Dowling and Boycott: Organization of the primate retina: Electron microscopy. *Proceedings of the Royal Society, 166*:80-111, 1966.

Dowling, J.E.: Organization of vertebrate retinas. The Jonas M. Friedenwald Memorial lecture. *Investigative Opthalmology, 655*-680, 1970.

Downing, J.: New experimental evidence of the effectiveness of I.T.A. in preventing disabilities of reading and spelling. *Developmental Medical Child Neurology, 11*:547, 555, 1969.

Drake, D.M.: *Perceptual correlates of impulsive and reflective behavior,* Doctoral dissertation, Harvard University, 1968.

Dreffin and Gilbert: Spatial relations ability and other characteristics of art laboratory students. *Journal of Applied Psychology, 32*:601-605, 1948.

Drew, A.L.: A neurological appraisal of familial congenital word-blindness. *Brain, 79*:440-460, 1956.

DuBois and Gleser: The Object-Aperture Test: a measure involving visualization in three dimensions. *American Psychology, 3*:363, 1948.

Dudek, Lester, Goldberg and Dyer: Relationship of prager measures to standard intelligence and motor scales. *Perceptual and Motor Skills, 28*:351-362, 1969.

Duffy, Clair and Egeland, *et al.*: Relationship of intelligence, visual-motor skills and psycholinguistic abilities with achievement in the third, fourth and fifth grades—a follow-up study. *Journal of Educational Psychology, 63*:358-362, August 1972.

Dunan, C.M.: L'espace visuel et l'espace tactile: Observations sur des aveugles. *Revue Philosophie, 25*:355-386, 1888.

Duncan and Eliot: Some variables affecting children's spatial conservation. *Child Development, 44*:828-830, 1973.

Durham, Guilford and Hoepfner: Abilities pertaining to classes and the learning of concepts. *Reports Psychological Laboratory,* No. 39, University of Southern California, 1966.

Durnford, N.: Right hemisphere specialization for depth perception reflected in visual field differences. *Nature, 231*:394-395, 1971.

Dusewioz and Kershner: The D-K scale of lateral dominance. *Perceptual and Motor Skills, 29*:282, 1969.

DuToit, B.M.: Pictorial depth perception and linguistic relativity. *Psychologia Africana*, 11:51-63, 1966.

Duyer, F.: Visual learning: An analysis by sex and grade level. *California Journal of Educational Research*, 22:170-177, 1971.

Dvorak, B.J.: The new USES general aptitude test battery. *Journal of Applied Psychology*, 31:372-376, 1947.

Dvoryashina, M.D.: Struktura pertseptivnogo prostraustva (novye issledovanya yaponskikh psekhologov). The structure of perceptual space (new investigations by Japanese psychologists). *Voprosy Psikhologii*, 15(2):161-7, 1969.

Dwyer, C.A.: Children's sex-role standards and sex-role identification and their relationship to achievement. Unpublished dissertation, University of California at Berkeley, 1972.

Dwyer, F.: Adapting visual illustrations for effective learning. *Harvard Educational Review*, 2:250-263, 1967.

Dye and Very: Growth changes in factorial structure by age and sex. *Genetic Psychology Monograph*, 78:55-88, 1968.

### E

Earle and Macrae: Tests of mechanical ability. *National Institute Ind. Psychol. Rep.*, 3, 1929.

Ebner and Myers: Corpus callosum and the interhemispheric transmission of tactual learning. *Journal of Neurophysiology*, 25:380-391, 1962.

Eddington, A.: *Space, Time and Gravitation*. Harper and Row, 1959.

Eig, J.: Effect of item orientation upon normal and dysfunctional children's spatial ability at two grade levels. Unpublished dissertation, University of Maryland, 1974.

Ekman and Bratfisch: Subjective distance and emotional involvement: a psychological mechanism. *Acta Psychologica*, 24:430-437, 1965.

Ekwall, G.: *Construct Validity of Mechanical Aptitude Tests*. Swedish Council on personnel administration, 1969.

El-Abd: H.A.A. el-S: A study of certain closure factors in relation to Guilford's structure of intellect. Unpublished dissertation, University of London, 1964.

Elias and Kinsbourne: Time course of identity and category matching by spatial orientation. *Journal of Experimental Psychology*, 95:117-183, September 1972.

Eliot, J.: The effects of age and training upon children's conceptualization of space. NICHD Report, January, 1967.

Eliot, J.: Children's spatial visualization, 1970 NCSS Yearbook, *Focus on Geography*, chapter 10.

Eliot, J.: On children's spatial representation. *Zeitschrift fur Padagogik*, January 1974.

Eliot and Dayton: Children's spatial egocentricism: do egocentric errors result from egocentricism? Unpublished manuscript, 1974.

Eliot and Dayton: Factors affecting perceptual accuracy on a task requiring the ability to identify viewpoints. *Journal of Genetic Psychology*, in press.

Elithorn, Kerr and Mott: A group version of a perceptual maze test. *British Journal of Psychology, 51*:19-26, 1960.

Elkind, Kolegher and Go: Studies in perceptual development: II. part-whole perception. *Child Development, 35*:81-90, 1964.

Elkind and Weiss: Studies in perceptual development, III: perceptual exploration. *Child Development, 38*:553-561, 1967.

Elkind and Flavell: *Studies in Cognitive Development.* Oxford University Press, 1969.

Elkind and Sameroff: Developmental psychology. *Annual Review of Psychology, 21*:191-238, 1970.

Elkind and Schoenfled: Identity and equivalence conservation. *Developmental Psychology, 6*:529-533, 1972.

Ellis, E.: Effects of pictorial mode on children's spatial visualization. Unpublished dissertation, University of Maryland, 1972.

Emmett, W.G.: Evidence for a space factor at II plus and earlier. *British Journal of Psychology.* (Statistical Section), 2:3-16, 1949.

Enstrom, E.A.: Left-handed child. *Today's Education, 58*:43-44, 1969.

Entwistte and Welsh: Correlates of school attainment at different ability levels. *British Journal of Educational Psychology, 39*:57-63, 1969.

Epstein, W.: Experimental investigation of the genesis of visual space perception. *Psychological Bulletin, 61*:115-128, 1964.

Erdmann, J.E.: *History of Philosophy, Macmillan,* 7, 1891.

Erickson, R.C.: Visual-haptic aptitude. *Journal of Industrial Teacher Education, 4*:48-55, 1967.

Esser, A.H.: Behavior and environment. *The use of space by animals and humans,* Plenum Press, 1971.

Estes, S.G.: A study of five tests of "spatial" ability. *Journal of Psychology, 13*:265-271, 1942.

Esty, E.T.: An investigation of children's concepts of certain aspects of topology. *Dissertation Abstract International, 3*:3773, February 1971.

Etaugh and Van Sickle: Discrimination of stereometric objects and photographs of objects by children. *Child Development, 42*:1580-1582, 1971.

Etter, E.: Investigation of Adult Observer's Sex and Physical Distance upon Children's Performance on a Perspective Task. Unpublished dissertation, University of Maryland, 1974.

Ettlinger and DeReuck: *Ciba Foundation Symposium on Functions of the Corpus Callosum.* Boston, Little, Brown and Co., 1965.

Ettlinger and Morton: Callosal section: Its effect on performance of a bimanual skill. *Science, 139*:485-486, 1963.

Evanechko and Maquire: Dimension of children's meaning space. *American Educational Research Association Journal, 9*:507-524, 1972.

Evans, J.R.: The relationship of unilateral usage and tactile sensitivity to right-left discrimination and spatial abilities. *Cortex, 5*:134-144, 1969.

Evarts, E.V.: Pyramidal tract activity associated with a conditioned hand movement in the monkey. *Journal of Neurophysiology, 29*:1011-1027, 1966.

Ewart and Carp: Recognition of tactual form by sighted and blind subjects. *American Journal of Psychology, 76*:488-492, 1963.

**F**

Fabian, A.A.: Vertical rotation in visual-motor performance—its relationship to reading reversals. *The Journal of Educational Psychology, 36*:129-154, 1945.

Faglioni, Scotti and Spinnler: The performance of brain-damaged patients in spatial localization of visual and tactile stimuli. *Brain, 91*:443-454, 1971.

Falk, C.T.: Object and pattern discrimination learning. *Child Development, 39*:923-931, 1968.

Fantz, R.L.: Origin of form perception. *Scientific American, 204*:66-72, 1961.

Farkas and Elkind: Distance and position effects on perceptual comparisons at five age levels. *Child Development, 45*:184-188, 1974.

Farnham-Diggory, D.S.: Symbol and synthesis in experimental "reading." *Child Development, 38*:221-231, 1967.

Farnham-Diggory, D.S.: Cognitive synthesis in Negro and white children. *Monographs of the Society for Research in Child Development, 35*:(2, serial No. 135), 1970.

Farnham-Diggory, D.S.: Development of equivalence systems. In Farnham-Diggory, *Information Processing in Children.* Academic Press, 1972, 43-65.

Fast, J.: *Body Language.* New York, Pocketbook Edition, 1971.

Faste, R.A.: The role of visualization in creative behaviour. *Engineering Education, 146*:124-127, 1972.

Faubian, Cleveland and Hassell: The influence of training on mechanical aptitude test-scores. *Educational and Psychological Measurement, 2*:91-94, 1942.

Fazekas and Haugan: Developmental dyslexia. *Medical Annals D.C., 38*:313-316, 1969.

Feffer, M.H.: The cognitive implications of role taking behavior. *Journal of Personality, 27*:152-168, 1959.

Feffer and Gouervitch: The cognitive aspects of role-taking in children. *Journal of Personality, 28*:383-396, 1960.

Feffer and Suchtoliff: Decentering implications of social interactions. *Journal of Personality and Social Psychology, 4*:4, 1966.

Feffer, M.: Symptom expression as a form of primitive decentering. *Psychological Review, 74*:16-28, 1967.

Feffer, M.: Developmental analysis of interpersonal behavior. *Psychological Review, 77*:197-214, 1970.

Feldman, D.H.: Study of fixed sequence of skill and concept acquisition requisite to map drawing. *Stanford Research and Development Center Memorandum, 38*, 1968.

Feldman and Snyder: Crystalling experiences: Occasions for change in cognitive development. Unpublished mimeograph, Yale University, 1972.

Fenseca and Kearl: *Comprehension of pictorial symbols: experiment in rural Brazil.* University of Wisconsin, Department of Agricultural Journalism, 1960.

Ferguson, G.O.: A series of form boards. *Journal of Experimental Psychology, 3*:47-58, 1920.

Ferguson and Maccoby: Interpersonal correlates of differential abilities. *Child Development, 37*:549-571, 1966.

Ferner, Horn and Suchenwirth: Determination of handedness in adults. *Medizinische Welt, 1*:33-35, 1970.

Feshbach and Roe: Empathy in six and seven-year-olds. *Child Development, 39*:133-145, 1968.

Filbey and Gazzaniga: Splitting the normal brain with reaction time. *Psychonomic Science, 17*:335-336, 1969.

Fildes and Myers: Left-handedness and the reversal of letters. *British Journal of Psychology, 3*:273-278, 1921.

Fildes, L.G.: Experiments on the problems of mirror-writing. *British Journal of Psychology*, 57-67, July 1923.

Fillmore, C.J.: Toward a theory of deixis. Paper presented at Pacific Conference on contrastive linguistic and language universals, University of Hawaii, 1971.

Fils, D.: Correlation of two tests of space perception with nonlanguage intelligence. *Journal of Experimental Education, 20*:113-119, 1951.

Finkel, D.L.: Developmental investigation of the visual processing of spatial information. Unpublished dissertation, Harvard University, 1970.

Fiorentini and Maffei: Binocular depth perception without geometrical cues. *Vision Research, 11*:1299-1305, November 1971.

Fishbein, Haygood and Frieson: Relevant and irrelevant saliency in concept learning. *American Journal of Psychology, 83*:544-553, 970.

Fisher, G.H.: Spatial localization by the blind. *American Journal of Psychology, 77*:2-14, 1964.

Fisher, G.H.: Development features of behavior and perception. 1: visual and factile-kinesthetic shape perception. *British Journal of Educational Psychology, 35*:69-78, 1965.

Fisher, Risley and Silverstein: Sex differences in the performance of mental retardates on WAIS. *Journal of Clinical Psychology, 17*:170, 1961.

Fisher, S.: Right-left gradients in body image . . . *Genetic Psychological Monographs, 61*:197, 1960.

Fitzgerald, H.E.: Autonomic pupillary reflex activity during early infancy and its relation to social and nonsocial visual stimuli. *Journal of Experimental Child Psychology, 6*:470-482, 1968.

Flanagan, J.C.: Job element aptitude classification tests. *Personnel Psychology, 7*, 1954.

Flannagan, J.C.: *Career Data Book.* American Institutes for Research, 1973.

Flaugher, R.: Project access research report No. 2; patterns of test performance by high school students of four ethnic identities. *ETS Research Report*, 1972.

Flavell and Dragnus: A microgenetic approach to perception and thought. *Psychological Bulletin*, 54:197-217, 1957.

Flavell, J.: *The Developmental Psychology of Jean Piaget*. Van Nostrand, 1963.

Flavell, Beach and Chinoky: Spontaneous verbal behavior in a memory task, *Child Development*, 37:283-299, 1966.

Flavell, *et al.*: *Development of Role-Taking and Communication Skills in Children*. Wiley, 1968.

Flavell, J.: Concept Development. In Mussen (Ed.) *Carmichael's Manual of Child Psychology*. Wiley, 1970, 983-1060.

Flavell, J.: The development of inferences about others. Paper read at the interdisciplinary conference on our knowledge of persons. *Person perception and interpersonal behavior*, State University of New York, 1971.

Fleishman, E.: Factor structure in relation to task difficulty in psychomotor performance. *Educational and Psychological Measurement*, 17:522-532, 1957.

Fleishman, E.A.: Testing for psychomotor abilities by means of apparatus tests. *Psychological Bulletin*, 50:241-262, 1953.

Fleishman and Rich: Role of kinesthetic and visual-spatial abilities in perceptual-motor learning. *Journal of Experimental Psychology*, 66:6-11, 1963.

Fleming, J.W.: Predicting trade school success. *Industrial Arts and Vocational Education*, 227:315-318, 1938.

Flick, G.: Sinistrality revisited: A perceptual-motor approach. *Child Development*, 37:613-622, 1966.

Flickinger and Rehage: Building time and space concepts. *Yearbook NCSS*, 20: 107-116, 1949.

Foley, I.P.: Empirical approaches to the problem of space perception. *Psychological Bulletin*, 35:409-457, 1938.

Foley, J.M.: The size-distance relation and intrinsic geometry of visual space-implications for processing. *Vision Research*, 12:323-332, February 1972.

Fontenot and Benton: Perception of direction in the right and left visual fields. *Neuropsychologoque*, 10:447-452, 1972.

Ford, L.H.: Predictive versus perceptual responses of Piaget's water-line task and their relation to distance conservation. *Child Development*, 41: 193-204, 1970.

Forman, G.E.: Development of jig-saw puzzle solving. *DARCEE Papers and Reports*, 5:Whole of No. 8, 1971.

Forman, G.E.: Early growth of logic:influences from bilateral symmetry of human anatomy. Paper presented at SRCD convention, Philadelphia, 1973.

Forness and Weil: Laterality in retarded readers with brain dysfunction. *Exceptional Child, 36*:684-685, 1970.

Forrai and Bankovi: Relations of hand clasping and arm folding to handedness in Hungarian children. *ACTA Genetic Med* Gemellol (Roma), *18*:166-174.

Forsman, R.: Age differences in the effects of stimulus complexity and symmetrical form on choice reaction and visual search performance. *Journal of Experimental Child Psychology, 5*:406-429, 1967.

Fournier, E.: Généralisation: internationelle d'un apprentiss age empirique de la notion de conservation of surface. Unpublished dissertation, University of Montreal, 1966.

Fournier, J.: The lefthanded child in psychomotor rehabilitation. *Review of Neuropsychiatry Infants, 17*:247-255, 1969.

Fox, F.H.: A description of language and perceptual function of culturally deprived children. *Dissertation Abstracts, 29*(12-A): 4323, 1969.

Fraisse and Vautrey: La perception de l'espace. *Enfance, 5*:102-119, 1952.

Fraisse and Piaget: *Intelligence*. Basic Books, 1967.

Frandsen and Hadley: The prediction of achievement in a radio training school. *Journal of Applied Psychology, 27*:303-310, 1943.

Fraser, A.: Visualization as a chief source of the psychology of Hobbes, Locke, Berkeley and Hume. *American Journal of Psychology,* 230, December 1891.

Freedman, S.: *The Neurophysiology of Spatially Oriented Behavior.* Dorsey Press, 1968.

Freeman, F.N.: *Mental tests: Their history, principles, and applications.* Boston, Houghton Mifflin, 1926.

Freeman, J.: The modeling of spatial relations. University of Maryland Computer Science Center, December 1973.

Freeman, R.B.Jr: A psychophysical metric for visual space perception. *Ergonomics, 13*:73-81, 1970.

Freeman, Mitchell and Milludot: A neural effect of partial visual deprivation in humans. *Science, 175*:1884-1886, 1972.

French, J.W.: The description of aptitude and achievement tests in terms of rotated factors. *Psychometric Monograph,* 5, 1951.

French, Ekstrom and Price: *Kit of Reference Tests for Cognitive Factors.* Educational Testing Service, 1963.

French, J.W.: Comparative prediction of highschool grades by pure-factor aptitude. Information and personality measures. *Educational and Psychological Measurement, 24*:321-329, 1964.

Fretz, B.R.: Factor structure of visuomotor performance of poorly coordinated boys. *Journal Motor Behavior, 11*:67-78, 1970.

Fried: Dyslexia and organization of Space. *Acta Paedopsychiatrica, 35*: 79-85, 1968.

Frisby, Vincent and Lancashire: *Tests for Engineering Apprentices. A Validation Study.* London, National Institute of Industrial Psychology, 1959.

Frith, U.: Why do children reverse letters. *British Journal of Psychology*, 62:459-468, 1971.

Frostig, M.: Visual perception in the Brain-injured child. *American Journal Orthopsychiatry*, 33:665-671, 1963.

Fruchter, B.: The factorial content of right-response scores and wrong-response scores in a battery of experimental aptitude tests. Unpublished dissertation, University of Southern California, 1948.

Fruchter, B.: *The factorial content of the airman classification battery: 1. Factor analysis of 1948 normative survey battery.* San Antonio, Tex., Human Resources Research Center, Lackland Air Force Base, November 1949. (Research Bulletin 49-1.)

Fruchter, B.: Extraction of factors by the Centroid method. *Air Force Technical Memorandum*, June, 1949, 13. Lackland Air Force base, San Antonio, Tex.

Fruchter, B.: Ability patterns in technical training criteria, *Journal of Applied Psychology*, 36:381-384, 1952.

Fruchter, B.: Orthogonal and oblique solutions of a battery of aptitude achievement, and background variables. *Educational and Psychological Measurement*, 12:20-38, 1952.

Fujiwara, S.: Study of interpersonal structure and empathy. *Japanese Journal of Psychology*, 35:277-287, 1965.

Furth, H.G.: Piaget's theory of knowledge: nature of representation and interiorization. *Psychological Review*, 75:143-154, 1968.

Furth, Youniss and Ross: Children's utilization of logical symbols. *Developmental Psychology*, 3:36-57, 1970.

Furth and Youniss: Influence of language on discovery and use of logical symbols. *British Journal of Psychology*, 56:381-390, 1965.

Fry, C.: Training children to communicate to listeners. *Child Development*, 37:675-686, 1966.

Fry, G.A.: Visual perception of space. *American Journal of Optomology*, Monograph 110, 1950.

## G

Gaffron, M.: Right and left in pictures. *Art Quarterly*, 13:312-331, 1950.

Gainer, W.L.: Ability wise subjects to discriminate between boys and girls of average intelligence. *California Journal of Educational Research*, 13:9-16, 1962.

Gainotti, G.: les manifestations de negligence et d'malterichou pour l'heme-space. *Cortex*, 4: 64-92, 1968.

Gainotti, Messerli and Tissot: Qualitative analysis of unilateral spatial neglect in relation to laterality of cerebral lesions. *Journal of Neurology Neurosurgery Psychiatry*, 35:545-550, August 1972.

Galton, F.: Statistics of Mental Imagery. *Mind*, 5: 300-318, 1880.

Galton, F.: *Hereditary Genius.* Macmillan, 1892.

Gamble, R.: An experimental study using semi-concrete and abstract materials in a paired-association learning task. *Dissertation Abstracts, 24*:1072-1073.

Gan Kova, Z.A.: The interrelation of action, image and speech in thinking of children of preschool age. *Problems of Psychology, 1*:26-35, 1960.

Garai and Scheinfeld: Sex differences in mental and behavioral traits. *Genetic Psychology Monograph, 77*:169-299, 1968.

Gardner, Howard and Perkins: Symbol systems: a philosophical, psychological and educational investigation. In D.R. Olson, *Media and Symbols*. 73rd Yearbook of the National Society for the Study of Education, in press.

Gardner, Jachson and Messick: Personality organization in cognitive controls and intellectual abilities. *Psychological Issues, 2*: Whole No. 8, 1960.

Gardner, M.: *The Ambidextrous Universe: left, right, and the fall of parity.* Mentor, 1969 (first printing, Basic Books, 1969).

Garling, T.: Studies in visual perception. *Scandinavian Journal of Psychology, 10*:250-268, 1969.

Garling, I.: Studies in visual perception of architectural spaces and rooms. Relation of judged depth to judged size of space under different view conditions. *Scandinavian Journal of Psychology. 11*:133-145, 1970.

Garner, W.R.: To perceive is to know. *American Psychologist, 21*:11-19, January 1966.

Garner, W.R.: Stimulus in information processing. *American Psychologist, 25*:350-358, 1970.

Garner and Feyoldy: Integrality and separation of stimulus dimensions. *Cognitive Psychology, 1*:225-241, 1970.

Garner and Plant: On the measurement of egocentricism. *British Journal of Educational Psychology, 42*:79-83, 1972.

Garnett, C.B.: *Kantian Philosophy of Space.* Kennikat Press, 1939.

Garrett, H.E.: A developmental theory of intelligence. *American Psychologist, 1*:372-378, 1946.

Garrod, S.: A memory model to account for comprehension of active and passive sentences in prose. Minor thesis, Princeton University, 1972.

Garron and Cheifetz: Stimulus rotation and visual scanning in SS with copying disability. *Perceptual and Motor Skills, 24*:1015-1024, June 1967.

Garron and Vander: Personality and intelligence in Turner's syndrome. *Archives General Psychiatry, 30*:239-257, 1967.

Garron, D.C.: Sex-linked, recessive inheritance of spatial and numerical abilities, and Turner's Syndrome. *Psychological Review, 77*:147-152, 1970.

Garry and Ascarillo: Teaching topological orientation and spatial orientation to congenitally blind children. *Journal of Education*, Boston University, *143*:1-48, 1960.

Garside, R.F.: The prediction of examination marks of mechanical engineering students at King's College. *British Journal of Psychology, 48*:219-220, 1957.

Garth, T.R.: IQ and achievement of mixed blood Indians. *Journal of Social Psychology*, 4:134-137, 1933.

Gates, A.I.: A study of the role of visual perception, intelligence and certain associative processes in reading and spelling. *Journal of Educational Psychology*, 17:433-445, 1926.

Gavurin: Anagram solving and spatial aptitude. *Journal of Psychology*, 65:65-68, 1965.

Gazzaniga, Bogan and Sperry: Laterality effects in somesthesis following cerebral commissurotomy in man. *Neuropsychologia*, 1:209-215, 1963

Gazzaniga, Bogen and Sperry: Observations on visual perception after disconnexion of the cerebral hemispheres in man. *Brain*, 88:221-236, 1965.

Gazzaniga, M.S.: Psychological properties of the disconnected hemispheres in man. *Science, 150*:372, 1965.

Gazzaniga, Bogen and Sperry: Dyspraxia following division of the cerebral commissures. *Archives of Neurology*, 16:606-612, 1967.

Gazzaniga, M.: Eye position and visual motor coordination. *Neuropsychologia*, 7:379-382, 1969.

Gazzaniga, M.S.; *Bisected Brain*. Appleton-Century-Crofts, 1970.

Gazzania and Hillyard: Language and speech capacity of the right hemisphere. *Neuropsychologia*, 9:273-80, September 1971.

Gedeon, B.: L'intelligence des relations spatiales: Aptitude aux mathematiques et aux sciences (Intelligence with respect to spatial relations: Aptitude for mathematics and science). *Bull Inst Pédag, 8*, Montreal, Saint-Georges, 1945.

Geffen, Bradshaw and Nettleton: Hemispheric asymmetry-verbal and spatial encoding of visual stimuli. *Journal of Experimental Psychology*, 95:25-31, September 1972.

Gelman, R.: Conservation acquisition: a problem of learning to attend to relevant attributes. *Journal of Experimental Child Development*, 7:167-187, 1969.

Geng and Mehl: Relationship between intelligence and special abilities. *Zeitschrift für Psychologie, 176*:103-128, 1969.

Geschwind and Levitsky: Human brain: Left-right asymmetries in temporal speech region. *Science, 161*:186, 1968.

Geschwind, N.: The organization of language and the brain. *Science, 170*:940-944, 1970.

Geschwind, N.: Language and the brain. *Scientific American*, April 1972.

Gesell, A., et al.: *The First Five Years of Life*, Harper, 1940.

Gesell, A.L.: Ontogenesis of infant behavior. In Carmichael's *Manual of Child Psychology*. Wiley, 1946, pages 295-331.

Gesell and Ames: Development of directionality in drawing. *Journal of Genetic Psychology, 68*:45-61, 1946.

Gesell and Ames: The development of handedness. *Journal of Genetic Psychology, 70*:155-175, 1947.

Ghareib, R.M. el.: *Factorial analysis of practical ability and its relation to other intellectual abilities and personality traits.* Ph.D. thesis, University of Edinburgh, 1949.

Ghent, L.: Perception of overlapping and embedded figures by children of different ages. *American Journal of Psychology, 69*:575-587, 1956.

Ghent, L.: Form and its orientation: a child's eye-view. *American Journal of Psychology, 74*:177-190, 1961.

Ghent, L.: Developmental changes in tactual thresholds on dominant and nondominant sides. *Journal of Comparative and Physiological Psychology, 54*:670-673, 1961.

Ghent, L.: *Stimulus orientation as a factor in the recognition of geometric forms by school-age children.* Paper presented at the meetings of the Eastern Psychological Association, 1963.

Ghiselli, E.E.: Tests for the selection of inspector-packers. *Journal of Applied Psychology, 26*:468-476, 1942.

Ghiselli, B.: Validity of personality inventories. *Journal of Applied Psychology, 37*:18-20, 1953.

Ghiselli, E.: Measurement of occupation aptitude. *University of California, Public Psychology, 8*(2):101-216, 1955.

Giangreco, C.J.: Hiskey-Nebraska test compared to several achievement tests. *American Annals Deal, 111*:566-577, 1966.

Gibson, Filbey and Gazzariga: Hemisphere differences as reflected by reaction time. *Federation Proceedings, 29*:658, 1970.

Gibson, E.: Improvement in perceptual judgment as a function of controlled practice or training. *Psychological Bulletin, 50*:401-431, 1953.

Gibson and Walk: The visual cliff. *Scientific American, 202*:64-71, 1960.

Gibson, Gibson, Pick and Osser: A developmental study of the discrimination of letter-like forms. *Journal of Comparative and Physiological Psychology, 55*:897-906, 1962.

Gibson, E.J.: Learning to read. *Science, 148*:1066-1072, 1965.

Gibson, E.: *Principles of Perceptual Learning and Development.* Appleton-Century-Crofts, 1969.

Gibson and Gibson: Continuous perspective transformations and the perception of rigid motion. *Journal of Experimental Psychology, 54*:129-138, 1957.

Gibson and Rodner: Adaptation, after-effect, and contrast in the perception of tilted lines. I. Quantitative studies. *Journal of Experimental Psychology, 20*:453-467, 1937.

Gibson, J.J.: *The perception of the visual world.* Boston, Houghton Mifflin, 1950.

Gibson, J.J.: What is form? *Psychological Review, 58*:403-412, 1951.

Gibson, J.: Visual field and visual world. *Psychological Review, 59*:149-151, 1952.

Gibson, J.: A theory of pictorial perception. *AV Communication Review, 2*:3-23, Winter 1954.

Gibson, J.: *Senses Considered as Perceptual Systems.* Houghton Mifflin, 1966.

Gibson, J.J.: On theories for visual space perception. A reply to Johansson. *Scandinavian Journal of Psychology, 11*:75-88, 1970.

Gilinsky, A.S.: Effect of altitude on the perception of size. *American Journal of Psychology, 68*:173-192, 1955.

Gilinsky, A.S.: Effect of growth on the perception of visual space. Eastern Psychological Association paper, 1960.

Gilinsky, Mayo and Jochnowitz: *Visual masking and tilt aftereffects as a function of tilt and angular separation between test and adaptation-line patterns.* Proceedings, 76th Annual Convention, APA, 1968.

Gilinsky, A.S.: Orientation-specific effects of patterns of adapting light on visual acuity. *Journal of the Optical Society of America, 58*:13-18, 1968.

Gilinsky and Doherty: Interocular transfer of orientation effects. *Science, 164*:454-455, April 25, 1969.

Gilliatt and Pratt: Disorders of perception and performance in a case of right-sided cerebral thrombosis. *Journal of Neurology, Neurosurgery, and Psychiatry, 15*:264-271, 1952.

Giraldo, M.: Egocentricism and moral development. Unpublished dissertation, Catholic University of America, 1972.

Gliner, Pick, Pick and Hales: Developmental investigation of visual and haptic preferences for shape and texture. *Society for Research Child Development Monograph, 130*, 1969.

Gloning, K., Harb, G., and Quatember, R.: Standardislevung Einer Untersuchungsmethode der Sogenannten "Prosopagnosie." *Neuropsychologia, 5*:99-101, 1967.

Glucksberg, Krauss and Weisberg: Referential communication in nursery school children. *Journal of Experimental Child Psychology, 3*:333-342, 1966.

Glucksberg and Krauss: What do people say after they have learned to talk? *Merrill-Palmer Quarterly, 13*:309-316, 1967.

Gogel, W.: Relative visual direction as a factor in relative distance perception. *Psychological Monograph, 70*:418, 1956.

Gogel, W.: Equidistance tendency and its consequences. *Psychological Bulletin, 64*:153-163, 1965.

Gogel and Mertens: Perceived depth between familiar objects. *Journal of Experimental Psychology, 77*:206-211, 1968.

Goins, J.T.: Visual perceptual abilities and early reading progress. *Supplementary Educational Monographs, 87*, Chicago, 1958.

Goldstein and Andrews: Perceptual uprightness and complexity of random shapes. *American Journal of Psychology, 75*:667-669, 1962.

Goldstein and Brooks: Recognition by children of inverted photographs of faces. *Child Development, 34*:1033-1040, 1963.

Goldstein and Chance: Recognition of children's faces. *Child Development, 35*:129-136, 1964.

Goldstein, A.G.: Learning of inverted and normally oriented faces in children and adults. *Psychonomic Science, 3*:447-448, 1965.

Goldstein and Mackenberg: Recognition of human faces from isolated facial features: A developmental study. *Psychonomic Science, 6*:149-150, 1966.

Goldstein and Sheerer: Abstract and concrete behavior, an experimental study with special tests. *Psychological Monographs, 53*:2, 1941.

Goldstein and Wicklund: The acquisition of the diagonal concept. *Child Development, 44*:210-213, 1973.

Goldstein, K.M.: *Tests of abstract and concrete thinking*. New York, Psychological Corporation, 1941.

Golla, Hutton, Walter and Grey: The objective study of mental imagery. 1. Physiological concomitants. *Journal of Mental Science, 89*:216-223, 1943.

Gollin, E.G.: Tactual form discrimination: A developmental comparison under conditions of spatial interference. *Journal of Experimental Psychology, 60*:126, 129, 1960.

Gollin, E.G.: Factors affecting recognition of incomplete objects. *Perceptual and Motor Skills, 15*:583-590, 1962.

Gombrich, Hochberg and Black: *Art, Perception, and Reality*. Johns Hopkins Press, 1972.

Gombrich, E.H.: *Art and Illusion*. Bollinger Foundation, 1960.

Gombrich, E.H.: The visual image. *Scientific American, 227*:82-97, 1972.

Gooch, A.G.: Some aspects of selection for technical courses in secondary schools. *The Vocational Aspect of Education, 14*:29, 154-159, 1962.

Goodman, C.H.: Factorial analysis of Thurstone's seven primary abilities. *Psychometrika, 8*:121-129, 1943.

Goodman, C.H.: A factorial analysis of Thurstone's sixteen primary mental abilities tests. *Psychometrika, 8*:141-151, 1943.

Goodman, C.H.: The MacQuarrie Test for mechanical ability. Time and motion analysis. *Journal of Applied Psychology, 34*:27-29, 1950.

Goodman, N.: *Languages of Art*, Bobbs-Merrill, 1968.

Goodman, N.: Seven structures on similarity. In Foster and Swanson, *Experience and Memory*, University of Massachusetts Press, 1970.

Goodnow and Bethon: Piaget's Tasks: the effects of schooling and intelligence. *Child Development, 37*:573-582, 1966.

Goodnow, J.J.: Effect of active handling. *Child Development, 40*:201-212, 1969.

Goodnow, J.J.: Problems in research on culture and thought. In Flavell and Elkind (Eds.), *Festschrift for Piaget, Oxford University Press*, in press.

Goodnow, J.J.: The role of modalities in perceptual and cognitive development. In J. Hill (Ed.), *Minnesota Symposia of Child Psychology*, Minneapolis, University of Minnesota Press, *5*:3-27, 1971.

Goodnow, J.J.: Matching auditory and visual series: modality problem or translation problem. *Child Development, 42*:1187-1201, 1971.

Goodnow, J.J.: Rules and repertoires, rituals and tricks of the trade. In Farnham-Diggory (Ed.), *Information processing in children*, Academic Press, 86-97, 1972.

Gordon, R.: An investigation into some of the factors that favour the formation of stereotyped images. *British Journal of Psychology, 39*:156-157, 1949.

Gottheil, Corey and Paredes: Psychological and physical dimensions of personal space. *Journal of Psychology, 69*:7-9, 1968.

Gottschalk and Bryden: Spatial organization of children's responses to a pictorial display. *Child Development, 35*:811-815, 1964.

Gough and Olton: Field independence as related to nonverbal measures of perceptual performance and cognitive ability. *Journal of Consulting Clinical Psychology, 38*:338-342, June 1972.

Gozova, A.P.: Spatial notions of deaf school children. In Boskis and Meohcheryakov (Ed.), *Sensory Defects and Mental Development*, International Congress of Psychology, Moscow, 1966.

Gragg and Gordon: *Validity of the Airman Classification Battery AC-1.* (2nd Ed.) San Antonio, Tex., Human Resources Research Center, Lackland Air Force Base, December 1950. (Research Bulletin 50-3.)

Graham, C.H.: Visual perception. In S.S. Stevens, *Handbook of Experimental Psychology.* New York, Wiley, 1951, 868-920.

Graham and Kendall: *Memory for designs test.* Department of Neurological Psychiatry, Washington University School of Medicine, 1948.

Graham, Berman and Ernhart: Development in preschool children of ability to copy forms. *Child Development, 31*:339-359, 1960.

Gratch and Landers: Stage IV of Piaget's theory of infant's object concepts: A longitudinal study. *Child Development, 42*:359-372, 1971.

Gray and Brumbach: Effect of daylight projection of film loops on learning badminton. *The Research Quarterly, 38*:562-569, 1967.

Graybiel, A.: Spatial disorientation in flight. *Military Surgery, 108*:287-294, 1951.

Green, Guilford, Christensen and Comrey: A factor-analytic study of reasoning abilities. *Psychometrika, 18*:135-160, 1953.

Green, B.: Intelligence and computer simulation. *Trans of N.Y. Academy of Sciences, 27*:55-63, 1964.

Greenfield, P.: Weaving skill, color terms, and pattern representation among the Zinacantecos of Southern Mexico, A developmental Study, in progress.

Gregg, F.M.: Are motor accompaniments necessary to orientational perception, *Journal of Psychology, 8*:63-97, 1931.

Gregory, R.L.: *The Intelligent Eye.* McGraw-Hill, 1971.

Griffith and Davidson: Long-term changes in intellect and behavior after hemispherectomy. *Journal of Neurology, Neurosurgery and Psychiatry, 29*:571-576, 1966.

Griffiths: Individual differences in Imagery. *Psychology Monographs, 172,* 1927.

Grimsley, Ruch, Warren and Ford: *Examiner's Manual, Employee Aptitude Survey, 5-Spatial Visualization.* Psychological Services, 1957.

Gross, Bender and Rocha-Miranda: Visual receptive fields of neurons in infertemporal cortex of monkey. *Science, 166:*1302-1306, 1969.

Grove, W.R.: An experimental study of the Kent-Shakow industrial formboard series. *Journal of Applied Psychology, 19:*467-473, 1935.

Grove, W.R.: Modification of the Kent-Shakow formboard series.*Journal of Psychology, 7:*385-397, 1939.

Growney and Weisstein: Spatial characteristics of Metacontrast. *Journal of Optical Society of America, 62:*690-696, May 1972.

Grunbaum, A.: *Philosophical Problem of Space and Time,* Knopf, 1963.

Guardo and Meisels: Child-parent spatial patterns. *Developmental Psychology, 5:*365, 1972.

Gudschinsky, S.: Recent trends in primer construction. *Fundamental and Adult Education, 11:*67-96, 1959.

Guilford and Zimmerman: Some AAF findings concerning aptitude factors. *Occupations, 26:*154-159, 1947.

Guilford and Lacy: (Eds.) *Printed classification tests. Army Air Forces Aviation Psychology Program Research Reports, Report No. 5.* Washington, D.C., Government Printing Office, 1947.

Guilford, Wayne and Zimmerman: The Guilford-Zimmerman aptitude survey. *Journal of Applied Psychology, 32:*1, February 1948.

Guilford, Green and Christensen: A factor-analytic study of reasoning abilities. II. Administration of tests and analysis of results. *Reproduction of the Psychology Laboratory, University of Southern California, 3,* 1951.

Guilford, Furchter and Zimmerman: Factor analysis of the Army Air Forces Sheppard Field battery of experimental aptitude tests. *Psychometrika, 17:*45-68, 1952.

Guilford, Christensen, Kettner, Green and Hertzka: Factor-analytic study of Navy reasoning tests with Air Force crew classification battery. *Educational and Psychological Measurement, 14:*301-325, 1954.

Guilford, J.: Structure of intellect. *Psychological Bulletin, 53:*267-293, 1956.

Guilford, J.: Three faces of intellect. *American Psychology, 14:*469-479, 1959.

Guilford, J.: *The Nature of Human Intelligence.* McGraw-Hill, 1967.

Guilford and Hoepfner: *Analysis of Intelligence.* McGraw-Hill, 1971.

Gur, Gur, and Harris: Cerebral activation, as measured by subject's lateral eye movements. Unpublished paper, Michigan State University, 1973.

Gusman, A.: Computer recognition of three-dimensional objects in a visual scene. *MIT project MAC technical Report MAC-TR-59,* December, 1968.

Guthrie, Brislin and Sinaiko: *Aptitudes and abilities of Vietnamese technicians: Implications for training.* Institute Defense Analysis, 1970.

# H

Hagan, M.: Picture perception. *Psychological Bulletin, 81*:471-497, 1974.

Halford, G.S.: Theory of acquisition of conservation. *Psychological Review,* 77:302-316, 1970.

Hall, E.T.: *The Silent Language.* New York, Fawcett Publications, Inc., 1959.

Hall, E.T.: *The Hidden Dimension.* New York, Doubleday and Co., Inc., 1966.

Hall, R.: The psycho-philosophy of history. *Main Currents, 29*: 2, 1972.

Halpin and Patterson: The performance of brain-injured children on the Goldstein-Scheerer Tests. *American Journal of Mental Deficiency, 59*: 91-99, 1954.

Halstead, H. *et al.*: Intelligence and personality in drug addicts: a pilot study. *British Journal of Addicts., 63*:237-240, 1968.

Halstead, W.C.: Chapter in *Cerebral Mechanisms in Behavior* (The Hixon Symposium). Edited by Lloyd A. Jeffress. London, J. Wiley & Sons, 1951.

Hamilton, N.: Differential response to instruction designed to call upon spatial and verbal aptitudes. *Technical Report No. 5, School of Education,* Stanford University, 1969.

Hammerton, T.: Some factors affecting learning and transfer of training in visual-motor skills. *British Journal of Psychology, 60*:369-371, 1969.

Handel and Buffardi: Pattern perception; integrating information presented in two modalities. *Science, 162*:1026-1028, 1968.

Handel, DeSoto and London: Reasoning and spatial representations. *Journal of Verbal Learning and Verbal Behavior,* 7:351-357, 1968.

Hanna, G.: Investigation of selected ability, interest and personality characteristics relevant to success in high school geometry. Unpublished dissertation, University of Southern California, 1965.

Hanna, G.S.: Empirical comparison of three geometry aptitude tests. *School Science and Mathematics, 68*:8-10, 1968.

Hannan, R.: *Concept formation in relation to the study of landforms among training college students.* M.Ed. Thesis, University of Leeds, 1963.

Hanvik: Note on rotations in the Bender Gestalt. *Journal of Clinical Psychology, 9*:399, 1953.

Harbran, R.K.: Just how important is mixed laterality? *Special Education of the Mentally Retarded,* 7:147-149, 1971.

Harcum and Jones: Letter-recognition within words flashed left and right of fixation. *Science, 138*:444-445, 1962.

Harcum and Finkel: Explanation of Mishkin and Forgays' result as a directional-reading conflict. *Canadian Journal of Psychology,* 17:224-234, 1963.

Harcum and Friedman: Reversal reading by Israeli observers of visual patterns without intrinsic directionality. *Canadian Journal of Psychology,* 17:361-869, 1963.

Harcum, E.R.: Visual hemifield differences as conflicts of direction of reading. *Journal of Educational Psychology, 72*:479-480, 1966.

Harnquist, K.: Relative changes in IQ from 13 to 18. *Scandinavian Journal of Psychology, 9*:65-82, 1968.

Harrell and Faubion: Selection tests for aviation mechanics. *Journal of Consulting Psychology, 4*:104-105, 1940.

Harris, A.: Lateral dominance, directional confusion and reading disability. *Journal of Psychology, 44*:283-294, 1957.

Harris, D.B.: *Children's Drawings as Measures of Intellectual Maturity.* Harcourt, Brace and World, 1963.

Harris and Gibson: Is orientation-specific color adaptation in human vision due to edge detectors, afterimages or "Dipoles?" *Science, 162*:1506-1507, 1968.

Harris and McKinney: *Directional preferences in the looking behavior of preschool children.* Mimeo, 10.

Harris, Strommen and Marshall: *Judged fronts, backs, and sides of various geometric figures and designs.* SRCD convention, 1973.

Harris and Strommen: Young children's self-referent and object-referent "front," "back," and "beside" placements of objects having front-back features and of objects lacking front-back features. Midwestern Psychological Association, 30 April, 1970. (also accepted for publication in *Merrill-Palmer Quarterly*).

Harris and Gutkin: *Adults' word associations and orientation judgments for geometric forms.* Unpublished paper, Michigan State University, 1971.

Harris and Schaller: Form and its orientation: reexamination of a child's eye-view. *American Journal of Psychology.* In press, 1971.

Harris and Strommen: The role of face and body cues in children's judgments of front, back, and side. Paper read at SRCD convention, 1971.

Harris, L.J.: Discrimination of left and right and development of the logic of relations. *Merril-Palmer Quarterly, 18*:307-320, 1972.

Harris, L.J.: Neuropsychological factors in spatial development. Paper read at SRCD convention, 1973.

Harris, L.J.: Recent studies of perception and cognition in human infants. Address to the *American Academy of Optometry*, San Francisco, 10 December 1973.

Harris, L.J.: Sex differences in spatial ability, in Kinsbourne, M (Ed). *Hemispheric Asymmetries of Function,* Cambridge University Press, 1975.

Hartigan, R.: Temporal-spatial scale. *Journal of Clinical Psychology,* 221-223, 1971.

Hartlage, L.C.: Differences in listening comprehension of the blind and sighted. *International Journal for the Education of the Blind, 13*: 1-7, 1963.

Hartlage, L.C.: Role of vision and the development of spatial ability. Unpublished dissertation, University of Louisville, 1967.

Hartlage: Sex-linked inheritance of spatial abilities. *Perceptual and Motor Skills, 31*:610, 1970.

Hartnett, Bailey and Gibson: Personal space as influenced by sex and type of movement. *Journal of Psychology*, 76:139-144, 1970.

Hartwell, J.J. *et al.*: Personal space as influenced by sex and type of movement. *Journal of Psychology*, 76:139-44, 1970.

Harway, N.I.: Judgment of distance in children and adults. *Journal of Experimental Psychology*, 65:385-390, 1963.

Hatwell, Y.: Perception tactite des formes et organization spatiale tactile. *Journal of Psychology*, 6:146-154, 1953.

Havinghurst and Janke: Relations between ability and social status in a midwestern community. *Journal of Educational Psychology*, 35:357-368. 1944.

Havinghurst and Breese: Relation between ability and social status in a midwestern city. *Journal of Educational Psychology*, 38:241-247, 1947.

Hay, Langdon and Pick: Spatial parameters of eye-hand adaptation to optical distortion. *Journal of Experimental Psychology*, 91:11-7, November 1971.

Hayashi and Bryden: Ocular dominance and perceptual asymmetry. *Perceptual and Motor Skills*, 25:605-612, 1967.

Haynes, J.: Factor-analytic study of performance on the Bender-Gestalt. *Journal of Consulting and Clinical Psychology*, 34(3):345-347, 1970.

Haynes and Carley: Relation of spatial abilities and selected personality traits. *Psychological Reports*, 26(1):214, 1970.

Head, H.: *Studies in Neurology*. Oxford Medical Publications, 1920.

Head, H.: *Aphasia and kindred disorders of speech*. Cambridge; the University Press, 1923, 95.

Healy and Fernald: Tests for practical mental classification. *Psychological Monograph*, 13:2, 1911.

Healy, W.: Pictorial completion test II. *Journal of Applied Psychology*, 5: 225-239, 1921.

Heamon, A.J.: Visual perception in Geography; a Study of Selected Aspects of Spatial Ability. Unpublished thesis, Reading University, 1966.

Hebb, D.O.: Intelligence in man after large removals of cerebral tissue. *Journal of General Psychology*, 21:437-446, 1939.

Hebb, D.O.: The effect of early and late brain injury upon test-scores and the nature of normal adult intelligence. *Proc. of the American Philosophical Society*, 85:275-92, 1942.

Hebb, D.O.: *The organization of behavior*. New York; John Wiley and Sons, Inc., 1949. (Science Editions.)

Hebb, D.O.: Concerning imagery. *Psychological Review*, 75:466-477, 1968.

Hecaen and Ajuriaguerra: L'apraxie de l'habillage. *Encephale*, 35:113-143, 1945.

Hecaen and Ajuriaguerra: Le syndrome praxique et gnosique au cours des lesions l' hemisphere droit. *Press Medicale*, 63:401-404, 1955.

Hecaen, H. and Angelergues, R.: Agnosia for faces (prosopagnosia). *Archives of Neurology*, 7:92-100, 1962.

Hecaen and Ajuriaguerra: *Left-Handedness: manual superiority and cerebral dominance.* New York; Grune & Stratton, 1964.

Hecaen and Assal: A comparison of constructive deficits following right and left hemispheric lesions. *Neuropsychologia, 8*:289-303, July 1970.

Hecaen, H.: Cerebral dominance in left-handed subjects. *Cortex, 7*:19-48, 1971.

Hector, Dlodlo and du Plessis: An experiment on silhouette recognition and projection with Bantu children of different ages. *Journal of National Institute and Personnel Research, 8*:195-8, 1961.

Hegion, A.G.: *Role playing and communication: a developmental study.* Unpublished doctoral dissertation, University of Minnesota, 1969.

Heglin, H.J.: Problemsolving set in different age groups. *Journal of Gerontology, 11*:310-317, 1956.

Heim and Simmonds: The shapes analysis: A test of spatial perception. *Perceptual and Motor Skills, 20*:158, 1965.

Heinonen, V.: Factor analytic study of transfer of training. *Scandinavian Journal of Psychology, 3*:177-188, 1962.

Held and Freedman: Plasticity in human sensorimotor control. *Science 142*:455-462, 1963.

Held and Hein: Movement-produced stimulation in the development of visually-guided behavior. *Journal of Comparative Psychology Physiology, 56*:872-876, 1963.

Held, R.: Two modes of processing spatially-distributed visual stimulation. In F.O. Schmitt (Ed.), The *Neurosciences: Second Study Program.* New York, Rockefeller University Press, 1971.

Heller, T.: *Blinden-Psychologie.* Engelman, 1904.

Helveston, Billips and Weber: Controlling eye-dominant hemisphere relationships as a factor in reading ability. *American Journal of Ophthalmology, 70*:96-100, 1970.

Henle, M.: Relation between logic and thinking. *Psychological Review, 69*:366-378, 1962.

Henry and Bishop: Simple cells of the striate cortex. In *Contributions to sensory physiology.* New York, Academic Press, 1971, 5.

Herkowitz, J.: Filmed test to assess elementary school-aged children's perception of figures which appear to move away from stationary backgrounds. *Perceptual and Motor Skills, 27*:643-6, October 1968.

Hermelin and O'Connor: Right and left handed reading of braille. *Nature, 231*:470, 1971.

Hermelin and O'Connor: Functional asymmetry in the reading of braille. *Neuropsyhologia, 9*:431-435, 1971.

Hermelin and O'Connor: Spatial coding in normal, autistic and blind children. *Perceptual and Motor Skills, 33*:127-132, 1971.

Hershensen, M.: Development of the perception of form. In Haber, *Contemporary theory and research in visual perception.* Holt, 1968.

Herskovits, Campbell, and Segall: *Cross-cultural Study of Perception*. Bobbs-Merrill, 1969.

Hertz, R.: *Death and the Right Hand*. Free Press, 1960.

Hertzka, Guilford, Christensen and Berger: Factor-analytic study of evaluative abilities. *Educational and Psychological Measurement, 14*:581-597, 1954.

Herzberg and Lepkin: Study of sex differences on primary mental abilities test. *Educational and Psychological Measurement, 14*:687-689, 1954.

Hess, E.H.: Shadows and depth perception. *Scientific American, 204*:138-148, 1961.

Higginson, G.D.: Examination of some phases of space perception. *Psychological Review, 44*:77-96, 1937.

High, W.S.: *Investigation of geographical orientation and its relationship to spatial visualization*, MA. thesis, San Jose College, 1951.

Hildreth, *et al.*: Body buffer zone. *American Journal of Psychiatry, 127*:77-81, June 1971.

Hill, Fischer and Warshay: Effects of drugs on visual perception. *American Journal of Optometry, 45*:454-457, 1968.

Hille, McCullum and Sceau: Relation of training in motor activity to development of right-left directionality in mentally retarded children: exploratory study. *Perceptual and Motor Skills, 24*:363-366, 1967.

Hills, J.: Factor-analyzed abilities and success in college mathematics. *Education and Psychological Measurement, 17*:615-622, 1957.

Himmelweit, H.T.: Student selection—an experimental investigation. *British Journal of Sociology, 1*:328-340, 1950.

Hirata and Osaka: Tachistoscopic recognition of Japanese letter materials in left and right visual fields. *Psychologia, 10*:7-18, 1967.

Hirsch and Spinelli: Visual experience modifies distribution of horizontally and vertically oriented receptive fields in cats. *Science, 168*:869-871, 1970.

Ho, K.: Exploratory Study of Spatial Dimensionality Across two Ethnic Groups at two age levels. Unpublished dissertation, University of Maryland, 1974.

Hobson, J.: Sex differences in primary mental abilities. *Journal of Educational Research, 41*:126-132, 1947.

Hochberg, Cleitman and Macbride: Visual threshold as a function of simplicity of form. *American Journal of Psychology, 60*:341-342, 1948.

Hockberg and Brooks: Pictorial recognition as an unlearned ability. *American Journal of Psychology, 75*:624-628, 1962.

Hockberg and Brooks: Psychophysics of form: reversible-perspective drawings of spatial objects. *American Journal of Psychology, 73*:337-354, 1960.

Hochberg and Galper: Recognition of faces: I. An exploration study. *Psychonomic Science, 9*:619-620, 1967.

Hochberg, J.: In the minds eye. In Haber, *Contemporary Theory and Research in Visual Perception*. Holt, Rinehart and Winston, 1968.

Hof, Legein and Reuter: Photopic and scotopic orientation acuity in man. *Pflueger Archives, 311*:195, 1969.

Hoffman, Guilford, Hoepfner and Doherty: A factor-analysis of the figural-cognition and figural-evaluation abilities. *Report from the Psychological Laboratory,* 40, University of Southern California, 1968.

Hoffman and Sattzstein: Parent discipline and the childs moral development. *Journal of Personality and Social Psychology, 5*:45-47, 1967.

Hohle, R.H.: Picture recognition latencies as a function of age and picture orientation. Paper read at SRCD convention, 1969.

Holden, A.: *Shapes, Space, and Symmetry.* Columbia University Press, 1972.

Holliday, F.: An investigation into selection of apprentices for the engineering industry. *Occupational Psychology, 14*:69-81, 1940.

Holliday, F.: Survey of an investigation into personnel selection for engineering industry. *Occupational Psychology, 16*:1-19, 1942.

Holliday, F.: The relations between psychological test-scores and subsequent proficiency of apprentices in the engineering industry. *Occupational Psychology, 17*:168-185, 1943.

Holzinger and Swineford: A study in factor analysis: The stability of a bi-factor solution. *Supplemental Educational Monograph, 48*, 1939.

Holzinger and Swineford: The relation of two bi-factors to achievement in geometry and other subjects. *Journal of Educational Psychology, 37*: 257-265, 1946.

Hooper, Fitzgerald and Papalia: Piagetian theory and the aging process. *Aging and Human Development, 2*:3-20, 1971.

Horn and Cattell: Age differences in primary mental ability factors. *Journal of Gerontology, 21*:210-220, 1966.

Horn, J.L.: Intelligence—why it grows, why it declines. *Transaction,* 23-31, 1967.

Horn and Bramble: Second-order ability structure revealed in rights and wrongs scores. *Journal Educational Psychology, 58*:115-122, 1967.

Horn and Cattell: Age differences in fluid and crystallized intelligence. *Acta Psychologica, 26*:107-129, 1967.

Horn, J.L.: Organization of abilities and the development of intelligence. *Psychological Review, 75*:242-259, 1968.

Horn, J.L.: Structure of intellect: primary abilities. In Dreger, (Ed.) *Multivariate Personality Research,* 1973.

Horn, W.: *Primary ability test.* Gottigen, Germany, 1960.

Horowitz, Duff and Stratton: Body buffer zone: Explorations of personal space. *Archives of General Psychiatry, 2*:651-656, 1964.

House and Zeaman: Transfer of a discrimination from objects to patterns. *Journal of Experimental Psychology, 59*:298-302, 1960.

House, B.: Discrimination of symmetrical and asymmetrical dot patterns by retardates. *Journal of Experimental Child Psychology, 3*:377-389, 1966.

Houssiadas, L.: Coordination of perspectives in children. *Archives Fuer Die Gesamte Psychologie, 117*:319-326, 1965.

Howard and Templeton: *Human Spatial Orientation,* New York, John Wiley and Sons, 1966.

Howard, I.P.: The spatial senses. In Carterette and Friedman (Eds.) *Handbook of Perception,* Academic Press, 1972.

Hubel and Wiesel: Receptive fields and functional architecture of monkey striate cortex. *Journal of Physiology, 195:*215-243, 1968.

Hudson, W.: Cultural problems in pictorial perception. *South African Journal of Science, 58:*189-195, 1962.

Hugh, S.C.: *Relationship of scores on various psychological tests to success in an industrial arts general shop course at the ninth grade level.* Unpublished Master's thesis, North Carolina State College, 1949.

Humphries and Shephard: Performance on several control-display arrangements as a function of age. *Canadian Journal of Psychology, 2:*231-238, 1955.

Humphries and Shephard: Age and training in the development of a perceptual-motor skill. *Perceptual and Motor Skills, 9:*3-11, 1959.

Hundal, P.S.: Organization of mental abilities at successive grade levels. *Indian Journal Psychology, 41:*65-72, 1966.

Hunter, I.M.L.: Solving three-term series problems. *British Journal of Psychology, 48:*286-298, 1957.

Hunter, I.M.L.: An exceptional talent for calculative thinking. *British Journal of Psychology, 53:*243-258, 1962.

Hunton, V.D.: The recognition of inverted pictures by children. *The Journal of Genetic Psychology, 86:*281-288, 1955.

Hunton, Hicks and Leslie: Discrimination of figural orientation by monkeys and children. *Perceptual and Motor Skills, 21:*55-59, 1965.

Hurwitz, Bibace and Wolff, *et al.*: Neuropsychological function of normal boys, delinquent boys, and boys learning problems. *Perceptual and Motor Skills, 35:*387-394, October 1972.

Huttenlocker, J.: Discrimination of figure orientation: Effects of relative position. *Journal of Comparative and Physiological Psychology, 63,* 1967.

Huttenlocker, Higgens, Milligan and Kauffman: Mystery of the 'Negative Equative' construction. *Journal of Verbal Learning and Verbal Behavior, 9:*334-341, 1970.

Huttenlocker and Higgins: Adjectives, comparatives, and syllogisms. *Psychological Review, 78:*487-504, 1971.

Huttenlocker and Higgins: On reasoning, congruence, and other matters. *Psychological Review, 79:*420-427, 1972.

Huttenlocker and Presson: *Mental rotation and the perspective problem.* Unpublished paper, 1973.

Hyman and Well: Judgments of similarity and spatial models. *Perception and Psychophysics, 2:*233-248, 1967.

Hyman and Well: Perceptual separability and spatial models. *Perception Psychophysics, 3:*161-165, 1968.

Hyman, J.A.: Performance of High and Low Imagers on Two Complex Tactile Discrimination Tasks. Unpublished doctoral dissertation, University of Western Ontario, 1966.

Hyman, L.: Symmetry, number, and partial identity in discrimination learning of dot patterns by retardates. Unpublished doctoral dissertation, University of Connecticut, 1965.

# I

Iakimanskaia, I.S.: *Some ways of diagnostics of spatial thinking development in school children.* Voprosy, Psikholgii, *3*:84-96, 1971.

Ingebretsen, K.: *A factor analysis of figural-evaluation abilities.* Unpublished dissertation, University of Southern California, 1969.

Ingram, D.: Motor asymmetries in young children. *Research Bulletin No. 269,* University of Western Ontario, 1973.

Inhelder and Piaget: *Early Growth of Logic in the Child.* Norton, 1969.

Inhelder, B.: Operational thought and symbolic images. *Society for Research in Development, Monograph, 100,* 1965.

Isard, W.: *Location and space economy. Wiley,* 1956.

Ittelson, Wm.: *Visual Space Perception. Springer,* 1960.

Ittelson, Wm.: *Environment and Cognition.* Seminar Press, 1973.

# J

Jackson, J.H.: Case of large cerebral tumor without optic neuritis and with left hemiplegia and imperception. *Royal Ophthalogical Hospital Report, 8*:434-444, 1876.

Jackson, J.H.: On the nature of the duality of the brain. *Brain, 38*:80-103, 1915.

Jackson, J.: Processing of sequentially presented shapes. *Developmental Psychology, 8*:46-50, 1973.

Jackson, Messick and Myers: Evaluation of group and individual forms of embedded-figures measures of field-independence. *Educational and Psychological Measurements, 24*:177-192, 1964.

Jager, A.O.: Dimenzionen der intelligenz. Gottingen, *Verlag fur Psychologie,* 1970.

Jahoda and Stacey: Susceptibility to geometrical illusions according to culture and professional training. *Perception and Psychophysics, 7*:179-184, 1970.

Jahoda, G.: Assessment of abstract behaviour in non-western culture. *Journal of Abnormal and Social Psychology, 53*:237-243, 1956.

Jahoda, G.: Geometric illusions and environment: a study in Ghana. *British Journal of Psychology, 57*:193-199, 1966.

Jahoda, G.: Retinal pigmentation, illusion susceptibility, and space perception, *International Journal of Psychology, 6*:199-208, 1971.

Janke and Havinghurst: Relations between ability and social status in midwestern community. *Journal of Educational Psychology, 36*:499-509,. 1945.

Janner, M.: *Concepts of Space: A History of Theories of Space in Physics.* Cambridge, Mass., 1969.

Jarvie, H.F.: Problem-solving defects following wounds of the brain. Paper read at B.P.S. Conference, Hull, *Quarterly Bulletin, B.P.S., 41*, 1960.

Jeffrey, W.E.: The effects of verbal and nonverbal responses in mediating an instrumental act. *Journal of Experimental Psychology, 45*:327-333, 1953.

Jeffrey, W.E.: Variables in early discrimination learning: I. Motor responses in the training of a left-right discrimination. *Child Development, 29*:269-275, 1958.

Jeffrey, W.E.: Discrimination of oblique lines by children. *Journal of Comparative and Physiological Psychology, 62*:154-156, 1966.

Jensen, B.T.: Reading habits and left-right orientation in profile drawings by Japanese children. *American Journal of Psychology*, 306-308, 1952.

Jensen, A.R.: Estimation of the limits of heritability of traits by comparison of monozygotic and dizygotic twins. *Proceedings National Academy Science*, 149-157, 1967.

Jensen, A.R.: *Genetics and Education.* Harper and Row, 1973.

Jensen, A.R.: Interaction of Level 1 and Level 2 abilities with race and socioeconomic status. *Journal of Educational Psychology*, in press.

Johansson, G.: (University of Uppsala Sweden). On theories for visual space perception. *Scandinavian Journal of Psychology, 11*(2):67-74, 1970.

Johansson and Rumar: Silhouette effects in night driving. *Scandinavian Journal of Psychology, 12*:80-89, 1971.

John, I.D.: Reexamination of block design rotation effect. *Perceptual and Motor Skills, 19*:175-189, 1964.

Johnson-Laird, P.N.: The Three-term series problem. *Cognition, 1*:57-82, 1972.

Jones, B.M.: Verbal and spatial intelligence in short and long term alcoholics. *Journal of Nervous and Mental Disorders, 153*:292-297, 1971.

Jones and Parsons: Specific vs. generalized deficits of abstracting ability in chronic alcoholics. *Archives of General Psychiatry, 26*:380-384, 1972.

Jones, I.V.: A factor analysis of the Stanford-Binet at four age levels. *Psychometrika, 14*:299-331, 1949.

Jones, P.: Sex differences in academic prediction. *Measurement and Evaluative Guidance, 3*:88-91, 1970.

Jones and Case: Validation of aptitude tests for engineering students. *Educational and Psychological Measurements, 15*: 502-508, 1955.

Jones, S.: Visual and verbal processes in problem solving. *Cognitive Psychology, 1*:201-214, 1970.

Judd, C.H.: Ambidexterity and Mirror Writing. In P. Monroe's *Cyclopedia of Education*, Macmillan, 1911.

Julesz, B.: Binocular depth perception without familiarity cues. *Science, 145*:356-362, 1964.

Julesz, B.: *Foundations of cyclopean perception*. Chicago, The University of Chicago Press, 1971.
Jung, R.: Summary of the Conference. In V.B. Mountcastles *Interhemispheric relations and Cerebral Dominance*. Johns Hopkins Press, 1962.

## K

Kagan, J.: The growth of the 'face' schema: theoretical significance and methodological issues. Paper read at American Psychological Association convention, 1965.
Kagan, J. and Kogan, N.: Individual variation in cognitive processes. In Mussen's *Carmichael's Manual of Child Psychology, 1*, Wiley, 1970, beginning page 1273.
Kagan, J.: Attention and psychological change. *Science, 170*:826-832, 1970.
Kahneman, Norman and Kubovy: Critical duration for the resolution of form: Centrally or peripherally determined? *Journal of Experimental Psychology, 73*:323-327, 1967.
Kailo, E.: Die Reaktionen des Sauglings auf das menschliche Gesicht. *Annales Univ. Aboensis, Ser. B*. Bd. 17, 1932 (cited in Gibson, 1969).
Kaliski, L.: Arithmetic and the brain-injured child. *Arithmetic Teacher, 9*:245-251, 1962.
Kamii, C.: Piaget-based curricula for early childhood education. Paper read at SRCD convention, Philadelphia, 1973.
Kant, I.: *Critique of Pure Reason*. William Benton, 1952 (1781).
Karp, S.: Field dependence and overcoming embeddedness. *Journal of Consulting Psychology, 27*:294-302, 1963.
Kasdorf and Schnall: Developmental differences in the integration of picture series: effects of variations in object-attribute relationships. *Human Development, 13*:188-200, 1970.
Katz and Deutach: Relation of auditory-visual shifting to reading achievement. *Perceptual and Motor Skills, 17*:327-332, 1963.
Keesey, U.T.: Effects of involuntary eye movements on visual acuity. *Journal of Optical Society of America, 50*:469-774, 1960.
Keir, G.: The progressive matrices as applied to school children. *British Journal of Psychology, 2*:140-150, 1949.
Kelley, H.P.: *An investigation to identify and analyze a spatial-relations factor in an airman population*. Unpublished master's thesis, University of Texas, 1951.
Kelley, T.L.: *Crossroads in the mind of man*. Stanford University Press, 1928.
Kellogg, R.: *Analysing children's art*, National Press, 1969.
Kennedy, J.: *Psychology of Picture Perception*, Jossy-Bass, 1973.
Kent and Shakow: Graded series of form boards. *Personality Journal, 7*: 115-120, 1928.
Kent, G.H.: Series of tasks for Dearborn Form Board No. 3. *Journal of Clinical Psychology, 35*:31-45, 1945.

Kenyon and Rice: Homing of the Layson Albatross. *Condor, 60*:3-6, 1958.

Keogh, B.K.: Pattern walking under three conditions of available visual cues. *American Journal of Mental Deficiency,* 74:376-381, 1969.

Keogh, B.K.: Preschool children's performance on measures of spatial organization, lateral preference and lateral usage. *Perceptual and Motor Skills, 34*:299-302, 1970.

Keogh, B.K.: Pattern copying under three conditions of an expanded spatial field. *Developmental Psychology, 4*:25-31, 1971.

Kerpelman and Pollock: Development changes in the location of form discrimination cues. *Perceptual and Motor Skills, 19*:375-382, 1964.

Kerpelman, L.C.: Stimulus dimensionality and manipulability in visual perceptual learning. *Child Development, 38*:563-571, 1967.

Kershner, J.R.: Children's spatial representation of directional movement and figure orientations along horizontal and vertical dimensions. *Perceptual and Motor Skills, 31*: 641-642, 1970.

Kershner, J.R.: Children's spatial representations and horizontal directionality. *Journal of Genetic Psychology, 116*:177-189, 1970.

Kershner, J.R.: Children's acquisition of visuospatial dimensionality. *Developmental Psychology, 5*:454-462, 1971.

Kershner and Kershner: Dual brain asymmetry: model for diagnosis and treatment of learning disorders. *Academic Therapy,* 1972, in press.

Kershner, J.R.: Effect of lateral preference on ability to conserve multiple spatial relations by the mentally retarded. *Perceptual and Motor Skills,* 1972, in press.

Kessen and Kessen: Behavior of children in a two-choice guessing problem. *Child Development, 32*:779-788, 1961.

Kettner, Guilford and Christensen: A factor—analytic investigation of factor called general reasoning. *Educational and Psychological Measurements, 16*:421-437, 1956.

Kettner, Guilford and Christensen: Relation of certain thinking factors to training criteria in U.S. Coast Guard Academy. *Educational and Psychological Measurement, 19*:381-394, 1959.

Kidd and Rivoire: Cultural-fair aspects of the development of spatial perception. *Journal of Genetic Psychology, 106*:101-111, 1965.

Kilbridge, Robbins and Freeman: Pictorial depth perception and education among Baganda school children. *Perceptual and Motor Skills, 26*:1116-1118, 1968.

Kilman, M.D.: Some factors related to mapreading ability. Unpublished dissertation, University of Southern California, 1969.

Kimura, D.: Cerebral dominance and the perception of verbal stimuli. *Canadian Journal of Psychology, 15*:166-171, 1961.

Kimura, D.: Some effects of temporal lobe damage on auditory perception. *Canadian Journal of Psychology, 15*:156-165, 1961.

Kimura, D.: Dual functional asymmetry of the brain in visual perception. *Neuropsychologia, 4*:275-285, 1966.

Kimura, D.: Spatial localization in left and right visual fields. *Canadian Journal of Psychology, 23*:445-458, 1969.

Kimura, D.: Speech lateralization in young children. *Journal of Comparative and Physiological Psychology, 56*:899-902, 1963.

Kimura and Vanderwolf: Relation between hand preference and the performance of individual finger movement by left and right hands. *Brain, 93*:769-774, 1970.

King, E.M.: Effects of different kinds of visual discrimination training on learning to read words. *Journal of Educational Psychology, 55*:325-333, 1964.

King, W.H.: Development of scientific concepts. *British Journal of Educational Psychology, 31*:1-20, 1961.

Kingsley, P.: Relationship between egocentricism and children's communication. Paper read at SRCD convention, 1971.

Kingsley and Hall: Training conservation through the use of learning sets, *Child Development, 38*:1111-1126, 1967.

Kinsbourne, M.: Cerebral basis of lateral asymmetries in attention. *Acta Psychologica, 55*:193-201, 1970.

Kinsbourne, M.: Eye and head turning indices of cerebral lateralization. *Science, 176*:539-541, 1972.

Kinzel, A.: Body-buffer zone. *American Journal of Psychiatry, 127*:99-104, 1970.

Kirssin and Harcum: Relative attensity of stimuli in left and right visual hemifields. *Perceptual and Motor Skills, 24*: 807-822, 1967.

Kisker, G.W.: Perceptual motor patterns following bilateral prefrontal lobotomy. *Archives of Neurology and Psychiatry, 50*:691-696, 1943.

Klahr and Wallace: An information processing analysis of some Piagetian experimental tasks. *Cognitive Psychology, 1*:358-387, 1970.

Klapper and Birch: Perceptual and action equivalence to objects and photographs in children. *Perceptual and Motor Skills, 29*:763-771, December 1969.

Kline, C.L.: A transcultural study of dyslexia: analysis of reading disabilities in 425 Chinese children simultaneously learning to read and write in English and Chinese. *American Orthopsychiatric Association*, San Francisco, March 26, 1970.

Klingberg, G.: Distinction between living and not living among 7-10-year-old children. *Journal of Genetic Psychology, 90*:227-238, 1957.

Knowlton, J. Q.: On the definition of a "picture." *Audiovisual Communication Review, 14*:154-201, 1966.

Knox and Kimura: Cerebral processing of nonverbal sounds in boys and girls. *Neuropsychologia, 8*:227-238, 1970.

Koch, H.: Some factors conditioning the social distance between the sexes. *Journal of Social Psychology, 20*:79-107, 1944.

Koch, H.: Relation of primary mental abilities in 4 and 5-year-olds to sex of child and characteristics of his siblings. *Child Development, 25*:209-223, 1954.

Koffka, K.: Some problems of space perception. In C. Murchinson (Ed.), *Psychologies of 1930*. London, Oxford University Press, 1930, 161-187.

Kohlberg, L.: Cognitive stages and preschool education. *Human Development*, *9*:5-17, 1966.

Kohlberg, Yaeger and Hjertholm: Private speech: four studies and a review of theories. *Child Development*, *39*:691-736, 1969.

Kohler, W.: *Gestalt Psychology*. New York, H. Liverright, 1929.

Kohler, I.: Formation and transformation of perceptual world. *Psychological Issues Monograph*, *3*, 1964.

Kohler and Emery: Figural aftereffects in the third dimension of visual space. *American Journal of Psychology*, *60*:159-201, 1947.

Kohns, S.C.: *Intelligence measurement: a psychological and statistical study based upon the block designs test*. New York, Macmillan, 1923.

Kohnstamm, C.: *Piaget's analysis of class inclusion*, Mouton, 1967.

Kolers, P.A.: Reading temporally and spatially transformed text. In Kenneth S. Goodman (Ed), *The Psycholinguistic Nature of the Reading Process*. Detroit, Wayne State University Press, 1968, 27-40.

Kolers and Eden: *Recognizing Patterns*. M.I.T. Press, 1968.

Kolers and Perkins: Orientation of letters and their speed of recognition. *Perception and Psychophysics*, *5*:275-280, 1969.

Kolers, P.A.: Formal characteristics of pictograms. *American Scientist*, *57*:348-363, 1969.

Kolers, P.A.: *Aspects of Motion Perception*. Pergamon, 1972.

Kolers, P.A.: A problem for theory. *Vision Research*, *12*:1057-1058, May 1972.

Korn, Wendt and Albe-Fessard: Somatic projection to the orbital cortex of the cat. *Electroencephalography and Clinical Neurophysiology*, *21*:209-226, 1966.

Kosslyn, Pick, and Fariello: Cognitive maps in children and men. *Child Development*, *45*:707-716, 1974.

El-Koussy, A.H.: Visual perception of space. *British Journal of Psychology*, Monograph Supplement, *20*:1-80, 1935.

El-Koussy, A.H.: Further examination of the "K" factor. *Proceedings of 12th International Congress of Psychology*, Edinburgh, 1948.

El-Koussy, A.H.: *Trends in research in spatial abilities*. International Colloquin on factor analysis, Paris, 1955.

Kralovich, A.M.: Relationship of perceiving, recognizing, distinguishing and relating in children's spatial visualization. Unpublished dissertation, University of Maryland, 1971.

Krathwohl, Living, Gilbert and Gronbach: Prediction of success in architectural courses. *American Psychology*, *7*:288-289, 1952.

Kraunak and Raskin: Influence of age and stimulus dimensionality on form preference by preschool children. *Developmental Psychology*, *4*(3):389-393, 1971.

Krauskopf, J.: Effects of retinal image motion on contrast thresholds for maintained vision. *Journal of the Optical Society of America, 47*:740-747, 1957.

Krauss and Rotter: Communication abilities of children as a function of status and age. *Merrill-Palmer Quarterly, 14*:161-173, 1968.

Krauthamer, G.: Form perception across sensory modalities. *American Psychologist, 14*:396, 1959.

Krumboltz and Christal: Short-term practice effects in tests of spatial aptitude. *Personnel and Guidance Journal,* 385-391, 1960.

Kubzansky, Rebelsky and Dorman: A developmental study of size, constancy for two versus three-dimensional stimuli. *Child-Development, 42*:633-635, 1971.

Kuffler, S.W.: Discharge patterns and functional organization of mammalian retina. *Journal of Neurophysiology, 16*:37-68, 1953.

Kugelmass and Lieblich: Perceptual exploration in Israeli children. *Child Development, 41*:1125-1131, 1970.

Kuhlman, C.K.: *Visual imagery in children.* Unpublished doctoral dissertation, Radcliffe College, Cambridge, Mass., 1960.

Kuhlman: Place of mental imagery. *American Journal of Psychology, 16*:337-356, 1905.

Kuhn, T.S.: *Copernican Revolution.* Vintage Books, 1957.

Kuhn, T.S.: *Structure of Scientific Revolution.* University of Chicago Press, 1962.

Kunnapas, T.M.: An analysis of the "vertical-horizontal" illusion. *Journal of Experimental Psychology, 49*:134-140, 1955.

Kunnapas, T.: Distance perception as a function of available visual cues. *Report from Psychology Laboratory,* University of Stockholm, 231, 1967.

## L

Lagrone, C.W.: Sex and personality differences in relation to feeling for direction. *Journal of Genetic Psychology, 81*:23-33, 1969.

Laithwaite, E.R.: The shape of things to come. *Proceedings of Institute for Electrical Engineers, 119*:61-68, 1972.

Lampel, A.K.: Child's memory for actional, locational and serial scenes. *Journal of Experimental Child Psychology, 15*:266-277, 1973.

Langley and Drew: Performance of retarded children in a liquid conservation task-protocol objectivity and visual screening. *American Journal of Mental Deficiency, 76*:729-732, May 1972.

Larsen, G.: Sequence of development of spatial concepts. Paper read at SRCD convention, 1969.

Lashley and Franks: The mechanism of vision: X. Postoperative disturbances of habits based on detail vision in the rat after lesions, the cerebral visual areas. *Journal of Comparative and Physiological Psychology, 17*:355-391, 1934.

Lashley, K.S.: Problem of serial order in behavior. In Jeffreso, *Cerebral Mechanisms in Behavior*. Wiley, 1951.

Laurendeau and Pinard: *The Development of the Concept of Space in the Child*. New York, International Universities Press, 1970.

Lawes, J.S.: The construction and validation of a spatial test. Abstract of master's thesis. *British Journal of Educational Psychology*, *31*:297-299, 1961.

Lawrenson and Bryant: Absolute and relative codes in young children. *Journal of Child Psychological Psychiatry*, *13*:23-35, March 1972.

Lawson, I.R.: Confusion in the house—the assessment of disorientation for the familiar in the home. *Psychiatric Quarterly*, *43*:225-239, 1969.

Lawson, Gulick and Park: Stereoscopic size-distance relationships from line-drawn and dot-matrix stereograms. *Journal of Experimental Psychology*, *92*:69-74, 1972.

Layton, W.: Predicting success in dental school. *Journal of Applied Psychology*, *37*:251-255, 1953.

Lee, T.: Perceived distance as a function of direction in the city. *Environment and Behavior*, *1*:40-51, 1970.

Lee, R.: Kung spatial organization: an ecological and historical perspective. *In Human Ecology*, *1*(2):1062, 1972.

Leech, G.N.: *Towards a semantic description of English*. Indiana University Press, 1969.

Leeuwenberg, E.L.: A perceptual coding language for visual and auditory patterns. *American Journal of Psychology*, *84*:307-349, 1971.

LeHew: *Imagery Characteristic of Retarded and Accelerated Readers*. Washington University, MA Thesis, 1936.

Lehman, R.A.: Hand preference and cerebral predominance in 24 rhesus monkeys. *Journal of Neurological Science*, *10*:185-192, 1970.

Lehn and Schnall: Further studies of the elasticity analoque of reversibility in relation to conservation judgments. Unpublished paper, 1973.

Leibman, M.: The effects of sex and race norms on personal space. *Environment and Behavior*, *2*:208-246, 1970.

Leibovic, Balsleu and Mathieson: Binocular space and its representation. *Journal of Theoretical Biology*, *28*:513-529, 1970.

Leibowitz, Graham and Parrish: The effect of hypnotic age regresion on size constancy. *American Journal of Psychology*, *85*:271-276, June, 1972.

Leidorman, P.H.: Imagery and sensory deprivation, An experimental study. *United States Air Force Technical Document Reprint*, 1962, 62-78.

LeMay and Culebras: Human Brain. *The New England Journal of Medicine*, *287*:168-170, 1972.

Lentz, W.: *Intersensory perception in children with language disorders*. Unpublished master's thesis, Colorado State University, 1965.

Leonard and Newman: Spatial orientation in the blind. *Nature*, *215*:1413-1414, 1967.

Leskow and Smock: Developmental changes in problem solving strategies; permutation. *Developmental Psychology,* 2:412-422, January 1970.

Lesser, Fifer and Clark: *Mental Abilities.* Comprehensive Research Project 1635, 1964.

Levin, S.: Compensated dys-perception. *South African Medical Journal,* 43:745-749, 1971.

Levinson, B.: A comparative study of the verbal and performance ability of monolingual and bilingual nature born Jewish preschool children of traditional parentage. *Journal of Genetic Psychology,* 97:93-112, 1960.

Levy-Agresti and Sperry: Differential perceptual capacities in major and minor hemispheres. *Proceedings of the National Academy of Sciences,* 61:1151, 1968.

Levy, J., Trevarthen, C., and Sperry, R.: Perception of bilateral chimeric figures folowing hemispheric deconnexion. *Brain,* 95:61-78, 1972.

Levy, J.: Possible basis for the evolution of lateral specialization of the human brain. *Nature (London)* 224:614-615.

Levy and Lam: Psychology of memory 1969: A bibliography. *Perceptual and Motor Skills,* 33:799-830, 1971.

Levy, Trevarthen and Sperry: Reception of bilateral chimeric figures following hemispheric deconnexion. *Brain,* 95:61-78, 1972.

Levy, W.H.: *Blindness and the blind.* London, Chapman and Hall, 1872.

Lewis, H.: Spatial representation as a correlate of development and a basis for picture preference. *Journal of Genetic Psychology,* 102:95-107, 1963.

Lewin, K.: Environmental forces in child behavior and development. In Muchison (Ed.) *Handbook of Child Psychology.* Worchester, 1933.

Lewis and Fishbein: Space perception in children. *Psychometric Society Convention,* St. Louis, 1969.

Liben, L.S.: Horizontality: Relation between operative level and long-term memory. Paper presented at SRCD Convention, Philadelphia, 1973.

Liberman, Cooper, Harris, MacNeilage and Studdert-Kennedy: Some observations on a model for speech perception. In Wathen- Dunn, S. (Ed.) *Models for the perception of speech and visual form.* Cambridge, M.I.T. Press, 1967.

Likert and Quasha: *Revised Minnesota Paper Form-Board Test.* New York, Psychological Corporation, 1941-8.

Lindauer, M.S.: *The orientation of form in abstract art.* American Psychological Association, Washington, D.C., September 1969.

Lindquist, E.F., *et al.*: *Educational Measurement.* Washington, American Council on Education, 1951.

Ling, B.C.: Form discrimination as a learning cue in infants. *Comparative Psychology Monograph,* 17:86, 1947.

Little, K.B.: Personal space. *Journal of Experimental Social Psychology,* 1:237-247, 1965.

Little, Ulehla and Henderson: Value congruence and interaction distances. *Journal of Social Psychology,* 75:249-253, 1968.

Little, K.B.: Cultural variations in social schemata. *Journal of Personality and Social Psychology, 10*:1-7, 1968.

Locke, J.: *Essay Concerning Human Understanding.* London, Thomas Davison, Whitefriars, 1828, 6.

Lockhead: Identification and the form of multidimensional discrimination of space. *Journal of Experimental Psychology, 85*:1-10, 1970.

Lombroso, C.: *The Man of Genius.* Scott, 1891.

London, I.D.: Research on sensory interaction in the Soviet Union. *Psychological Bulletin, 51*:531-568, 1954.

London, I.D.: Russian report on the post-operative newly seeing. *American Journal Psychology, 73*:478-482, 1960.

Long: Reasoning ability in children. *Journal of Psychology, 12*:21-44, 1941.

Long and Welch: Influence of levels of abstractness. *Journal of Psychology, 13*:41-59, 1942.

Long and Looft: Directionality in children. *Developmental Psychology, 6*: 375-380, 1972.

Loranger and Misiak: The performance of aged females on fine nonlanguage tests of intellectual functions. *Journal of Clinical Psychology, 16*:189-191, 1960.

Lorenz, K.Z.: The role of Gestalt perception in animal and human behavior. *Symposium on Aspects of Form* (edited by L.L. Whyte). London, Lund Humphries, 1951.

Lotze, H.: *Metaphysic.* Oxford, Claredon Press, 1887.

Lotze, H.: *Microcosmus; An Essay Concerning Man and His Relation to the World.* New York, *1*:316-321, 1887.

Lowenfeld, V.: Tests for visual and haptic aptitudes. *American Journal of Psychology, 58*:100-111, 1945.

Lowenfeld and Brittan: *Creative and mental growth.* Macmillan, 1964.

Lowrey, R.A.: Distance concepts of urban residents. *Environment and Behavior, 2*:52-73, 1970.

Lueddeckens, F.: *Rechts-und-Linkshandigkeit,* Engelman, 1900.

Lumsden, E.A., Jr.; Implications of the equivalence of mirror-image stimuli for object constancy. *Psychonomic Science, 19*:55-56, 1970.

Lundberg, Bratfisch and Ekman: Emotional involvement and subjective distance—a summary of investigations. *Journal of Social Psychology, 87*:169-177, August 1972.

Lunneborg, P.: Birth order and sex of sibling effects on intellectual abilities. *Journal of Consulting and Clinical Psychology, 37*:445, 1971.

Lunzer, E.: Some points of Piagetian theory in the light of experimental criticism. *Journal of Child Psychology and Psychiatry, 1*:191-202, 1960.

Lunzer and Vinh-Bang: *Conservations spatiales, e'tudes d'espistemologie Genetique.* University of France, 1965, 9.

Lunzer and Morris: *Development in Human Learning. Staples Press, 2*:9, 1968.

Lunzer, E.A.: Translator's Introduction. In Inhelder and Piaget's *Early Growth of Logic in the Child*. Norton, 1969.

Luria, Karpov and Yarbus: Disturbances of active visual perception with lesions of frontal lobes. *Cortex*, 2:202-212, 1966.

Luria, A.R.: *Mind of the Mnemonist*. Basic Books, 1968.

Luria, A.R.: *Higher Cortical Functions in Man*. Basic Books, 1966.

Luria, A.R.: Speech development and the formation of mental processes. In Cole and Maltzman, *Handbook of Contemporary Soviet Psychology*. Basic Books, 1969, 121-162.

Luria, Simernitskaya and Tubylevich: The structure of psychological processes in relation to cerebral organization. *Neuropsychologia*, 8:13-19, 1970.

Luria, A.R.: Functional organization of the brain. *Scientific American*, 66-78, February 1970.

# M

MacArthur, R.S.: Assessing intellectual potential of native Canadian pupils: a summary. *Alberta Review of Educational Research*, 14:115-122, 1968.

MacLeod and Pick: *Studies in Perception: Essays in Honor of J.J. Gibson*. Cornell University Press, in press.

Maccoby and Bee: Some speculations concerning the lag between perceiving and performing. *Child Development*, 36:367-377, 1965.

Maccoby, E.: *Development of Sex Differences*. Stanford University Press, 1966.

Mackay, Brazendale and Wilson: Concepts of horizontal and vertical. *Developmental Psychology*, 7:232-237, 1972.

Mackworth and Morandi: The gaze selects informative information without pictures. *Perception and Psychophysics*, 2:547-552, 1967.

Mackworth and Bruner: How adults and children search and recognize pictures. *Human Development*, 13:149-177, 1970.

Macquarrie, T.W.: A mechanical ability test. *Journal of Personnel Research*, 5:329-337, 1927.

Madsen and Shapira: Behavior of three ethnic groups. *Developmental Psychology*, 3:16-20, 1970.

Maffei and Campbell: Neurophysiological localization of vertical and horizontal visual coordinates. *Science*, 167:386-387, 1970.

Magnussen, S.: Reversibility of perspective in normal and stabilized viewing. *Scandinavian Journal of Psychology*, 11:153-156, 1970.

Mahaffy and Bernard: *Kant's critical philosophy for English readers*. London, Macmillan, 1889, 6.

Makita, K.: Rarity of reading disability in Japanese children. *American Journal of Orthopsychiatry*, 38:599-614, 1968.

Malis, Pribram and Kruger: Action potentials in motor cortex. *Journal of Neurophysiology*, 16:161-167, 1953.

Malmo, R.B.: Psychological aspects of frontal gyrectomy and frontal lobotomy in mental patients. *Research publication of the Association of Nervous and Mental Disorders*, 27:537-564, 1948.

Mandes and Ghent: *The effect of stimulus orientation on the recognition of geometric forms by adults.* Paper presented at the meetings of the American Psychological Associations, 1963.

Marrie and Campbell: Neurophysiological localization of vertical and horizontal coordinates in man. *Science*, 167:386-387, 1970.

Marshall and Talbott: Recent evidence for neural mechanisms in vision leading to a general theory of sensory acuity. In J. Cattell (Ed.) *Biological symposia. Visual mechanisms*, edited by Heinrich Kluever. New York, Ronald Press, 1942, 7.

Marshall, J.C.: Some problems and paradoxes associated with recent accounts of hemispheric specialization. *Neuropsychologia*, 11:463-470, 1973.

Martin and Wreekers: Ravens coloured progressive matrices and the Wechsler intelligence scale for children. *Journal of Consulting Psychology*, 18:143-144, 1954.

Martin, B.L.: Spatial visualization abilities of Central Washington State College prospective teachers of Mathematics. Unpublished dissertation, Oregon State University, 1966.

Martin, B.L.: Spatial visualization abilities of perspective mathematics teachers. *Journal of Research in Science Teaching*, 5:11, 1968.

Martin, R.: *Lehrbuch der Anthropologie.* Fischer, 1957-1960.

Martin, W.T.: Analysis of abstracting function in reasoning using an experimental test. *Psychological Reports*, 21:593-98, 1967.

Masangkay, Feenstra, and Tayag: *Coordination of Perceptives among Filipino Children.* Occasional paper #10, Language Study Center, Philippine Normal College, Manilla, Philippines, D406, 1971.

Masangkay, McCluskey, Sims-Knight and Flavell: Early Development of Inferences about the visual percepts of others. *Child Development*, 45:357-366, 1974.

Maslow, Frostig, Lefever, Welty and Whittlesey: Frostig developmental test visual perception: 1963 standardization. *Perceptual and Motor Skills*, 19:463-499, 1964.

Mayo and Bell: A note on the taxonomy of Witken's field-independence measures. *British Journal of Psychology*, 63:255-6, May 1972.

McCallum, D.I.: *The relationship between psychological test-scores and Mathematical attainment.* M.Ed. Thesis, University of Leicester, 1972.

McCollough, C.: Color Adaptation of edge detectors in the human visual system. *Science*, 149:1115-1116, 1965.

McDonnel and Duffett: Vision and touch—a reconsideration of conflict between the two senses. *Canadian Journal of Psychology*, 26:171-180, June 1972.

McFarlane, M.: A study of practical ability. *British Journal of Psychological Monograph Supplement*, 8, 1935,

McFarland, Clashson, Wapner and Werner: *Relation between perceptual properties of objects in space and one's own body.* Paper read at American Psychological Association convention, 1961.

McFie, J.: The effects of hemispherectomy on intellectual functioning in cases of infantile hemiplegia. *Journal of Neurological Neurosurgery Psychiatry,* 24:240-249, 1961.

McFie, J.: Factors of the brain. *Bulletin of British Psychological Society,* 25:11-14, 1972.

McFie, J.: The effect of education on African performance in a group of intellectual tests. *British Journal of Educational Psychology, 31*:232-240, 1961.

McGehee and Moffie: Psychological tests in the selection of enrollees in engineering, science, management, defense training courses. *Journal of Applied Psychology, 26*:504-586, 1942.

McGlone and Davidson: Relationship between cerebral speech laterality and spatial ability. *Neuropsychologia, 11*:105-113, 1973.

McGlone and Kertesz: Sex differences in cerebral processing of visio-spatial tasks. *Cortex, 9*:313-320, 1973.

McGrady, H.J.: Verbal and nonverbal functions in school children with speech and language disorders. Unpublished doctoral dissertation, Northwestern University, 1964.

McGrady, H.J.: Language pathology and learning disabilities. In H.R. Myklebust (Ed.), *Progress in Learning Disabilities,* New York, Grune and Stratton, 199-233, 1968.

McGraw and Joreskog: Factor invariance of ability measures in groups differing in intelligence and socioeconomic status. *British Journal of Mathematical Statistical Psychology,* 24:154-168, 1971.

McGrew and McGrew: Changes in children's spacing behavior. *Human Development, 15*:359-372, 1972.

McGrew: Social and spatial density. *Journal of Child Psychology and Psychiatry,* 2:187-195, 1970.

McGuire, C.: Sex role and community variables in test performances. *Journal of Educational Psychology, 52*:61-73, 1961.

McKeever and Huling: Lateral dominance in tachistoscopic word recognitions of children at two levels of ability. *Quarterly Journal of Experimental Psychology,* 22:600-604, 1970.

McKeever and Huling: Left-cerebral hemisphere superiority in tachistoscopic word-recognition performances. *Perceptual and Motor Skills, 30*: 736-766, 1970.

McKellar: *Thinking and Imagination.* Basic Books, 1958.

McKim, R.H.: Visual thinking and the design process. *Engineering Education,* 795-799, 1968.

McKinney, J.P.: Hand scheme in children. *Psychonomic Science, 1*:99-100, 1964.

McLuhan: *Understanding Media.* McGraw-Hill, 1964.

McMahon, Montgomery and Ross: Symposium on research on engineering apprentices. Proceedings of the annual conference of B.P.S. Liverpool, B.P.S. *Quarterly Bulletin, 44*:4-5, 1961.

McMahon, S.: Selection and follow-up of engineering apprentices. *Occupational Psychology, 36*:53-58, 1962.

McRae, Branch and Milner: Occipital horns and cerebral dominance. *Neurology, 18*:95-98, 1968.

McReynolds and Worchel: Geographic orientation in the blind. *Journal of Genetic Psychology, 51*:221-236, 1954.

Meehling, O.: Tachistoscoptic visual hemifield presentation of verbal and nonverbal stimuli. *International Neuropsychological Society*, New Orleans, 1973.

Mehler, J.: Studies in language and thought development. In Huxley and Ingram, *Language Acquisition: Models and Methods*. Academic Press, 1971.

Mehrabian, A.: Relationship of attitude to seated posture, orientation, and distance. *Journal of Personality and Social Psychology, 10*:26-30, 1968.

Meier, M.J.: Effects of focal cerebral lesions on contralateral visuomotor adaptation to reversal and inversion of visual feedback. *Neuropsychologia, 8*:269-279, 1970.

Meisels and Guardo: Development of personal space schemata. *Child Development, 40*:1167-1178, 1969.

Meisels and Wapner: Interaction of factors affecting space localization. *Journal of Experimental Psychology, 79*:430-437, 1969.

Meisels and Canter: Personal space and personality characteristics: a nonconfirmation. *Psychological Reports, 27*:287-290, 1970.

Meister, D.: Comparative study of figure-ground discrimination in preschool children and adults. *Journal of Genetic Psychology, 74*:311-323, 1959.

Mellone, M.A.: A factorial study of picture tests for young children. *British Journal of Psychology, 35*:9-16, 1944.

Mendicino, N.C.: Mechanical reasoning and space perception. *Personnel and Guidance Journal, 36*:335-338, 1958.

Meredith, P.: Number-space and measurement. *Educational Sciences, 4*:37-55, 1970.

Meuris, G.: Structure of PMA of Belgian secondary school students. *Journal of Educational Measurement, 7*:191-197, 1970.

Meuris, G.: *Test Sr*. University Catholique de Lorvain, 1973.

Meux, M.O.: Role of reasoning and spatial abilities in performance at three difficulty levels of the embedded figures test. *Dissertation Abstracts, 21*:1625, 1960.

Meyer, D.: Retrieval of semantic information. *Cognitive Psychology, 1*:242-300, 1970.

Meyer, E.: la représéntation des relations spatiales chez l'enfant. *Cahiers de pedagogie experimentale et de psychologie de l'enfant*, 1935.

Meyer, M.E.: Stimulus control for bird orientation. *Psychological Bulletin,* 62:165-179, 1964.

Michael, C.R.: Retinal processing of visual image. *Scientific American, 220:* 104-114, 1969.

Michael, W.B.: The nature of space and visualization abilities: Some recent findings based on factor analysis studies. *Transactions of the New York Academy of Sciences, 11:*275-281, 1949.

Michael, Zimmerman and Guilford: An investigation of two hypotheses regarding the nature of the spatial relations and visualization factors. *Educational and Psychological Measurements, 10:*187-213, 1950.

Michael, W.B.: Factor analyses of tests and criteria: A comparative study of two AAF pilot populations. *Psychological Monograph, 63:*298, 1950.

Michael, Zimmerman and Guilford: An investigation of the nature of the spatial relations and visualization factors in two high school samples. *Educational and Psychological Measurement, 11:*561-577, 1951.

Michael, Guilford, Fruchter and Zimmerman: Description of spatial visualization abilities. *Educational and Psychological Measurement,* 1957.

Michael, Jones and Haney: Development and validation of test battery for selection of nurses. *Educational and Psychological Measurement, 19:*641-643, 1959.

Micholte, A.: *Perception of Causality.* Basic Books, 1963.

Mickish, V.: Relationship of viewing skills and visual perception. Unpublished dissertation, Arizona State University, 1970.

Midlarsky, E.: Aiding responses: an analysis and review. *Merrill-Palmer Quarterly, 14:*229-269, 1968.

Mill, J.S.: *Examination of Sir William Hamilton's philosophy, and of the principal philosophical questions discussed in his writing.* New York, Henry Holt, 1877.

Millar, S.: Visual and Haptic cue utilization by preschool children: The recognition of visual and haptic stimuli presented separately and together. *Journal of Experimental Child Psychology, 12:*88-94, 1971.

Millar, S.: Development of visual and kinaesthetic judgments of distance. *British Journal of Psychology, 63:*271-282, 1972.

Miller, E.: Handedness and the patterns of human ability. *British Journal of Psychology, 62:*111-112, 1971.

Miller, J.: Measuring perspective ability. *Journal of Geography, 46:* 167-171, 1967.

Miller, Boismier and Hooks: Training in spatial conceptualization: teacher directed activities, automated and combined programs. *Journal of Experimental Education, 38:*87-92, 1969.

Miller and Miller: A successful attempt at training children in coordination of perspective space. *Paper for AERA Convention,* Minneapolis, March, 1970.

Miller, R.: Cross-cultural research in the perception of pictorial materials. *Psychological Bulletin, 80:*135-150, 1973.

Milner, Branch and Rasmussen: Observations on cerebral dominance. In A.V.S. DeReuck and M. O'Connor (Eds.), *Ciba Foundation Symposium on Disorders of Language*, London, 200-214, 1964.

Milner, Branch and Rasmussen: Evidence for bilateral speech representation in some nonrighthanders. *Transactions of the American Neurological Association*, 91:306-308, 1966.

Milner, B.: Lateralized suppression of dichotically presented digits after commissural section in man. *Science, 161*:184-186, 1968.

Milner, B.: Visual recognition and recall after right temporal lobe excision in man. *Neuropsychologia, 6*:191-209, 1968.

Milner, B.: Interhemispheric differences in the localization of psychological processes in man. *British Medical Bulletin, 27*:272-277, 1971 .

Milner and Taylor: Right-hemisphere superiority in tactile pattern-recognition after cerebral commissurotomy-evidence for nonverbal memory. *Neuropsychologia, 10*:1-15, April 1972.

Minami, H.: Determinant factors of visual space perception. *Japanese Journal of Psychology, 15*:153-180, 1940.

Minnigerode and Carey: Development of mechanisms underlying spatial perspectives. *Child Development, 45*:496-498, 1974.

Minsky and Papert: *Research at the laboratory in vision, language and other problems of intelligence.* MIT, Artificial Intelligence memo, 252, January 1972.

Mitchelmore, M.C.: Spatial ability and three-dimensional drawing. Unpublished paper, Ohio State University, 1972.

Mitchelmore, M.C.: Influence of sex and culture on spatial ability. Unpublished paper, Ohio State University, 1973.

Moeller and Goodnow: Orientation called "right-side-up: effects of stimulus alignment. *Psychological Science, 16*:213-215, 1969.

Moffie, D.J.: A nonverbal approach to the Thurstone Primary Mental Abilities. Unpublished Ph.D., Thesis, Pennsylvania State College, 1940.

Moir, D.: Egocentricism and the emergence of conventional morality in preadolescent girls. Unpublished thesis, University of Canterbury, New Zealand, 1971.

Molfese, D.L.: Cerebral asymmetry in infant, children, and adults. Unpublished dissertation, Pennsylvania State University, 1972.

Money, J.: Dyslexia: A postconference review. In Money, J. (Ed.), *Reading Disability: Progress and Research Needs in Dyslexia.* Baltimore, The Johns Hopkins Press, 9-33, 1962.

Money, J.: Cytogenetic and psycho-sexual incongruities with a note on space-form blindness. *American Journal of Psychiatry, 119*:820-827, 1963.

Money, J.: Two cytogenetic syndromes: Psychologic comparisons intelligence and specific factor quotients. *Journal of Psychiatric Research, 2*: 223-231, 1964.

Money, J.: *A Standardized Road-Map Test of Direction Sense (manual).* Baltimore, Johns Hopkins Press, 1965.

Money, J.: On learning and not learning to read. In Money, J. (Ed.), *The Disabled Reader*. Baltimore, The Johns Hopkins Press, 1966.

Money and Mittenthal: Lack of personality pathology in Turner's syndrome. *Behavioral Genetics*, 1:43-46, 1970.

Monk, E.S.: *Dissertation abstracts*, 1967. Reading reversal, right-left discrimination and lateral preference. Unpublished doctoral dissertation, Teachers College, Columbia University, 1966.

Montgomery, G.W.G.: Predicting success in engineering. *Occupational Psychololgy*, 36:59-68, 1962.

Moore and Peel: Predicting aptitude for dentistry. *Occupational Psychology*, 25:192-199, 1951.

Moore, O.K.: Problem solving and the perception of persons. In Taguiri and Petrullo (Eds.), *Person perception and interpersonal behavior*, Stanford University Press, 131-150, 1958.

Moore, A.D.: Letter to the editor. *Scientific American*, 229:6, 1973.

Moore, M.K.: Genesis of object permanence. Paper presented at SCCD Convention, Philadelphia 1973.

Moore, MacNaughton and Osburn: Ethnic differences within an industrial selection battery. *Personnel Psychology*, 22:473-482, 1969.

Morgan, W.J.: The scores on the revised Minnesota Paper Form Board test at different grade levels of a technical-industrial high school. *Journal of Genetic Psychology*, 64:159-162, 1944.

Morris, B.B.: Effects of order and trial on necker cube reversals under free and presistive instructions. *Perceptual and Motor Skills*, 33:235-240, 1971.

Morris, C.M.: A critical analysis of certain performance tests. *Journal of Genetic Psychology*, 54:85-105, 1939.

Morrow, R.S.: An analysis of the relations among tests of musical, artistic and mechanical abilities. *Journal of Psychology*, 5:253-263, 1938.

Morrow, R.S.: An experimental analysis of the theory of independent abilities. *Journal of Educational Psychology*, 32:495-512, 1941.

Moscovitch and Catlin: Interhemispheric transmission of information: measurement in normal man. *Psychonomic Science*, 18:211-213, 1970.

Mottram and Faulds: Adaptation of a piagetian spatial perception study applied cross-culturally. *Perceptual and Motor Skills*, 37:348-350, 1973.

Mountcastle, V.B.: (Ed.), *Interhemispheric Relations and Cerebral Dominance*. Johns Hopkins University Press, 1962.

Moyles, Tuddenham and Block: Simplicity-complexity or symmetry-asymmetry? A re-analysis of the Barron-Welsh Art Scales. In, J. Hogg, (Ed.), *Psychology and the Visual Arts*. Baltimore, Penguin, 375-382, 1969.

Mowbray and Luria: Labeling and children's visual imagery. *Developmental Psychology*, 9:1-8, 1973.

Muehl, S.: The effects of visual discrimination pretraining on learning to read a vocabulary list. *Journal of Educational Psychology*, 51:217-221, 1960.

Muehl and Kremenak: Ability to match information within and between auditory and visual sense modalities and subsequent reading achievement. *Journal of Educational Psychology*, 57:230-239, 1966.

Mundy-Castle: Pictorial depth perception in Ghanian children. *International Journal of Psychology*, 1:290-300, 1966.

Munroe and Munroe: Effect of environmental experience on spatial ability in an East African society. *Journal of Social Psychology*, 83:15-22, 1971.

Munsinger and Kessen: Uncertainty, structure and preferences. *Psychological Monographs*, 78, 1964.

Munsinger and Kessen: Stimulus variability and cognitive change. *Psychological Review*, 73:164-178, 1966.

Munsinger and Forsman: Symmetry, development and tachistoscopic recognition. *Journal of Experimental Child Psychology*, 3:168-176, 1966.

Murphy, L.W.: The relation between mechanical ability tests and verbal and nonverbal intelligence tests. *Journal of Psychology*, 2:353-366, 1936.

Murray, F.B.: Conservation of illusion, distorted lengths and areas. *Journal of Educational Psychology*, 56:62-66, 1965.

Murray, F.B.: Acquistition of conservation. *Developmental Psychology*, 6:1-6, 1972.

Murray and Fetzer: Operational thought and syllogistic reasoning. *Second Conference on Research in Child Development*, Williamsburg, Va., 1972.

Murray, J.: Analysis of geometric ability. *Journal of Educational Psychology*, 40:118-124, 1949.

Myers, C.T.: Validation of six spatial relations tests. *Educational Testing Service Research Bulletin*, 53-15, 1953.

Myers, C.T.: A note on spatial relations pretest and posttest. *Educational and Psychological Measurement*, 13:596-600, 1953.

Myers, C.T.: Comparative effectiveness of spatial test directions. *Educational Testing Service Research Memorandum*, 53-11, 1953.

Myers, C.T.: Observations and opinions concerning spatial relations tests. *Educational Testing Service Research Memorandum*, 57-7, 1957.

Myers, C.T.: Effects of training in mechanical drawing on spatial relations test scores as predictors of engineering drawing grades. *Educational Testing Service Research Bulletin*, 58-4, 1958.

Myers, C.T.: Observations of problem solving in spatial relations tests. *Educational Testing Service Research Bulletin*, 58-16, 1958.

Myers and Dingman: Structure of abilities at preschool ages. *Psychological Bulletin*, 27:514-532, 1960.

Myklebust and Boshes: Psychoneurological learning disorders in children. *Archives of Pediatrics*, 77:247-256, 1960.

## N

Nadien, Schaeffer and Schmeidler: Mood as a confounding variable in eye dominance, field dependence and reading. *Perceptual and Motor Skills*, 29:277-278, 1969.

Nakahama, H.: Contralateral and ipsilateral cortical responses from somatic afferent nerves. *Journal of Neurophysiology, 21*:611-632, 1958.

Nebes, R.: Investigations of lateralization of function in the disconnected hemispheres of man. *Dissertations Abstracts International,* 71-16220.

Nebes, R.: Superiority of the minor hemisphere in commissurotomized man for the perception of part-whole relations. *Cortex, 7*:333-349, 1971.

Neimark and Lewis: Development of logical problem-solving strategies. *Child Development, 38*:107-117, 1967.

Neimark, Slotnick and Ulrick: Development of memorization strategies. *Developmental Psychology, 5*:427-432 ,1971.

Neisser, U.: Visual search. *Scientific American, 210*:6, 94-102, 1964.

Niesser and Beller: Searching through word lists. *British Journal of Psychology, 56*:349-358, 1965.

Neisser, U.: *Cognitive Psychology.* Appleton-Century-Croft, 1967.

Nelson and MacDonald: Lateral organization, perceived depth, and title preference in pictures. *Perceptual and Motor Skills, 33*:983-986, 1971.

Newbigging, P.L.: Relationship between reversible perspective and embedded figures. *Canadian Journal of Psychology, 8*:204-208, 1954.

Newman, C.V.: Children's size judgments in a picture with suggested depth. *Nature, 223*:418-420, 1969.

Newman, C.V.: The influence of visual texture density gradients on relative distance judgments. *Quarterly Journal of Experimental Psychology, 23*:225-233, 1971.

Newman, C.V.: Familiar and relative size cues and surface texture as determinants of relative distance judgments. *Journal of Experimental Psychology 96*:37-42, November 1972.

Newman, J.: The prediction of shopwork performance in an adult rehabilitation program: The Kent-Shakow industrial formboard series. *Psychology Records, 5*:343-352, 1945.

Newman, O.: *Defensible Space.* MacMillan, 1972.

Newton, I.: *Mathematical Principles of Natural Philosophy.* William Benton, 1952 (1686).

Nicholls, J.V.: Reading disabilities in the young—the ophthalmologist role. *Canadian Journal of Ophthalmology, 4*:223-230, 1969.

Nishikawa, Y.: Relationship between binocular space and physical space. *Japanese Journal of Psychology, 40*: 24-36, 1969.

Nodelman, C.: Conservation of substance and field-independence. *Graduate Research in Education and Related Disciplines, 1*:3-34, 1965.

Notcutt, B.: The measurement of Zulu intelligence. *Journal of Social Research, 1*:195-206, 1950.

Nuttin, J.: The intellectual ability of youth in different socioeconomic classes. *Mededel. Kon. Vlaamse Akad.* K1. Lett., 27(7), 1965.

Nutzhorn, H.: Re-education of left-handers. *Deutsch Med. Wschr. (Ger),* 95, 1970.

# O

O'Bryan and MacArther: A factor-analytic study of Piagetian reversibility. *Alberta Journal of Educational Research, 13*:211-220, 1967.

O'Bryan and MacArther: Reversibility, intelligence and creativity in nine-year-old boys. *Child Development, 40*:33-45, 1969.

O'Bryan, K.G.: Eye movements, perceptual activity and conservation development. *Journal of Experimental and Child Psychology, 12*:157-169, October 1971.

O'Connor, J.: *Structural Visualization,* Human Engineering Laboratory, Boston, 1943.

O'Connor, J.: Fathers and daughters: Abstract visualization. *Bulletin,* Human Engineering Laboratory, 104.

Odum and Mumbaver: Relevant dimension in problem solving. *Developmental Psychology, 4*:135-140, 1971.

Odom and Guzman: Development of hierarchies of dimensional salience. *Developmental Psychology, 6*:271-287, 1972.

Okonji, M.O.: Culture and children's understanding of geometry. *International Journal of Psychology, 6*:121-128, 1971.

Oldendorf and Crandal: Bilateral cerebral circulation curves obtained by intravenous injection of radioisotopes. *Journal of Neurosurgery, 18*:195-199, 1961.

Oleron, P.: *Les composants de l'intelligence d'apres les recherches factorielles,* Presses Universitaire de France, Paris, 1957.

Olson, A.: Factor analytic studies of the Frostig developmental test of visual perception. *Journal of Special Education, 2*:429-433, 1968.

Olson and Attneave: What variables produce similarity grouping. *American Journal of Psychology, 83*:1-21, 1970.

Olson, N.H.: Neurological dysfunction and reading disability: types of disorders. *Reading Teacher, 22*:157-162, 1968.

Olson and Pagliuso: From perceiving to performing: an aspect of cognitive growth. *Ontario Journal of Educational Research, 10*, 1968.

Olson, D.R.: *Cognitive Development.* Academic Press, 1970.

Olson, D.R.: Information-processing limitations of mentally retarded children. *American Journal of Mental Deficiency, 75*:478-486, 1971.

Olson, D.R.: Language use for communicating, instructing and thinking. In Carroll and Freedle, *Language comprehension and the acquisition of knowledge.* Winston, 1972.

Olson, D.R.: Media, modes and symbol systems. In Olson (Ed.), *Media and Symbols: The forms of expression, communication and education.* 73rd Yearbook of National Society for Study of Education, University of Chicago, 1974.

Olson and Filby: On the comprehension of active and passive sentences. *Cognitive Psychology, 3*:631-681, 1972.

Olson and Laxar: Asymmetries in processing the terms "right" and "left." *Journal of experimental Psychology,* in press.

Olson and Hildyard: The role of long and short-term memory in the verification of active and passive sentences. In preparation.

Ombredane, Bertelson and Beniest-Noirot: Speed and accuracy of performance of an African native population and of Belgian children on a paper-and-pencil perceptual task. *Journal of Social Psychology*, 47:327-337, 1958.

Ono, H.: Apparent distance as a function of familiar size. *Journal of Experimental Psychology*, 79:109-115, 1969.

Orbach, J.: Retinal locus as a factor in the recognition of visually perceived words. *American Journal of Psychology*, 555-562, 1952.

Orbach, J.: Differential recognition of Hebrew and English words in right and left visual fields as a function of cerebral dominance and reading habits. *Neuropsychologia*, 5:127-136, 1967.

Orbach, J.: Perceptual reversals, eye blinks and "preferred orientation." *Perceptual and Motor Skills*, 29:902, 1969.

Ornstein, R.E.:*The Psychology of Consciousness.* Viking, 1973.

Orton, S.T.: "Word blindness" in school children. *Archives of Neurological and Psychiatric*, 14:581-615, 1925.

Orton, S.T.: Specific reading disability—strephosymbolia. *Journal of American Medical Association*, 90:1095-1099, 1928.

Orton, S.T.: Visual functions in strephosymbolia. *Archives of Ophthalmology*, 30:707-717, 1943.

Osborne and Lindsey: A longitudinal investigation of change in the factorial composition of intelligence with age in young school children. *Journal of Genetic Psychology*, 110:49-58, 1967.

Osgood, Suci and Tannenbaum: *Measurement of Meaning.* University of Illinois Press, 1957.

Osgood, C.E.: Exploration in semantic space. *Journal of Social Issues*, 27: 5-64, 1971.

Oswald, I.: Number-forms and kindred visual images. *Journal of General Psychology*, 63:81-88, 1960.

Over and Over: Kinaesthetic judgments of direction. *Quarterly Journal of Experimental Psychology*, 19:337-340, 1967.

Overton and Jackson: Representation of imagined objects in action sequences. *Child Development*, 44:309-314, 1973.

Owens, W.A.: Age and mental abilities: A longitudinal study. *Genetic and Psychological Monograph*, 48:3-54, 1953.

Owens, W.A.: Age and mental ability: A second adult follow-up. *Journal of Educational Psychology*, 57:311-325, 1966.

Oxlade, M.N.: Further experience with selection tests for power sewing machine operators. *Bulletin of Industrial Psychology and Personnel Practice*, 8:1, Australia, 1951.

# P

Painter, G.: Effect of rhythmic and sensory motor activity on perceptual motor spatial activities of kindergarten children. *Exceptional Children,* 33:113-116, 1966.

Paivio, A.: Mental imagery in associative learning and memory. *Psychological Review,* 76:241-263, 1969.

Paivio, A.: *Imagery and Verbal Processes.* Holt, Rinehart and Winston, 1971.

Palow, W.P.: (University of Florida) A study of the ability of public school students to visualize particular perspectives of selected solid figures. *Dissertation Abstracts International,* 31:78-79, 1970.

Palted, G.M.: A study of spatial ability in high school pupils and its relation to success in architecture course, Dissertation. *Department of Psychological Foundations,* NCERT, Delhi, 1967.

Pantle and Sekuler: Contrast response of human visual mechanism—sensitive to orientation and direction of motion. *Vision Research,* 9:397-406, March, 1969.

Paoluzzi and Bravaccio: Ripartizoine tra 1 due emisferi delle anomalita EEG focalizzate. *Atti XVI Congress Naz. Neurologia,* V. 111 Rome, 367-372, 1967.

Paraskevopoulos, I.: Symmetry, recall and preference in relation to chronological age. *Journal of Experimental Child Psychology,* 6:254-264, 1968.

Paraskevopoulos, I.: Effects of redundancy on information-reduction tasks. *Journal of Experimental Child Psychology,* 7:195-202, 1969.

Parisi and Antinucci: Lexical competence. In Flores d'Arcias and Levelt, W.J.M. *Advances in Psycholinquistics.* North-Holland Publishing Company, 1970.

Parker and Day: Use of perceptual, functional and abstract attributes in multiple classification. *Developmental Psychology,* 5: 312-319, 1971.

Parlee, M.: Comments on Broverman hypothesis. *Psychological Review,* 79: 180-184, 1972.

Parsons, B.S.: *Left-handedness.* New York, Macmillan Co., 1924.

Pastore, N.: Perceiving as innately determined. *Journal of Genetic Psychology,* 96:93-99, 1960.

Pastore, N.: The orientation of the cerebral image in Descartes' theory of visual perception. *Journal History of Behavioral Science.* 5:385-389, 1969.

Patson, N.: Prediction of construction achievement using Saddler test. *Dexterity Questionnaire,* and four spatial relations tests. Unpublished master's thesis, Iowa State College, 1952.

Patterson, C.H.: Predicting success in trade and vocational school courses; Review of the literature. *Educational and Psychological Measurements,* 16:352-400, 1956.

Patton, Towe and Kennedy: Activation of pyradimal tract neurons by ipsilateral cutaneous stimuli. *Journal of Neurophysiology,* 25:501-514, 1962.

Pavelko, A.E.: Development of spatial representations in children. Unpublished thesis, Purdue University, 1967.

Pawlik: Concept and calculations in human cognitive abilities. In Cattell, *Handbook of Multivariate Experimental Psychology.* Rand McNally, 1966.

Payne, J.F.: Comparative study of mental ability. *British Journal of Educational Psychology, 39:*326-327, 1969.

Pear, T.: *Remembering and Forgetting.* London, Methuen, 1922.

Pear, T.: Privileges and limitations of visual imagery. *British Journal of Psychology, 14:*363-373, 1925.

Pear, T.: The revelance of visual imagery in the process of thinking. I. *British Journal of Psychology, 18:*1-14, 1927.

Pear, T.: The place of imagery in mental processes. *Psychological Abstracts, 12:*729, 1938.

Pear and Cohen: Simple and complex imagery in individual subjects. *Psychological Record, 21:*25-33, 1971.

Pearson, Alpers and Weisenburg: Aphasia: a study of normal control cases. *Archives of Neurology and Psychiatry, 19:*281-295, 1928.

Pedde, M.L.: Children's Concepts of Base Area Symbols. Unpublished thesis, University of Alberta, 1966.

Pelecanos, M.: Some Greek data on handedness, hand clasping and arm folding. *Human Biology, 41:*275-278, 1969.

Pepper, S.C.: *World Hypotheses.* University of California Press, 1942.

Perky, C.W.: Experimental study of imagination. *American Journal of Psychology, 21:*422-452, 1910.

Perlo and Rak: Developmental dyslexia in adults. *Neurology, 21:*1231-1235, 1971.

Personnel Research Division, Human Resources Research Center: *Research Report No. 13 for Quarter ending September 1949.* United States Air Force Air Training Command Indoctrination Division, 1 October, 1949.

Peterson, Danner and Flavell: Developmental changes in children's response to three indications of communicative failure. *Child Development,* in press.

Petrie, A.: Personality changes after prefrontal leucotomy. *British Journal of Medical Psychology, 22:*200-207, 1939.

Petrie, A.: The selection of medical students. *Lancet, 255:*325-327, 1948.

Piaget, J.: *Judgment and Reasoning in the Child.* London, Routledge and Kegan Paul Ltd., 1928.

Piaget and Lambercier: Recherches sur le development des perceptions. *Archives Psychologic Geneve, 29:*255-308, 1942.

Piaget and Lambercier: la comparaison visuelle des hauteurs a distances variables. *Archives de psychologie, 29:*173-253, 1943.

Piaget, J.: *Child's Construction of Reality.* Basic Books, 1954.

Piaget, Inhelder and Szeminska: *Childs Conception of Geometry.* Kegan-Paul, 1960.

Piaget, J.: *Play, Dreams, and Imitation in Childhood.* Norton, 1962.

Piaget, J.: *Origins of Intelligence.* Norton, 1963.

Piaget, J.: *Child's Conception of Time.* Basic Books, 1969.

Piaget, J.: *Child's Conception of Physical Causality.* Littlefield, Adams, 1969.

Piaget and Inhelder: *Mental Imagery in the Child.* Basic Books, 1970.

Piaget, J.: *Biology and Knowledge.* University of Chicago Press, 1971.

Piaget, J.: Perceptual and cognitive structures in the development of space. *14th International Congress of Psychology,* Montreal.

Piaget and Taponier: Recherches sur le development des perceptions. *Archives Psychologic Geneve,* 35:269-400, 1956.

Piaget, J.: Response to Brian Sutton-Smith. *Psychological Review,* 73:111-112, 1966.

Piaget, J.: Piaget's theory. In Mussen (Ed.), *Carmichael's Manual of Child Psychology.* Wiley, 1970.

Pick, A.D.: Improvement of visual and tactual form discrimination. *Journal of Experimental Psychology.* 69:331-369, 1965.

Pick and Pick: A developmental study of tactual discrimination in blind and sighted children and adults. *Psychonomic Science,* 6:367-368, 1966.

Pick, Klein and Pick: Visual and tactual identification of form orientation. *Journal of Experim ntal Child Psychology,* 4:391-397, 1966.

Pick, Pick and Klein: 'erceptual integration in children. In L.P. Lipsitt and C.C. Spiker (Eds.). *Advances in Child Development and Behavior.* New York, Academic, 3:191-223, 1967.

Pick, H.L.: Systems of perceptual and perceptual-motor development. In J. Hill (Ed.). *Minnesota Symposia of Child Psychology,* Minn., University of Minnesota Press, 4:199-219, 1970.

Pick and Pick: Sensory and perceptual development. In Mussen, (Ed.), *Carmichael's Manual of Child Psychology.* Wiley, 773-848, 1970.

Pick, H.L.: Mapping children mapping space. Paper read at APA convention. Hawaii, September, 1972.

Pick, Acredolo and Gronseth: Children's knowledge of the spatial layout of their homes. Paper presented at SRCD convention, 1973.

Piercy and Smyth: Right hemisphere dominance for certain nonverbal intellectual skills. *Brain,* 85:775-790, 1962.

Pieron, H.: Essais en vue de l'etablissement d'une fiche d'aptitude technique. *Bull. Inst. nat. d'orient. prof.,* 4:189-194, 1932.

Pieron, H.: Essais en vue de l'etablissement d'une fiche d'aptitude technique (Experiments to establish a test for technical aptitude.) *Bull. Inst. nat. d'orient. prof.,* 5:29-37, 1933.

Pike, R.: How children answer questions about perceived events, pictures and statements. Unpublished dissertation, University of Toronto, 1973.

Pimsleur and Bonkowski: Transfer of verbal material across sense modalities. *Journal of Educational Psychology,* 52:104-107, 1961.

Pinard and Laurendeau: Topological nature of early spatial concepts. *International Journal of Psychology,* 1:243-255, 1966.

Pines, M.: *The Brain Changers: Scientists and the New Mind Control.* Harcourt, Brace Jovanovich, 1973.

Pintner and Paterson: *A Scale of Performance Tests.* New York, D. Appleton, 1917.

Pirenne, M.H.: *Optics, Painting and Photography.* Cambridge University Press, 1970.

Pizzemiglio, L.: Development of the hemispheric dominance in children from 5 to 10 years of age and their relations with the development of cognitive processes. *Brain Research, 31*:363-364, 1971.

Platner, E.: *Philosophische Aphorisman.* Leipzig, 466, 1973.

Podell and Phillips: A developmental analysis of cognition as observed in dimensions of Rorschach and objective test performance. *Journal of Personality, 27*:439-463, 1959.

Poincare, H.: *Foundations of Science.* Science Press, 1946.

Poincare, H.: *Science and Hypothesis.* Dover, 1952.

Pollack and Kiev: Spatial orientation and psychotherapy. *Journal of Nervous and Mental Diseases, 137*:93-97, 1963.

Pollack and Spence: Subjective pictorial information and visual search. *Perception and Psychophysics, 3*:41-44, 1968.

Poole, H.: Urbanization upon scientific concept at  inment among Hausa children. *British Journal of Educational Psycholo  ', 38*:57-63, 1968.

Poole, H.: Restructuring the perceptual world of Af  .:an children. *Teacher Education in New Countries, 10*:165-172, 1969.

Poole and Stanley: A factorial and predictive study of spatial abilities. *Australian Journal of Psychology, 24*:317-320, 1972.

Popper, K.R.: *Logic of Scientific Discovery.* Basic Books, 1959.

Popper, K.R.: *Conjectures and Refutations.* Basic Books, 1963.

Porteus and Peters: Maze test validation and psychosurgery. *Genetic Psychology Monograph, 36*, 1947.

Porteus, S.D.: *The Maze Test and Mental Differences.* Vineland, Smith, 1933.

Poruben, A., Jr.: Validation and standardization of the AGO General Mechanical Aptitudes Test for the selection of civilian employees in War Department installations. *Educational and Psychological Measurement, 10*:254-262, 1950.

Posner, M.I.: Characteristics of visual and kinesthetic memory codes. *Journal of Experimental Psychology, 75*:103-107, 1967.

Potegal, M.: A note on spatial-motor deficits in patients with Huntington's disease—A test of a hypothesis. *Neuropsychologia, 9*:233-235, June 1971.

Potter and Levy: Spatial enumeration without counting. *Child Development, 265-273*, March 1968.

Pratt, C.C.: Experimental studies of thought and reasoning. *Psychological Bulletin, 25*:550-561, 1928.

Pratt, R.T.: Unilateral ECT as a test for cerebral dominance with a strategy for treating left-handers. *British Journal of Psychiatry, 119*:79-83, 1971.

Prechtl, H.F.R.: The directed head turning response and allied movements of the human infant. *Behavior, 13*:212-242, 1958.

Pribram, K.: Discussion. In Mountcastle, V.B. *Interhemispheric and Cerebral Dominance.* Johns Hopkins Press, 1962.

Pribram, K.: *Languages of the brain.* Prentice-Hall, 1971.

Price, E.J.J.: The nature of the practical factor (F). *British Journal of Psychology, 30*:341-351, 1940.

Price, J.R.: Set, satiation and confusion: A reply to Sadler and Mufferd. *Perceptual and Motor Skills, 33*:703-707, 1971.

Prior, F.M.: *The place of maps in the junior school, a study of the junior school child's understanding of maps in relation to spatial concepts.* M.A. Thesis, University of Birmingham, 1959.

Proshansky, Ittelson and Rivlin: *Environmental Psychology.* Holt, Rinehart and Winston, 1971.

Provins, K.A.: Handedness and skill. *Quarterly Journal of Experimental Psychology, 8*:79-95, 1956.

Provins, K.A.: Effect of training and handedness on the performance of two simple motor skills. *Quarterly Journal of Experimental Psychology, 10*: 29-39, 1958.

Pufall, P.B.: Acquisition and generalization of spatial order conservation. Unpublished dissertation, Catholic University, 1969.

Pufall, P.B.: Relations between egocentricism and coordinate reference systems. Paper presented at SRCD Convention, 1973.

Pufall and Shaw: Analysis of the development of children's spatial reference systems. *Cognitive Psychology, 5*:151-175, 1973.

Punwar, A.: Spatial visualization, reading, spelling, and mathematical abilities in second and third-grade children. *American Journal of Occupational Therapy, 24*:495-499, 1970.

Pylyshyn, Z.W.: What the mind's eye tells the mind's brain: a critique of mental imagery. *Psychological Bulletin, 80*:1-24, 1973.

**Q**

Quasha and Likert: The Revised Minnesota Paper Form Board Test. *Journal of Educational Psychology, 28*:197-204, 1937.

Quereshi, M.Y.: Patterns of psycholinguistic development during early and middle childhood. *Educational and Psychological Measurement, 27*:353-365, 1967.

**R**

Radaker, L.D.: Visual imagery of retarded children and rels to memory for word forms. *Exceptional Children, 27*, 1961.

Radke-Yarrow and Campbell: Person perception in children. *Merrill-Palmer Quarterly, 9*:57-72, 1963.

Raju: Note on imagery types. *Indiana Journal of Psychology, 42*:86-88, 1946.

Rainville and Dusek: Euclidean and noneucliden illusions. *Perceptual and Motor Skills, 34*:916, June 1972.

Ramalingaswami, P.: Use of block design test among illiterate low economic group of people. *Indian Journal of Psychology,* 40:153-160, 1965.

Ranucci, E.: Effect of a study of solid geometry on certain aspects of space perception abilities. Unpublished dissertation, teachers college, Columbia, 1952.

Ratliff, F.: The role of physiological nystagmus in monocular acuity. *Journal of Psychology,* 43:163-172, 1952.

Raven, J.C.: *Progressive Matrices,* Lewis, 1962.

Rawls, Trego, McGaffey and Rawls: Personal space as a predictor of performance under close working conditions. *Journal of Social Psychology,* 86:261-267, 1972.

Ray-Chowdhury, K.: Imagery and performance tests of intelligence. *Indian Psychological Bulletin,* 2:25-30, 1957.

Reed, H.O.: The Midget Wiggly Block test for mechanical ability. *Industrial Arts Vocational Education,* 30:153-154, 1941.

Reese, H.W.: Imagery in children's learning: A symposium. *Psychological Bulletin,* 73:385-421, 1970.

Reese, H.W.: Implications of Mnemonic research for cognitive theory. Paper presented at SRCD Convention, Southeastern Conference, 1970.

Reichard, S.: Mental organization and age level. *Archives Psychology, 295,* New York, 1944.

Reichenbach, H.: *Philosophy of space and time.* New York, 1958.

Remmers and Smith: Reliability and practice effect in the O'Connor Wiggly Block test, *Journal of Applied Psychology,* 20:591-598, 1936.

Rennels, M.: Instructional methodology in art education upon achievement on spatial tasks by disadvantaged Negro youths. *Journal of Negro Education,* 39:116-123, 1970.

Rennert, H.: Vertical displacement of the visual angle in schizophrenic creative art. Spatial conception anomalies. *Psychiatric Neurology Medical Psychology,* 21:325-329, 1969.

Renz and Smock: *Some Methodological problems in the study of perceptual and cognitive factors in the development of space concepts.* APA Convention, 1970.

Rey, Pond, and Evans: Clinical and electroencephalogephic studies of the temporal lobe function. *Proceedings of the Royal Society of Medicine,* 42:891-904, 1949.

Rice, C.: The orientation of plane figures as a factor in their perception by children. *Child Development,* 1:111-143, 1930.

Rice, J.A.: Right-left discrimination: systematic reversal in bright children. *Journal of Learning Disabilities,* 1:26-31, 1968.

Rice, J.A.: Confusion in laterality: A validity study with bright and dull children. *Journal of Learning Disabilities,* 2:29-34, 1969.

Richard, H.: Contre-verification experimentale d'une etude sur la mise en relation des perspectives. Unpublished thesis, University of Montreal, 1962.

Richards, W.: Factors affecting depth perception. Air Force Office of Scientific Research, Washington, D.C., 1973.

Richardson, A.: *Mental Imagery.* Springer, 1969.

Rieger, C.: Ueber Apparate in dem Hirn. *Arb. psychiat. Klin. Wurzburg,* 5:176-197, 1909.

Rife, D.C.: Handedness with special reference to twins. *Genetics,* 25:178-186, 1940.

Riggs, L.A.: Visual acuity. In C.H. Grahni (Ed.), *Vision and Visual Perception,* New York, Wiley, 1965.

Riviore, J.L.: Development of reference systems in children. Unpublished dissertation, University of Arizona, 1961.

Roberts, L.: *Machine perception of 3ᵈ solids.* TR 315, Lincoln Laboratory, MIT, 1963.

Robinson, A.: The relation of visual imagery to operational thinking in children. Unpublished dissertation, Catholic University, 1970.

Robinson, L.T.: An exploratory study of the utilization of spatial concepts by children. *Dissertation Abstracts International, 31:* 1631, 1970.

Rockway, A.M.: Cognitive factors in adolescent person perception development. *Developmental Psychology,* 1:630, 1969.

Rodda, M.: Experimental techniques in diagnosing temporal sequence problems. *Sound,* 2:31-33, 1968.

Rodger, A.: A Borstal experiment in vocational guidance. *Industrial Health Research Board Reprint,* 78: 1937.

Rogers, Volkmann, Reese and Kaufman: *Accuracy and variability of direct estimates of hearing from large display screens.* Memorandum Rep. 166-I-MHCI. Special Devices Center, O.N.R., 1947.

Rogers, E.M.: *Physics for the Inquiring Mind.* Princeton University Press, 1960.

Roff, M.: *Personnel Selection and Classification Procedures: Perceptual tests,* Project 21-02-009, United States Air Force School of aviation medicine, April, 1950.

Roff, M.F.: *Personnel selection and classification procedures: Spatial tests, a factorial analysis.* United States Air Force School of Aviation Medicine, Randolph Field, Texas, 1951, Project 21-29-002.

Roff, M.: A factorial study of tests in the perceptual area. *Psychometric Monograph, 8,* 1952.

Roff, M.: *Pilot candidate selection research program: V: A factorial study of motor aptitudes.* United States Air Force School of Aviation Medicine, Report, 1953, 21-29-008.

Rose, Blank and Bridger: Intermodal and intramodal retention of visual and tactile information in young children. *Developmental Psychology,* 6:482-486, 1972.

Rosenberger, P.B.: Visual matching and clinical findings among good and poor readers. *American Journal of Disturbed Children,* 119:103-110, 1970.

Rosenhan, D.: Some origins of concern for others. In Mussen *et al.*, *Trends and Issues in Developmental Psychology*, Holt, 1969.

Rosenweig, M.R.: Discrimination of interaural time—differences at the auditory cortex. *Federal Proceedings, 10*:111, 1951.

Ross, J.: Predicting practical skill in engineering apprentices. *Occupational Psychology, 36*:69-74, 1962.

Roth, M.: Disorders of body image caused by lesions of right parietal lobe. *Brain, 4*:625-629, 1949.

Rothenberg, B.: Childrens social sensitivity. *Child Development, 2*:335-350, 1970.

Royer, D.: Copie de geste et recherche de symetrie dans une epreive delocalisation de sites topographiques. Unpublished Thesis, University of Montreal, 1964.

Royer, F.L.: Spatial orientational and figural information in free recall of visual figures. *Journal of Experimental Psychology, 91*:326-332, 1971.

Rubin, K.: Egocentric communication and popularity. *Developmental Psychology, 7*:364, 1972.

Rudel and Teuber: Discrimination of direction of line in children. *Journal of Comparative and Physiological Psychology, 56*:892-898, 1963.

Rudel and Teuber: Decrement of visual and haptic Muller-Lyer illusion on repeated trials: A study of crossmodal transfer. *Quarterly Journal of Experimental Psychology, 15*:1-15, 1963.

Rudel and Teuber: Crossmodal transfer of shape discrimination by children. *Neuropsychologia, 2*:1-8, 1964.

Rudel, Denckla, and Spalten: Functional asymmetry of Braille letter learning in normal, sighted children. *Brain*, in press.

Rummelhart and Abrahamson: Toward a theory of analogical reasoning. Unpublished manuscript, University of California at San Diego, 1970.

Rushdoony: Child's ability to read maps. *Journal of Geography, 67*:213-222, 1968.

Rusmore, J.T.: Comparison of an "industrial" problem solving task and an assembly task. *Journal of Applied Psychology, 28*:129-131, 1944.

Russell, W.R.: Functions of the frontal lobes. *Lancet,* 356-360, 1948.

Ryan and Ryan: Geographical orientation. *American Journal of Psychology 53*:204-215, 1940.

Ryan and Schwartz: Speed of perception as a function of mode of representation. *American Journal of Psychology, 69*:60-69, 1956.

### S

Saarni, C.I.: Piagetian operations and field independence as factors in children's problem-solving performance. *Child Development, 44*:338-345, 1973.

Sabatino and Cramblett: Encephalitis virus infection in children. *Developmental Medical Child Neurology, 10*:331-337, 1968.

Salk, L.: The role of the heartbeat in the relations between mother and infant, *Scientific American, 228*:24-29, 1973.

Salkind, N.: A developmental study of a spatial measure. Unpublished dissertation, University of Maryland, 1973.

Salomon, G.: *Heuristic models for the generation of aptitude-treatment interaction hypotheses.* University of Jerusalem, October, 1971.

Salomon, G.: Can we affect cognitive skills through the visual media? Unpublished mimeograph, Hebrew University, 1972.

Saltz and Sigel: Concept overdiscrimination in children. *Journal of Experimental Psychology*, 73:1-8, 1967.

Samuels, Butters and Goodglass: Visual memory deficits following cortical and limbic lesions-effect of field of presentation. *Physiological Behavior*, 6:447-452, April 1971.

Sanders, Laurendeau, and Bergson: Aging and the concept of space. *Journal of Gerontology*, 21:281-286, 1966.

Sandstrom, E.: Sex differences in localization and orientation. *Acta Psychologica*, 9:82-96, 1953.

Sayed, F.B., et al.: *The cognitive factors in geometrical ability.* Ph.D. Thesis, University of Reading, 1951.

Scandura, J.: Role of rules in behavior. *Psychological Review.* 77:516-533, 1970.

Scagnelli, P.: Relationships among visual imagery, language, and haptics in spatial perception. *Dissertation Abstracts International, 30*:3875, 1970.

Schaffer, M.C.: Parent-child Similarity in Psychological Differentiation. Unpublished dissertation, Purdue University, 1969.

Schaie, and Strother: A cross-sequential study of age changes in cognitive behavior. *Psychological Bulletin,* 70:671-680, 1968.

Schaller, M.J.: The role of intrinsic features in the judgment of upright orientation of two-dimensional forms. Unpublished doctoral dissertation, Michigan State University, 1971.

Schaller and Harris: *Children's same—different judgments of various transformations of letter-like forms using the method of paired comparisons: Effects of transformation and age of child.* Paper presented at SRCD Convention, Santa Monica, 1969.

Schaub, Alma de Vries: On the intensity of images. *American Journal of Psychology*, 2C:346-368, 1911.

Schell and Satz: "Nonverbal" visual half-field perception and hemispheric asymmetry. *American Psychological Association Proceedings 78th Annual Convention,* 5:187-188, 1970.

Schiller, B.: Verbal, numerical, and spatial abilities of young children. *Archives of Psychology, 161*, 1934.

Schiller, B.: The factor pattern yield of twelve tests of intelligence, *Journal of Genetic Psychology, 16*:311-321, 1937.

Schlaegal, T.: Method of imagery in blind as compared to sighted adolescents. *Journal of Genetic Psychology*, 83:265-277, 1953.

Schmeidler, G.R.: Visual imagery correlated to a measure of creativity. *Journal of consulting psychology, 29*:78-80, 1965.

Schmidt, F.L.: *Spatial Ability—The Feminine Achilles Heel.* Publisher unknown.

Schnall, M.: Spatio-temporal integration in progressively changing patterns. In Wapner and Kaplan (Eds.), *Heinz Werner,* Clark University Press, 1966.

Schnall, M.: Global errors in children's reproductions of progressively changing pictures. *American Journal of Psychology, 80:*213-220, 1967.

Schnall, M.: Age differences in the integration of progressive by changing visual patterns. *Human Development, 11:*287-295, 1968.

Schnall and Kemper: Modes of organizing progressively changing stimulation. *American Journal of Psychology, 81:*375-383, 1968.

Schnall, M.: Representations and reproductions in children's drawings, proceedings, 77th Annual Convention. *American Psychological Association,* 1969.

Schnall, Alter, Swanland and Schivertzer: A sensory-motor context affecting performance in a conservation task. *Child Development, 43,* 1972.

Schnall and Lenk: Empirical analoge of reversibility affecting conservation of weight judgments. Unpublished paper, 1972.

Schnoll and Kemper: Modes of organizing progressively changing stimulation. *American Journal of Psychology, 81:*375-383, 1968.

Schrier, Povar and Vaughan: Measurement of eye orientation of monkeys during visual discrimination. *Behavior Research Methods and Instrumentation, 2:*55-62, 1970.

Schroth, M.L.: Spatial aptitude and its relationship to art judgment. *Perceptual and Motor Skills, 24:*746, 1967.

Schultz, R.S.: Preliminary study of an industrial revision of the revised Minnesota Paper Form Board Test. *Journal of Applied Psychology, 24:* 463-467, 1940.

Schwartz, P.A.: *Aptitude tests for use in the developing nations and development of manpower screening tests for the developing nations.* American Institutes for Research. Pittsburgh, 1961, 1964.

Schwartz, T.: Spatial and temporal orientation in the Admiralty Islands (Manus). *Paper read at American Anthropological Association,* Pittsburgh, Pa., November, 1966.

Schweitzer and Schnall: Sequence effects in the abstraction of concept of progressive change. *Human Development, 13:*201-212, 1970.

Schwitzgebel, R.: The performance of Dutch and Zulu Adults on selected perceptual tasks. *Journal of Social Psychology,* 1962.

Scott: Imagery. *Journal of General Psychology.* 1271-1278, 1936.

Scott, M.S.: Absence of interference effects in preschool children's picture recognition. *Journal of Genetic Psychology, 122:*121-126, 1973.

Scoval, T.: Foreign accents, language acquisition, and cerebral dominance. *Language Learning, 20:*237-246, 1970.

Seashore, Buxton and McCollom: Multiple factorial analysis of fine motor skills. *American Journal Psychology, 53:*251-259, 1940.

Secor, W.B.: Visual Reading—A study in mental imagery. *American Journals of Psychology, 11*:225-266, 1899.

Seeman, E.: Development of the pictorial aptitude in children. *Journal of Personality, 34*:209-221, 1933.

Segal and Michael: Relaxation and the 'Perky Effect,' The influence of body position on judgments of images. *American Journal of Psychology, 80*: 257-262, 1967.

Segal, Campbell and Herskovits: *The influence of culture on visual perception.* New York, Bobbs-Merrill, Inc., 1969.

Seinen and Werff: Van Der Observation of facial asymmetry. *Nederl T Psychol* (Dut), *24*:551-558, September 1969.

Sekuler and Rosenblith: Discrimination of direction of line and the effect of stimulus alignment. *Psychonomic Science, 1*:143-144, 1964.

Sekuler and Abrams: Visual sameness: a choice-time analysis of pattern recognition processes. *Journal of Experimental Psychology, 77*:232-238, 1968.

Sekuler and Houlihan: Discrimination of mirror-images: Choice time analysis of human adult performance. *Quarterly Journal of Experimental Psychology, 20*:204-207, 1968.

Sekuler and Erlebacher: The two illusions of muller-lyer: Confusion theory reexamined. *American Journal of Psychology, 84*:477-486, 1971.

Selfridge and Neisser: Pattern recognition by machine. *Scientific American, 203*:60-68, 1960.

Selman, R.: Relationship of role-taking ability to the development of moral judgment in children. *Child Development, 42*:79-91, 1971.

Selman, R.: Taking another's perspective: Role-taking development in early childhood. *Child Development, 42*:1721-1734, 1971.

Selman, R.: Structural analysis of the ability to take another perspective. Paper presented at SRCD Convention, 1973.

Semmes, Weinstein, Ghent and Teuber: *Somatosensory Changes after Penetrating Brain Wounds in a Man.* Cambridge, Harvard University Press, 1:91, 1960.

Semmes, J.: Hemispheric specialization. *Neuropsychologica, 6*:11-26, 1968.

Serpell, R.: Attention theory copying orientation. *African Social Research, 9*:660-668, 1970.

Seymour, P.H.K.: Response latencies in judgments of spatial location. *British Journal of Psychology, 60*:31-39, 1969.

Shafer and Lilly: Dominance in relation to achievement. *Academic Therapy, 6*:177-185, 1970.

Shai, Goodglass and Barton: Recognition of tachistoscopically presented verbal and nonverbal material after unilateral cerebral damage. *Neuropsychologia, 10*:185-191, July 1972.

Shantz, C.U.: Developmental study of Piaget's theory of logical multiplication. *Merrill-Palmer Quarterly,* 1966.

Shantz, C.U.: Egocentricism in children, its generality and correlates. Unpublished manuscript. *Merrill-Palmer Institute,* 1968.

Shapiro, M.B.: Rotation of drawings by illiterate Africans. *Journal of Social Psychology, 52:*17-30, 1960.

Shaver, P.R.: Interference with spatial memory during problem solving. Unpublished dissertation, University of Michigan, 1970.

Shaw, B.: *Visual symbols survey, Report on the recognition of drawings in Kenya.* African Medical and Research Foundation, 1969.

Shayeoft, M.F.: High school years, growth in cognitive skills. *American Institute of Research,* 1967.

Shedd, C.L.: Ptolemy rides again or dyslexia doesn't exist. *Alabama Journal of Medical Science, 54:*481-503, 1968.

Sheehan, P.W.: Accuracy and vividness of visual images. *Perceptual and Motor Skills, 23:*391-398, 1966.

Sheehan, P.W.: Functional similarity of imaging to perceiving. *Perceptual and Motor Skills, 23:*1011-1033, 1966.

Sheehan, P.W.: *The Function and Nature of Imagery.* Academic Press, 1972.

Shemyakin, F.N.: Orientation in space. *Psychological Science in United Soviet Socialist Republic.* Office of Technical Services, *62:*11083, 1962.

Shepard, Hovland and Jenkins: Learning and memorization of classifications. *Psychological Monograph, 75:*517, 1961.

Shepard, R.N.: Analysis of proximities as a technique for the studying of information processing in man. *Human factors, 5:*33-48, 1963.

Shepard and Chipman: Second-order isomorphism of internal representations: shapes of states. *Cognitive Psychology, 1:*1-17, 1970.

Shepard and Metzler: Mental rotation of three-dimensional objects. *Science, 171:*701-703, 1971.

Shepard, R.N.: Studies of the form, formation, and transformation of internal representations. E. Galanter (Ed.), *Cognitive Mechanisms,* Washington, D.C., V.H., Winston & Sons, in press.

Shepard and Feng: A chronometric study of mental paper folding. *Cognitive Psychology, 3:*228-243, 1972.

Sherman, J.A.: Problem of sex differences in space perception and aspects of intellectual functioning. *Psychological Review, 4:*290-299, 1967.

Sherman and McWhinnie: Flash-room method-drawing training for freshman architectural students. *Acta Psychology, 31:*158-168, 1969.

Shif, Z.: Development of children in schools for the mentally retarded. In Cole and Maltzman (Eds.), *Handbook of Contemporary Soviet Psychology.* Basic Books, 1969.

Shidely, T.: Visual contours in homogeneous space. *Science, 150:*348-350, 1965.

Short: Objective study of visual imagery. *British Journal of Psychology, 44:* 35-51, 1953.

Shugart, Souder and Bunker: Relationship between vertical space perception and a dynamic nonlocomotor balance task. *Perceptual and Motor Skills, 34:*43-46, 1972.

Siebeck, H.: *Geschichte der Psychologie*. Gotha, Friedrich Andreas Perthes, 6, 1880.

Siegel and Kresh: Children's ability to operate within a matrix. *Developmental Psychology*, 232-239, 1971.

Siegel and Barber: Visual and haptic dimensional preference for planometric stimuli. *Perceptual and Motor Skills, 36*:383-390, 1973.

Siegel and Ozkaptan: Manipulative completion of bisected geometrical form by nursery school children. *American Journal of Psychology, 66*:626-628, 1953.

Siemankowski and MacKnight: Spatial cognition, a success prognosticator in College science courses, paper presented at National Association for Research in Science Teaching convention, 1971.

Sigel, I.: The distancing hypothesis: a hypothesis crucial to acquisition of representational thought. Unpublished paper, Merrill-Palmer Institute, 1968.

Sigel, *et al.*: *Logical thinking in children*. Holt, Rinehart and Winston, 1968.

Silverman, R.: Comparing effects of two versus three- dimensional art activity upon spatial visualization, aesthetic judgment and art interest. Unpublished. Stanford University, 1962.

Silverman, Adevai and McGough: Some relationships between handedness and perception. *Journal of Phychosomatic Research, 10*:151-158, 1966.

Simon and Newell: Computer simulation of human thinking and problem solving. In W. Kessen and C. Kuhlman (Eds.), Thought In The Young Child. *Monographs of the Society for Research in Child Development,* 27:137-150, 1962.

Sinclair, C.: Dominance patterns of young children, a follow-up study. *Perceptual and Motor Skills, 32*:142, 1971.

Singer and Montegomery: Comment on roles of activation and inhibition in sex differences in cognitive abilities. *Psychological Review, 76*:325-327, 1969.

Siqueland and Lipsitt: Conditioned head-turning in human newborns. *Journal Experimental Child Psychology, 3*:356-376, 1966.

Sitkei and Meyers: Comparative structure of intellect in middle and lower class four-year-olds of two ethnic groups. *Developmental Psychology, 1*: 529-604, 1969.

Skager, Schultz and Klein: Points of view about preference as tools in the analysis of creative products. *Perceptual and Motor Skills, 22*:83-94, 1966.

Slater, P.: Some group tests of spatial judgment or practical ability. *Occupational Psychology, 14*:39-55, 1940.

Slater and Bennett: The development of spatial judgment and its relation to some educational problems. *Occupational Psychology, 17*:139-155, 1943.

Slater, P.: Evidence on selection for technical schools. *Occupational Psychology, 21*:135-140, 1947.

Slater, P.: Mr. Slater replies to Dr. Adcock. *Occupational Psychology, 23·* 2, 1949.

Smedslund, J.: Concrete reasoning: a study of intellectual development. *Society for Research in Child Development Monograph, 29,* No. 93, 1964.

Smedslund, J.: Microanalysis of concrete reasoning: theoretical overview. *Scandinavian Journal of Psychology,* 7:164-167, 1966.

Smedslund, J.: Psychological diagnostics. *Psychological Bulletin,* 71:237-248, 1969.

Smith, A.: Nondominant hemispherectomy. *Neurology, 19:*442-445, 1969.

Smith, A.J.: Speech and other functions after left (sominant) hemispherectomy. *Journal of Neurology, Neurosurgery, and Psychiatry,* 29:407-417, 1966.

Smith, G.M.: Group factors in mental tests similar in material or in structure. *Archives of Psychology, 156,* 1933.

Smith, J.M.: Which hand is the eye of the blind? *Genetic Psychology Monographs, 5:*213-252, 1929.

Smith, Lott and Cronnell: The effect of type size and case alternation on word identification. *American Journal of Psychology,* 82:248-253, June 1969.

Smith, K.U.: Experimental analysis of the associative mechanism of the human brain in learning functions. *Journal of Comparative and Physiological Psychology,* 45:66-79, 1952.

Smith and Greene: A critical period in maturation of performance with space—displaced vision. *Perceptual and Motor Skills,* 17:627-639, 1963.

Smith and Smith: Developmental studies of spatial judgments by children and adults. *Perceptual and Motor Skills,* 22:3-73, 1966.

Smith, I.M.: Measuring spatial ability in school pupils. *Occupational Psychology,* 22:150-159, 1948.

Smith, I.M.: Development of a spatial test. *Durham Research Review, 5:*19-33, 1954.

Smith, I.M.: The validity of tests of spatial ability as predictors of success on technical courses. *British Journal of Educational Psychology, 30:* 138-145, 1960.

Smith, I.M.: A reply to Mr. Gooch. *The Vocational Aspect of Education, 15:*18-21, 1963.

Smith, I.M.: *Spatial Ability, Its Educational and Social Significance.* Knapp, 1964.

Smith and Taylor: Factorial study of a hypothesis about nature of spatial ability. *Durham Research Review, 18:*149-165, 1967.

Smith, I.M.: Spatial ability and its relevance to technical education. *Technical Education Abstracts,* 9:4, 1969.

Smith, I.M.: Use of diagnostic tests for assessing the abilities of overseas students attending institutions of further education. *Vocational Aspects of Education, 51:*1-8, 1970.

Smith, I.M.: Use of diagnostic tests for assessing the abilities of overseas students attending institutions of further education. *Vocational Aspects of Education, 54:*39-48, 1971.

Smith and Gulich: A statistical theory of dynamic contour perception. *Psychological Review, 69*:91-108, 1962.

Smithells, R.W.: Hand and foot preference in thalidomide children. *Archives of Disturbed Children, 45*:274, 1970.

Smock and Cox: Children's ability to reproduce space relations as a function of transformation of field configuration and perceptual mode. *Paper Presented at American Educational Research Association Convention*, 1969.

Smothergill, Martin and Pick: Perceptual-Motor performance under rotation of central field. *Journal of Experimental Psychology, 87*:64-70, 1971.

Smothergill, D.: Spatial localization at three age levels. *Developmental Psychology, 8*:62-66, 1973.

Smothergill, D.: Spatial development in children: mental manipulation of form images. Paper presented at SRCD Convention, 1973.

Snyder and Mortimer: Diagnosis and treatment-Dyslexia. *Pediatrics, 44*:601-605, October 1969.

Snyder, C.R.: *Attentional demands of spatial uncertainty*. Western Psychological Association, Los Angeles, April 1970.

Snyder and Mortimer: Dyslexia. *Pediatrics, 45*:344-345, 1970.

Solkoff, N.: Race of experimenter in research with children. *Developmental Psychology, 7*:70-75, 1972.

Sommer, R.: Studies in personal space. *Sociometry, 22*:247-260, 1959.

Sommer, R.: *Personal Space: The Behavioral Basis of Design*. Englewood Cliffs, N.J., Prentice-Hall, 1969.

Spaulding, S.: Communication potential of pictorial illustrations. *Audio-Visual Communications Review, 4*:31-46, 1954.

Spearman, C.: General intelligence, objectively determined and measured. *American Journal of Psychology, 15*:201-293, 1904.

Spearman, C.: *The abilities of man: Their nature and measurement*. New York; Macmillan, 1927.

Spearman and Jones: *Human Abilities*. Macmillan, 1950.

Spencer, H.: *The principles of psychology*. New York; Appleton, 1899.

Spencer, J.: A preliminary inquiry into engineering drawing comprehension. *Occupational Psychology, 37*:181-195, 1963.

Sperry, R. W.: The Great Cerebral Commisure. *Scientific American, 210*:44-52, 1964.

Sperry, R.: Split-brain approach to learning problems. In G. Quarton, T. Melnechuk, and F. Schmitt (Eds.), *The Neurosciences: A Study Program*. Rockefeller University Press, New York, 1967, 714-722.

Spinelli and Barrett: Visual receptive field organization of single units in the cat's visual cortex. *Experimental Neurology, 24*:76-98, 1969.

Spitz, H.: Effects of symmetry on the reproduction of dot patterns by mental retardates and equal MA normals. *American Journal of Mental Deficiency, 69*:101-106, 1964.

Spitz, R.A. and Wolf, K.M.: The smiling response: a contribution to the ontogenesis of social relations. *Genetic Psychology Monographs, 34*:57-125, 1946.

Springbett, B.M.: The subjective edge. *American Journal of Psychology*, 74: 101-103, 1961.

Stafford, R.E.: Similarities in parent-child test scores. *Educational Testing Service Research Bulletin*, 63:11, 1963.

Stallings, W.M.: Effects of teaching descriptive geometry on spatial relations test scores. Research report No. 280, Office of Instructional Resources, University of Illinois. 1968.

Start and Richardson: Imagery and mental practice. *British Journal of Educational Psychology*, 34:280-284, 1964.

Staub, E.: Helping a person in distress: influence of implicit and explicit "rules." *Journal of Personality and Social Psychology*, 17:137-144, 1971.

Stea and Downs: From the outside looking in at the inside looking out. *Environment and Behavior*, 2:3-12, 1970.

Stearns and Borkowski: The development of conservation and horizontal vertical space perception in mental retardates. *American Journal of Mental Deficiency*, 73:785-790, 1969.

Steinfeld, G.J.: The effect of retinal orientation on the recognition of novel and familiar shapes. *Journal of General Psychology*, 82:223-239, 1970.

Steinzor, B.: The spatial factor in face-to-face discussion groups. *Journal of Abnormal Social Psychology*, 45:552-555, 1950.

Stephens, E.W.: A comparison of New England norms with national norms on the Revised Minnesota Paper Form Board Test—Series AA. *Occupations*, 24:101-104, 1945.

Stephens and McLaughlin: Normals and retardates on Piagetian reasoning assessments as function of verbal ability. *Perceptual and Motor Skills*, 32:868-870, 1971.

Stephens, W.: Reading readiness and eye-hand preference patterns in first grade children. *Exceptional Children*, 33:481-488, 1967.

Stephens, B.: Development of reasoning. *Moral Judgment and Moral Conduct*. HEW Grant, 1972.

Stephenson, W.: Tetrad differences for verbal subtests relative to nonverbal sub-tests. *British Journal of Education Psychology*, 22:334-350, 1931.

Stevenson and McBee: Learning of object and pattern discrimination by children. *Journal of Comparative and Physiological Psychology*, 51:752-754, 1958.

Stewart and Smith: The Alpha rhythm, imagery and spatial and verbal abilities. *Durham Research Review*, 2:2-10, 1959.

Stewart, J.C.: An Experimental Investigation of Imagery. Unpublished dissertation, University of Toronto, 1965.

Stewart, V.M.: Cross-cultural test of the 'carpentered environment' hypothesis. Unpublished dissertation, Northwestern University, 1971.

Stool, E.: Geometric concept formation in kindergarten children. Unpublished disseration, Stanford University, 1962.

Stotland, E.: *Empathy and Birth Order*. University of Nebraska Press, 1971.

Stout, G.F.: *A Annual of Psychology*. London, W.B. Clive, 1913.

Stoy, E.G.: Tests for mechanical drawing aptitude. *Personnel Journal, 6*:93-101, 1927.

Stoy, E.G.: Additional tests for mechanical drawing aptitude. *Personnel Journal, 6*:361-366, 1928.

Stratton, G.M.: *Experimental Psychology and its Bearing upon Culture.* New York, Macmillan, 122-141, 1903.

Strayer, Bigelow and Ames: "I," "You," and point of view. Unpublished study, Simon Fraser University, 1973.

Stringer, P.: The role of spatial ability in a first year architecture course. *Art, 2*:23-33, 1971.

Stuart and Breslow: Question of constitutional influence upon perceptual style. *Perceptual and Motor Skills, 20*:419-420, 1965.

Stuit, Dickson, Jordan and Schloerb: *Predicting success in professional schools.* Washington, American Council on Education, 1949.

Subirana, A.: The prognosis in aphasia in relation to cerebral dominance and handedness. *Brain, 81*:415-425, 1958.

Subirana, A.: The relationship between handedness and language function *International Journal of Neurology, 4*:215-234, 1964.

Subirana, A.: Handedness and cerebral dominance: In P. Vinken and G. Bruyn (Eds.), *Handbook of Clinical Neurology,* Amsterdam, North-Holland Publishing Co., 248-272, 1969.

Suchenwirth, R.: Origin of handedness and its significance for the physiopathology of the hemispheres. *Nervenarzt, 40*:509-517, 1969.

Suinn, Dauterman and Shapiro: Stanford Ohwaki-Kohs tactile block design intelligence test for the blind. *New Outlooks for the Blind, 60*:77-79, 1966.

Sullivan and Hunt: Interpersonal and objective decentering. *Journal of Genetic psychology, 110*:199-210, 1967.

Sullivan, Georgeson and Oatley: Channels for spatial frequency selection and the defection of single bars by the human visual system. *Vision Research, 12*:383-394, 1972.

Sully, J.: *The human mind.* New York; Appleton, 1892.

Supa, Cotzin and Dallenbach: Facial vision: The perception of obstacles by the blind. *American Journal of Psychology, 57*:133-183, 1944.

Super, D.E.: *Appraising Vocational Fitness.* Harper, 1949.

Super and Bachrach: *Scientific careers and vocational development theory.* Teachers College, 1957.

Suppes, P.: Mathematical concept formation in children. *American Psychologist,* February 1966.

Sutherland, N.S.: Visual discrimination of orientation by octupus: mirror-images. *British Journal of Psychology, 51*:9-18, 1960.

Sweeney, E.J.: Sex differences in problem solving. Stanford University, Unpublished dissertation, 1954.

Swineford, F.: A study in factor analysis: The nature of the general, verbal and spatial bi-factors. *Supplementary Education Monograph, 67,* 1948.

Swink, J.R.: Intersensory comparisons of reaction time using an electro-pulse tactile stimulus. *Human Factors, 8*:143-145, 1966.

Swinson: Development of cognitive skills and role-taking. Unpublished dissertation, Boston University, 1965.

Symmes and Rapoport: Unexpected reading failure. *American Journal of Orthopsychiatry, 41*:321-322, 1971.

Szeminska: Evolution of thought. In *Society for Research in Child Development Monograph, 30*:47-57, 1965.

Sziklai, C.: Underwater studies of spatial orientation. Unpublished dissertation, Clark University, 1966.

## T

Takala, M.: Asymmetries of the visual space. *Academia Sientiarumfennica Annales, 72,* 1951.

Tampieri, G.: If problema dell-indifferenze infantile per l'orientamento nello spazio visivo. *Revista di Psicologia, 57*:105-177, 1963.

Tanaka, Yo: Children's representation of spatial transformation. *Japanese Journal of Educational Psychology, 16*:87-99, 1968.

Tanaka, Yo: Role of mediators in the epistemic observation: especially on spatial representation. *Japanese Journal of Educational Psychology,* 1972.

Tate, M.W.: Individual difference in speed of response in mental test materials of varying degrees of difficulty. *Educational and Psychological Measurement, 8*:352-374, 1948.

Taylor and Warrington: Visual agnosia, A single case report. *Cortex, 7*: 152-161, 1971.

Taylor, C.C.: A study of the nature of spatial ability and its relationship to attainment in geography. *British Journal of Educational Psychology, 30*:266-270, 1960.

Taylor, D.: Creative design through functional visualization. *Journal of Creative Behavior, 3*:122-127, 1969.

Taylor, D.: Differential rates of cerebral maturation between sexes and between hemispheres. *Lancet, 2*:140-142, 1969.

Taylor and Wales: A developmental study of form discrimination in pre-school children. *Quarterly Journal of Experimental Psychology, 22*: 720-734, 1970.

Teegarden, L.: Tests for the tendency to reversal in reading. *Journal of Educational Research, 27*:81-97, 1933.

Teets, J.: *Comparison of two socioeconomic classes on performance of Piagetean tasks.* Master's Thesis, West Virginia University, 1968.

Teller, P.: Discussion and extension of Manfred Bierwisch's work on German adjectivals. *Foundations of Language, 5*:185-217, 1969.

Terman, L.M.: *The measurement of intelligence.* Boston, Houghton Mifflin, 1916.

Terrance, H.S.: Discrimination learning with and without "errors". *Journal of Experimental Child Psychology, 6*:1-27, 1963.

Teuber, H.H.: Perception. In J. Field, H.W. Magoun and V.E. Hall (Eds.), *Handbook of Physiology*, Washington, D.C. American Physiological society, *8*:1595-1668, 1960.

Teuber, H.: Space perception and its disturbance after brain injury in man. *Neuropsychologia, 1*:47-57, 1963.

Thomas, H.: Spatial models and multidimensional scaling of random shapes. *American Journal of Psychology, 81*:551-558, 1968.

Thomas, H.: Development of water-level representation. Paper read at SRCD convention, 1971.

Thomas, R.M.: Rationale for the measurement in the visual arts. *Educational and Psychological Measurement, 25*:163-189, 1965.

Thompson, S.W.: Cerebral blood-flow assessment with radioisotope method. *Archives of Neurology, 10*:12-20, 1964.

Thomson, G.H.: *The factorial analysis of human ability. Boston*, Houghton Mifflin, 1939.

Thor, Winters and Hoats: Vertical eye movement and space perception: a developmental study. *Journal of Experimental Psychology, 82*:165-167, 1969.

Thorndike, E.L.: *Educational Psychology*. New York, Lemcke and Buechner, 1903.

Thorndike, E.L.: On the organization of the intellect. *Psychological Review, 28*:141-151, 1921.

Thouless, R.H.: A racial difference in perception. *Journal of Abnormal Social Psychology, 4*:330-339, 1933.

Thurmond and Alluisi: An extension of the information-deductive analysis of form. *Psychonomic Science, 7*:157-158, 1967.

Thurmond and Hancock: Effects of figural complexity on the identity of different solid and outlined shapes. *Psychonomic Science, 15*:315-317, 1969.

Thurstone, L.L.: *The vectors of mind*. Chicago, University of Chicago Press, 1935.

Thurstone, L.L.: Primary mental abilities. *Psychometric Monograph, 1*, 1938.

Thurstone, L.L.: Experimental study of simple structure. *Psychometrika, 5*:153-168, 1940.

Thurstone and Thurstone: *Factorial studies of intelligence*. Chicago, University of Chicago Press, 1941.

Thurstone: *A Factorial Study of Perception*. University of Chicago, 1944.

Thurstone and Thurstone: Mechanical aptitude: Report of the first year of the study. *Psychometric Monograph, 47*, 1947.

Thurstone, L.L.: *Multiple-factor analysis*. Chicago, University of Chicago Press, 1947.

Thurstone, L.L.: Primary mental abilities. *Science, 108*:585, 1948.

Thurstone, L.L.: Mechanical aptitude, analysis of group tests. *Psychometric Laboratory*, University of Chicago, *55*, 1949.

Thurstone, L.L.: Mechanical aptitude, description of group tests. *Psychometric Laboratory*, University of Chicago, *54*, 1949.

Thurstone, L.L.: Mechanical aptitude. *Report from Psychological Laboratory*, Chicago University, *57*, 1950.

Thurstone, L.L.: Some primary abilities in visual thinking. *Report from Psychological Laboratory*, Chicago University, *59*, 1950.

Thurstone, L.L.: Analysis of mechanical aptitude. *Report from Psychological Laboratory*, Chicago University, *62*, 1951.

Thurstone, L.L.: *Tests for spatial visualization*. University of North Carolina, 1952.

Thurstone, J.: *Flags; A test of space thinking*. Chicago, Education Industry Service, 1956.

Tighe, T.: Concept formation and art. *Psychonomic Science*, *12*:363-364, 1968.

Tillman, Bashaw and Bradley: Reanalysis and critique of "Sensory discrimination" as an ability component of the blind. *Perceptual and Motor Skills*, *29*:283-290, 1969.

Tillman and Smock: Copying errors by children as a function of stimulus size and mode of presentation. *Perceptual and Motor Skills*, *33*:743-746, 1971.

Tinker, M.A.: Speed, power and level in the Revised Minnesota Paper Form Board Test. *Journal of Genetic Psychology*, *64*:93-97, 1944.

Titchener, E.B.: *Textbook of psychology*. New York, MacMillan, 1910.

Tizard and Loos: Learning of spatial relations test by adult imbeciles. *American Journal of Mental Deficiency*, *59*:85-90, 1954.

Tobin, M.J.: Conservation of substance in the blind and partially sighted. *British Journal of Educational Psychology*, *42*:192-197, June 1972.

Todd, J.W.: Reaction to multiple stimuli. *Archives of Psychology*, *25*, 1912.

Tolman, E.C.: Cognitive maps in rats and men. *Psychological Review*, *55*:189-208, 1948.

Tonnis, D.: Asymmetry of motor development in infants and its clinical significance. *Zbl Neurochir (Ger)*, *31*:26-30, 1970.

Torrance, E.P.: Tendency to produce unusual visual perspective as a predictor of creative achievement. *Perceptual and Motor Skills*, *34*:911-915, June 1972.

Toulmin and Goodfield: *Fabric of the Heavens*. Harper and Row, 1961.

Towler, J.: Egocentrism: A key to map-reading ability. *Social Education*, *35*:893-898, 1971.

Townsend, E.: A study of copying ability in children. *Genetic Psychological Monograph*, *43*:3-51, 1951.

Trabasso, Rollins and Shaughnessy: Storage and verification stages in processing concepts. *Cognitive Psychology*, *2*:239-289, 1971.

Travers, R.: *Design of pictures for teaching children in elementary school*. Mimeographed Paper.

Trembly, D.: The paper folding test. *Human Engineering Laboratory Bulletin*, 100.

Trumbull, R.: A study of relationships between factors of personality and intelligence. *Journal of Social Psychology, 38*:161-173, 1953.

Tschirgi, R.: Spatial perception and the central nervous system symmetry. *Arquivos de Neuropsiquiatria, 16*:364-366, 1958.

Tuddenham, R.: Jean Piaget and the world of the child. *American Psychology, 21*:207-217, 1966.

Tuddenham, R.: A Piagetian test of cognitive development. In Dochell, *On Intelligence.* Methuen, 1970.

Tunturi, A.R.: Study on the pathway from the medial geniculate body to the acoustic cortex in the dog. *American Journal of Physiology, 147*: 311-319, 1946.

Turkewitz and Birch.: Neurobehavioral organization of the human newborn. In Hellmuth, J. *Exceptional Infant*, Brunner-Mazel, 1971.

Turkewitz, Gordon and Birch: Head turning in the human neonate: effects of prandial condition and lateral preference. *Journal of Comparative and Physiological Psychology, 59*:189-192, 1965.

Turkewitz, Moreau and Birch: Head position and receptor organization in the human neonate. *Journal of Experimntal Child Psychology, 4*:169-177, 1966.

Turkewitz, Moreau, Davis and Birch: Factors affecting lateral differentiation in the human newborn. *Journal of Experimental Child Psychology, 8*:483-493, 1969.

Turner, M.L.: The learning of symmetry principles and their transfer to tests of spatial ability. Unpublished doctoral dissertation, University of California, Berkeley, 1967-1968.

Tyson, M.C.: Pilot study of remedial visuomotor training. *Special Education,* 22-24, 1963.

## U

Ufrich, J.: The case for the syllogism in plane geometry. *Mathematics Teacher, 56*:311-315, 1953.

Ulrich, L.: Egocentric depth and size estimates of stereoscoptic forms. Paper presented at Eastern Psychological Association meeting, Philadelphia, April 1969.

United States Airforce: (Payne, Rohles, Cobb) *Spatial Visualization tests,* 2:1204, 1952.

Urner, L.H.: The Development of a Tridimensional Spatial Relations Test to Measure the Drafting Ability of Industrial Arts Students. Unpublished Master's Dissertation, Kansas State Teachers College, 1949.

Updegraff, R.: *Visual perception of distance.* University of Iowa Studies in Child Welfare, 4:4, 1930.

Uzgiris: Situational generality of conservation. *Child Development 35*:831-841, 1964.

# V

Vandenberg, S.G.: How stable are hereditary estimates? *American Journal of Physical Anthropology,* 20:331-338, 1962.

Vandenberg, S.G.: The hereditary abilities study: hereditary components in a psychological test battery. *American Journal of Human Genetics,* 14:220-237, 1962.

Vandenberg, S.G.: Innate abilities, one or many. *Acta Geneticae Medicae et Gemellologiae,* 14:41-47, 1965.

Vandenberg, S.G.: Contributions of twin research to psychology. *Psychological Bulletin,* 66:327-352, 1966.

Vandenberg, S.G.: Hereditary factors in psychological variables in man. In J. Spuhler, *Behavioral Consequences of Genetic Diversity,* Aldine, 1967.

Vandenberg, S.G.: A twin study of spatial ability. *Multivariate Behavioral Research,* 4:273-294, 1969.

Van der linderie, F.J.: Intelligence and school achievement in young school children. *Netherlands Tychschrift voor de psydiologie,* 25:278-301, 1970.

Van Voorhis, W.: *Improvement of Spatial Perception Ability by Training.* University Michrofilms, 1942.

Vaughan and Costa: Performance with patients with lateralized cerebral lesions. *Journal of Nervous and Mental Diseases,* 134:237-243, 1962.

Vaughn, K.W.: The Yale Scholastic Aptitude Tests as predictors of success in college engineering. *Journal Engineering Education,* 34:572-582, 1944.

Vereechen, P.: *Spatial Development.* Groningen, Walters, 1961.

Verhage, F.: *Intelligentie Leetijd.* Van Gorkum, 1964.

Vernon, M.D.: Different types of perceptual ability. *British Journal of Psychology,* 38:69-89, 1947.

Vernon, P.E.: Psychological tests in the Royal Navy, Army and American Test S. *Occupational Psychology,* 1-22, April 1941.

Vernon, P.E.: Ability factors and environmental influences. *American Psychologist,* 20:723-733, 1965.

Vernon, P.E.: *Intelligence and Cultural Environment,* Methuen, 1969.

Very, P.: Differential factor structures in mathematical ability. *Genetic Psychological Monograph,* 75:169-207, 1967.

Vinh-Bang and Lunzer: Etudes d'epistemotogie genetique, volume 19. *Conservations spatials,* University of Paris Press, 1965.

Vinken and Bruyn: *Handbook of Clinical Neurology: Disorders of Speech, Perception, and Symbolic Behaviour.* North-Holland Publishing Co., Amsterdam, 1969.

Virsu and Weintraub: Perceived curvature of arcs and dot patterns as a function of curvature arc length, and instructions. *Quarterly Journal of Experimental Psychology,* 23:373-380, November 1971.

Vitz and Todd: Model of perception of simple geometric figures. *Psychological Review,* 78:207-228, 1971.

Vlietstra, A.: Development of exploratory and search behaviours in perception and problemsolving. Unpublished paper, University of Kansas, 1972.

Von Bonin, G.: Anatomical asymmetries of the cerebral hemispheres. In V.B. Mountcastle, (Ed.), *Interhemispheric Relations and Cerebral Dominance*, Baltimore, The Johns Hopkins Press, 1-6, 1962,

Von Senden: *Space and Sight.* Free Press, 1960.

Voth, Cancro and Rennick: Autokinesis and central nervous system disease. *Disorders of the Nervous System, 32*:744-747, November 1971.

Vurpillot and Brautt: Etude experimentale surla formation des schemes empiriques. *Annee Psychologique, 59*:381-394, 1959.

Vurpillot, Elaine: The development of scanning strategies and their relation to visual differentiation. *Journal of Experimental Child Psychology, 6*: 632-650, 1968.

Vygotsky, L.S.: *Thought and Language.* M.I.T. Press, 1962.

## W

Wada, J.: Interhemispheric sharing and shift of cerebral speech function. 9th International Congress of Neurology, New York, 1969.

Waern, Y.: Structure in similarity matrices. A graphic approach. *Scandinavian Journal of Psychology, 13*:5-16, 1972.

Wales and Campbell: On the development of comparison and the comparison of development. In Flores d'Arcais and Levelt, W.J., *Advances in Psycholinquistics*, North-Holland, 1970.

Walk and Gibson: Comparative and analytic study of visual depth perception. *Psychological Monograph, 75*:15, 1961.

Walk, R.D.: Concept formation and arts. *Psychonomic Science, 9*:237-238, 1967.

Walk, R.D.: Monocular compared to binocular depth perception. *Science, 162*:473-475, 1968.

Walk, et al.: Artistic style as concept formation. *Merrill-Palmer Quarterly,* 1971.

Wallach and O'Connell: Memory effect of visual perception of 3d form. *Journal of Experimental Psychology, 45*:360-368, 1953.

Wallach and McKenna: On size-perception in the absence of cues for distance. *American Journal of Psychology, 73*:458-460, 1960.

Wallach and Moore: Modification of stereoscoptic depth perception. *American Journal of Psychology, 76*:191-204, 1963.

Wallon, H.: *Origines de la pensee chez l'enfant.* Presses Universitaires de France, 1947.

Walsh and Dangelo: Effectiveness of the Frostig program. *Perceptual and Motor Skills, 32*:944-946, 1971.

Walter and Yeager: Visual imagery and electroencephalographic changes. *E.E.G. Clinical Neurophysiology, 8*:193-199, 1956.

Walter and Doan: Perceptual and cognitive functioning in retarded readers. *Journal of Consulting Psychology, 26*:355-361, 1962.

Waltz, D.: *Shedding light on shadows*. M.I.T., A.I. Vision Flash, *29*, 1972.

Warbruton, F.W.: British Intelligence Scale. In Dockrell (Ed.) *On Intelligence*, Methuen, 1970.

Warhadpande and Khullar: BMP. *Factoral analysis of intelliqeve tests*. Mana, 1963, 89-100.

War Manpower Commission. Division of occupational analysis: Staff Factor analysis of occupational aptitude tests. *Educational and Psychological Measurement, 5*:147-155, 1945.

Warm and Clark: Effects of absolute and differential orientation on tactual pattern. *Psychonomic Science, 17*:124, 1969.

Warren and Pick: The eye, the ear, the hand: who's ahead. Paper read at SRCD Convention, 1969.

Warren, D.: Intermodality interactions in spatial localization. *Cognitive Psychology, 1*:114-133, 1970.

Warren, D.: Early versus late blindness. Paper read at SRCD Convention, 1973.

Warren, H.C.: Magnetic sense of direction. *Psychological Bulletin, 5*:376-377, 1908.

Warrington, James and Kinsbourne: Drawing disability in relation to laterality of cerebral lesion. *Brain, 89*:53-82, 1966.

Warrington and James: Disorders of visual perception of patients with localized cerebral lesions. *Neuropsychologica, 5*:253-266, 1967.

Warrington and Rabin: Perceptual matching in patients with cerebral lesions. *Neuropsychologia, 8*:75-89, 1970.

Washburn, Hatt and Holt: The correlation of a test of control of visual imagery with estimated geometrical ability. *American Journal of Psychology, 34*:103-105, 1923.

Watker, H.E.: Selected time-space concepts of 7-8 year old children. Unpublished master's thesis, Rutgers University, 1952.

Watson, J.S.: *Orientation-specific age changes in responsiveness to the face stimulus in young infants*. Paper read at APA, Chicago, 1965.

Watson, J.S.: Perception of object orientation in infants. *Merrill-Palmer Quarterly of Behavior and Development, 12*:73-94, 1966.

Webb, E.W.: *The relation of certain factors of imagery and immediate memory of geometrical ability*. M.A. Thesis, University of London, 1949.

Webb, S.: Prediction of achievement in 1st year dental students. *Educational and Psychological Measurement, 16*:543-548, 1956.

Webb, T.E.: Stereoscopic contour perception in mental retardation. *American Journal of Mental Deficiency, 76*:699-702, May 1972.

Weber, C.O.: Stephosymbolia and reading disability. *Journal of Abnormal Psychology, 39*:356-361, 1944.

Weber and Castleman: The time it takes to imagine. *Perception and Psychological Physics, 8*:165-168, 1970.

Weber, Kelley and Little: Is visual imagery sequencing under verbal control? *Journal of Experimental Psychology, 96*:354-362, 1972.

Webster, W.G.: Functional asymmetry between the cerebral hemispheres. *Neuropsychologia 10*:75-87, 1972.

Wechler, David and Hagin: The problem of axial rotation in reading disability. *Perceptual and Motor Skills, 19*:319-326, 1964.

Wedell, K.: The visuospatial perception of cerebral-palsied children. Paper read to the South-West of England Branch of the British Psychological Society B.P.S. *Quarterly Bulletin, 39*:24, 1959.

Weinheimer, S.: Egocentricism and social influence in children. *Child Development, 43*:567-578, 1972.

Weintraub, S.: Research; eye-hand preference and reading. *Reading Teacher, 21*:369, 1968.

Weisenburg and McBride: *Aphasia: Clinical and Psychological Study.* Oxford University Press, 1935.

Weiss, A.A.: Directionality in 4 Bender-Gestalt figures. *Perceptual and Motor Skills, 29*:59-62, August 1969.

Weiss, I.: Prediction of academic success in dental school. *Journal of Applied Psychology, 36*:11-14, 1952.

Welch, L.: Aspects of hierarchial development of concepts. *Journal of Psychology, 22*:359-378, 1940.

Wenkart, A.: Spatiality—a concern for the psychoanalyst. *American Journal of Psychoanalysis, 30*:145-154, 1970.

Werdelin, I.: *Geometrical ability and the space factors in boys and girls.* University of Lund Press, Sweden, 1961.

Werdelin and Stjernberg: Relationship between difficulty and factor loadings of some visual-perceptual tests. *Scandinavian Journal of Psychology, 12*:21-28, 1971.

Werner and Strauss: Pathology of figure background relation in the child. *Journal of Abnormal and Social Psychology, 36*:58-67, 1941.

Werner and Wapner: Changes in psychological distance under conditions of danger. *Journal of Personality, 24*:153-167, 1954.

Wernicke, K.: *Der Aphasische Symptomencomplex.* Cogn und Weigert, 1874.

Wertheimer, M.: Hebb and Senden on the role of learning in perception. *American Journal of Psychology, 64*:133-137, 1951.

Wertheimer, M.: Psychomotor coordination of auditory and visual space at birth. *Science, 134*, 1962.

Wesman, A.G.: Separation of sex groups in test reporting. *Journal of Educational Psychology, 40*:223-229, 1949.

Whipple, G.M.: *Manual of mental and physical tests, Part I: Simpler Processes.* Baltimore, Warwick & York, 1914.

White, M.J.: Laterality differences in perception: A review. *Psychological Bulletin, 72*:387-405, December 1969.

White and Saltz: Measurement of reproducibility. *Psychological Bulletin, 54*:81-99, 1957.

Wickelgren, L.W.: Convergence in the human newborn. *Journal of Experimental Child Psychology, 5*:74-85, 1967.

Wiesel and Hubel: Spatial and chromatic interactions in the lateral geniculate body of the rhesus monkey. *Journal of Neurophysiology, 29*:1115-1156, 1966.

Wilcox and Teghtsoonian: The control of relative size by pictorial depth cues in children and adults. *Journal of Experimental Child Psychology, 11*:413-429, 1971.

Williams, J.P.: Training kindergarten children to discriminate letterlike forms. *American Educational Research Journal, 6*:501-514, 1969.

Wilson and Burgess: Construction puzzle B as an ability test. *Journal of Educational Psychology, 36*:53-60, 1945.

Winestine, M.C.: Twinship and psychological differentiation. *Journal of American Academy of Child Psychiatry, 8*:436-455, 1969.

Wit, O.C.: Sex differences in perception. Unpublished dissertation, University of Utrecht, 1955.

Witelson, S.F.: Hemispheric specialization for linquistic and nonlinquistic tactile perception using a dichotomous stimulation technique. *Cortex,* 1973, in press.

Witelson and Pallie: Left hemisphere specialization for language in the human newborn. *Brain,* 1973, in press.

Witkin, Patterson and Goodenough: *Psychological Differentiation.* Wiley, 1962.

Witkin, Goodenough and Karp: Stability of cognitive style from childhood to young adulthood. *Journal of Personality and Social Psychology, 7*:291-300, 1967.

Witkin, Birnbaum, Lomonaco, Lehr and Herman: Cognitive patterning in congenitally totally blind children. *Child Development, 39*:767-786, 1968.

Wittenborn, J.R.: Mechanical ability, its nature and measurement, I. An analysis of the variables employed in the preliminary Minnesota experiment. *Educational Psychological Measurement, 5*:241-260, 1945.

Wittenborn, J.R.: Mechanical ability, its nature and measurement, II. Manual dexterity. *Educational Psychological Measurement, 5*:395-409, 1945.

Wober, M.: *Notes on administering psychological tests in Africa.* Bulletin, BPS, 20:25-34, 1967.

Wohlwill, J.: Developmental studies of perception. *Psychological Bulletin, 57*:249-288, 1960.

Wohlwill, J.: The perspective illusion: perceived size and distance in fields varying in suggested depth, in children and adults. *Journal of Experimental Psychology, 64*:300-310, 1962.

Wohlwill, J.: The development of over-constancy in space perception. In Lipsitt and Spiker (Eds.), *Advances in Child Development and Behavior.* Academic Press, 1963, 265-312.

Wohlwill, J.: Changes in distance judgments as a function of corrected and uncorrected practice. *Perceptual and Motor Skills, 19*:403-413, 1964.

Wohlwill, J.: Texture of the stimulus field and age as variables in the perception of relative distance in photographic slides. *Journal of Experimental Child Psychology, 2*:163-177, 1965.

Wohlwill, J.: Responses to class-inclusion questions for verbally and pictorially presented items. *Child Development, 39*:449-465, 1968.

Wohlwill, J.: The age variable in psychological research. *Psychological Review,* 77:49-64, 1970.

Wohlwill, J.: Effect of correlated visual and tactual feedback on auditory pattern learning at different age levels. *Journal of Experimental Psychology, 11*:213-218, 1971.

Wold, R.M.: Transformational training. *Academic Therapy Quarterly, 3*: 90-95, 1967-68.

Wold, R.M.: Dominance—fact or fantasy: its significance in learning disabilities. *Journal of the American Optometric Association, 39*:908-915, 1968.

Wolf, C.W.: Dyslexic children: the physician's role in the identification of specific dyslexia. *Journal of the Kansas Medical Society,* 71:101-103, 1970.

Wolfe, L.R.: Effects of spatial visualization training upon spatial ability and arithmetic achievement. Unpublished dissertation, State University of New York, Albany, 1970.

Wolfe, R.: The role of conceptual systems in cognitive functioning at varying levels of age and intelligence. *Journal of Personality,* 108-123, 1963.

Wolff, P.: Mirror-image confusability in adults *Journal of Experimental Psychology, 91*:268-272, 1971.

Wolff and Levin: The role of overt activity in children's imagery production. *Child Development, 43*:537-547, June 1972.

Wolfle, D.: Factor analysis. *Psychometric Monographs.* University of Chicago Press, *3,* 1940.

Woo, T.L.: On the asymmetry of the human skull. *Biometrika, 22*:324-352, 1931.

Wood, D.J.: Nature and development of problem-solving strategies. Unpublished dissertation, University of Nottingham, 1969.

Woodring, P.D.: Investigation of direction orientation. Unpublished dissertation, Ohio University, 1939.

Woodring, P.D.: Technique for investigation of direction. *Michigan Academy of Arts and Sciences, 24*:147-152, 1938.

Woodrow, H.: The common factors in fifty-two mental tests. *Psychometrika, 4*:99-108, 1939.

Woodward, W.M.: Concepts of space in the mentally subnormal studied by Piaget's method. *British Journal of Sociological and Clinical Psychology, 1*:25-37, 1962.

Woodworth and Wells: Association tests. *Psychological Monograph, 13*: 5, 1911.

Woolsey and Fairman: Contralateral, ipsilateral, and bilateral representation of cutaneous receptors in somatic areas 1 and 11 of the cerebral cortex of pig, sheep, and other mammals. *Surgery, 19*:684-702, 1946.

Wooster, M.: Certain factors in the development of a new test of spatial co-ordination. *Psychological Monograph, 32:*4, 1923.

Worchel and Dallenbach: Facial vision: Perception of obstacles by the deaf-blind. *American Journal of Psychology, 60:*502-553, 1947.

Worchel, P.: Spatial perception and orientation in the blind. *Psychological Monographs, 65:*352, 1951.

Worsten, H.: Recherches sur le developpement des perceptions. *Archives of Psychology, 32:*1-144, 1947.

Wright and Mikkonen: The influence of alcohol on the detection of light signals in different part of the visual field. *Scandinavian Journal of Psychology, 11:*167-175, 1970.

Wright, R.E.: A factor analysis of the original Stanford-Binet scale. *Psychometrika, 4:*209-220, 1939.

Wright and Jimmerson: Intellectual sequelae of hemophilus influenzae meningitis. *Journal of Abnormal Psychology,* 77:181-183, April 1971.

Wrigley, J.: The factorial nature of ability in elementary mathematics. *British Journal of Psychology,* 28:61-78, 1958.

Wundt, W.: *Lectures on Human and Animal Psychology.* New York; Macmillan, 1896.

Wussler, M.: Cerebral dominance, psycholinguistic skills and reading disability. *Perceptual and Motor Skills, 31:*419-425, 1970.

Wyatt and Tursky: Skin potential levels in right and left-handed males. *Psychophysiology, 6:*133-137, September 1969.

Wyke, M.: Postural arm drift associated with brain lesions in man. *Archives of Neurology, 15:*329-334, 1966.

Wyke, M.: Effect of brain lesions on the rapidity of arm movement. *Neurology, 17:*1113-1120, 1967.

Wyke, M.: The effect of brain lesion in the performance of an arm-hand precision task. *Neuropsychologia, 6:*125-134, 1968.

Wyke, M.: The effects of brain lesions on the performance of bilateral arm movements. *Neuropsychologia, 9:*33-42, 1971.

## Y

Yacorzynski, Boshes and Davis: Psychological changes produced by frontal lobotomy. *Research Publications of the Association for research in Nervous and Mental Disease,* 27:642-657, 1948.

Yates and Barr: Selection for secondary technical courses—A report of a pilot investigation. *Educational Research, 2:*143, 1960.

Yela, M.: Application of the concept of simple structure to Alexander's data. *Psychometric Monograph, 49,* 1948.

Yin, R.K.: Looking at upside-down faces. *Eastern Psychological Association.* April 1969.

Yin, R.: Face recognition in brain-injured patients: a dissociable ability? *Neuropsychologia, 8:*395-402, 1970.

Youfon, C.: A study of the development of children's ability to perceive depth in static two dimensional pictures. *Dissertation Abstracts,* 1969, 3470.

Young, W.G.: Visuospatial ability, dental aptitude tests and multiple-choice practical examinations in oral pathology. *Journal of Dental Education, 36:*48-56, 1972.

Youniss and Furth: Role of language and experience on use of logical symbols. *British Journal of Phychology, 58:*435-443, 1967.

Youniss and Robertson: Projective visual imagery as a function of age and deafness. *Child Development, 41:*215-224, 1970.

Yudin, L.W.: Rutgers drawing test and intelligence: A preliminary comparative study. *Perceptual and Motor Skills, 24:*1038, 1967.

## Z

Zachert, V.: Factor analysis of Army, Navy and Air Force classification batteries. *Research Bulletin* 52-12, Lackland Air Force Base, 1952.

Zahalkova, Vrzal and Kloboukova, et al.: Dyslexia and serum-uric-acid. *Lancet, 2:*651, September 1969.

Zahalkova, Vrzal and Koboukova: Genetic aspect of the dyslexia child. *Cesk Pediat* (Cze), *25:*135-138, March 1970.

Zangwill, Macfie and Piercy: Visual spatial agnosia. *Brain, 73:* 167, 1950.

Zangwill, O.L.: *Cerebral Dominance and its Relation to Psychological Function.* London, Oliver and Boyd, 1960.

Zangwill, O.L.: The current status of cerebral dominance. Chapter VIII in *Disorders of communication,* Vol. XLII. Association for Research in Nervous and Mental Diseases, 1964.

Zaporozhets: Development of perception in the preschool child. In *European Research in Cognitive Development.* Society for Research in Child Development Monograph, 1965, 100.

Zaslow, R.W.: Reversals in children as a function of midline body orientation. *Journal of Educational Psychology, 57:*133-139, 1966.

Zeaman and House: Role of attention in retardate discrimination learning. In Ellis (Ed.), *Handbook of Mental Deficiency,* McGraw-Hill, 1963.

Zechmeister and Mckillip: Recall of place on the page. *Journal of Educational Psychology, 63:*446-453, October 1972.

Zeigler and Leibowitz: Apparent visual size as a function of distance for children and adults. *American Journal of Psychology, 70:*106, 1957.

Zeller, E.: *A history of Greek philosophy.* London; Longmans, 1886.

Zeman, S.: A summary of research concerning laterality and reading. *Journal of the Reading Specialist, 6:*116-123, 1967.

Zimmerman, Canfield and Wilson: Effect of increased positive radial acceleration upon human abilities. *Research Report to the office of Naval Research,* Contract Nbori, 70, 1948.

Zimmerman, W.S.: The Isolation, Definition, and Measurement of Spatial and Visualization abilities. Unpublished dissertation, University of Southern California, 1949.

Zimmerman, W.S.: Revised orthogonal solution for Thurstone's original, PMA Test Battery. *Psychometrica, 18*:77-93, 1953.

Zimmerman, W.S.: Influence of item complexity upon the factor composition of a spatial visualization test. *Educational Psychological Measurement, 14*:106-119, 1954.

Zimmerman, W.S.: Hypotheses concerning the nature of spatial factors. *Educational and Psychological Measurement, 14*: 396-400, 1954.

Zimmerman, N.: Stereoscoptic depth perception and accuracy in anticipating landing position of moving objects in 3ᵈ space. *American Association of Health*, Physical Educational and Records, Convention, Chicago, 1970.

Zinchenko, *et al.*: Formation and development of perceptual activity. *Society Psychology and Psychiatry, 1*:3-12, 1963.

Zinchenko, V.P.: Perceptual and memory elements of creativity. *Voprosy Psikhologii, 14*:3-7, 1968.

# INDEX

## A

Abilities
 mechanical, 58, 175
 numerical, 69, 182
 spatial orientation, 42, 58, 87, 101, 108,
  179, 183
 spatial visualization, 58, 61, 63, 84, 88,
  125, 150, 162, 177, 193
Arnheim, R., 83, 148
Aristotle, 112-114, 132, 147
Aronson, E., 47, 49, 185
Asymetries, 14, 21, 28, 33, 36, 48, 86, 90,
 108, 146, 150
Audition, 14-17, 31, 35, 44, 51
 auditory-visual discrepancy, 47, 124

## B

Ball, W., 48-49
Benton, A.L., 6-7, 13, 25, 52, 178
Bergson, H., 135-136
Bock, R., 61, 193
Bower, T.G.R., 49, 120-123, 131, 183, 185
Brain, W., 8-9
Broadbent, D., 14
Broca, P., 6, 32, 51
Brooks, L., 83-84
Bryant, P., 96-98, 107

## C

Carmon, A., 13, 24, 56
Causality, 133-135, 139, 150
Clark, H., 70, 73-79, 84-88, 93
Classification, 141-147
Comprehension, 59, 71, 95
Conservation, 166, 173-174, 190
Cortex, 5, 29-30, 32, 130
Culture, 85, 94, 98, 107, 116, 164, 172, 187

## D

Development, 16, 73, 109, 145-146
Dimensionality, 23, 58-62, 73, 81, 85-87,
 118, 132, 148, 166-167, 183

Discrimination of left-right, 17-23, 171,
 176, 194
Disorders
 general, 19-22, 44, 177, 186
 spatial, 8-9, 14, 51, 56, 62, 170, 178
Dominance
 cerebral, 16, 31-35, 43-50, 76
 hand, 25-28, 30, 53, 171

## E

Einstein, A., 116-119, 147
Elkind, D., 121, 171
Evolution, 5, 40

## F

Fantz, R., 121
Forman, G., 111-155
French, J., 58, 187

## G

Geschwind, N., 29-30, 32-33
Gessell, A., 25, 146
Gestalt, 25, 43
Ghent, L., 22, 178
Gibson, E., 14, 42, 45
Goodman, N., 70
Guilford, J., 58-59

## H

Handedness, 7, 18-23, 25, 31, 109, 194
Harris, L., 5-55, 184, 194
Hecaen, H., 9-10, 13, 43
Hemisphere
 laterization, 13, 17, 34-39, 54, 56, 171,
  176, 194
 left, 6, 14-15, 17, 20, 27, 31, 41-43, 55,
  69, 76, 82
 right, 6, 12, 14, 22-23, 30, 32, 39-41,
  69, 76
Hermelin, B., 19-20
Hologram, 132, 149
Huttenlocker, J., 79, 178-186

**I**

Imagery
  body, 27, 119, 125, 171
  visual, 58-59, 73, 79, 115, 125, 138, 163, 172, 186, 188
Infancy, 25, 32-33, 46-48, 54, 91, 120-123, 131, 136, 184
Ingram, D., 21, 53
Intelligence, 45, 57, 69, 152, 172

**J**

Jackson, H., 7, 9, 32

**K**

Kimura, D., 11, 20-24, 69

**L**

Language
  spatial, 82, 84-88, 162
  verbal, 10, 21, 43, 45, 88-96, 169, 177
Levy, J., 24, 41
Linquistic processes, 10, 23-26, 43, 50, 70-73, 76, 83-84, 96, 107, 109, 177
Luria, A., 26, 44, 82

**M**

McCrae, D., 31
Memory, 52
Migration, 42
Molfese, D., 35-36
Money, J., 61-63

**N**

Newton, I., 114-116, 133, 147
Notational systems, 77

**O**

Object concept, 49, 120-126, 131, 143
Oldendorf, W., 37
Olson, D., 67-110, 128, 151, 179
Osgood, C., 81-82

**P**

Paoluzzi, C., 37-38, 55
Perception
  depth, 13, 69, 131, 148
  distance, 12-13, 49, 191-192
  facial, 43-46, 48-50, 121
  form, 8, 149, 170, 180
  haptic-tactile, 17, 21-23, 26, 54

  line, 12, 24, 87, 96, 104, 108, 130-131, 149, 165, 170, 183
  shape, 169-170, 180, 183
  training, 64, 163, 180, 191
Phylogentic scale, 5, 40
Piaget, J., 45, 63, 87-88, 116, 123-129, 133-135, 171, 181, 190
Poincare, H., 78, 116, 125, 150
Position
  head, 33-36, 55
  object, 107, 120-126, 171
Pribram, K., 29, 130, 132

**R**

Reasoning, 58, 69, 79, 127, 144, 193
Representation, 67, 71, 87, 96, 108, 126, 149, 164, 191
Rudel, R., 21, 91, 96, 98

**S**

Semmes, J., 39-41, 51, 56
Sex differences, 61, 65, 84, 165, 172, 193
Shepard, R., 63, 73, 75, 77, 110
Smith, I., 57
Smith, J., 18, 20, 53
Social class differences, 59-60, 166, 184
Space
  definition, 76, 128, 135
  egocentric, 88-89, 161, 186, 189-190, 192
  euclidean, 78, 67-88, 93-94, 132, 148, 151
  personal, 174
  processes, 50, 73-78, 80, 83
State, 126, 139

**T**

Thurstone, L., 58, 68-69, 81
Time, 51, 135-141, 148, 150, 179
Topology, 93, 98, 130-131
Turkewitz, G., 33-34, 55

**V**

Vandenberg, S., 57-66
Visual field, 11-14, 38, 53
von Bonin, G., 28-29
Vygotski, L., 44, 89, 143

**W**

Wallace, G., 43-44
Wertheimer, M., 46
Witelson, S., 22, 25, 33, 54